HISTORICAL SKETCH
OF THE CHEROKEE

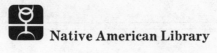 **Native American Library**

Herman J. Viola, General Editor
Director, National Anthropological Archives
National Museum of Natural History
Smithsonian Institution

HISTORICAL SKETCH
OF THE CHEROKEE

by
James Mooney

Foreword by
W. W. Keeler
Chief of the Cherokee Nation

Introduction by
Richard Mack Bettis
President, Tulsa Tsa-La-Gi-Ya
Cherokee Community

A Smithsonian Institution Press Book

Aldine Publishing Company, *Chicago*

First published 1975 by
Aldine Publishing Company
529 South Wabash Avenue
Chicago, Illinois 60605

ISBN: 0–202–01136–4 Clothbound edition
ISBN: 0–202–01137–2 Paperbound edition

Library of Congress Catalog Card Number 75–20706

Printed in the United States of America

CONTENTS

List of Illustrations

PREFACE

The Bureau of American Ethnology was created in 1879 to collect, record, and document the history and culture of Indian tribes, especially in the United States. Data were published in 200 Bulletins and 81 Annual Reports, which were discontinued when the Bureau was amalgamated with the Department of Anthropology, National Museum of Natural History, Smithsonian Institution, in 1965.

This reorganization affected Archives of the Bureau of American Ethnology, which contained many documents of historic and scientific importance. In 1969, the name was changed to the National Anthropological Archives and activities were expanded. Collections are growing and representatives selected by Indian tribes are assisting in their documentation while receiving guidance in the acquisition, preservation, and use of archival materials.

The Native American Library, in which this book appears, is designed to make old and new data more accessible. It will contain both reprints from Bureau of American Ethnology publications with new introductions by Indians, and original works written or edited by Indians. Requests for reprints are initiated by the governing bodies of native American groups; copies are made available to members of the sponsoring tribe at cost and to other native American groups on a non-profit basis. In this way, we hope to assist in the wider dissemination to and by Indians of information on their heritage, which is also a significant part of the heritage of all other Americans.

Herman J. Viola
Director, National Anthropological Archives

FOREWORD

Since 1907, when Oklahoma became a state, the Cherokee Nation as a political entity ceased to exist. The Federal government, believing that the continuation of political bodies within the Five Civilized Tribes might ultimately bring about problems in the newly formed state, had provided that the Tribes could no longer legally elect their own leaders. All Principal Chiefs were either appointed directly by the President or through the Secretary of the Interior. The government did not try to develop the resources of the Indian people and kept them under tight control.

In 1971, a law was passed that again permitted the Cherokee to elect their own chief. We feel that we are now making significant gains, but have yet to reach our potential, which is as great as that of any other people. With approximately $2,000,000 from the residual funds of a claim of approximately $13,700,000 against the U.S. government, the Cherokee Nation started various programs that have grown and developed. We now own two office buildings; one is the Tribal Business Office, the other is leased to the Bureau of Indian Affairs. A third building under construction will house the Tribe's education programs. We also own and operate a motor inn with an adjoining arts and crafts shop and restaurant. We have three industrial buildings which shelter a garment manufacturing company (employing Cherokee people), the Cherokee Nation Builders Corporation (Cherokee Indian construction crews), and our skills-training programs. A service station provides on-the-job training for Cherokee people interested in this type of work.

The Tribe publishes a weekly newspaper with subscribers from all over the United States and abroad. The Tribe also has a Housing Authority and is managing several low-rent housing projects and an apartment complex. The Cherokee Nation Industries is doing assembly-line production for companies such as Western Electric, Corvus, and IBM. We have a Cherokee National Historical Society and a Cherokee Foundation under which we operate the Tsa-La-Gi Indian Village, a recreation of a pre-Civil War Cherokee Indian village. We also have an amphitheater, where the "Trail of Tears" drama is reenacted during the summer months, and a newly opened Cherokee Nation Museum. These attractions, we feel, have helped to promote tourism in Northeastern Oklahoma as well as aid the economy of the Cherokee people. The Cherokee Tribe has revised its old constitution, which was first written in 1839. The revised constitution was approved by vote during the summer of 1975. We also are publishing a complete Cherokee dictionary.

Our Tribe has members all over the world in all types of work. It is estimated that there are 135,000 living descendants of the original 1907 Dawes Commission enrollees. Basically, our objectives are to develop in every way possible our human resources and to continue to keep alive the culture and heritage of the Cherokee people. We hope that our efforts to retain our history, culture, and heritage will inspire young Cherokees to have pride in their blood, for when we fail to keep our culture we lose a part of ourselves. We can never do our best work when we are trying to be someone else. We accept the challenge to add to the progress of mankind to reach the potential made available to us by our Creator. This will bear fruit, for we know history will reveal that the Cherokees have had an important part in the continuing progress of this great nation and that there will always be a Cherokee people surviving to the end of this earth.

James Mooney has provided us with an accurate account of our people in the nineteenth century. Knowledge such as this will allow our young people to expand on their rich heritage and take pride in preparing for their own future.

W. W. Keeler
Chief of the Cherokee Nation

INTRODUCTION

Any sincere writer who undertakes to comment on the work of James Mooney must do so somewhat in awe and with a humble awareness of the responsibility before him. In his Historical Sketch, the reprint of which follows, Mooney points up the Anglo-European attitude of his day—that the Cherokee were the most important of the Indian tribes in terms of size, commercial intercourse, and the ability to live and deal with diverse groups. While there may be weighted elements of personal judgment in his evaluation of the Cherokee, upon reading the whole of Mooney's work, one comes to live more comfortably with his analysis as being one of fact.

One of the more succinct statements that illustrates Mooney's thought about the nature of the Cherokee is his comment that "unlike most other Indians, Cherokees are not conservative." In this, he means that the Cherokee, more easily than other tribes, made the transition from ancient tradition to methods, tools, and ways that they recognized as superior and useful. However, this is not to imply that there was a total and willing transition by all members of the tribe. Indeed, conservative groups fought every attempt and suggestion to get them to give up the ways of their fathers and assimilate into the dominant race. One of the conservative groups was the Ketoowah (Kituwha) band. Their very purpose was to counteract the influx of whites and the influence of white culture and politics. That group has never ceased to exist, and remnants of their beliefs, purposes, and ancient legends have been passed down to a few followers in the present generation, both in North Carolina and Oklahoma.

Mooney did not speculate on why the Cherokee were able to make the transition more easily than other tribes and it may now be too late to determine adequate and acceptable reasons. We might begin, however, with the suggestion by Adair and others that the Cherokee were one of the Lost Tribes of Israel and, therefore, their historical origins and legends meshed with the religious teachings offered by missionaries. There is also the legend of the returning "Great White Father" which was prevalent among Central American and many other tribes. Most anthropologists now connect the Cherokee with the great Central American civilizations. The mounds at Etowah and other places, as well as cultural and language patterns, suggest this conclusion and reflect elements of the splendor of those ancient cultures.

Another reason for their easy transition may lie in the makeup of Cherokee society, which divided its members into "peace" and "war" groups. There were white towns (peace towns) and there red towns (war towns). Priests conducted the activities necessary to the functions of the white towns, and they were superior in rank over the war leaders except when the tribe was at war. Even then, the war chiefs planned and executed military acts only after the proper religious rituals were conducted. Since the higher aim of the Cherokee culture was peace, it seems plausible to this writer that the Cherokee tried wherever possible and by every means available to maintain and promote peace and harmony. This atmosphere was conducive to trade, political relations, and intermarriage with other groups.

Indeed, the ready acceptance of whites with genuine interest into tribal society is evidenced by some of the greatest Cherokee leaders. John Ross was only one-eighth Cherokee; Sequoyah's father was German; and Sam Houston, who was all white, was adopted as a son by Chief Jolly and married a Cherokee.

Mooney wrote his history of the Cherokee at a time of great transition. Most of the ancient and traditional practices—"sacred myths" and "national legends," as he refers to them—had ceased to exist as the way of life by his day. Apparently from the time of their first contact with the whites, the Cherokee were a willing people and were able to cross the usually long bridge from "heathenism" to a superior civilization in a very short period of years. Probably two things, in addition to their willingness and the background mentioned above, made this rapid transition possible. One was intermarriage, for it allowed leaders to move easily between both worlds. The other was the development of writing by Sequoyah, which made teaching everyone possible. The Cherokee proved to be eager learners. Through the use of the Sequoyah syllabary the tribe had a national newspaper, school texts, the Bible, a constitution, and legal and other books in the native language.

Since most of the traditional culture was either gone or waning for the tribe as a whole, it was not available for Mooney to study and describe. This comment is offered for the understanding of, and not in defense of, what follows. For example, Mooney summarily mentions in his writings the seven clans of the Cherokee. Other writers disagree with him and among themselves as to the names of the clans. It is in these ancient and traditional areas of history that one finds a void in the writings of Mooney as well as others. Again, I do not criticize Mooney for such voids; rather, I am attempting to show why such a lack of information exists in his work.

When one has grown up holding the writings of James Mooney on the Cherokee in a reverence that is usually reserved for scripture, it is difficult to disassociate oneself from strongly positive feelings and to be critical. But volume after volume of additional reading has failed to produce any serious contradiction of Mooney's historical picture of my native tribe. Indeed, isolated facts and whole studies turn up repeatedly to strengthen his account. The detailed data he presented have even been successfully used in recent years as the basis for precedent-setting land-settlement cases argued before the U.S. Supreme Court.

Mooney's descriptions of treaties, his maps and biographical sketches, and his extensive accounts of interaction between the Cherokee and the people of the United States have been found impeccable in their accuracy. These events occurred during Mooney's own time, and all cross comparisons have served to authenticate his ideas and to increase respect for his work. In reviewing many contributions by other authors on Cherokee history, one consistently finds that none is more followed or quoted than Mooney. His work has become the source for most of what is known and available about the history of the Cherokee Nation today.

It should be noted that Mooney did not study from the distance of the classroom. He lived with, ate with, even spoke with the Cherokee in their native tongue, and thus learned about his subject firsthand. No doubt this is why his work evidences accuracy in repeated tests. I can attest that Mooney did learn the language very well for a U-Ne-Ga, a white man, who did not grow up speaking it. He employed the language throughout his writing.

Although this work is the most accepted and best known history of the Cherokee, only a few members of the tribe have read it in its entirety because the Bureau of American Ethnology Annual Report in which it appears is found in few public libraries and private collections. Since most of the Cherokee do not know a great deal of their past culture, I am glad that this reprint will be easily available to every tribal member and serious student of Cherokee history. If I might philosophize to this extent only, I feel that many of the Indians' present problems in American society, even alcohol and drug problems (just to name two), are poignantly related to identity problems. A "nobody" seeks to escape his unhappy state. A people who do not know who they are and where they are from cannot walk erect with the pride of one who knows the achievements of his ancestors. Anglo-European culture has demanded that the Indian forget and leave behind his past as being unworthy of continuation or even remembrance. No textbook in any public school reports more than a pitifully few incidents of Cherokee history. It is therefore hoped that this reprint can recreate for many Cherokee, and for Indians of other tribes as well, a fuller understanding of their truly remarkable heritage and place in history.

Richard Mack Bettis
President
Tulsa Tsa-La-Gi-Ya Cherokee Community

The Traditionary Period

The Cherokee were the mountaineers of the South, holding the entire Allegheny region from the interlocking head-streams of the Kanawha and the Tennessee southward almost to the site of Atlanta, and from the Blue ridge on the east to the Cumberland range on the west, a territory comprising an area of about 40,000 square miles, now included in the states of Virginia, Tennessee, North Carolina, South Carolina, Georgia, and Alabama. Their principal towns were upon the headwaters of the Savannah, Hiwassee, and Tuckasegee, and along the whole length of the Little Tennessee to its junction with the main stream. Itsâtǐ, or Echota, on the south bank of the Little Tennessee, a few miles above the mouth of Tellico river, in Tennessee, was commonly considered the capital of the Nation. As the advancing whites pressed upon them from the east and northeast the more exposed towns were destroyed or abandoned and new settlements were formed lower down the Tennessee and on the upper branches of the Chattahoochee and the Coosa.

As is always the case with tribal geography, there were no fixed boundaries, and on every side the Cherokee frontiers were contested by rival claimants. In Virginia, there is reason to believe, the tribe was held in check in early days by the Powhatan and the Monacan. On the east and southeast the Tuscarora and Catawba were their inveterate enemies, with hardly even a momentary truce within the historic period; and evidence goes to show that the Sara or Cheraw were fully as hostile. On the south there was hereditary war with the Creeks, who claimed nearly the whole of upper Georgia as theirs by original possession, but who were being gradually pressed down toward the Gulf until, through the mediation of the United States, a treaty was finally made fixing the boundary between the two tribes along a line running about due west from the mouth of Broad river on the Savannah. Toward the west, the Chickasaw on the lower Tennessee and the Shawano on the Cumberland repeatedly turned back the tide of Cherokee invasion from the rich central valleys, while the powerful Iroquois in the far north set up an almost unchallenged claim of paramount lordship from the Ottawa river of Canada southward at least to the Kentucky river.

1

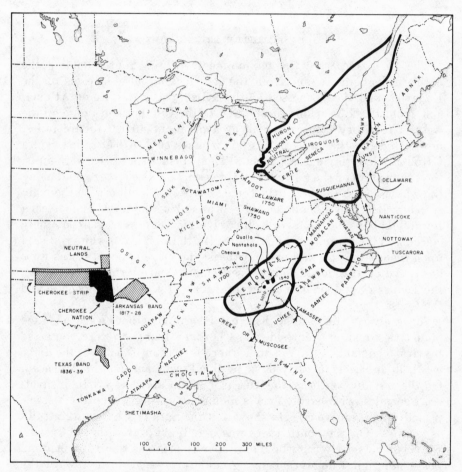

The Cherokee and Their Neighbors

Remnant eastern lands and the location of the Cherokee Nation are indicated in black. Other areas held at various times west of the Mississippi River are shown by hachure. Cognate Iroquoian tribes occupied the regions defined by the wide lines. (Redrawn from the original map compiled by Mooney and published as Plate II in the 19th Annual Report of the Bureau of American Ethnology.)

On the other hand, by their defeat of the Creeks and expulsion of the Shawano, the Cherokee made good the claim which they asserted to all the lands from upper Georgia to the Ohio river, including the rich hunting grounds of Kentucky. Holding as they did the great mountain barrier between the English settlements on the coast and the French or Spanish garrisons along the Mississippi and the Ohio, their geographic position, no less than their superior number, would have given them the balance of power in the South but for a looseness of tribal organization in striking contrast to the compactness of the Iroquois league, by which for more than a century the French power was held in check in the north. The English, indeed, found it convenient to recognize certain chiefs as supreme in the tribe, but the only real attempt to weld the whole Cherokee Nation into a political unit was that made by the French agent, Priber, about 1736, which failed from its premature discovery by the English. We frequently find their kingdom divided against itself, their very number preventing unity of action, while still giving them an importance above that of neighboring tribes.

The proper name by which the Cherokee call themselves (1)[1] is Yûñ′wiyă′, or Ani′-Yûñ′wiyă′ in the third person, signifying "real people," or "principal people," a word closely related to Oñwe-hoñwe, the name by which the cognate Iroquois know themselves. The word properly denotes "Indians," as distinguished from people of other races, but in usage it is restricted to mean members of the Cherokee tribe, those of other tribes being designated as Creek, Catawba, etc., as the case may be. On ceremonial occasions they frequently speak of themselves as Ani′-Kitu′hwagĭ, or "people of Kĭtu′hwa," an ancient settlement on Tuckasegee river and apparently the original nucleus of the tribe. Among the western Cherokee this name has been adopted by a secret society recruited from the full-blood element and pledged to resist the advances of the white man's civilization. Under the various forms of Cuttawa, Gattochwa, Kittuwa, etc., as spelled by different authors, it was also used by several northern Algonquian tribes as a synonym for Cherokee.

Cherokee, the name by which they are commonly known, has no meaning in their own language, and seems to be of foreign origin. As used among themselves the form is Tsa′lăgĭ′ or Tsa′răgĭ′. It first appears as Chalaque in the Portuguese narrative of De Soto's expedition, published originally in 1557, while we find Cheraqui in a French document of 1699, and Cherokee as an English form as early, at least, as 1708. The name has thus an authentic history of 360 years. There is evidence that it is derived from the Choctaw word *choluk* or *chiluk*, signifying a pit or cave, and comes to us through the so-called Mobilian trade language, a corrupted Choctaw jargon formerly used as the

---

[1] See the notes to the historical sketch.

medium of communication among all the tribes of the Gulf states, as far north as the mouth of the Ohio (2). Within this area many of the tribes were commonly known under Choctaw names, even though of widely differing linguistic stocks, and if such a name existed for the Cherokee it must undoubtedly have been communicated to the first Spanish explorers by De Soto's interpreters. This theory is borne out by their Iroquois (Mohawk) name, Oyata'ge'ronoñ', as given by Hewitt, signifying "inhabitants of the cave country," the Allegheny region being peculiarly a cave country, in which "rock shelters," containing numerous traces of Indian occupancy, are of frequent occurrence. Their Catawba name also, Mañterañ, as given by Gatschet, signifying "coming out of the ground," seems to contain the same reference. Adair's attempt to connect the name Cherokee with their word for fire, *atsila*, is an error founded upon imperfect knowledge of the language.

Among other synonyms for the tribe are Rickahockan, or Recnahecrian, the ancient Powhatan name, and Tallige', or Tallige'wi, the ancient name used in the Walam Olum chronicle of the Lenape'. Concerning both the application and the etymology of this last name there has been much dispute, but there seems no reasonable doubt as to the identity of the people.

Linguistically the Cherokee belong to the Iroquoian stock, the relationship having been suspected by Barton over a century ago, and by Gallatin and Hale at a later period, and definitely established by Hewitt in 1887.[1] While there can now be no question of the connection, the marked lexical and grammatical differences indicate that the separation must have occurred at a very early period. As is usually the case with a large tribe occupying an extensive territory, the language is spoken in several dialects, the principal of which may, for want of other names, be conveniently designated as the Eastern, Middle, and Western. Adair's classification into "Ayrate" (*e'ladĭ*), or low, and "Ottare" (*â'talĭ*), or mountainous, must be rejected as imperfect.

The Eastern dialect, formerly often called the Lower Cherokee dialect, was originally spoken in all the towns upon the waters of the Keowee and Tugaloo, head-streams of Savannah river, in South Carolina and the adjacent portion of Georgia. Its chief peculiarity is a rolling *r*, which takes the place of the *l* of the other dialects. In this dialect the tribal name is Tsa'răgĭ', which the English settlers of Carolina corrupted to Cherokee, while the Spaniards, advancing from the south, became better familiar with the other form, which they wrote as Chalaque. Owing to their exposed frontier position, adjoining the white settlements of Carolina, the Cherokee of this division

[1] Barton, Benj. S., New Views on the Origin of the Tribes and Nations of America, p. xlv, passim; Phila., 1797; Gallatin, Albert, Synopsis of Indian Tribes, Trans. American Antiquarian Society, II, p. 91; Cambridge, 1836; Hewitt, J. N. B., The Cherokee an Iroquoian Language, Washington, 1887 (MS in the archives of the Bureau of American Ethnology).

were the first to feel the shock of war in the campaigns of 1760 and 1776, with the result that before the close of the Revolution they had been completely extirpated from their original territory and scattered as refugees among the more western towns of the tribe. The consequence was that they lost their distinctive dialect, which is now practically extinct. In 1888 it was spoken by but one man on the reservation in North Carolina.

The Middle dialect, which might properly be designated the Kituhwa dialect, was originally spoken in the towns on the Tuckasegee and the headwaters of the Little Tennessee, in the very heart of the Cherokee country, and is still spoken by the great majority of those now living on the Qualla reservation. In some of its phonetic forms it agrees with the Eastern dialect, but resembles the Western in having the *l* sound.

The Western dialect was spoken in most of the towns of east Tennessee and upper Georgia and upon Hiwassee and Cheowa rivers in North Carolina. It is the softest and most musical of all the dialects of this musical language, having a frequent liquid *l* and eliding many of the harsher consonants found in the other forms. It is also the literary dialect, and is spoken by most of those now constituting the Cherokee Nation in the West.

Scattered among the other Cherokee are individuals whose pronunciation and occasional peculiar terms for familiar objects give indication of a fourth and perhaps a fifth dialect, which can not now be localized. It is possible that these differences may come from foreign admixture, as of Natchez, Taskigi, or Shawano blood. There is some reason for believing that the people living on Nantahala river differed dialectically from their neighbors on either side (3).

The Iroquoian stock, to which the Cherokee belong, had its chief home in the north, its tribes occupying a compact territory which comprised portions of Ontario, New York, Ohio, and Pennsylvania, and extended down the Susquehanna and Chesapeake bay almost to the latitude of Washington. Another body, including the Tuscarora, Nottoway, and perhaps also the Meherrin, occupied territory in northeastern North Carolina and the adjacent portion of Virginia. The Cherokee themselves constituted the third and southernmost body. It is evident that tribes of common stock must at one time have occupied contiguous territories, and such we find to be the case in this instance. The Tuscarora and Meherrin, and presumably also the Nottoway, are known to have come from the north, while traditional and historical evidence concur in assigning to the Cherokee as their early home the region about the headwaters of the Ohio, immediately to the southward of their kinsmen, but bitter enemies, the Iroquois. The theory which brings the Cherokee from northern Iowa and the Iroquois from Manitoba is unworthy of serious consideration. (4)

The most ancient tradition concerning the Cherokee appears to be the Delaware tradition of the expulsion of the Talligewi from the north, as first noted by the missionary Heckewelder in 1819, and published more fully by Brinton in the Walam Olum in 1885. According to the first account, the Delawares, advancing from the west, found their further progress opposed by a powerful people called Alligewi or Talligewi, occupying the country upon a river which Heckewelder thinks identical with the Mississippi, but which the sequel shows was more probably the upper Ohio. They were said to have regularly built earthen fortifications, in which they defended themselves so well that at last the Delawares were obliged to seek the assistance of the "Mengwe," or Iroquois, with the result that after a warfare extending over many years the Alligewi finally received a crushing defeat, the survivors fleeing down the river and abandoning the country to the invaders, who thereupon parceled it out amongst themselves, the "Mengwe" choosing the portion about the Great lakes while the Delawares took possession of that to the south and east. The missionary adds that the Allegheny (and Ohio) river was still called by the Delawares the Alligewi Sipu, or river of the Alligewi. This would seem to indicate it as the true river of the tradition. He speaks also of remarkable earthworks seen by him in 1789 in the neighborhood of Lake Erie, which were said by the Indians to have been built by the extirpated tribe as defensive fortifications in the course of this war. Near two of these, in the vicinity of Sandusky, he was shown mounds under which it was said some hundreds of the slain Talligewi were buried.[1] As is usual in such traditions, the Alligewi were said to have been of giant stature, far exceeding their conquerors in size.

In the Walam Olum, which is, it is asserted, a metrical translation of an ancient hieroglyphic bark record discovered in 1820, the main tradition is given in practically the same way, with an appendix which follows the fortunes of the defeated tribe up to the beginning of the historic period, thus completing the chain of evidence. (5)

In the Walam Olum also we find the Delawares advancing from the west or northwest until they come to "Fish river"—the same which Heckewelder makes the Mississippi (6). On the other side, we are told, "The Talligewi possessed the East." The Delaware chief "desired the eastern land," and some of his people go on, but are killed by the Talligewi. The Delawares decide upon war and call in the help of their northern friends, the "Talamatan," i. e., the Wyandot and other allied Iroquoian tribes. A war which continues through the terms of four successive chiefs, when victory declares for the invaders, and "all the Talega go south." The country is then divided, the Talamatan taking the northern portion, while the Delawares "stay south of the lakes." The chronicle proceeds to tell how, after eleven more chiefs have ruled, the Nanticoke and Shawano separate from the

---

[1] Heckewelder, John, Indian Nations of Pennsylvania, pp. 47–49, ed. 1876.

parent tribe and remove to the south. Six other chiefs follow in succession until we come to the seventh, who "went to the Talega mountains." By this time the Delawares have reached the ocean. Other chiefs succeed, after whom "the Easterners and the Wolves"—probably the Mahican or Wappinger and the Munsee—move off to the northeast. At last, after six more chiefs, "the whites came on the eastern sea," by which is probably meant the landing of the Dutch on Manhattan in 1609 (7). We may consider this a tally date, approximating the beginning of the seventeenth century. Two more chiefs rule, and of the second we are told that "He fought at the south; he fought in the land of the Talega and Koweta," and again the fourth chief after the coming of the whites "went to the Talega." We have thus a traditional record of a war of conquest carried on against the Talligewi by four successive chiefs, and a succession of about twenty-five chiefs between the final expulsion of that tribe and the appearance of the whites, in which interval the Nanticoke, Shawano, Mahican, and Munsee branched off from the parent tribe of the Delawares. Without venturing to entangle ourselves in the devious maze of Indian chronology, it is sufficient to note that all this implies a very long period of time—so long, in fact, that during it several new tribes, each of which in time developed a distinct dialect, branch off from the main Lenape' stem. It is distinctly stated that all the Talega went south after their final defeat; and from later references we find that they took refuge in the mountain country in the neighborhood of the Koweta (the Creeks), and that Delaware war parties were still making raids upon both these tribes long after the first appearance of the whites.

Although at first glance it might be thought that the name Tallige-wi is but a corruption of Tsalagi, a closer study leads to the opinion that it is a true Delaware word, in all probability connected with *waloh* or *walok*, signifying a cave or hole (Zeisberger), whence we find in the Walam Olum the word *oligonunk* rendered as "at the place of caves." It would thus be an exact Delaware rendering of the same name, "people of the cave country," by which, as we have seen, the Cherokee were commonly known among the tribes. Whatever may be the origin of the name itself, there can be no reasonable doubt as to its application. "Name, location, and legends combine to identify the Cherokees or Tsalaki with the Tallike; and this is as much evidence as we can expect to produce in such researches."[1]

The Wyandot confirm the Delaware story and fix the identification of the expelled tribe. According to their tradition, as narrated in 1802, the ancient fortifications in the Ohio valley had been erected in the course of a long war between themselves and the Cherokee, which resulted finally in the defeat of the latter.[2]

The traditions of the Cherokee, so far as they have been preserved,

[1] Brinton, D. G., Walam Olum, p. 231; Phila., 1885.
[2] Schoolcraft, H. R., Notes on the Iroquois, p. 162; Albany, 1847.

supplement and corroborate those of the northern tribes, thus bringing the story down to their final settlement upon the headwaters of the Tennessee in the rich valleys of the southern Alleghenies. Owing to the Cherokee predilection for new gods, contrasting strongly with the conservatism of the Iroquois, their ritual forms and national epics had fallen into decay even before the Revolution, as we learn from Adair. Some vestiges of their migration legend still existed in Haywood's time, but it is now completely forgotten both in the East and in the West.

According to Haywood, who wrote in 1823 on information obtained directly from leading members of the tribe long before the Removal, the Cherokee formerly had a long migration legend, which was already lost, but which, within the memory of the mother of one informant—say about 1750—was still recited by chosen orators on the occasion of the annual green-corn dance. This migration legend appears to have resembled that of the Delawares and the Creeks in beginning with genesis and the period of animal monsters, and thence following the shifting fortune of the chosen band to the historic period. The tradition recited that they had originated in a land toward the rising sun, where they had been placed by the command of "the four councils sent from above." In this pristine home were great snakes and water monsters, for which reason it was supposed to have been near the sea-coast, although the assumption is not a necessary corollary, as these are a feature of the mythology of all the eastern tribes. After this genesis period there began a slow migration, during which "towns of people in many nights' encampment removed," but no details are given. From Heckewelder it appears that the expression, "a night's encampment," which occurs also in the Delaware migration legend, is an Indian figure of speech for a halt of one year at a place.[1]

In another place Haywood says, although apparently confusing the chronologic order of events: "One tradition which they have amongst them says they came from the west and exterminated the former inhabitants; and then says they came from the upper parts of the Ohio, where they erected the mounds on Grave creek, and that they removed thither from the country where Monticello (near Charlottesville, Virginia) is situated."[2] The first reference is to the celebrated mounds on the Ohio near Moundsville, below Wheeling, West Virginia; the other is doubtless to a noted burial mound described by Jefferson in 1781 as then existing near his home, on the low grounds of Rivanna river opposite the site of an ancient Indian town. He himself had opened it and found it to contain perhaps a thousand disjointed skeletons of both adults and children, the bones piled in successive layers, those near the top being least decayed. They showed no signs

[1] Heckewelder, Indian Nations, p. 47, ed. 1876.

[2] Haywood, John, Natural and Aboriginal History of Tennessee, pp. 225–226; Nashville, 1823.

of violence, but were evidently the accumulation of long years from the neighboring Indian town. The distinguished writer adds: "But on whatever occasion they may have been made, they are of considerable notoriety among the Indians: for a party passing, about thirty years ago [i. e., about 1750], through the part of the country where this barrow is, went through the woods directly to it without any instructions or enquiry, and having staid about it some time, with expressions which were construed to be those of sorrow, they returned to the high road, which they had left about half a dozen miles to pay this visit, and pursued their journey."[1] Although the tribe is not named, the Indians were probably Cherokee, as no other southern Indians were then accustomed to range in that section. As serving to corroborate this opinion we have the statement of a prominent Cherokee chief, given to Schoolcraft in 1846, that acccording to their tradition his people had formerly lived at the Peaks of Otter, in Virginia, a noted landmark of the Blue ridge, near the point where Staunton river breaks through the mountains.[2]

From a careful sifting of the evidence Haywood concludes that the authors of the most ancient remains in Tennessee had spread over that region from the south and southwest at a very early period, but that the later occupants, the Cherokee, had entered it from the north and northeast in comparatively recent times, overrunning and exterminating the aborigines. He declares that the historical fact seems to be established that the Cherokee entered the country from Virginia, making temporary settlements upon New river and the upper Holston, until, under the continued hostile pressure from the north, they were again forced to remove farther to the south, fixing themselves upon the Little Tennessee, in what afterward became known as the middle towns. By a leading mixed blood of the tribe he was informed that they had made their first settlements within their modern home territory upon Nolichucky river, and that, having lived there for a long period, they could give no definite account of an earlier location. Echota, their capital and peace town, "claimed to be the eldest brother in the nation," and the claim was generally acknowledged.[3] In confirmation of the statement as to an early occupancy of the upper Holston region, it may be noted that "Watauga Old Fields," now Elizabethtown, were so called from the fact that when the first white settlement within the present state of Tennessee was begun there, so early as 1769, the bottom lands were found to contain graves and other numerous ancient remains of a former Indian town which tradition ascribed to the Cherokee, whose nearest settlements were then many miles to the southward.

While the Cherokee claimed to have built the mounds on the upper

---

[1] Jefferson, Thomas, Notes on Virginia, pp. 136-137; ed. Boston, 1802.

[2] Schoolcraft, Notes on the Iroquois, p. 163, 1847.

[3] Haywood, Natural and Aboriginal History of Tennessee, pp. 233, 236, 269, 1823.

The boundaries of Cherokee country east of the Mississippi River according to the original claim, at the close of the Revolution, and after the final cession. (Redrawn from the map compiled by Mooney and published as Plate III in the 19th Annual Report of the Bureau of American Ethnology.)

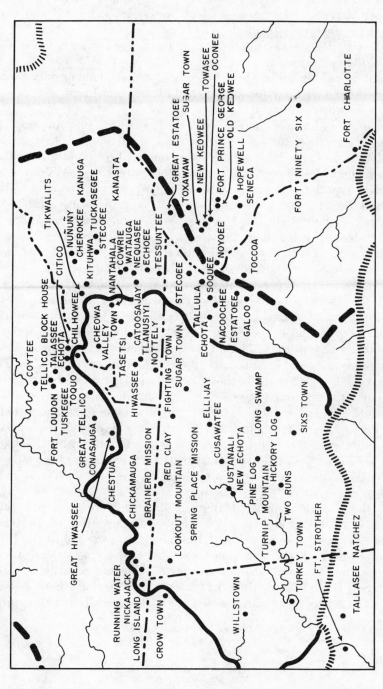

Cherokee towns and other settlements in the southern part of the territory originally claimed by the tribe. (Redrawn from Plate III; cf. Map 2.)

Ohio, they yet, according to Haywood, expressly disclaimed the author-
ship of the very numerous mounds and petroglyphs in their later home
territory, asserting that these ancient works had exhibited the same
appearance when they themselves had first occupied the region.[1] This
accords with Bartram's statement that the Cherokee, although sometimes utilizing the mounds as sites for their own town houses, were as
ignorant as the whites of their origin or purpose, having only a general tradition that their forefathers had found them in much the same
condition on first coming into the country.[2]

Although, as has been noted, Haywood expresses the opinion that
the invading Cherokee had overrun and exterminated the earlier
inhabitants, he says in another place, on halfbreed authority, that
the newcomers found no Indians upon the waters of the Tennessee,
with the exception of some Creeks living upon that river, near the
mouth of the Hiwassee, the main body of that tribe being established
upon and claiming all the streams to the southward.[3] There is
considerable evidence that the Creeks preceded the Cherokee, and
within the last century they still claimed the Tennessee, or at least
the Tennessee watershed, for their northern boundary.

There is a dim but persistent tradition of a strange white race preceding the Cherokee, some of the stories even going so far as to locate
their former settlements and to identify them as the authors of the
ancient works found in the country. The earliest reference appears
to be that of Barton in 1797, on the statement of a gentleman whom
he quotes as a valuable authority upon the southern tribes. "The
Cheerake tell us, that when they first arrived in the country which
they inhabit, they found it possessed by certain 'moon-eyed people,'
who could not see in the day-time. These wretches they expelled."
He seems to consider them an albino race.[4] Haywood, twenty-six
years later, says that the invading Cherokee found "white people"
near the head of the Little Tennessee, with forts extending thence down
the Tennessee as far as Chickamauga creek. He gives the location of
three of these forts. The Cherokee made war against them and
drove them to the mouth of Big Chickamauga creek, where they
entered into a treaty and agreed to remove if permitted to depart in
peace. Permission being granted, they abandoned the country. Elsewhere he speaks of this extirpated white race as having extended into
Kentucky and probably also into western Tennessee, according to the
concurrent traditions of different tribes. He describes their houses,
on what authority is not stated, as having been small circular structures

---

[1] Haywood, Nat. and Aborig. Hist. Tennessee, pp. 226, 234, 1823.
[2] Bartram, Wm., Travels, p. 365; reprint, London, 1792.
[3] Haywood, op. cit., pp. 234-237.
[4] Barton, New Views, p. xliv, 1797.

of upright logs, covered with earth which had been dug out from the inside.[1]

Harry Smith, a halfbreed born about 1815, father of the late chief of the East Cherokee, informed the author that when a boy he had been told by an old woman a tradition of a race of very small people, perfectly white, who once came and lived for some time on the site of the ancient mound on the northern side of Hiwassee, at the mouth of Peachtree creek, a few miles above the present Murphy, North Carolina. They afterward removed to the West. Colonel Thomas, the white chief of the East Cherokee, born about the beginning of the century, had also heard a tradition of another race of people, who lived on Hiwassee, opposite the present Murphy, and warned the Cherokee that they must not attempt to cross over to the south side of the river or the great leech in the water would swallow them.[2] They finally went west, "long before the whites came." The two stories are plainly the same, although told independently and many miles apart.

THE PERIOD OF SPANISH EXPLORATION—1540–?

The definite history of the Cherokee begins with the year 1540, at which date we find them already established, where they were always afterward known, in the mountains of Carolina and Georgia. The earliest Spanish adventurers failed to penetrate so far into the interior, and the first entry into their country was made by De Soto, advancing up the Savannah on his fruitless quest for gold, in May of that year.

While at Cofitachiqui, an important Indian town on the lower Savannah governed by a "queen," the Spaniards had found hatchets and other objects of copper, some of which was of finer color and appeared to be mixed with gold, although they had no means of testing it.[3] On inquiry they were told that the metal had come from an interior mountain province called Chisca, but the country was represented as thinly peopled and the way as impassable for horses. Some time before, while advancing through eastern Georgia, they had heard also of a rich and plentiful province called Coça, toward the northwest, and by the people of Cofitachiqui they were now told that Chiaha, the nearest town of Coça province, was twelve days inland. As both men and animals were already nearly exhausted from hunger and hard travel, and the Indians either could not or would not furnish sufficient provision for their needs, De Soto determined not to attempt the passage of the mountains then, but to push on at once to Coça, there to rest and recuperate before undertaking further exploration. In the mean-

---

[1] Haywood, Nat. and Aborig. Hist. Tennessee, pp. 166, 234–235, 287–289, 1823.
[2] See story, "The Great Leech of Tlanusi'yĭ," p. 328.
[3] Garcilaso de la Vega, La Florida del Inca, pp. 129, 133–134; Madrid, 1723.

time he hoped also to obtain more definite information concerning the mines. As the chief purpose of the expedition was the discovery of the mines, many of the officers regarded this change of plan as a mistake, and favored staying where they were until the new crop should be ripened, then to go directly into the mountains, but as the general was "a stern man and of few words," none ventured to oppose his resolution.[1] The province of Coça was the territory of the Creek Indians, called Ani'-Kusa by the Cherokee, from Kusa, or Coosa, their ancient capital, while Chiaha was identical with Chehaw, one of the principal Creek towns on Chattahoochee river. Cofitachiqui may have been the capital of the Uchee Indians.

The outrageous conduct of the Spaniards had so angered the Indian queen that she now refused to furnish guides and carriers, whereupon De Soto made her a prisoner, with the design of compelling her to act as guide herself, and at the same time to use her as a hostage to command the obedience of her subjects. Instead, however, of conducting the Spaniards by the direct trail toward the west, she led them far out of their course until she finally managed to make her escape, leaving them to find their way out of the mountains as best they could.

Departing from Cofitachiqui, they turned first toward the north, passing through several towns subject to the queen, to whom, although a prisoner, the Indians everywhere showed great respect and obedience, furnishing whatever assistance the Spaniards compelled her to demand for their own purposes. In a few days they came to "a province called Chalaque," the territory of the Cherokee Indians, probably upon the waters of Keowee river, the eastern head-stream of the Savannah. It is described as the poorest country for corn that they had yet seen, the inhabitants subsisting on wild roots and herbs and on game which they killed with bows and arrows. They were naked, lean, and unwarlike. The country abounded in wild turkeys ("gallinas"), which the people gave very freely to the strangers, one town presenting them with seven hundred. A chief also gave De Soto two deerskins as a great present.[2] Garcilaso, writing on the authority of an old soldier nearly fifty years afterward, says that the "Chalaques" deserted their towns on the approach of the white men and fled to the mountains, leaving behind only old men and women and some who were nearly blind.[3] Although it was too early for the new crop, the poverty of the people may have been more apparent than real, due to their unwillingness to give any part of their stored-up provision to the unwelcome strangers. As the Spaniards were greatly in need of corn for themselves and their horses, they made no stay, but hurried on. In a few days they arrived

---

[1] Gentleman of Elvas, Publications of the Hakluyt Society, IX, pp. 52, 58, 64; London, 1851.
[2] Ibid., p. 60.
[3] Garcilaso, La Florida del Inca, p. 136, ed. 1723.

at Guaquili, which is mentioned only by Ranjel, who does not specify whether it was a town or a province—i. e., a tribal territory. It was probably a small town. Here they were welcomed in a friendly manner, the Indians giving them a little corn and many wild turkeys, together with some dogs of a peculiar small species, which were bred for eating purposes and did not bark.[1] They were also supplied with men to help carry the baggage. The name Guaquili has a Cherokee sound and may be connected with *wa'gulĭ'*, "whippoorwill," *uwă'gi'lĭ*, "foam," or *gi"lĭ*, "dog."

Traveling still toward the north, they arrived a day or two later in the province of Xuala, in which we recognize the territory of the Suwali, Sara, or Cheraw Indians, in the piedmont region about the head of Broad river in North Carolina. Garcilaso, who did not see it, represents it as a rich country, while the Elvas narrative and Biedma agree that it was a rough, broken country, thinly inhabited and poor in provision. According to Garcilaso, it was under the rule of the queen of Cofitachiqui, although a distinct province in itself.[2] The principal town was beside a small rapid stream, close under a mountain. The chief received them in friendly fashion, giving them corn, dogs of the small breed already mentioned, carrying baskets, and burden bearers. The country roundabout showed greater indications of gold mines than any they had yet seen.[1]

Here De Soto turned to the west, crossing a very high mountain range, which appears to have been the Blue ridge, and descending on the other side to a stream flowing in the opposite direction, which was probably one of the upper tributaries of the French Broad.[3] Although it was late in May, they found it very cold in the mountains.[4] After several days of such travel they arrived, about the end of the month, at the town of Guasili, or Guaxule. The chief and principal men came out some distance to welcome them, dressed in fine robes of skins, with feather head-dresses, after the fashion of the country. Before reaching this point the queen had managed to make her escape, together with three slaves of the Spaniards, and the last that was heard of her was that she was on her way back to her own country with one of the runaways as her husband. What grieved De Soto most in the matter was that she took with her a small box of pearls, which he had intended to take from her before releasing her, but had left with her for the present in order "not to discontent her altogether."[5]

Guaxule is described as a very large town surrounded by a number of small mountain streams which united to form the large river down which the Spaniards proceeded after leaving the place.[6] Here, as

[1] Ranjel, in Oviedo, Historia General y Natural de las Indias, I, p. 562; Madrid, 1851.
[2] Garcilaso, La Florida del Inca, p. 137, 1723.   [4] Ranjel, op. cit., I, p. 562.
[3] See note 8, De Soto's route.   [5] Elvas, Hakluyt Society, IX, p. 61, 1851.
[6] Garcilaso, op. cit., p. 139.

elsewhere, the Indians received the white men with kindness and hospitality—so much so that the name of Guaxule became to the army a synonym for good fortune.[1]   Among other things they gave the Spaniards 300 dogs for food, although, according to the Elvas narrative, the Indians themselves did not eat them.[2]   The principal officers of the expedition were lodged in the "chief's house," by which we are to understand the townhouse, which was upon a high hill with a roadway to the top.[3]   From a close study of the narrative it appears that this "hill" was no other than the great Nacoochee mound, in White county, Georgia, a few miles northwest of the present Clarkesville.[4] It was within the Cherokee territory, and the town was probably a settlement of that tribe.   From here De Soto sent runners ahead to notify the chief of Chiaha of his approach, in order that sufficient corn might be ready on his arrival.

Leaving Guaxule, they proceeded down the river, which we identify with the Chattahoochee, and in two days arrived at Canasoga, or Canasagua, a frontier town of the Cherokee.   As they neared the town they were met by the Indians, bearing baskets of "mulberries,"[5] more probably the delicious service-berry of the southern mountains, which ripens in early summer, while the mulberry matures later.

From here they continued down the river, which grew constantly larger, through an uninhabited country which formed the disputed territory between the Cherokee and the Creeks.   About five days after leaving Canasagua they were met by messengers, who escorted them to Chiaha, the first town of the province of Coça.   De Soto had crossed the state of Georgia, leaving the Cherokee country behind him, and was now among the Lower Creeks, in the neighborhood of the present Columbus, Georgia.[6]   With his subsequent wanderings after crossing the Chattahoochee into Alabama and beyond we need not concern ourselves (8).

While resting at Chiaha De Soto met with a chief who confirmed what the Spaniards had heard before concerning mines in the province of Chisca, saying that there was there "a melting of copper" and of another metal of about the same color, but softer, and therefore not so much used.[7]   The province was northward from Chiaha, somewhere in upper Georgia or the adjacent part of Alabama or Tennessee, through all of which mountain region native copper is found.   The other mineral, which the Spaniards understood to be gold, may have been iron pyrites, although there is some evidence that the Indians occasionally found and shaped gold nuggets.[6]

---

[1] Ranjel, in Oviedo, Historia, I, p. 563, 1851.
[2] Elvas, Biedma, and Ranjel all make special reference to the dogs given them at this place; they seem to have been of the same small breed ("perrillos") which Ranjel says the Indians used for food.
[3] Garcilaso, La Florida del Inca, p. 139, 1723.   [4] See note 8, De Soto's route.
[5] See Elvas, Hakluyt Society, IX, p. 61, 1851; and Ranjel, op. cit., p. 563.
[6] See note 8, De Soto's route.   [7] Elvas, op. cit., p. 64.

Accordingly two soldiers were sent on foot with Indian guides to find Chisca and learn the truth of the stories. They rejoined the army some time after the march had been resumed, and reported according to the Elvas chronicler, that their guides had taken them through a country so poor in corn, so rough, and over so high mountains that it would be impossible for the army to follow, wherefore, as the way grew long and lingering, they had turned back after reaching a little poor town where they saw nothing that was of any profit. They brought back with them a dressed buffalo skin which the Indians there had given them, the first ever obtained by white men, and described in the quaint old chronicle as " an ox hide as thin as a calf's skin, and the hair like a soft wool between the coarse and fine wool of sheep."[1]

Garcilaso's glowing narrative gives a somewhat different impression. According to this author the scouts returned full of enthusiasm for the fertility of the country, and reported that the mines were of a fine species of copper, and had indications also of gold and silver, while their progress from one town to another had been a continual series of feastings and Indian hospitalities.[2] However that may have been, De Soto made no further effort to reach the Cherokee mines, but continued his course westward through the Creek country, having spent altogether a month in the mountain region.

There is no record of any second attempt to penetrate the Cherokee country for twenty-six years (9). In 1561 the Spaniards took formal possession of the bay of Santa Elena, now Saint Helena, near Port Royal, on the coast of South Carolina. The next year the French made an unsuccessful attempt at settlement at the same place, and in 1566 Menendez made the Spanish occupancy sure by establishing there a fort which he called San Felipe.[3] In November of that year Captain Juan Pardo was sent with a party from the fort to explore the interior. Accompanied by the chief of "Juada" (which from Vandera's narrative we find should be "Joara," i. e., the Sara Indians already mentioned in the De Soto chronicle), he proceeded as far as the territory of that tribe, where he built a fort, but on account of the snow in the mountains did not think it advisable to go farther, and returned, leaving a sergeant with thirty soldiers to garrison the post. Soon after his return he received a letter from the sergeant stating that the chief of Chisca—the rich mining country of which De Soto had heard—was very hostile to the Spaniards, and that in a recent battle the latter had killed a thousand of his Indians and burned fifty houses with almost no damage to themselves. Either the sergeant or his chronicler must have been an unconscionable liar, as it was asserted that all this was done with only fifteen men. Immediately afterward, according to the same story, the sergeant marched with twenty men about a day's

---

[1] Elvas, Hakluyt Society, IX, p. 66, 1851.   [2] Garcilaso, La Florida del Inca, p. 141, ed. 1723.
[3] Shea, J. G., in Winsor, Justin, Narrative and Critical History of America, II, pp. 260, 278; Boston, 1886.

distance in the mountains against another hostile chief, whom he found in a strongly palisaded town, which, after a hard fight, he and his men stormed and burned, killing fifteen hundred Indians without losing a single man themselves. Under instructions from his superior officer, the sergeant with his small party then proceeded to explore what lay beyond, and, taking a road which they were told led to the territory of a great chief, after four days of hard marching they came to his town, called Chiaha (Chicha, by mistake in the manuscript translation), the same where De Soto had rested. It is described at this time as palisaded and strongly fortified, with a deep river on each side, and defended by over three thousand fighting men, there being no women or children among them. It is possible that in view of their former experience with the Spaniards, the Indians had sent their families away from the town, while at the same time they may have summoned warriors from the neighboring Creek towns in order to be prepared for any emergency. However, as before, they received the white men with the greatest kindness, and the Spaniards continued for twelve days through the territories of the same tribe until they arrived at the principal town (Kusa?), where, by the invitation of the chief, they built a small fort and awaited the coming of Pardo, who was expected to follow with a larger force from Santa Elena, as he did in the summer of 1567, being met on his arrival with every show of hospitality from the Creek chiefs. This second fort was said to be one hundred and forty leagues distant from that in the Sara country, which latter was called one hundred and twenty leagues from Santa Elena.[1]

In the summer of 1567, according to previous agreement, Captain Pardo left the fort at Santa Elena with a small detachment of troops, and after a week's travel, sleeping each night at a different Indian town, arrived at "Canos, which the Indians call Canosi, and by another name, Cofetaçque" (the Cofitachiqui of the De Soto chronicle), which is described as situated in a favorable location for a large city, fifty leagues from Santa Elena, to which the easiest road was by a river (the Savannah) which flowed by the town, or by another which they had passed ten leagues farther back. Proceeding, they passed Jagaya, Gueza, and Arauchi, and arrived at Otariyatiqui, or Otari, in which we have perhaps the Cherokee ä'tärï or ä'tälï, "mountain". It may have been a frontier Cherokee settlement, and, according to the old chronicler, its chief and language ruled much good country. From here a trail went northward to Guatari, Sauxpa, and Usi, i. e., the Wateree, Waxhaw (or Sissipahaw?), and Ushery or Catawba.

Leaving Otariyatiqui, they went on to Quinahaqui, and then, turning to the left, to Issa, where they found mines of crystal (mica?). They came next to Aguaquiri (the Guaquili of the De Soto chronicle), and then to Joara, "near to the mountain, where Juan Pardo arrived

[1] Narrative of Pardo's expedition by Martinez, about 1568, Brooks manuscripts.

with his sergeant on his first trip." This, as has been noted, was the Xuala of the De Soto chronicle, the territory of the Sara Indians, in the foothills of the Blue ridge, southeast from the present Asheville, North Carolina. Vandera makes it one hundred leagues from Santa Elena, while Martinez, already quoted, makes the distance one hundred and twenty leagues. The difference is not important, as both statements were only estimates. From there they followed "along the mountains" to Tocax (Toxaway?), Cauchi (Nacoochee?), and Tanasqui—apparently Cherokee towns, although the forms can not be identified—and after resting three days at the last-named place went on "to Solameco, otherwise called Chiaha," where the sergeant met them. The combined forces afterward went on, through Cossa (Kusa), Tasquiqui (Taskigi), and other Creek towns, as far as Tascaluza, in the Alabama country, and returned thence to Santa Elena, having apparently met with a friendly reception everywhere along the route. From Cofitachiqui to Tascaluza they went over about the same road traversed by De Soto in 1540.[1]

We come now to a great gap of nearly a century. Shea has a notice of a Spanish mission founded among the Cherokee in 1643 and still flourishing when visited by an English traveler ten years later,[2] but as his information is derived entirely from the fraudulent work of Davies, and as no such mission is mentioned by Barcia in any of these years, we may regard the story as spurious (10). The first mission work in the tribe appears to have been that of Priber, almost a hundred years later. Long before the end of the sixteenth century, however, the existence of mines of gold and other metals in the Cherokee country was a matter of common knowledge among the Spaniards at St. Augustine and Santa Elena, and more than one expedition had been fitted out to explore the interior.[3] Numerous traces of ancient mining operations, with remains of old shafts and fortifications, evidently of European origin, show that these discoveries were followed up, although the policy of Spain concealed the fact from the outside world. How much permanent impression this early Spanish intercourse made on the Cherokee it is impossible to estimate, but it must have been considerable (11).

THE COLONIAL AND REVOLUTIONARY PERIOD—1654–1784

It was not until 1654 that the English first came into contact with the Cherokee, called in the records of the period Rechahecrians, a corruption of Rickahockan, apparently the name by which they were known to the Powhatan tribes. In that year the Virginia colony, which had only recently concluded a long and exterminating war with the Powhatan, was thrown into alarm by the news that a great body of

---

[1] Vandera narrative, 1569, in French, B. F., Hist. Colls. of La., new series, pp. 289–292; New York, 1875.
[2] Shea, J. G., Catholic Missions, p. 72; New York, 1855.
[3] See Brooks manuscripts, in the archives of the Bureau of American Ethnology.

six or seven hundred Rechahecrian Indians—by which is probably meant that number of warriors—from the mountains had invaded the lower country and established themselves at the falls of James river, where now is the city of Richmond. The assembly at once passed resolutions "that these new come Indians be in no sort suffered to seat themselves there, or any place near us, it having cost so much blood to expel and extirpate those perfidious and treacherous Indians which were there formerly." It was therefore ordered that a force of at least 100 white men be at once sent against them, to be joined by the warriors of all the neighboring subject tribes, according to treaty obligation. The Pamunkey chief, with a hundred of his men, responded to the summons, and the combined force marched against the invaders. The result was a bloody battle, with disastrous outcome to the Virginians, the Pamunkey chief with most of his men being killed, while the whites were forced to make such terms of peace with the Rechahecrians that the assembly cashiered the commander of the expedition and compelled him to pay the whole cost of the treaty from his own estate.[1] Owing to the imperfection of the Virginia records we have no means of knowing the causes of the sudden invasion or how long the invaders retained their position at the falls. In all probability it was only the last of a long series of otherwise unrecorded irruptions by the mountaineers on the more peaceful dwellers in the lowlands. From a remark in Lederer it is probable that the Cherokee were assisted also by some of the piedmont tribes hostile to the Powhatan. The Peaks of Otter, near which the Cherokee claim to have once lived, as has been already noted, are only about one hundred miles in a straight line from Richmond, while the burial mound and town site near Charlottesville, mentioned by Jefferson, are but half that distance.

In 1655 a Virginia expedition sent out from the falls of James river (Richmond) crossed over the mountains to the large streams flowing into the Mississippi. No details are given and the route is uncertain, but whether or not they met Indians, they must have passed through Cherokee territory.[2]

In 1670 the German traveler, John Lederer, went from the falls of James river to the Catawba country in South Carolina, following for most of the distance the path used by the Virginia traders, who already had regular dealings with the southern tribes, including probably the Cherokee. He speaks in several places of the Rickahockan, which seems to be a more correct form than Rechahecrian, and his narrative and the accompanying map put them in the mountains of North Carolina, back of the Catawba and the Sara and southward from the head of Roanoke river. They were apparently on hostile terms with the tribes to the eastward, and while the traveler was stopping at an Indian

---

[1] Burk, John, History of Virginia, II, pp. 104–107; Petersburg, 1805.

[2] Ramsey, J. G. M., Annals of Tennessee, p. 37; Charleston, 1853 (quoting Martin, North Carolina, I, p. 115, 1853).

village on Dan river, about the present Clarksville, Virginia, a delegation of Rickahockan, which had come on tribal business, was barbarously murdered at a dance prepared on the night of their arrival by their treacherous hosts. On reaching the Catawba country he heard of white men to the southward, and incidentally mentions that the neighboring mountains were called the Suala mountains by the Spaniards.[1] In the next year, 1671, a party from Virginia under Thomas Batts explored the northern branch of Roanoke river and crossed over the Blue ridge to the headwaters of New river, where they found traces of occupancy, but no Indians. By this time all the tribes of this section, east of the mountains, were in possession of firearms.[2]

The first permanent English settlement in South Carolina was established in 1670. In 1690 James Moore, secretary of the colony, made an exploring expedition into the mountains and reached a point at which, according to his Indian guides, he was within twenty miles of where the Spaniards were engaged in mining and smelting with bellows and furnaces, but on account of some misunderstanding he returned without visiting the place, although he procured specimens of ores, which he sent to England for assay.[3] It may have been in the neighborhood of the present Lincolnton, North Carolina, where a dam of cut stone and other remains of former civilized occupancy have recently been discovered (11). In this year, also, Cornelius Dougherty, an Irishman from Virginia, established himself as the first trader among the Cherokee, with whom he spent the rest of his life.[4] Some of his descendants still occupy honored positions in the tribe.

Among the manuscript archives of South Carolina there was said to be, some fifty years ago, a treaty or agreement made with the government of that colony by the Cherokee in 1684, and signed with the hieroglyphics of eight chiefs of the lower towns, viz, Corani, the Raven (Kâ'lanû); Sinnawa, the Hawk (Tlă'nuwă); Nellawgitehi, Gorhaleke, and Owasta, all of Toxawa; and Canacaught, the great Conjuror, Gohoma, and Caunasaita, of Keowa. If still in existence, this is probably the oldest Cherokee treaty on record.[5]

What seems to be the next mention of the Cherokee in the South Carolina records occurs in 1691, when we find an inquiry ordered in regard to a report that some of the colonists " have, without any proclamation of war, fallen upon and murdered " several of that tribe.[6]

In 1693 some Cherokee chiefs went to Charleston with presents for the governor and offers of friendship, to ask the protection of South Carolina against their enemies, the Esaw (Catawba), Savanna (Shawano),

---

[1] Lederer, John, Discoveries, pp. 15, 26, 27, 29, 33, and map; reprint, Charleston, 1891; Mooney, Siouan Tribes of the East (bulletin of Bureau of Ethnology), pp. 53–54, 1894.

[2] Mooney, op. cit., pp. 34–35.

[3] Document of 1699, quoted in South Carolina Hist. Soc. Colls., I, p. 209; Charleston, 1857.

[4] Haywood, Nat. and Aborig. Hist. Tennessee, p. 233, 1823.

[5] Noted in Cherokee Advocate, Tahlequah, Indian Territory, January 30, 1845.

[6] Document of 1691, South Carolina Hist. Soc. Colls., I, p. 126.

and Congaree, all of that colony, who had made war upon them and
sold a number of their tribesmen into slavery. They were told that
their kinsmen could not now be recovered, but that the English desired
friendship with their tribe, and that the Government would see that
there would be no future ground for such complaint.[1] The promise
was apparently not kept, for in 1705 we find a bitter accusation brought
against Governor Moore, of South Carolina, that he had granted commissions to a number of persons "to set upon, assault, kill, destroy,
and take captive as many Indians as they possible [sic] could," the
prisoners being sold into slavery for his and their private profit. By
this course, it was asserted, he had "already almost utterly ruined the
trade for skins and furs, whereby we held our chief correspondence
with England, and turned it into a trade of Indians or slave making,
whereby the Indians to the south and west of us are already involved
in blood and confusion." The arraignment concludes with a warning
that such conditions would in all probability draw down upon the colony
an Indian war with all its dreadful consequences.[2] In view of what
happened a few years later this reads like a prophecy.

About the year 1700 the first guns were introduced among the Cherokee, the event being fixed traditionally as having occurred in the girl-
hood of an old woman of the tribe who died about 1775.[3] In 1708 we
find them described as a numerous people, living in the mountains
northwest from the Charleston settlements and having sixty towns, but
of small importance in the Indian trade, being "but ordinary hunters
and less warriors."[4]

In the war with the Tuscarora in 1711–1713, which resulted in the
expulsion of that tribe from North Carolina, more than a thousand
southern Indians reenforced the South Carolina volunteers, among
them being over two hundred Cherokee, hereditary enemies of the
Tuscarora. Although these Indian allies did their work well in the
actual encounters, their assistance was of doubtful advantage, as they
helped themselves freely to whatever they wanted along the way, so
that the settlers had reason to fear them almost as much as the hostile
Tuscarora. After torturing a large number of their prisoners in the
usual savage fashion, they returned with the remainder, whom they
afterward sold as slaves to South Carolina.[5]

Having wiped out old scores with the Tuscarora, the late allies of
the English proceeded to discuss their own grievances, which, as we
have seen, were sufficiently galling. The result was a combination

[1] Hewat, South Carolina and Georgia, I, p. 127, 1778.

[2] Documents of 1705, in North Carolina Colonial Records, II, p. 904; Raleigh, 1886.

[3] Haywood, Nat. and Aborig. Tenn., p. 237, 1823; with the usual idea that Indians live to extreme
old age, Haywood makes her 110 years old at her death, putting back the introduction of firearms
to 1677.

[4] Letter of 1708, in Rivers, South Carolina, p. 238, 1856.

[5] Royce, Cherokee Nation, Fifth Ann. Rep. Bureau of Ethnology, p. 140, 1888; Hewat, op. cit.,p. 216
et passim.

against the whites, embracing all the tribes from Cape Fear to the Chattahoochee, including the Cherokee, who thus for the first time raised their hand against the English. The war opened with a terrible massacre by the Yamassee in April, 1715, followed by assaults along the whole frontier, until for a time it was seriously feared that the colony of South Carolina would be wiped out of existence. In a contest between savagery and civilization, however, the final result is inevitable. The settlers at last rallied their whole force under Governor Craven and administered such a crushing blow to the Yamassee that the remnant abandoned their country and took refuge with the Spaniards in Florida or among the Lower Creeks. The English then made short work with the smaller tribes along the coast, while those in the interior were soon glad to sue for peace.[1]

A number of Cherokee chiefs having come down to Charleston in company with a trader to express their desire for peace, a force of several hundred white troops and a number of negroes under Colonel Maurice Moore went up the Savannah in the winter of 1715–16 and made headquarters among the Lower Cherokee, where they were met by the chiefs of the Lower and some of the western towns, who reaffirmed their desire for a lasting peace with the English, but refused to fight against the Yamassee, although willing to proceed against some other tribes. They laid the blame for most of the trouble upon the traders, who "had been very abuseful to them of late." A detachment under Colonel George Chicken, sent to the Upper Cherokee, penetrated to "Quoneashee" (Tlanusi'yĭ, on Hiwassee, about the present Murphy) where they found the chiefs more defiant, resolved to continue the war against the Creeks, with whom the English were then trying to make peace, and demanding large supplies of guns and ammunition, saying that if they made a peace with the other tribes they would have no means of getting slaves with which to buy ammunition for themselves. At this time they claimed 2,370 warriors, of whom half were believed to have guns. As the strength of the whole Nation was much greater, this estimate may have been for the Upper and Middle Cherokee only. After "abundance of persuading" by the officers, they finally "told us they would trust us once again," and an arrangement was made to furnish them two hundred guns with a supply of ammunition, together with fifty white soldiers, to assist them against the tribes with which the English were still at war. In March, 1716, this force was increased by one hundred men. The detachment under Colonel Chicken returned by way of the towns on the upper part of the Little Tennessee, thus penetrating the heart of the Cherokee country.[2]

---

[1] Hewat, South Carolina and Georgia, I, p. 216 et passim, 1778.
[2] See Journal of Colonel George Chicken, 1715–16, with notes, in Charleston Yearbook, pp. 313–354, 1894.

Steps were now taken to secure peace by inaugurating a satisfactory trade system, for which purpose a large quantity of suitable goods was purchased at the public expense of South Carolina, and a correspondingly large party was equipped for the initial trip.[1] In 1721, in order still more to systematize Indian affairs, Governor Nicholson of South Carolina invited the chiefs of the Cherokee to a conference, at which thirty-seven towns were represented. A treaty was made by which trading methods were regulated, a boundary line between their territory and the English settlements was agreed upon, and an agent was appointed to superintend their affairs. At the governor's suggestion, one chief, called Wrosetasatow (?)[2] was formally commissioned as supreme head of the Nation, with authority to punish all offenses, including murder, and to represent all Cherokee claims to the colonial government. Thus were the Cherokee reduced from their former condition of a free people, ranging where their pleasure led, to that of dependent vassals with bounds fixed by a colonial governor. The negotiations were accompanied by a cession of land, the first in the history of the tribe. In little more than a century thereafter they had signed away their whole original territory.[3]

The document of 1716 already quoted puts the strength of the Cherokee at that time at 2,370 warriors, but in this estimate the Lower Cherokee seem not to have been included. In 1715, according to a trade census compiled by Governor Johnson of South Carolina, the tribe had thirty towns, with 4,000 warriors and a total population of 11,210.[4] Another census in 1721 gives them fifty-three towns with 3,510 warriors and a total of 10,379,[5] while the report of the board of trade for the same year gives them 3,800 warriors,[6] equivalent, by the same proportion, to nearly 12,000 total. Adair, a good authority on such matters, estimates, about the year 1735, when the country was better known, that they had "sixty-four towns and villages, populous and full of children," with more than 6,000 fighting men,[7] equivalent on the same basis of computation to between 16,000 and 17,000 souls. From what we know of them in later times, it is probable that this last estimate is very nearly correct.

By this time the colonial government had become alarmed at the advance of the French, who had made their first permanent establishment in the Gulf states at Biloxi bay, Mississippi, in 1699, and in 1714 had built Fort Toulouse, known to the English as "the fort at

---

[1] Journal of South Carolina Assembly, in North Carolina Colonial Records, II, pp. 225–227, 1886.

[2] For notice, see the glossary.

[3] Hewat, South Carolina and Georgia, I, pp. 297–298, 1778; Royce, Cherokee Nation, in Fifth Ann. Rep. Bureau of Ethnology, p. 144 and map, 1888.

[4] Royce, op. cit., p. 142.

[5] Document of 1724, in Fernow, Berthold, Ohio Valley in Colonial Days, pp. 273–275; Albany, 1890.

[6] Report of Board of Trade, 1721, in North Carolina Colonial Records, II, p. 422, 1886.

[7] Adair, James, American Indians, p. 227; London, 1775.

the Alabamas," on Coosa river, a few miles above the present Montgomery, Alabama. From this central vantage point they had rapidly extended their influence among all the neighboring tribes until in 1721 it was estimated that 3,400 warriors who had formerly traded with Carolina had been "entirely debauched to the French interest," while 2,000 more were wavering, and only the Cherokee could still be considered friendly to the English.[1] From this time until the final withdrawal of the French in 1763 the explanation of our Indian wars is to be found in the struggle between the two nations for territorial and commercial supremacy, the Indian being simply the cat's-paw of one or the other. For reasons of their own, the Chickasaw, whose territory lay within the recognized limits of Louisiana, soon became the uncompromising enemies of the French, and as their position enabled them in a measure to control the approach from the Mississippi, the Carolina government saw to it that they were kept well supplied with guns and ammunition. British traders were in all their towns, and on one occasion a French force, advancing against a Chickasaw palisaded village, found it garrisoned by Englishmen flying the British flag.[2] The Cherokee, although nominally allies of the English, were strongly disposed to favor the French, and it required every effort of the Carolina government to hold them to their allegiance.

In 1730, to further fix the Cherokee in the English interest, Sir Alexander Cuming was dispatched on a secret mission to that tribe, which was again smarting under grievances and almost ready to join with the Creeks in an alliance with the French. Proceeding to the ancient town of Nequassee (Nĭkwăsĭ', at the present Franklin, North Carolina), he so impressed the chiefs by his bold bearing that they conceded without question all his demands, submitting themselves and their people for the second time to the English dominion and designating Moytoy,[3] of Tellico, to act as their "emperor" and to represent the Nation in all transactions with the whites. Seven chiefs were selected to visit England, where, in the palace at Whitehall, they solemnly renewed the treaty, acknowledging the sovereignty of England and binding themselves to have no trade or alliance with any other nation, not to allow any other white people to settle among them, and to deliver up any fugitive slaves who might seek refuge with them. To confirm their words they delivered a "crown", five eagle-tails, and four scalps, which they had brought with them. In return they received the usual glittering promises of love and perpetual friendship, together with a substantial quantity of guns, ammunition, and red paint. The treaty being concluded in September,

---

[1] Board of Trade report, 1721, North Carolina Colonial Records, II, p. 422, 1886.
[2] Pickett, H. A., History of Alabama, pp. 234, 280, 288; reprint, Sheffield, 1896.
[3] For notice, see the glossary.

they took ship for Carolina, where they arrived, as we are told by
the governor, "in good health and mightily well satisfied with His
Majesty's bounty to them."[1]

In the next year some action was taken to use the Cherokee and
Catawba to subdue the refractory remnant of the Tuscarora in North
Carolina, but when it was found that this was liable to bring down the
wrath of the Iroquois upon the Carolina settlements, more peaceable
methods were used instead.[2]

In 1738 or 1739 the smallpox, brought to Carolina by slave ships,
broke out among the Cherokee with such terrible effect that, according
to Adair, nearly half the tribe was swept away within a year.   The
awful mortality was due largely to the fact that as it was a new and
strange disease to the Indians they had no proper remedies against it,
and therefore resorted to the universal Indian panacea for "strong"
sickness of almost any kind, viz, cold plunge baths in the running
stream, the worst treatment that could possibly be devised.   As the
pestilence spread unchecked from town to town, despair fell upon the
nation.   The priests, believing the visitation a penalty for violation of
the ancient ordinances, threw away their sacred paraphernalia as things
which had lost their protecting power.   Hundreds of the warriors
committed suicide on beholding their frightful disfigurement.   "Some
shot themselves, others cut their throats, some stabbed themselves
with knives and others with sharp-pointed canes; many threw themselves with sullen madness into the fire and there slowly expired, as if
they had been utterly divested of the native power of feeling pain."[3]
Another authority estimates their loss at a thousand warriors, partly
from smallpox and partly from rum brought in by the traders.[4]

About the year 1740 a trading path for horsemen was marked out
by the Cherokee from the new settlement of Augusta, in Georgia, to
their towns on the headwaters of Savannah river and thence on to the
west.   This road, which went up the south side of the river, soon
became much frequented.[4]   Previous to this time most of the trading
goods had been transported on the backs of Indians.   In the same
year a party of Cherokee under the war chief Kâ'lanû. "The Raven,"
took part in Oglethorpe's expedition against the Spaniards of Saint
Augustine.[5]

In 1736 Christian Priber, said to be a Jesuit acting in the French
interest, had come among the Cherokee, and, by the facility with which
he learned the language and adapted himself to the native dress and

[1]Hewat, South Carolina and Georgia, II, pp. 3–11, 1779; treaty documents of 1730, North Carolina
Colonial Records, III, pp. 128–133, 1886; Jenkinson, Collection of Treaties, II, pp. 315–318; Drake, S. G.,
Early History of Georgia: Cuming's Embassy; Boston, 1872; letter of Governor Johnson, December 27,
1730, noted in South Carolina Hist. Soc. Colls., I, p. 246, 1857.

[2] Documents of 1731 and 1732, North Carolina Colonial Records, III, pp. 153, 202, 345, 369, 393, 1886.

[3] Adair, American Indians, pp. 232–234, 1775.

[4] Meadows (?), State of the Province of Georgia, p. 7, 1742, in Force Tracts, I, 1836.

[5] Jones, C. C., History of Georgia, I, pp. 327, 328; Boston, 1883.

mode of life, had quickly acquired a leading influence among them. He drew up for their adoption a scheme of government modeled after the European plan, with the capital at Great Tellico, in Tennessee, the principal medicine man as emperor, and himself as the emperor's secretary.   Under this title he corresponded with the South Carolina government until it began to be feared that he would ultimately win over the whole tribe to the French side.   A commissioner was sent to arrest him, but the Cherokee refused to give him up, and the deputy was obliged to return under safe-conduct of an escort furnished by Priber.   Five years after the inauguration of his work, however, he was seized by some English traders while on his way to Fort Toulouse, and brought as a prisoner to Frederica, in Georgia, where he soon afterward died while under confinement.   Although his enemies had represented him as a monster, inciting the Indians to the grossest immoralities, he proved to be a gentleman of polished address, extensive learning, and rare courage, as was shown later on the occasion of an explosion in the barracks magazine.   Besides Greek, Latin, French, German, Spanish, and fluent English, he spoke also the Cherokee, and among his papers which were seized was found a manuscript dictionary of the language, which he had prepared for publication— the first, and even yet, perhaps, the most important study of the language ever made.   Says Adair: "As he was learned and possessed of a very sagacious penetrating judgment, and had every qualification that was requisite for his bold and difficult enterprise, it was not to be doubted that, as he wrote a Cheerake dictionary, designed to be published at Paris, he likewise set down a great deal that would have been very acceptable to the curious and serviceable to the representatives of South Carolina and Georgia, which may be readily found in Frederica if the manuscripts have had the good fortune to escape the despoiling hands of military power."   He claimed to be a Jesuit, acting under orders of his superior, to introduce habits of steady industry, civilized arts, and a regular form of government among the southern tribes, with a view to the ultimate founding of an independent Indian state.   From all that can be gathered of him, even though it comes from his enemies, there can be little doubt that he was a worthy member of that illustrious order whose name has been a synonym for scholarship, devotion, and courage from the days of Jogues and Marquette down to De Smet and Mengarini.[1]

Up to this time no civilizing or mission work had been undertaken by either of the Carolina governments among any of the tribes within their borders.   As one writer of the period quaintly puts it, "The gospel spirit is not yet so gloriously arisen as to seek them more than theirs," while another in stronger terms affirms, "To the shame of

[1] Adair, American Indians, pp. 240–243, 1775; Stevens, W. B., History of Georgia, I, pp. 104–107; Phila., 1847.

the Christian name, no pains have ever been taken to convert them to Christianity; on the contrary, their morals are perverted and corrupted by the sad example they daily have of its depraved professors residing in their towns."[1] Readers of Lawson and other narratives of the period will feel the force of the rebuke.

Throughout the eighteenth century the Cherokee were engaged in chronic warfare with their Indian neighbors. As these quarrels concerned the whites but little, however momentous they may have been to the principals, we have but few details. The war with the Tuscarora continued until the outbreak of the latter tribe against Carolina in 1711 gave opportunity to the Cherokee to cooperate in striking the blow which drove the Tuscarora from their ancient homes to seek refuge in the north. The Cherokee then turned their attention to the Shawano on the Cumberland, and with the aid of the Chickasaw finally expelled them from that region about the year 1715. Inroads upon the Catawba were probably kept up until the latter had become so far reduced by war and disease as to be mere dependent pensioners upon the whites. The former friendship with the Chickasaw was at last broken through the overbearing conduct of the Cherokee, and a war followed of which we find incidental notice in 1757,[2] and which terminated in a decisive victory for the Chickasaw about 1768. The bitter war with the Iroquois of the far north continued, in spite of all the efforts of the colonial governments, until a formal treaty of peace was brought about by the efforts of Sir William Johnson (12) in the same year.

The hereditary war with the Creeks for possession of upper Georgia continued, with brief intervals of peace, or even alliance, until the United States finally interfered as mediator between the rival claimants. In 1718 we find notice of a large Cherokee war party moving against the Creek town of Coweta, on the lower Chattahoochee, but dispersing on learning of the presence there of some French and Spanish officers, as well as some English traders, all bent on arranging an alliance with the Creeks. The Creeks themselves had declared their willingness to be at peace with the English, while still determined to keep the bloody hatchet uplifted against the Cherokee.[3] The most important incident of the struggle between the two ·tribes was ·probably the battle of Tali'wa about the year 1755.[4]

By this time the weaker coast tribes had become practically extinct, and the more powerful tribes of the interior were beginning to take the alarm, as they saw the restless borderers pushing every year farther into the Indian country. As early as 1748 Dr Thomas Walker, with a company of hunters and woodsmen from Virginia, crossed the moun-

[1] Anonymous writer in Carroll, Hist. Colls. of South Carolina, II, pp. 97–98, 517, 1836.

[2] Buckle, Journal, 1757, in Rivers, South Carolina, p. 57, 1856.

[3] Barcia, A. G., Ensayo Chronologico para la Historia General de la Florida, pp. 335, 336, Madrid, 1723.

[4] For more in regard to these intertribal wars see the historical traditions.

tains to the southwest, discovering and naming the celebrated Cumberland gap and passing on to the headwaters of Cumberland river. Two years later he made a second exploration and penetrated to Kentucky river, but on account of the Indian troubles no permanent settlement was then attempted.[1] This invasion of their territory awakened a natural resentment of the native owners, and we find proof also in the Virginia records that the irresponsible borderers seldom let pass an opportunity to kill and plunder any stray Indian found in their neighborhood.

In 1755 the Cherokee were officially reported to number 2,590 warriors, as against probably twice that number previous to the great smallpox epidemic sixteen years before. Their neighbors and ancient enemies, the Catawba, had dwindled to 240 men.[2]

Although war was not formally declared by England until 1756, hostilities in the seven year's struggle between France and England, commonly known in America as the " French and Indian war," began in April, 1754, when the French seized a small post which the English had begun at the present site of Pittsburg, and which was afterward finished by the French under the name of Fort Du Quesne. Strenuous efforts were made by the English to secure the Cherokee to their interest against the French and their Indian allies, and treaties were negotiated by which they promised assistance.[3] As these treaties, however, carried the usual cessions of territory, and stipulated for the building of several forts in the heart of the Cherokee country, it is to be feared that the Indians were not duly impressed by the disinterested character of the proceeding. Their preference for the French was but thinly veiled, and only immediate policy prevented them from throwing their whole force into the scale on that side. The reasons for this preference are given by Timberlake, the young Virginian officer who visited the tribe on an embassy of conciliation a few years later:

I found the nation much attached to the French, who have the prudence, by familiar politeness—which costs but little and often does a great deal—and conforming themselves to their ways and temper, to conciliate the inclinations of almost all the Indians they are acquainted with, while the pride of our officers often disgusts them. Nay, they did not scruple to own to me that it was the trade alone that induced them to make peace with us, and not any preference to the French, whom they loved a great deal better. . . . The English are now so nigh, and encroached daily so far upon them, that they not only felt the bad effects of it in their hunting grounds, which were spoiled, but had all the reason in the world to apprehend being swallowed up by so potent neighbors or driven from the country inhabited by their fathers, in which they were born and brought up, in fine, their native soil, for which all men have a particular tenderness and affection.

[1] Walker, Thomas, Journal of an Exploration, etc., pp. 8, 35–37; Boston, 1888; Monette (Valley of the Miss. I, p. 317; New York, 1848) erroneously makes the second date 1758.

[2] Letter of Governor Dobbs, 1755, in North Carolina Colonial Records, v. pp. 320, 321, 1887.

[3] Ramsey, Tennessee, pp. 50–52, 1853; Royce, Cherokee Nation, in Fifth Ann. Rep. Bur. of Ethnology, p. 145, 1888.

He adds that only dire necessity had induced them to make peace with the English in 1761.[1]

In accordance with the treaty stipulations Fort Prince George was built in 1756 adjoining the important Cherokee town of Keowee, on the headwaters of the Savannah, and Fort Loudon near the junction of Tellico river with the Little Tennessee, in the center of the Cherokee towns beyond the mountains.[2]   By special arrangement with the influential chief, Ata-kullakulla (Ătă'-gûl″kălû'),[3] Fort Dobbs was also built in the same year about 20 miles west of the present Salisbury, North Carolina.[4]

The Cherokee had agreed to furnish four hundred warriors to cooperate against the French in the north, but before Fort Loudon had been completed it was very evident that they had repented of their promise, as their great council at Echota ordered the work stopped and the garrison on the way to turn back, plainly telling the officer in charge that they did not want so many white people among them.   Ata-kullakulla, hitherto supposed to be one of the stanchest friends of the English, was now one of the most determined in the opposition.   It was in evidence also that they were in constant communication with the French.   By much tact and argument their objections were at last overcome for a time, and they very unwillingly set about raising the promised force of warriors.   Major Andrew Lewis, who superintended the building of the fort, became convinced that the Cherokee were really friendly to the French, and that all their professions of friendship and assistance were "only to put a gloss on their knavery."   The fort was finally completed, and, on his suggestion, was garrisoned with a strong force of two hundred men under Captain Demeré.[5]   There was strong ground for believing that some depredations committed about this time on the heads of Catawba and Broad rivers, in North Carolina, were the joint work of Cherokee and northern Indians.[6]   Notwithstanding all this, a considerable body of Cherokee joined the British forces on the Virginia frontier.[7]

Fort Du Quesne was taken by the American provincials under Washington, November 25, 1758.   Quebec was taken September 13, 1759, and by the final treaty of peace in 1763 the war ended with the transfer of Canada and the Ohio valley to the crown of England.   Louisiana had already been ceded by France to Spain.

Although France was thus eliminated from the Indian problem, the

---

[1] Timberlake, Henry, Memoirs, pp. 73, 74; London, 1765.

[2] Ramsey, Tennessee, p. 51, 1853; Royce, Cherokee Nation, in Fifth Ann. Rept. Bur. of Ethnology, p. 145, 1888.

[3] For notice see Ătă'-gûl″kălû', in the glossary.

[4] Ramsey, op. cit., p. 50.

[5] Letters of Major Andrew Lewis and Governor Dinwiddie, 1756, in North Carolina Colonial Records v, pp. 585, 612–614, 635, 637, 1887; Ramsey, op. cit., pp. 51, 52.

[6] Letter of Governor Dobbs, 1756, in North Carolina Colonial Records, v, p. 604, 1887.

[7] Dinwiddie letter, 1757, ibid., p. 765.

Indians themselves were not ready to accept the settlement. In the north the confederated tribes under Pontiac continued to war on their own account until 1765. In the South the very Cherokee who had acted as allies of the British against Fort Du Quesne, and had voluntarily offered to guard the frontier south of the Potomac, returned to rouse their tribe to resistance.

The immediate exciting cause of the trouble was an unfortunate expedition undertaken against the hostile Shawano in February, 1756, by Major Andrew Lewis (the same who had built Fort Loudon) with some two hundred Virginia troops assisted by about one hundred Cherokee. After six weeks of fruitless tramping through the woods, with the ground covered with snow and the streams so swollen by rains that they lost their provisions and ammunition in crossing, they were obliged to return to the settlements in a starving condition, having killed their horses on the way. The Indian contingent had from the first been disgusted at the contempt and neglect experienced from those whom they had come to assist. The Tuscarora and others had already gone home, and the Cherokee now started to return on foot to their own country. Finding some horses running loose on the range, they appropriated them, on the theory that as they had lost their own animals, to say nothing of having risked their lives, in the service of the colonists, it was only a fair exchange. The frontiersmen took another view of the question however, attacked the returning Cherokee, and killed a number of them, variously stated at from twelve to forty, including several of their prominent men. According to Adair they also scalped and mutilated the bodies in the savage fashion to which they had become accustomed in the border wars, and brought the scalps into the settlements, where they were represented as those of French Indians and sold at the regular price then established by law. The young warriors at once prepared to take revenge, but were restrained by the chiefs until satisfaction could be demanded in the ordinary way, according to the treaties arranged with the colonial governments. Application was made in turn to Virginia, North Carolina, and South Carolina, but without success. While the women were still wailing night and morning for their slain kindred, and the Creeks were taunting the warriors for their cowardice in thus quietly submitting to the injury, some lawless officers of Fort Prince George committed an unpardonable outrage at the neighboring Indian town while most of the men were away hunting.[1] The warriors could no longer be restrained. Soon there was news of attacks upon the back settlements of Carolina, while on the other side of the mountains two soldiers of the Fort Loudon garrison were killed. War seemed at hand.

---

[1] Adair, American Indians, 245–246, 1775; North Carolina Colonial Records, v, p. xlviii, 1887; Hewat, quoted in Ramsey, Tennessee, p. 54, 1853.

At this juncture, in November, 1758, a party of influential chiefs, having first ordered back a war party just about to set out from the western towns against the Carolina settlements, came down to Charleston and succeeded in arranging the difficulty upon a friendly basis. The assembly had officially declared peace with the Cherokee, when, in May of 1759, Governor Lyttleton unexpectedly came forward with a demand for the surrender for execution of every Indian who had killed a white man in the recent skirmishes, among these being the chiefs of Citico and Tellico. At the same time the commander at Fort Loudon, forgetful of the fact that he had but a small garrison in the midst of several thousands of restless savages, made a demand for twenty-four other chiefs whom he suspected of unfriendly action. To compel their surrender orders were given to stop all trading supplies intended for the upper Cherokee.

This roused the whole Nation, and a delegation representing every town came down to Charleston, protesting the desire of the Indians for peace and friendship, but declaring their inability to surrender their own chiefs. The governor replied by declaring war in November, 1759, at once calling out troops and sending messengers to secure the aid of all the surrounding tribes against the Cherokee. In the meantime a second delegation of thirty-two of the most prominent men, led by the young war chief Oconostota (Âgăn-stâta),[1] arrived to make a further effort for peace, but the governor, refusing to listen to them, seized the whole party and confined them as prisoners at Fort Prince George, in a room large enough for only six soldiers, while at the same time he set fourteen hundred troops in motion to invade the Cherokee country. On further representation by Ata-kullakulla (Ătă′-gûl″kălû′), the civil chief of the Nation and well known as a friend of the English, the governor released Oconostota and two others after compelling some half dozen of the delegation to sign a paper by which they pretended to agree for their tribe to kill or seize any Frenchmen entering their country, and consented to the imprisonment of the party until all the warriors demanded had been surrendered for execution or otherwise. At this stage of affairs the smallpox broke out in the Cherokee towns, rendering a further stay in their neighborhood unsafe, and thinking the whole matter now settled on his own basis, Lyttleton returned to Charleston.

The event soon proved how little he knew of Indian temper. Oconostota at once laid siege to Fort Prince George, completely cutting off communication at a time when, as it was now winter, no help could well be expected from below. In February, 1760, after having kept the fort thus closely invested for some weeks, he sent word one day by an Indian woman that he wished to speak to the commander, Lieutenant Coytmore. As the lieutenant stepped out from the stockade

---

[1] For notices see the glossary.

to see what was wanted, Oconostota, standing on the opposite side of the river, swung a bridle above his head as a signal to his warriors concealed in the bushes, and the officer was at once shot down. The soldiers immediately broke into the room where the hostages were confined, every one being a chief of prominence in the tribe, and butchered them to the last man.

It was now war to the end. Led by Oconostota, the Cherokee descended upon the frontier settlements of Carolina, while the warriors across the mountains laid close siege to Fort Loudon. In June, 1760, a strong force of over 1,600 men, under Colonel Montgomery, started to reduce the Cherokee towns and relieve the beleaguered garrison. Crossing the Indian frontier, Montgomery quickly drove the enemy from about Fort Prince George and then, rapidly advancing, surprised Little Keowee, killing every man of the defenders, and destroyed in succession every one of the Lower Cherokee towns, burning them to the ground, cutting down the cornfields and orchards, killing and taking more than a hundred of their men, and driving the whole population into the mountains before him. His own loss was very slight. He then sent messengers to the Middle and Upper towns, summoning them to surrender on penalty of the like fate, but, receiving no reply, he led his men across the divide to the waters of the Little Tennessee and continued down that stream without opposition until he came in the vicinity of Echoee (Itse'yĭ), a few miles above the sacred town of Nĭkwăsĭ', the present Franklin, North Carolina. Here the Cherokee had collected their full force to resist his progress, and the result was a desperate engagement on June 27, 1760, by which Montgomery was compelled to retire to Fort Prince George, after losing nearly one hundred men in killed and wounded. The Indian loss is unknown.

His retreat sealed the fate of Fort Loudon. The garrison, though hard pressed and reduced to the necessity of eating horses and dogs, had been enabled to hold out through the kindness of the Indian women, many of whom, having found sweethearts among the soldiers, brought them supplies of food daily. When threatened by the chiefs the women boldly replied that the soldiers were their husbands and it was their duty to help them, and that if any harm came to themselves for their devotion their English relatives would avenge them.[1] The end was only delayed, however, and on August 8, 1760, the garrison of about two hundred men, under Captain Demeré, surrendered to Oconostota on promise that they should be allowed to retire unmolested with their arms and sufficient ammunition for the march, on condition of delivering up all the remaining warlike stores.

The troops marched out and proceeded far enough to camp for the night, while the Indians swarmed into the fort to see what plunder they might find. "By accident a discovery was made of ten bags of

---

[1] Timberlake, Memoirs, p. 65, 1765.

powder and a large quantity of ball that had been secretly buried in the fort, to prevent their falling into the enemy's hands" (Hewat). It is said also that cannon, small arms, and ammunition had been thrown into the river with the same intention (Haywood). Enraged at this breach of the capitulation the Cherokee attacked the soldiers next morning at daylight, killing Demeré and twenty-nine others at the first fire. The rest were taken and held as prisoners until ransomed some time after. The second officer, Captain Stuart (13), for whom the Indians had a high regard, was claimed by Ata-kullakulla, who soon after took him into the woods, ostensibly on a hunting excursion, and conducted him for nine days through the wilderness until he delivered him safely into the hands of friends in Virginia. The chief's kindness was well rewarded, and it was largely through his influence that peace was finally brought about.

It was now too late, and the settlements were too much exhausted, for another expedition, so the fall and winter were employed by the English in preparations for an active campaign the next year in force to crush out all resistance. In June 1761, Colonel Grant with an army of 2,600 men, including a number of Chickasaw and almost every remaining warrior of the Catawba,[1] set out from Fort Prince George. Refusing a request from Ata-kullakulla for a friendly accommodation, he crossed Rabun gap and advanced rapidly down the Little Tennessee along the same trail taken by the expedition of the previous year. On June 10, when within two miles of Montgomery's battlefield, he encountered the Cherokee, whom he defeated, although with considerable loss to himself, after a stubborn engagement lasting several hours. Having repulsed the Indians, he proceeded on his way, sending out detachments to the outlying settlements, until in the course of a month he had destroyed every one of the Middle towns, 15 in all, with all their granaries and cornfields, driven the inhabitants into the mountains, and "pushed the frontier seventy miles farther to the west."

The Cherokee were now reduced to the greatest extremity. With some of their best towns in ashes, their fields and orchards wasted for two successive years, their ammunition nearly exhausted, many of their bravest warriors dead, their people fugitives in the mountains, hiding in caves and living like beasts upon roots or killing their horses for food, with the terrible scourge of smallpox adding to the miseries of starvation, and withal torn by factional differences which had existed from the very beginning of the war—it was impossible for even brave men to resist longer. In September Ata-kullakulla, who had all along done everything in his power to stay the disaffection, came down to Charleston, a treaty of peace was made, and the

---

[1] Catawba reference from Milligan, 1763, in Carroll, South Carolina Historical Collections, II, p. 519, 1836.

war was ended.   From an estimated population of at least 5,000 warriors some years before, the Cherokee had now been reduced to about 2,300 men.[1]

In the meantime a force of Virginians under Colonel Stephen had advanced as far as the Great island of the Holston—now Kingsport, Tennessee—where they were met by a large delegation of Cherokee, who sued for peace, which was concluded with them by Colonel Stephen on November 19, 1761, independently of what was being done in South Carolina.   On the urgent request of the chief that an officer might visit their people for a short time to cement the new friendship, Lieutenant Henry Timberlake, a young Virginian who had already distinguished himself in active service, volunteered to return with them to their towns, where he spent several months.   He afterward conducted a delegation of chiefs to England, where, as they had come without authority from the Government, they met such an unpleasant reception that they returned disgusted.[2]

On the conclusion of peace between England and France in 1763, by which the whole western territory was ceded to England, a great council was held at Augusta, which was attended by the chiefs and principal men of all the southern Indians, at which Captain John Stuart, superintendent for the southern tribes, together with the colonial governors of Virginia, North Carolina, South Carolina, and Georgia, explained fully to the Indians the new condition of affairs, and a treaty of mutual peace and friendship was concluded on November 10 of that year.[3]

Under several leaders, as Walker, Wallen, Smith, and Boon, the tide of emigration now surged across the mountains in spite of every effort to restrain it,[4] and the period between the end of the Cherokee war and the opening of the Revolution is principally notable for a number of treaty cessions by the Indians, each in fruitless endeavor to fix a permanent barrier between themselves and the advancing wave of white settlement.   Chief among these was the famous Henderson purchase in 1775, which included the whole tract between the Kentucky and Cumberland rivers, embracing the greater part of the present state of Kentucky.   By these treaties the Cherokee were shorn of practically all their ancient territorial claims north of the present Tennessee line and east of the Blue ridge and the Savannah, including much of their best hunting range; their home settlements were, however, left still in their possession.[5]

---

[1] Figures from Adair, American Indians, p. 227, 1775.   When not otherwise noted this sketch of the Cherokee war of 1760–61 is compiled chiefly from the contemporary dispatches in the Gentleman's Magazine, supplemented from Hewat's Historical account of South Carolina and Georgia, 1778; with additional details from Adair, American Indians; Ramsey, Tennessee; Royce, Cherokee Nation; North Carolina Colonial Records, v, documents and introduction; etc.

[2] Timberlake, Memoirs, p. 9 et passim, 1765.

[3] Stevens, Georgia, II, pp. 26–29, 1859.   [4] Ramsey, Tennessee, pp. 65–70, 1853.

[5] Royce, Cherokee Nation, in Fifth Ann. Rep. Bur. of Ethnology, pp. 146–149, 1888.

As one consequence of the late Cherokee war, a royal proclamation had been issued in 1763, with a view of checking future encroachments by the whites, which prohibited any private land purchases from the Indians, or any granting of warrants for lands west of the sources of the streams flowing into the Atlantic.[1]   In 1768, on the appeal of the Indians themselves, the British superintendent for the southern tribes, Captain John Stuart, had negotiated a treaty at Hard Labor in South Carolina by which Kanawha and New rivers, along their whole course downward from the North Carolina line, were fixed as the boundary between the Cherokee and the whites in that direction. In two years, however, so many borderers had crossed into the Indian country, where they were evidently determined to remain, that it was found necessary to substitute another treaty, by which the line was made to run due south from the mouth of the Kanawha to the Holston, thus cutting off from the Cherokee almost the whole of their hunting grounds in Virginia and West Virginia.   Two years later, in 1772, the Virginians demanded a further cession, by which everything east of Kentucky river was surrendered; and finally, on March 17, 1775, the great Henderson purchase was consummated, including the whole tract between the Kentucky and Cumberland rivers.   By this last cession the Cherokee were at last cut off from Ohio river and all their rich Kentucky hunting grounds.[2]

While these transactions were called treaties, they were really forced upon the native proprietors, who resisted each in turn and finally signed only under protest and on most solemn assurances that no further demands would be made.   Even before the purchases were made, intruders in large numbers had settled upon each of the tracts in question, and they refused to withdraw across the boundaries now established, but remained on one pretext or another to await a new adjustment.   This was particularly the case on Watauga and upper Holston rivers in northeastern Tennessee, where the settlers, finding themselves still within the Indian boundary and being resolved to remain, effected a temporary lease from the Cherokee in 1772.   As was expected and intended, the lease became a permanent occupancy, the nucleus settlement of the future State of Tennessee.[3]

Just before the outbreak of the Revolution, the botanist, William Bartram, made an extended tour of the Cherokee country, and has left us a pleasant account of the hospitable character and friendly disposition of the Indians at that time.   He gives a list of forty-three towns then inhabited by the tribe.[4]

The opening of the great Revolutionary struggle in 1776 found the Indian tribes almost to a man ranged on the British side against the

[1] Royce, Cherokee Nation, op. cit., p. 149; Ramsey, Tennessee, p. 71, 1853.
[2] Ramsey, op. cit., pp. 93–122; Royce, op. cit. pp. 146–149.
[3] Ramsey, op. cit., pp. 109–122; Royce, op. cit. p. 146 et passim.
[4] Bartram, Travels, pp. 366–372, 1792.

Americans. There was good reason for this. Since the fall of the French power the British government had stood to them as the sole representative of authority, and the guardian and protector of their rights against constant encroachments by the American borderers. Licensed British traders were resident in every tribe and many had intermarried and raised families among them, while the border man looked upon the Indian only as a cumberer of the earth. The British superintendents, Sir William Johnson in the north and Captain John Stuart in the south, they knew as generous friends, while hardly a warrior of them all was without some old cause of resentment against their backwoods neighbors. They felt that the only barrier between themselves and national extinction was in the strength of the British government, and when the final severence came they threw their whole power into the British scale. They were encouraged in this resolution by presents of clothing and other goods, with promises of plunder from the settlements and hopes of recovering a portion of their lost territories. The British government having determined, as early as June, 1775, to call in the Indians against the Americans, supplies of hatchets, guns, and ammunition were issued to the warriors of all the tribes from the lakes to the gulf, and bounties were offered for American scalps brought in to the commanding officer at Detroit or Oswego.[1] Even the Six Nations, who had agreed in solemn treaty to remain neutral, were won over by these persuasions. In August, 1775, an Indian "talk" was intercepted in which the Cherokee assured Cameron, the resident agent, that their warriors, enlisted in the service of the king, were ready at a signal to fall upon the back settlements of Carolina and Georgia.[2] Circular letters were sent out to all those persons in the back country supposed to be of royalist sympathies, directing them to repair to Cameron's headquarters in the Cherokee country to join the Indians in the invasion of the settlements.[3]

In June, 1776, a British fleet under command of Sir Peter Parker, with a large naval and military force, attacked Charleston, South Carolina, both by land and sea, and simultaneously a body of Cherokee, led by Tories in Indian disguise, came down from the mountains and ravaged the exposed frontier of South Carolina, killing and burning as they went. After a gallant defense by the garrison at Charleston the British were repulsed, whereupon their Indian and Tory allies withdrew.[4]

About the same time the warning came from Nancy Ward (14), a noted friendly Indian woman of great authority in the Cherokee Nation, that seven hundred Cherokee warriors were advancing in two divisions against the Watauga and Holston settlements, with the design of

---

[1] Ramsey, Tennessee, pp. 143–150, 1853; Monette, Valley of the Mississippi, I, pp. 400, 401, 431, 432, and II, pp. 33, 34, 1846; Roosevelt, Winning of the West, I, pp. 276–281, and II, pp. 1–6, 1889.

[2] Ramsey, op. cit., p. 143.

[3] Quoted from Stedman, in Ramsey, op. cit., p. 162.

[4] Ramsey, op. cit., p. 162.

destroying everything as far up as New river. The Holston men from both sides of the Virginia line hastily collected under Captain Thompson and marched against the Indians, whom they met and defeated with signal loss after a hard-fought battle near the Long island in the Holston (Kingsport, Tennessee), on August 20. The next day the second division of the Cherokee attacked the fort at Watauga, garrisoned by only forty men under Captain James Robertson (15), but was repulsed without loss to the defenders, the Indians withdrawing on news of the result at the Long island. A Mrs. Bean and a boy named Moore were captured on this occasion and carried to one of the Cherokee towns in the neighborhood of Tellico, where the boy was burned, but the woman, after she had been condemned to death and everything was in readiness for the tragedy, was rescued by the interposition of Nancy Ward. Two other Cherokee detachments moved against the upper settlements at the same time. One of these, finding all the inhabitants securely shut up in forts, returned without doing much damage. The other ravaged the country on Clinch river almost to its head, and killed a man and wounded others at Black's station, now Abingdon, Virginia.[1]

At the same time that one part of the Cherokee were raiding the Tennessee settlements others came down upon the frontiers of Carolina and Georgia. On the upper Catawba they killed many people, but the whites took refuge in the stockade stations, where they defended themselves until General Rutherford (16) came to their relief. In Georgia an attempt had been made by a small party of Americans to seize Cameron, who lived in one of the Cherokee towns with his Indian wife, but, as was to have been expected, the Indians interfered, killing several of the party and capturing others, who were afterward tortured to death. The Cherokee of the Upper and Middle towns, with some Creeks and Tories of the vicinity, led by Cameron himself, at once began ravaging the South Carolina border, burning houses, driving off cattle, and killing men, women, and children without distinction, until the whole country was in a wild panic, the people abandoning their farms to seek safety in the garrisoned forts. On one occasion an attack by two hundred of the enemy, half of them being Tories, stripped and painted like Indians, was repulsed by the timely arrival of a body of Americans, who succeeded in capturing thirteen of the Tories. The invasion extended into Georgia, where also property was destroyed and the inhabitants were driven from their homes.[2]

Realizing their common danger, the border states determined to strike such a concerted blow at the Cherokee as should render them passive while the struggle with England continued. In accord with this plan of cooperation the frontier forces were quickly mobilized and

---

[1] Ramsey, Tennessee, pp. 150–159, 1853.
[2] Roosevelt, Winning of the West, I, pp. 293–297, 1889.

in the summer of 1776 four expeditions were equipped from Virginia, North Carolina, South Carolina, and Georgia, to enter the Cherokee territory simultaneously from as many different directions.

In August of that year the army of North Carolina, 2,400 strong, under General Griffith Rutherford, crossed the Blue ridge at Swannanoa gap, and following the main trail almost along the present line of the railroad, struck the first Indian town, Stikâ'yĭ, or Stecoee, on the Tuckasegee, near the present Whittier. The inhabitants having fled, the soldiers burned the town, together with an unfinished townhouse ready for the roof, cut down the standing corn, killed one or two straggling Indians, and then proceeded on their mission of destruction. Every town upon Oconaluftee, Tuckasegee, and the upper part of Little Tennessee, and on Hiwassee to below the junction of Valley river—thirty-six towns in all—was destroyed in turn, the corn cut down or trampled under the hoofs of the stock driven into the fields for that purpose, and the stock itself killed or carried off. Before such an overwhelming force, supplemented as it was by three others simultaneously advancing from other directions, the Cherokee made but poor resistance, and fled with their women and children into the fastnesses of the Great Smoky mountains, leaving their desolated fields and smoking towns behind them. As was usual in Indian wars, the actual number killed or taken was small, but the destruction of property was beyond calculation. At Sugartown (Kûlsetsi'yĭ, east of the present Franklin) one detachment, sent to destroy it, was surprised, and escaped only through the aid of another force sent to its rescue. Rutherford himself, while proceeding to the destruction of the Hiwassee towns, encountered the Indians drawn up to oppose his progress in the Waya gap of the Nantahala mountains, and one of the hardest fights of the campaign resulted, the soldiers losing over forty killed and wounded, although the Cherokee were finally repulsed (17). One of the Indians killed on this occasion was afterward discovered to be a woman, painted and armed like a warrior.[1]

On September 26 the South Carolina army, 1,860 strong, under Colonel Andrew Williamson, and including a number of Catawba Indians, effected a junction with Rutherford's forces on Hiwassee river, near the present Murphy, North Carolina. It had been expected that Williamson would join the northern army at Còwee, on the Little Tennessee, when they would proceed together against the western towns, but he had been delayed, and the work of destruction in that direction was already completed, so that after a short rest each army returned home along the route by which it had come.

The South Carolina men had centered by different detachments in

[1] See no. 110, "Incidents of Personal Heroism." For Rutherford's expedition, see Moore, Rutherford's Expedition, in North Carolina University Magazine, February, 1888; Swain, Sketch of the Indian War in 1776, ibid., May, 1852, reprinted in Historical Magazine, November, 1867; Ramsey, Tennessee, p. 164, 1853; Roosevelt, Winning of the West, I, pp. 294–302, 1889, etc.

the lower Cherokee towns about the head of Savannah river, burning one town after another, cutting down the peach trees and ripened corn, and having an occasional brush with the Cherokee, who hung constantly upon their flanks. At the town of Seneca, near which they encountered Cameron with his Indians and Tories, they had destroyed six thousand bushels of corn, besides other food stores, after burning all the houses, the Indians having retreated after a stout resistance. The most serious encounter had taken place at Tomassee, where several whites and sixteen Cherokee were killed, the latter being all scalped afterward. Having completed the ruin of the Lower towns, Williamson had crossed over Rabun gap and descended into the valley of the Little Tennessee to cooperate with Rutherford in the destruction of the Middle and Valley towns. As the army advanced every house in every settlement met was burned—ninety houses in one settlement alone—and detachments were sent into the fields to destroy the corn, of which the smallest town was estimated to have two hundred acres, besides potatoes, beans, and orchards of peach trees. The·stores of dressed deerskins and other valuables were carried off. Everything was swept clean, and the Indians who were not killed or taken were driven, homeless refugees, into the dark recesses of Nantahala or painfully made their way across to the Overhill towns in Tennessee, which were already menaced by another invasion from the north.[1]

In July, while Williamson was engaged on the the upper Savannah, a force of two hundred Georgians, under Colonel Samuel Jack, had marched in the same direction and succeeded in burning two towns on the heads of Chattahoochee and Tugaloo rivers, destroying the corn and driving off the cattle, without the loss of a man, the Cherokee having apparently fallen back to concentrate for resistance in the mountains.[2]

The Virginia army, about two thousand strong, under Colonel William Christian (18), rendezvoused in August at the Long island of the Holston, the regular gathering place on the Tennessee side of the mountains. Among them were several hundred men from North Carolina, with all who could be spared from the garrisons on the Tennessee side. Paying but little attention to small bodies of Indians, who tried to divert attention or to delay progress by flank attacks, they advanced steadily, but cautiously, along the great Indian warpath (19) toward the crossing of the French Broad, where a strong force of Cherokee was reported to be in waiting to dispute their passage. Just before reaching the river the Indians sent a Tory trader

---

[1] For Williamson's expedition, see Ross Journal, with Rockwell's notes, in Historical Magazine, October, 1876; Swain, Sketch of the Indian War in 1776, in North Carolina University Magazine for May, 1852, reprinted in Historical Magazine, November, 1867; Jones, Georgia, II, p. 246 et passim, 1883; Ramsey, Tennessee, 163–164, 1853; Roosevelt, Winning of the West, I, pp. 296-303, 1889.

[2] Jones, op. cit., p. 246; Ramsey, op. cit., p. 163; Roosevelt, op. cit., p. 295.

with a flag of truce to discuss terms. Knowing that his own strength was overwhelming, Christian allowed the envoy to go through the whole camp and then sent him back with the message that there could be no terms until the Cherokee towns had been destroyed. Arriving at the ford, he kindled fires and made all preparations as if intending to camp there for several days. As soon as night fell, however, he secretly drew off half his force and crossed the river lower down, to come upon the Indians in their rear. This was a work of great difficulty; as the water was so deep that it came up almost to the shoulders of the men, while the current was so rapid that they were obliged to support each other four abreast to prevent being swept off their feet. However, they kept their guns and powder dry. On reaching the other side they were surprised to find no enemy. Disheartened at the strength of the invasion, the Indians had fled without even a show of resistance. It is probable that nearly all their men and resources had been drawn off to oppose the Carolina forces on their eastern border, and the few who remained felt themselves unequal to the contest.

Advancing without opposition, Christian reached the towns on Little Tennessee early in November, and, finding them deserted, proceeded to destroy them, one after another, with their outlying fields. The few lingering warriors discovered were all killed. In the meantime messages had been sent out to the farther towns, in response to which several of their head men came into Christian's camp to treat for peace. On their agreement to surrender all the prisoners and captured stock in their hands and to cede to the whites all the disputed territory occupied by the Tennessee settlements, as soon as representatives of the whole tribe could be assembled in the spring, Christian consented to suspend hostilities and retire without doing further injury. An exception was made against Tuskegee and another town, which had been concerned in the burning of the boy taken from Watauga, already noted, and these two were reduced to ashes. The sacred "peace town," Echota (20), had not been molested. Most of the troops were disbanded on their return to the Long island, but a part remained and built Fort Patrick Henry, where they went into winter quarters.[1]

From incidental notices in narratives written by some of the participants, we obtain interesting side-lights on the merciless character of this old border warfare. In addition to the ordinary destruction of war—the burning of towns, the wasting of fruitful fields, and the killing of the defenders—we find that every Indian warrior killed was scalped, when opportunity permitted; women, as well as men, were shot down and afterward "helped to their end"; and prisoners taken were put up at auction as slaves when not killed on the spot. Near Tomassee a small

---

[1] For the Virginia-Tennessee expedition see Roosevelt, Winning of the West, I, pp. 303–305, 1889; Ramsey, Tennessee, pp. 165–170, 1853.

party of Indians was surrounded and entirely cut off. "Sixteen were found dead in the valley when the battle ended. These our men scalped." In a personal encounter "a stout Indian engaged a sturdy young white man, who was a good bruiser and expert at gouging. After breaking their guns on each other they laid hold of one another, when the cracker had his thumbs instantly in the fellow's eyes, who roared and cried '*canaly*'—enough, in English. 'Damn you,' says the white man, 'you can never have enough while you are alive.' He then threw him down, set his foot upon his head, and scalped him alive; then took up one of the broken guns and knocked out his brains. It would have been fun if he had let the latter action alone and sent him home without his nightcap, to tell his countrymen how he had been treated." Later on some of the same detachment (Williamson's) seeing a woman ahead, fired on her and brought her down with two serious wounds, but yet able to speak. After getting what information she could give them, through a half-breed interpreter, "the informer being unable to travel, some of our men favored her so far that they killed her there, to put her out of pain." A few days later "a party of Colonel Thomas's regiment, being on a hunt of plunder, or some such thing, found an Indian squaw and took her prisoner, she being lame, was unable to go with her friends. She was so sullen that she would, as an old saying is, neither lead nor drive, and by their account she died in their hands; but I suppose they helped her to her end." At this place—on the Hiwassee—they found a large town, having "upwards of ninety houses, and large quantities of corn," and "we encamped among the corn, where we had a great plenty of corn, peas, beans, potatoes, and hogs," and on the next day "we were ordered to assemble in companies to spread through the town to destroy, cut down, and burn all the vegetables belonging to our heathen enemies, which was no small undertaking, they being so plentifully supplied." Continuing to another town, "we engaged in our former labor, that is, cutting and destroying all things that might be of advantage to our enemies. Finding here curious buildings, great apple trees, and white-man-like improvements, these we destroyed." [1]

While crossing over the mountains Rutherford's men approached a house belonging to a trader, when one of his negro slaves ran out and "was shot by the Reverend James Hall, the chaplain, as he ran, mistaking him for an Indian." [2] Soon after they captured two women and a boy. It was proposed to auction them off at once to the highest bidder, and when one of the officers protested that the matter should be left to the disposition of Congress, "the greater part swore bloodily that if they were not sold for slaves upon the spot they would kill and

---

[1] Ross Journal, in Historical Magazine, October, 1867.
[2] Swain, Sketch of the Indian War of 1776, in Historical Magazine, November, 1867.

scalp them immediately." The prisoners were accordingly sold for about twelve hundred dollars.[1]

At the Wolf Hills settlement, now Abingdon, Virginia, a party sent out from the fort returned with the scalps of eleven warriors. Having recovered the books which their minister had left behind in his cabin, they held a service of prayer for their success, after which the fresh scalps were hung upon a pole above the gate of the fort. The barbarous custom of scalping to which the border men had become habituated in the earlier wars was practiced upon every occasion when opportunity presented, at least upon the bodies of warriors, and the South Carolina legislature offered a bounty of seventy-five pounds for every warrior's scalp, a higher reward, however, being offered for prisoners.[2] In spite of all the bitterness which the war aroused there seems to be no record of any scalping of Tories or other whites by the Americans (21).

The effect upon the Cherokee of this irruption of more than six thousand armed enemies into their territory was well nigh paralyzing. More than fifty of their towns had been burned, their orchards cut down, their fields wasted, their cattle and horses killed or driven off, their stores of buckskin and other personal property plundered. Hundreds of their people had been killed or had died of starvation and exposure, others were prisoners in the hands of the Americans, and some had been sold into slavery. Those who had escaped were fugitives in the mountains, living upon acorns, chestnuts, and wild game, or were refugees with the British.[3] From the Virginia line to the Chattahoochee the chain of destruction was complete. For the present at least any further resistance was hopeless, and they were compelled to sue for peace.

By a treaty concluded at DeWitts Corners in South Carolina on May 20, 1777, the first ever made with the new states, the Lower Cherokee surrendered to the conqueror all of their remaining territory in South Carolina, excepting a narrow strip along the western boundary. Just two months later, on July 20, by treaty at the Long island, as had been arranged by Christian in the preceding fall, the Middle and Upper Cherokee ceded everything east of the Blue ridge, together with all the disputed territory on the Watauga, Nolichucky, upper Holston, and New rivers. By this second treaty also Captain James Robertson was appointed agent for the Cherokee, to reside at Echota, to watch their movements, recover any captured property, and prevent their correspondence with persons unfriendly to the American cause. As the Federal government was not yet in perfect operation these treaties

---

[1] Moore's narrative, in North Carolina University Magazine, February, 1888.

[2] Roosevelt, Winning of the West, I, pp. 285, 290, 303, 1889.

[3] About five hundred sought refuge with Stuart, the British Indian superintendent in Florida, where they were fed for some time at the expense of the British government (Jones, Georgia, II, p. 246, 1883).

were negotiated by commissioners from the four states adjoining the Cherokee country, the territory thus acquired being parceled out to South Carolina, North Carolina, and Tennessee.[1]

While the Cherokee Nation had thus been compelled to a treaty of peace, a very considerable portion of the tribe was irreconcilably hostile to the Americans and refused to be a party to the late cessions, especially on the Tennessee side. Although Ata-kullakulla sent word that he was ready with five hundred young warriors to fight for the Americans against the English or Indian enemy whenever called upon, Dragging-canoe (Tsiyu-gûnsi′nĭ), who had led the opposition against the Watauga settlements, declared that he would hold fast to Cameron's talk and continue to make war upon those who had taken his hunting grounds. Under his leadership some hundreds of the most warlike and implacable warriors of the tribe, with their families, drew out from the Upper and Middle towns and moved far down upon Tennessee river, where they established new settlements on Chickamauga creek, in the neighborhood of the present Chattanooga. The locality appears to have been already a rendezvous for a sort of Indian banditti, who sometimes plundered boats disabled in the rapids at this point while descending the river. Under the name "Chickamaugas" they soon became noted for their uncompromising and never-ceasing hostility. In 1782, in consequence of the destruction of their towns by Sevier and Campbell, they abandoned this location and moved farther down the river, where they built what were afterwards known as the "five lower towns," viz, Running Water, Nickajack, Long Island, Crow town, and Lookout Mountain town. These were all on the extreme western Cherokee frontier, near where Tennessee river crosses the state line, the first three being within the present limits of Tennessee, while Lookout Mountain town and Crow town were respectively in the adjacent corners of Georgia and Alabama. Their population was recruited from Creeks, Shawano, and white Tories, until they were estimated at a thousand warriors. Here they remained, a constant thorn in the side of Tennessee, until their towns were destroyed in 1794.[2]

The expatriated Lower Cherokee also removed to the farthest western border of their tribal territory, where they might hope to be secure from encroachment for a time at least, and built new towns for themselves on the upper waters of the Coosa. Twenty years after-

---

[1] Royce, Cherokee Nation, in Fifth Ann. Rep. Bureau of Ethnology, p. 150 and map, 1888; Ramsey, Tennessee, pp. 172–174, 1853; Stevens, Georgia, II, p. 144, 1859; Roosevelt, Winning of the West, I, p. 306, 1889.

[2] Ramsey, op. cit., pp. 171–177, 185–186, 610 et passim; Royce, op. cit., p. 150; Campbell letter, 1782, and other documents in Virginia State Papers, III, pp. 271, 571, 599, 1883, and IV, pp. 118, 286, 1884; Blount letter, January 14, 1793, American State Papers: Indian Affairs, I, p. 431, 1832. Campbell says they abandoned their first location on account of the invasion from Tennessee. Governor Blount says they left on account of witches.

ward Hawkins found the population of Willstown, in extreme western Georgia, entirely made up of refugees from the Savannah, and the children so familiar from their parents with stories of Williamson's invasion that they ran screaming from the face of a white man (22).[1]

In April, 1777, the legislature of North Carolina, of which Tennessee was still a part, authorized bounties of land in the new territory to all able-bodied men who should volunteer against the remaining hostile Cherokee. Under this act companies of rangers were kept along the exposed border to cut off raiding parties of Indians and to protect the steady advance of the pioneers, with the result that the Tennessee settlements enjoyed a brief respite and were even able to send some assistance to their brethren in Kentucky, who were sorely pressed by the Shawano and other northern tribes.[2]

The war between England and the colonies still continued, however, and the British government was unremitting in its effort to secure the active assistance of the Indians. With the Creeks raiding the Georgia and South Carolina frontier, and with a British agent, Colonel Brown, and a number of Tory refugees regularly domiciled at Chickamauga,[3] it was impossible for the Cherokee long to remain quiet. In the spring of 1779 the warning came from Robertson, stationed at Echota, that three hundred warriors from Chickamauga had started against the back settlements of North Carolina. Without a day's delay the states of North Carolina (including Tennessee) and Virginia united to send a strong force of volunteers against them under command of Colonels Shelby and Montgomery. Descending the Holston in April in a fleet of canoes built for the occasion, they took the Chickamauga towns so completely by surprise that the few warriors remaining fled to the mountains without attempting to give battle. Several were killed, Chickamauga and the outlying villages were burned, twenty thousand bushels of corn were destroyed and large numbers of horses and cattle captured, together with a great quantity of goods sent by the British Governor Hamilton at Detroit for distribution to the Indians. The success of this expedition frustrated the execution of a project by Hamilton for uniting all the northern and southern Indians, to be assisted by British regulars, in a concerted attack along the whole American frontier. On learning, through runners, of the blow that had befallen them, the Chickamauga warriors gave up all idea of invading the settlements, and returned to their wasted villages.[4] They, as well as the Creeks, however, kept in constant communication with

---

[1] Hawkins, manuscript journal, 1796, with Georgia Historical Society.
[2] Ramsey, Tennessee, pp. 174–178, 1853.
[3] Campbell letter, 1782, Virginia State Papers, III, p. 271, 1883.
[4] Ramsey, op. cit, pp. 186–188; Roosevelt, Winning of the West, II, pp. 236–238, 1889.   Ramsey's statements, chiefly on Haywood's authority, of the strength of the expedition, the number of warriors killed, etc., are so evidently overdrawn that they are here omitted.

the British commander in Savannah. In this year also a delegation of Cherokee visited the Ohio towns to offer condolences on the death of the noted Delaware chief, White-eyes.[1]

In the early spring of 1780 a large company of emigrants under Colonel John Donelson descended the Holston and the Tennessee to the Ohio, whence they ascended the Cumberland, effected a junction with another party under Captain James Robertson, which had just arrived by a toilsome overland route, and made the first settlement on the present site of Nashville. In passing the Chickamauga towns they had run the gauntlet of the hostile Cherokee, who pursued them for a considerable distance beyond the whirlpool known as the Suck, where the river breaks through the mountain. The family of a man named Stuart being infected with the smallpox, his boat dropped behind, and all on board, twenty-eight in number, were killed or taken by the Indians, their cries being distinctly heard by their friends ahead who were unable to help them. Another boat having run upon the rocks, the three women in it, one of whom had become a mother the night before, threw the cargo into the river, and then, jumping into the water, succeeded in pushing the boat into the current while the husband of one of them kept the Indians at bay with his rifle. The infant was killed in the confusion. Three cowards attempted to escape, without thought of their companions. One was drowned in the river; the other two were captured and carried to Chickamauga, where one was burned and the other was ransomed by a trader. The rest went on their way to found the capital of a new commonwealth.[2] As if in retributive justice, the smallpox broke out in the Chickamauga band in consequence of the capture of Stuart's family, causing the death of a great number.[3]

The British having reconquered Georgia and South Carolina and destroyed all resistance in the south, early in 1780 Cornwallis, with his subordinates, Ferguson and the merciless Tarleton, prepared to invade North Carolina and sweep the country northward to Virginia. The Creeks under McGillivray (23), and a number of the Cherokee under various local chiefs, together with the Tories, at once joined his standard.

While the Tennessee backwoodsmen were gathered at a barbecue to contest for a shooting prize, a paroled prisoner brought a demand from Ferguson for their submission; with the threat, if they refused, that he would cross the mountains, hang their leaders, kill every man found in arms and burn every settlement. Up to this time the mountain men had confined their effort to holding in check the Indian enemy, but now, with the fate of the Revolution at stake, they felt

---

[1] Heckewelder, Indian Nations, p. 327, reprint of 1876.
[2] Donelson's Journal, etc., in Ramsey, Tennessee, pp. 197–203, 1853; Roosevelt, Winning of the West, II, pp. 324–340, 1889.
[3] Ibid., II, p. 337.

that the time for wider action had come.   They resolved not to await the attack, but to anticipate it.   Without order or authority from Congress, without tents, commissary, or supplies, the Indian fighters of Virginia, North Carolina, and Tennessee quickly assembled at the Sycamore shoals of the Watauga to the number of about one thousand men under Campbell of Virginia, Sevier (24) and Shelby of Tennessee, and McDowell of North Carolina.   Crossing the mountains, they met Ferguson at' Kings mountain in South Carolina on October 7, 1780, and gained the decisive victory that turned the tide of the Revolution in the South.[1]

It is in place here to quote a description of these men in buckskin, white by blood and tradition, but half Indian in habit and instinct, who, in half a century of continuous conflict, drove back Creeks, Cherokee, and Shawano, and with one hand on the plow and the other on the rifle redeemed a wilderness and carried civilization and free government to the banks of the Mississippi.

"They were led by leaders they trusted, they were wonted to Indian warfare, they were skilled as horsemen and marksmen, they knew how to face every kind of danger, hardship, and privation.   Their fringed and tasseled hunting shirts were girded by bead-worked belts, and the trappings of their horses were stained red and yellow.   On their heads they wore caps of coon skin or mink skin, with the tails hanging down, or else felt hats, in each of which was thrust a buck tail or a sprig of evergreen.   Every man carried a small-bore rifle, a toma-hawk, and a scalping knife.   A very few of the officers had swords, and there was not a bayonet nor a tent in the army."[2]

To strike the blow at Kings mountain the border men had been forced to leave their own homes unprotected.   Even before they could cross the mountains on their return the news came that the Cherokee were again out in force for the destruction of the upper settlements, and their numerous small bands were killing, burning, and plundering in the usual Indian fashion.   Without loss of time the Holston settle-ments of Virginia and Tennessee at once raised seven hundred mounted riflemen to march against the enemy, the command being assigned to Colonel Arthur Campbell of Virginia and Colonel John Sevier of Tennessee.

Sevier started first with nearly three hundred men, going south along the great Indian war trail and driving small parties of the Cherokee before him, until he crossed the French Broad and came upon seventy of them on Boyds creek, not far from the present Sevier-ville, on December 16, 1780.   Ordering his men to spread out into a half circle, he sent ahead some scouts, who, by an attack and feigned retreat, managed to draw the Indians into the trap thus prepared,

---

[1] Roosevelt, Winning of the West, II, pp. 241-294, 1889; Ramsey, Tennessee, pp. 208-249, 1853.
[2] Roosevelt, op. cit., p. 256.

with the result that they left thirteen dead and all their plunder, while not one of the whites was even wounded.[1]

A few days later Sevier was joined by Campbell with the remainder of the force. Advancing to the Little Tennessee with but slight resistance, they crossed three miles below Echota while the Indians were watching for them at the ford above. Then dividing into two bodies, they proceeded to destroy the towns along the river. The chiefs sent peace talks through Nancy Ward, the Cherokee woman who had so befriended the whites in 1776, but to these overtures Campbell returned an evasive answer until he could first destroy the towns on lower Hiwassee, whose warriors had been particularly hostile. Continuing southward, the troops destroyed these towns, Hiwassee and Chestuee, with all their stores of provisions, finishing the work on the last day of the year. The Indians had fled before them, keeping spies out to watch their movements. One of these, while giving signals from a ridge by beating a drum, was shot by the whites. The soldiers lost only one man, who was buried in an Indian cabin which was then burned down to conceal the trace of the interment. The return march was begun on New Year's day. Ten principal towns, including Echota, the capital, had been destroyed, besides several smaller villages, containing in the aggregate over one thousand houses, and not less than fifty thousand bushels of corn and large stores of other provision. Everything not needed on the return march was committed to the flames or otherwise wasted. Of all the towns west of the mountains only Talassee, and one or two about Chickamauga or on the headwaters of the Coosa, escaped. The whites had lost only one man killed and two wounded. Before the return a proclamation was sent to the Cherokee chiefs, warning them to make peace on penalty of a worse visitation.[2]

Some Cherokee who met them at Echota, on the return march, to talk of peace, brought in and surrendered several white prisoners.[3] One reason for the slight resistance made by the Indians was probably the fact that at the very time of the invasion many of their warriors were away, raiding on the Upper Holston and in the neighborhood of Cumberland gap.[4]

Although the Upper or Overhill Cherokee were thus humbled, those of the middle towns, on the head waters of Little Tennessee, still continued to send out parties against the back settlements. Sevier

---

[1] Roosevelt, Winning of the West, II, pp. 298–300, 1889; Ramsey, Tennessee, pp. 261–264, 1853. There is great discrepancy in the various accounts of this fight, from the attempts of interested historians to magnify the size of the victory. One writer gives the Indians 1,000 warriors. Here, as elsewhere, Roosevelt is a more reliable guide, his statements being usually from official documents.

[2] Roosevelt, op. cit., pp. 300–304; Ramsey, op. cit., pp. 265–268; Campbell, report, January 15, 1781, in Virginia State Papers, I, p. 436. Haywood and others after him make the expedition go as far as Chickamauga and Coosa river, but Campbell's report expressly denies this.

[3] Ramsey, op. cit., p. 266.

[4] Roosevelt, op. cit., p. 302.

determined to make a sudden stroke upon them, and early in March of the same year, 1781, with 150 picked horsemen, he started to cross the Great Smoky mountains over trails never before attempted by white men, and so rough in places that it was hardly possible to lead horses.   Falling unexpectedly upon Tuckasegee, near the present Webster, North Carolina, he took the town completely by surprise, killing several warriors and capturing a number of women and children.   Two other principal towns and three smaller settlements were taken in the same way, with a quantity of provision and about 200 horses, the Indians being entirely off their guard and unprepared to make any effective resistance.   Having spread destruction through the middle towns, with the loss to himself of only one man killed and another wounded, he was off again as suddenly as he had come, moving so rapidly that he was well on his homeward way before the Cherokee could gather for pursuit.[1]   At the same time a smaller Tennessee expedition went out to disperse the Indians who had been making headquarters in the mountains about Cumberland gap and harassing travelers along the road to Kentucky.[2]   Numerous indications of Indians were found, but none were met, although the country was scoured for a considerable distance.[3]   In summer the Cherokee made another incursion, this time upon the new settlements on the French Broad, near the present Newport, Tennessee.   With a hundred horsemen Sevier fell suddenly upon their camp on Indian creek, killed a dozen warriors, and scattered the rest.[4]   By these successive blows the Cherokee were so worn out and dispirited that they were forced to sue for peace, and in midsummer of 1781 a treaty of peace—doubtful though it might be—was negotiated at the Long island of the Holston.[5]   The respite came just in time to allow the Tennesseeans to send a detachment against Cornwallis.

Although there was truce in Tennessee, there was none in the South. In November of this year the Cherokee made a sudden inroad upon the Georgia settlements, destroying everything in their way.   In retaliation a force under General Pickens marched into their country, destroying their towns as far as Valley river.   Finding further progress blocked by heavy snows and learning through a prisoner that the Indians, who had retired before him, were collecting to oppose him in the mountains, he withdrew, as he says, "through absolute necessity," having accomplished very little of the result expected.   Shortly afterward the Cherokee, together with some Creeks, again invaded Georgia,

[1] Campbell, letter, March 28, 1781, in Virginia State Papers, I, p. 602, 1875; Martin, letter, March 31, 1781, ibid., p. 613; Ramsey, Tennessee, p. 268, 1853; Roosevelt, Winning of the West, II, pp. 305–307, 1889.

[2] Campbell, letter, March 28, 1781, in Virginia State Papers, I, p. 602, 1875.

[3] Ramsey, op. cit., p. 269.

[4] Ibid.; Roosevelt, op. cit., p. 307.

[5] Ibid.; Ramsey, op. cit., pp. 267, 268.   The latter authority seems to make it 1782, which is evidently a mistake.

but were met on Oconee river and driven back by a detachment of American troops.[1]

The Overhill Cherokee, on lower Little Tennessee, seem to have been trying in good faith to hold to the peace established at the Long island. Early in 1781 the government land office had been closed to further entries, not to be opened again until peace had been declared with England, but the borderers paid little attention to the law in such matters, and the rage for speculation in Tennessee lands grew stronger daily.[2] In the fall of 1782 the chief, Old Tassel of Echota, on behalf of all the friendly chiefs and towns, sent a pathetic talk to the governors of Virginia and North Carolina, complaining that in spite of all their efforts to remain quiet the settlers were constantly encroaching upon them, and had built houses within a day's walk of the Cherokee towns. They asked that all those whites who had settled beyond the boundary last established should be removed.[3] As was to have been expected, this was never done.

The Chickamauga band, however, and those farther to the south, were still bent on war, being actively encouraged in that disposition by the British agents and refugee loyalists living among them. They continued to raid both north and south, and in September, 1782, Sevier, with 200 mounted men, again made a descent upon their towns, destroying several of their settlements about Chickamauga creek, and penetrating as far as the important town of Ustana'li, on the head-waters of Coosa river, near the present Calhoun, Georgia. This also he destroyed. Every warrior found was killed, together with a white man found in one of the towns, whose papers showed that he had been active in inciting the Indians to war. On the return the expedition halted at Echota, where new assurances were received from the friendly element.[4] In the meantime a Georgia expedition of over 400 men, under General Pickens, had been ravaging the Cherokee towns in the same quarter, with such effect that the Cherokee were forced to purchase peace by a further surrender of territory on the head of Broad river in Georgia.[5] This cession was concluded at a treaty of peace held with the Georgia commissioners at Augusta in the next year, and was confirmed later by the Creeks, who claimed an interest in the same lands, but was never accepted by either as the voluntary act of their tribe as a whole.[6]

By the preliminary treaty of Paris, November 30, 1782, the long Revolutionary struggle for independence was brought to a close, and the Cherokee, as well as the other tribes, seeing the hopelessness of con-

---

[1] Stevens, Georgia, II, pp. 282–285, 1859; Jones, Georgia, II, p. 503, 1883.
[2] Roosevelt, Winning of the West, II, p. 311, 1889.
[3] Old Tassel's talk, in Ramsey, Tennessee, p. 271, 1853, and in Roosevelt, op. cit., p. 315.
[4] Ramsey, op. cit., p. 272; Roosevelt, op. cit., p. 317 et passim.
[5] Stevens, op. cit., pp. 411–415.
[6] Royce, Cherokee Nation, in Fifth Ann. Rep. Bureau of Ethnology, p. 151, 1888.

tinuing the contest alone, began to sue for peace.   By seven years of constant warfare they had been reduced to the lowest depth of misery, almost indeed to·the verge of extinction.   Over and over again their towns had been laid in ashes and their fields wasted.   Their best warriors had been killed and their women and children had sickened and starved in the mountains.   Their great war chief, Oconostota, who had led them to victory in 1780, was now a broken old man, and in this year, at Echota, formally resigned his office in favor of his son, The Terrapin.   To complete their brimming cup of misery the smallpox again broke out among them in 1783.[1]   Deprived of the assistance of their former white allies they were left to their own cruel fate, the last feeble resistance of the mountain warriors to the advancing tide of settlement came to an end with the burning of Cowee town,[2] and the way was left open to an arrangement.   In the same year the North Carolina legislature appointed an agent for the Cherokee and made regulations for the government of traders among them.[3]

RELATIONS WITH THE UNITED STATES

FROM THE FIRST TREATY TO THE REMOVAL—1785–1838

Passing over several unsatisfactory and generally abortive negotiations conducted by the various state governments in 1783–84, including the treaty of Augusta already noted,[4] we come to the turning point in the history of the Cherokee, their first treaty with the new government of the United States for peace and boundary delimitation, concluded at Hopewell (25) in South Carolina on November 28, 1785. Nearly one thousand Cherokee attended, the commissioners for the United States being Colonel Benjamin Hawkins (26), of North Carolina; General Andrew Pickens, of South Carolina; Cherokee Agent Joseph Martin, of Tennessee, and Colonel Lachlan McIntosh, of Georgia.   The instrument was signed by thirty-seven chiefs and principal men, representing nearly as many different towns.   The negotiations occupied ten days, being complicated by a protest on the part of North Carolina and Georgia against the action of the government commissioners in confirming to the Indians some lands which had already been appropriated as bounty lands for state troops without the consent of the Cherokee.   On the other hand the Cherokee complained that 3,000 white settlers were at that moment in occupancy of unceded land between the Holston and the French Broad.   In spite of their protest these intruders were allowed to remain, although the territory was not acquired by treaty until some years later.   As finally arranged the treaty left the Middle and Upper towns, and those in the vicinity

---

[1] See documents in Virginia State Papers, III, pp. 234, 398, 527, 1883.
[2] Ramsey, Tennessee, p. 280, 1853.   [3] Ibid., p. 275.
[4] See Royce, Cherokee Nation, op. cit., pp. 151, 152; Ramsey, op. cit., p. 299 et passim.

of Coosa river, undisturbed, while the whole country east of the Blue ridge, with the Watauga ard Cumberland settlements, was given over to the whites.   The general boundary followed the dividing ridge between Cumberland river and the more southern waters of the Tennessee eastward to the junction of the two forks of Holston, near the present Kingsport, Tennessee, thence southward to the Blue ridge and southwestward to a point not far from the present Atlanta, Georgia, thence westward to the Coosa river and northwestward to a creek running into Tennessee river at the western line of Alabama, thence northward with the Tennessee river to the beginning.   The lands south and west of these lines were recognized as belonging to the Creeks and Chickasaw.   Hostilities were to cease and the Cherokee were taken under the protection of the United States.   The proceedings ended with the distribution of a few presents.[1]

While the Hopewell treaty defined the relations of the Cherokee to the general government and furnished a safe basis for future negotiation, it yet failed to bring complete peace and security.   Thousands of intruders were still settled on Indian lands, and minor aggressions and reprisals were continually occurring.   The Creeks and the northern tribes were still hostile and remained so for some years later, and their warriors, cooperating with those of the implacable Chickamauga towns, continued to annoy the exposed settlements, particularly on the Cumberland.   The British had withdrawn from the South, but the Spaniards and French, who claimed the lower Mississippi and the Gulf region and had their trading posts in west Tennessee, took every opportunity to encourage the spirit of hostility to the Americans.[2] But the spirit of the Cherokee nation was broken and the Holston settlements were now too surely established to be destroyed.

The Cumberland settlements founded by Robertson and Donelson in the winter of 1779–80 had had but short respite.   Early in spring the Indians—Cherokee, Creeks, Chickasaw, and northern Indians—had begun a series of attacks with the design of driving these intruders from their lands, and thenceforth for years no man's life was safe outside the stockade.   The long list of settlers shot down at work or while hunting in the woods, of stock stolen and property destroyed, while of sorrowful interest to those most nearly concerned, is too tedious for recital here, and only leading events need be chronicled.   Detailed notice may be found in the works of local historians.

On the night of January 15, 1781, a band of Indians stealthily approached Freeland's station and had even succeeded in unfastening

---

[1] Indian Treaties, p. 8 et passim, 1837.   For a full discussion of the Hopewell treaty, from official documents, see Royce, Cherokee Nation, in Fifth Ann. Rep. Bureau of Ethnology, pp. 152–158, 1888, with map; Treaty Journal, etc., American State Papers; Indian Affairs, I, pp. 38–44, 1832; also Stevens, Georgia, II, pp. 417–429, 1859; Ramsey, Tennessee, pp. 336, 337, 1853; see also the map accompanying this work.

[2] Ramsey, op. cit., pp. 459–461; Agent Martin and Hopewell commissioners, ibid., pp. 318–336; Bledsoe and Robertson letter, ibid., p. 465; Roosevelt, Winning of the West, II, p. 368, 1899.

the strongly barred gate when Robertson, being awake inside, heard the noise and sprang up just in time to rouse the garrison and beat off the assailants, who continued to fire through the loopholes after they had been driven out of the fort. Only two Americans were killed, although the escape was a narrow one.[1]

About three months later, on April 2, a large body of Cherokee approached the fort at Nashville (then called Nashborough, or simply "the Bluff"), and by sending a decoy ahead succeeded in drawing a large part of the garrison into an ambush. It seemed that they would be cut off, as the Indians were between them and the fort, when those inside loosed the dogs, which rushed so furiously upon the Indians that the latter found work enough to defend themselves, and were finally forced to retire, carrying with them, however, five American scalps.[2]

The attacks continued throughout this and the next year to such an extent that it seemed at one time as if the Cumberland settlements must be abandoned, but in June, 1783, commissioners from Virginia and North Carolina arranged a treaty near Nashville (Nashborough) with chiefs of the Chickasaw, Cherokee, and Creeks. This treaty, although it did not completely stop the Indian inroads, at least greatly diminished them. Thereafter the Chickasaw remained friendly, and only the Cherokee and Creeks continued to make trouble.[3]

The valley towns on Hiwassee, as well as those of Chickamauga, seem to have continued hostile. In 1786 a large body of their warriors, led by the mixed-blood chief, John Watts, raided the new settlements in the vicinity of the present Knoxville, Tennessee. In retaliation Sevier again marched his volunteers across the mountain to the valley towns and destroyed three of them, killing a number of warriors; but he retired on learning that the Indians were gathering to give him battle.[4] In the spring of this year Agent Martin, stationed at Echota, had made a tour of inspection of the Cherokee towns and reported that they were generally friendly and anxious for peace, with the exception of the Chickamauga band, under Dragging-canoe, who, acting with the hostile Creeks and encouraged by the French and Spaniards, were making preparations to destroy the Cumberland settlements. Notwithstanding the friendly professions of the others, a party sent out to obtain satisfaction for the murder of four Cherokee by the Tennesseeans had come back with fifteen white scalps, and sent word to Sevier that they wanted peace, but if the whites wanted war they would get it.[5] With lawless men on both sides it is evident that peace was in jeopardy. In August, in consequence of further killing and reprisals, commissioners of the new "state of Franklin," as Tennessee was now

---

[1] Roosevelt, Winning of the West, II, p. 353, 1889.
[2] Ibid., p. 355, 1889; Ramsey, Tennessee, pp. 452–454, 1853.
[3] Ibid., pp. 358–366, 1889.   [4] Ibid., p. 341, 1853.
[5] Martin letter of May 11, 1786, ibid., p. 342.

called, concluded a negotiation, locally known as the "treaty of
Coyatee," with the chiefs of the Overhill towns.   In spite of references
to peace, love, and brotherly friendship, it is very doubtful if the era
of good will was in any wise hastened by the so-called treaty, as the
Tennesseeans, who had just burned another Indian town in reprisal for
the killing of a white man, announced, without mincing words, that
they had been given by North Carolina—against which state, by the
way, they were then in organized rebellion—the whole country north
of the Tennessee river as far west as the Cumberland mountain, and
that they intended to take it "by the sword, which is the best right to
all countries."   As the whole of this country was within the limits of
the territory solemnly guaranteed to the Cherokee by the Hopewell
treaty only the year before, the chiefs simply replied that Congress
had said nothing to them on the subject, and so the matter rested.[1]
The theory of state's rights was too complicated for the Indian understanding.

While this conflict between state and federal authority continued,
with the Cherokee lands as the prize, there could be no peace.   In
March, 1787, a letter from Echota, apparently written by Agent
Martin, speaks of a recent expedition against the Cherokee towns,
and the confusion and alarm among them in consequence of the daily
encroachments of the "Franklinites" or Tennesseeans, who had proceeded to make good their promise by opening a land office for the sale
of all the lands southward to Tennessee river, including even a part of the
beloved town of Echota.   At the same time messengers were coming
to the Cherokee from traders in the foreign interest, telling them that
England, France, and Spain had combined against the Americans and
urging them with promises of guns and ammunition to join in the
war.[2]   As a result each further advance of the Tennessee settlements,
in defiance as it was of any recognized treaty, was stubbornly contested by the Indian owners of the land.   The record of these encounters, extending over a period of several years, is too tedious for recital.
"Could a diagram be drawn, accurately designating every spot sig-
nalized by an Indian massacree, surprise, or depredation, or courageous
attack, defense, pursuit, or victory by the whites, or station or fort
or battlefield, or personal encounter, the whole of that section of
country would be studded over with delineations of such incidents.
Every spring, every ford, every path, every farm, every trail, every
house nearly, in its first settlement, was once the scene of danger,
exposure, attack, exploit, achievement, death."[3]   The end was the
winning of Tennessee.

In the meantime the inroads of the Creeks and their Chickamauga

---

[1] Reports of Tennessee commissioners and replies by Cherokee chiefs, etc., 1786, in Ramsey, Tennessee, pp. 343–346, 1853.

[2] Martin (?) letter of March 25, 1787, ibid., p. 359.

[3] Ibid., p. 370.

allies upon the Georgia frontier and the Cumberland settlements around Nashville became so threatening that measures were taken for a joint campaign by the combined forces of Georgia and Tennessee ("Franklin"). The enterprise came to naught through the interference of the federal authorities.[1] All through the year 1788 we hear of attacks and reprisals along the Tennessee border, although the agent for the Cherokee declared in his official report that, with the exception of the Chickamauga band, the Indians wished to be at peace if the whites would let them. In March two expeditions under Sevier and Kennedy set out against the towns in the direction of the French Broad. In May several persons of a family named Kirk were murdered a few miles south of Knoxville. In retaliation Sevier raised a large party and marching against a town on Hiwassee river— one of those which had been destroyed some years before and rebuilt— and burned it, killing a number of the inhabitants in the river while they were trying to escape. He then turned, and proceeding to the towns on Little Tennessee burned several of them also, killing a number of Indians. Here a small party of Indians, including Abraham and Tassel, two well-known friendly chiefs, was brutally massacred by one of the Kirks, no one interfering, after they had voluntarily come in on request of one of the officers. This occurred during the temporary absence of Sevier. Another expedition under Captain Fayne was drawn into an ambuscade at Citico town and lost several in killed and wounded. The Indians pursued the survivors almost to Knoxville, attacking a small station near the present Maryville by the way. They were driven off by Sevier and others, who in turn invaded the Indian settlements, crossing the mountains and penetrating as far as the valley towns on Hiwassee, hastily retiring as they found the Indians gathering in their front.[2] In the same summer another expedition was organized against the Chickamauga towns. The chief command was given to General Martin, who left White's fort, now Knoxville, with four hundred and fifty men and made a rapid march to the neighborhood of the present Chattanooga, where the main force encamped on the site of an old Indian settlement. A detachment sent ahead to surprise a town a few miles farther down the river was fired upon and driven back, and a general engagement took place in the narrow pass between the bluff and the river, with such disastrous results that three captains were killed and the men so badly demoralized that they refused to advance. Martin was compelled to turn back, after burying the dead officers in a large townhouse, which was then burned down to conceal the grave.[3]

In October a large party of Cherokee and Creeks attacked Gillespie's station, south of the present Knoxville. The small garrison was

---

[1] Ramsey, Tennessee, pp. 393–399, 1853.   [2] Ibid., pp. 417–423, 1853.
[3] Ibid., pp. 517–519, and Brown's narrative, ibid., p. 515.

overpowered after a short resistance, and twenty-eight persons, including several women and children, were killed.   The Indians left behind
a letter signed by four chiefs, including John Watts, expressing
regret for what they called the accidental killing of the women and
children, reminding the whites of their own treachery in killing
Abraham and the Tassel, and defiantly concluding, "When you move
off the land, then we will make peace."   Other exposed stations were
attacked, until at last Sevier again mustered a force, cleared the
enemy from the frontier, and pursued the Indians as far as their
towns on the head waters of Coosa river, in such vigorous fashion that
they were compelled to ask for terms of peace and agree to a surrender
of prisoners, which was accomplished at Coosawatee town, in upper
Georgia, in the following April.[1]

Among the captives thus restored to their friends were Joseph
Brown, a boy of sixteen, with his two younger sisters, who, with
several others, had been taken at Nickajack town while descending
the Tennessee in a flatboat nearly a year before.   His father and the
other men of the party, about ten in all, had been killed at the time,
while the mother and several other children were carried to various
Indian towns, some of them going to the Creeks, who had aided the
Cherokee in the capture.   Young Brown, whose short and simple
narrative is of vivid interest, was at first condemned to death, but was
rescued by a white man living in the town and was afterward adopted
into the family of the chief, in spite of the warning of an old Indian
woman that if allowed to live he would one day guide an army to
destroy them.   The warning was strangely prophetic, for it was
Brown himself who guided the expedition that finally rooted out the
Chickamauga towns a few years later.   When rescued at Coosawatee
he was in Indian costume, with shirt, breechcloth, scalp lock, and
holes bored in his ears.   His little sister, five years old, had become
so attached to the Indian woman who had adopted her, that she
refused to go to her own mother and had to be pulled along by force.[2]
The mother and another of the daughters, who had been taken by the
Creeks, were afterwards ransomed by McGillivray, head chief of the
Creek Nation, who restored them to their friends, generously refusing
any compensation for his kindness.

An arrangement had been made with the Chickasaw, in 1783, by
which they surrendered to the Cumberland settlement their own claim
to the lands from the Cumberland river south to the dividing ridge of
Duck river.[3]   It was not, however, until the treaty of Hopewell, two
years later, that the Cherokee surrendered their claim to the same
region, and even then the Chickamauga warriors, with their allies, the

[1] Ramsey, Tennessee, pp. 515, 519.
[2] Brown's narrative, etc., ibid., pp. 508–516.
[3] Ibid., pp. 459, 489.

hostile Creeks and Shawano, refused to acknowledge the cession and continued their attacks, with the avowed purpose of destroying the new settlements. Until the final running of the boundary line, in 1797, Spain claimed all the territory west of the mountains and south of Cumberland river, and her agents were accused of stirring up the Indians against the Americans, even to the extent of offering rewards for American scalps.[1] One of these raiding parties, which had killed the brother of Captain Robertson, was tracked to Coldwater, a small mixed town of Cherokee and Creeks, on the south side of Tennessee river, about the present Tuscumbia, Alabama. Robertson determined to destroy it, and taking a force of volunteers, with a couple of Chickasaw guides, crossed the Tennessee without being discovered and surprised and burnt the town. The Indians, who numbered less than fifty men, attempted to escape to the river, but were surrounded and over twenty of them killed, with a loss of but one man to the Tennesseeans. In the town were found also several French traders. Three of these, who refused to surrender, were killed, together with a white woman who was accidentally shot in one of the boats. The others were afterward released, their large stock of trading goods having been taken and sold for the benefit of the troops. The affair took place about the end of June, 1787. Through this action, and an effort made by Robertson about the same time to come to an understanding with the Chickamauga band, there was a temporary cessation of hostile inroads upon the Cumberland, but long before the end of the year the attacks were renewed to such an extent that it was found necessary to keep out a force of rangers with orders to scour the country and kill every Indian found east of the Chickasaw boundary.[2]

The Creeks seeming now to be nearly as much concerned in these raids as the Cherokee, a remonstrance was addressed to McGillivray, their principal chief, who replied that, although the Creeks, like the other southern tribes, had adhered to the British interest during the Revolution, they had accepted proposals of friendship, but while negotiations were pending six of their people had been killed in the affair at Coldwater, which had led to a renewal of hostile feeling. He promised, however, to use his best efforts to bring about peace, and seems to have kept his word, although the raids continued through this and the next year, with the usual sequel of pursuit and reprisal. In one of these skirmishes a company under Captain Murray followed some Indian raiders from near Nashville to their camp on Tennessee river and succeeded in killing the whole party of eleven warriors.[3] A treaty of peace was signed with the Creeks in 1790, but, owing to the intrigues of the Spaniards, it had little practical effect,[4] and not

[1] Bledsoe and Robertson letter of June 12, 1787, in Ramsey, Tennessee, p. 465, 1853.

[2] Ibid., with Robertson letter, pp. 465–476.

[3] Ibid., pp. 479–486.

[4] Monette, Valley of the Mississippi, I, p. 505, 1846.

until Wayne's decisive victory over the confederated northern tribes
in 1794 and the final destruction of the Nickajack towns in the same
year did real peace came to the frontier.

By deed of cession of February 25, 1790, Tennessee ceased to be a
part of North Carolina and was organized under federal laws as " The
Territory of the United States south of the Ohio river," preliminary
to taking full rank as a state six years later.   William Blount (27)
was appointed first territorial governor and also superintendent for the
southern Indians, with a deputy resident with each of the four principal tribes.[1]   Pensacola, Mobile, St. Louis, and other southern posts
were still held by the Spaniards, who claimed the whole country south
of the Cumberland, while the British garrisons had not yet been withdrawn from the north.   The resentment of the Indians at the occupancy
of their reserved and guaranteed lands by the whites was sedulously
encouraged from both quarters, and raids along the Tennessee frontier were of common occurrence.   At this time, according to the
official report of President Washington, over five hundred families of
intruders were settled upon lands belonging rightly to the Cherokee,
in addition to those between the French Broad and the Holston.[2]
More than a year before the Secretary of War had stated that "the
disgraceful violation of the treaty of Hopewell with the Cherokee
requires the serious consideration of Congress.   If so direct and manifest contempt of the authority of the United States be suffered with
impunity, it will be in vain to attempt to extend the arm of government to the frontiers.   The Indian tribes can have no faith in such
imbecile promises, and the lawless whites will ridicule a government
which shall on paper only make Indian treaties and regulate Indian
boundaries."[3]   To prevent any increase of the dissatisfaction, the
general government issued a proclamation forbidding any further
encroachment upon the Indian lands on Tennessee river; notwithstanding which, early in 1791, a party of men descended the river in
boats, and, landing on an island at the Muscle shoals, near the present
Tuscumbia, Alabama, erected a blockhouse and other defensive works.
Immediately afterward the Cherokee chief, Glass, with about sixty
warriors, appeared and quietly informed them that if they did not at
once withdraw he would kill them.   After some parley the intruders
retired to their boats, when the Indians set fire to the buildings and
reduced them to ashes.[4]

To forestall more serious difficulty it was necessary to negotiate a
new treaty with a view to purchasing the disputed territory.   Accordingly, through the efforts of Governor Blount, a convention was held
with the principal men of the Cherokee at White's fort, now Knox-

[1] Ramsey, Tennessee, pp. 522, 541, 561, 1853.
[2] Washington to the Senate, August 11, 1790, American State Papers: Indian Affairs, I, p. 83, 1832.
[3] Secretary Knox to President Washington, July 7, 1789, ibid., p. 53.
[4] Ramsey, op. cit., pp. 550, 551.

ville, Tennessee, in the summer of 1791. With much difficulty the Cherokee were finally brought to consent to a cession of a triangular section in Tennessee and North Carolina extending from Clinch river almost to the Blue ridge, and including nearly the whole of the French Broad and the lower Holston, with the sites of the present Knoxville, Greenville, and Asheville. The whole of this area, with a considerable territory adjacent, was already fully occupied by the whites. Permission was also given for a road from the eastern settlements to those on the Cumberland, with the free navigation of Tennessee river. Prisoners on both sides were to be restored and perpetual peace was guaranteed. In consideration of the lands surrendered the Cherokee were to receive an annuity of one thousand dollars with some extra goods and some assistance on the road to civilization. A treaty was signed by forty-one principal men of the tribe and was concluded July 2, 1791. It is officially described as being held "on the bank of the Holston, near the mouth of the French Broad," and is commonly spoken of as the "treaty of Holston."

The Cherokee, however, were dissatisfied with the arrangement, and before the end of the year a delegation of six principal chiefs appeared at Philadelphia, then the seat of government, without any previous announcement of their coming, declaring that when they had been summoned by Governor Blount to a conference they were not aware that it was to persuade them to sell lands; that they had resisted the proposition for days, and only yielded when compelled by the persistent and threatening demands of the governor; that the consideration was entirely too small; and that they had no faith that the whites would respect the new boundary, as they were in fact already settling beyond it. Finally, as the treaty had been signed, they asked that these intruders be removed. As their presentation of the case seemed a just one and it was desirable that they should carry home with them a favorable impression of the government's attitude toward them, a supplementary article was added, increasing the annuity to eight thousand five hundred dollars. On account of renewed Indian hostilities in Ohio valley and the desire of the government to keep the good will of the Cherokee long enough to obtain their help against the northern tribes, the new line was not surveyed until 1797.[1]

As illustrating Indian custom it may be noted that one of the principal signers of the original treaty was among the protesting delegates, but having in the meantime changed his name, it appears on the supplementary paragraph as "Iskagua, or Clear Sky, formerly Nenetooyah, or Bloody Fellow."[2] As he had been one of the prin-

---

[1] Indian Treaties, pp. 34–38, 1837; Secretary of War, report, January 5, 1798, in American State Papers, I, pp. 628–631, 1832; Ramsey, Tennessee, pp. 554–560, 1853; Royce, Cherokee Nation, Fifth Ann. Rep. Bureau of Ethnology, pp. 158–170. with full discussion and map, 1888.

[2] Indian Treaties, pp. 37, 38, 1837.

cipal raiders on the Tennessee frontier, the new name may have been symbolic of his change of heart at the prospect of a return of peace.

The treaty seems to have had little effect in preventing Indian hostilities, probably because the intruders still remained upon the Indian lands, and raiding still continued. The Creeks were known to be responsible for some of the mischief, and the hostile Chickamaugas were supposed to be the chief authors of the rest.[1] Even while the Cherokee delegates were negotiating the treaty in Philadelphia a boat which had accidentally run aground on the Muscle shoals was attacked by a party of Indians under the pretense of offering assistance, one man being killed and another severely wounded with a hatchet.[2]

While these negotiations had been pending at Philadelphia a young man named Leonard D. Shaw, a student at Princeton college, had expressed to the Secretary of War an earnest desire for a commission which would enable him to accompany the returning Cherokee delegates to their southern home, there to study Indian life and characteristics. As the purpose seemed a useful one, and he appeared well qualified for such a work, he was accordingly commissioned as deputy agent to reside among the Cherokee to observe and report upon their movements, to aid in the annuity distributions, and to render other assistance to Governor Blount, superintendent for the southern tribes, to study their language and home life, and to collect materials for an Indian history. An extract from the official instructions under which this first United States ethnologist began his work will be of interest. After defining his executive duties in connection with the annuity distributions, the keeping of accounts and the compiling of official reports, Secretary Knox continues—

A due performance of your duty will probably require the exercise of all your patience and fortitude and all your knowledge of the human character. The school will be a severe but interesting one. If you should succeed in acquiring the affections and a knowledge of the characters of the southern Indians, you may be at once useful to the United States and advance your own interest.

You will endeavor to learn their languages; this is essential to your communications. You will collect materials for a history of all the southern tribes and all things thereunto belonging. You will endeavor to ascertain their respective limits, make a vocabulary of their respective languages, teach them agriculture and such useful arts as you may know or can acquire. You will correspond regularly with Governor Blount, who is superintendent for Indian affairs, and inform him of all occurrences. You will also cultivate a correspondence with Brigadier-General McGillivray [the Creek chief], and you will also keep a journal of your proceedings and transmit them to the War Office. . . . You are to exhibit to Governor Blount the Cherokee book and all the writings therein, the messages to the several tribes of Indians, and these instructions.

Your route will be hence to Reading; thence Harris's ferry [Harrisburg, Pennsylvania] to Carlisle; to —— ferry on the Potomac; to Winchester; to Staunton; to

---

[1] Ramsey, Tennessee, p. 557, 1853.
[2] Abel deposition, April 16, 1792, American State Papers; Indian Affairs, I, p. 274, 1832.

————, and to Holston. I should hope that you would travel upwards of twenty miles each day, and that you would reach Holston in about thirty days.[1]

The journey, which seemed then so long, was to be made by wagons from Philadelphia to the head of navigation on Holston river, thence by boats to the Cherokee towns. Shaw seems to have taken up his residence at Ustanali, which had superseded Echota as the Cherokee capital. We hear of him as present at a council there in June of the same year, with no evidence of unfriendliness at his presence.[2] The friendly feeling was of short continuance, however, for a few months later we find him writing from Ustanali to Governor Blount that on account of the aggressive hostility of the Creeks, whose avowed intention was to kill every white man they met, he was not safe 50 yards from the house. Soon afterwards the Chickamauga towns again declared war, on which account, together with renewed threats by the Creeks, he was advised by the Cherokee to leave Ustanali, which he did early in September, 1792, proceeding to the home of General Pickens, near Seneca, South Carolina, escorted by a guard of friendly Cherokee. In the following winter he was dismissed from the service on serious charges, and his mission appears to have been a failure.[3]

To prevent an alliance of the Cherokee, Creeks, and other southern Indians with the confederated hostile northern tribes, the government had endeavored to persuade the former to furnish a contingent of warriors to act with the army against the northern Indians, and special instruction had been given to Shaw to use his efforts for this result. Nothing, however, came of the attempt. St Clair's defeat turned the scale against the United States, and in September, 1792, the Chickamauga towns formally declared war.[4]

In November of this year the governor of Georgia officially reported that a party of lawless Georgians had gone into the Cherokee Nation, and had there burned a town and barbarously killed three Indians, while about the same time two other Cherokee had been killed within the settlements. Fearing retaliation, he ordered out a patrol of troops to guard the frontier in that direction, and sent a conciliatory letter to the chiefs, expressing his regret for what had happened. No answer was returned to the message, but a few days later an entire family was found murdered—four women, three children, and a young man—all scalped and mangled and with arrows sticking in the bodies, while, according to old Indian war custom, two war clubs were left upon

[1] Henry Knox, Secretary of War, Instructions to Leonard Shaw, temporary agent to the Cherokee Nation of Indians, February 17, 1792, in American State Papers: Indian Affairs, I, 247, 1832; also Knox, letters to Governor Blount, January 31 and February 16, 1792, ibid., pp. 245, 246.

[2] Estanaula conference report, June 26, 1792, ibid., p. 271; Deraque, deposition, September 15, 1792, ibid., p. 292; Pickens, letter, September 12, 1792, ibid., p. 317.

[3] See letters of Shaw, Casey, Pickens, and Blount, 1792–93, ibid., pp. 277, 278, 317, 436, 437, 440.

[4] Knox, instructions to Shaw, February 17, 1792, ibid., p. 247; Blount, letter, March 20, 1792, ibid., p. 263; Knox, letters, October 9, 1792, ibid., pp. 261, 262.

the ground to show by whom the deed was done. So swift was savage vengeance.[1]

Early in 1792 a messenger who had been sent on business for Governor Blount to the Chickamauga towns returned with the report that a party had just come in with prisoners and some fresh scalps, over which the chiefs and warriors of two towns were then dancing; that the Shawano were urging the Cherokee to join them against the Americans; that a strong body of Creeks was on its way against the Cumberland settlements, and that the Creek chief, McGillivray, was trying to form a general confederacy of all the Indian tribes against the whites. To understand this properly it must be remembered that at this time all the tribes northwest of the Ohio and as far as the heads of the Mississippi were banded together in a grand alliance, headed by the warlike Shawano, for the purpose of holding the Ohio river as the Indian boundary against the advancing tide of white settlement. They had just cut to pieces one of the finest armies ever sent into the West, under the veteran General St Clair (28), and it seemed for the moment as if the American advance would be driven back behind the Alleghenies.

In the emergency the Secretary of War directed Governor Blount to hold a conference with the chiefs of the Chickasaw, Choctaw, and Cherokee at Nashville in June to enlist their warriors, if possible, in active service against the northern tribes. The conference was held as proposed, in August, but nothing seems to have come of it, although the chiefs seemed to be sincere in their assurances of friendship. Very few of the Choctaw or Cherokee were in attendance. At the annuity distribution of the Cherokee, shortly before, the chiefs had also been profuse in declarations of their desire for peace.[2] Notwithstanding all this the attacks along the Tennessee frontier continued to such an extent that the blockhouses were again put in order and garrisoned. Soon afterwards the governor reported to the Secretary of War that the five lower Cherokee towns on the Tennessee (the Chickamauga), headed by John Watts, had finally declared war against the United States, and that from three to six hundred warriors, including a hundred Creeks, had started against the settlements. The militia was at once called out, both in eastern Tennessee and on the Cumberland. On the Cumberland side it was directed that no pursuit should be continued beyond the Cherokee boundary, the ridge between the waters of Cumberland and Duck rivers. The order issued by Colonel White, of Knox county, to each of his captains shows how great was the alarm:

---

[1] Governor Telfair's letters of November 14 and December 5, with inclosure, 1792, American State Papers: Indian Affairs, I, pp. 332, 336, 337, 1832.

[2] Ramsey, Tennessee, pp. 562–563, 598, 1853.

KNOXVILLE, *September 11, 1792.*

SIR: You are hereby commanded to repair with your company to Knoxville, equipped, to protect the frontiers; there is imminent danger. Bring with you two days' provisions, if possible; but you are not to delay an hour on that head.

I am, sir, yours,

JAMES WHITE.[1]

About midnight on the 30th of September, 1792, the Indian force, consisting of several hundred Chickamaugas and other Cherokee, Creeks, and Shawano, attacked Buchanan's station, a few miles south of Nashville. Although numbers of families had collected inside the stockade for safety, there were less than twenty able-bodied men among them. The approach of the enemy alarmed the cattle, by which the garrison had warning just in time to close the gate when the Indians were already within a few yards of the entrance. The assault was furious and determined, the Indians rushing up to the stockade, attempting to set fire to it, and aiming their guns through the port holes. One Indian succeeded in climbing upon the roof with a lighted torch, but was shot and fell to the ground, holding his torch against the logs as he drew his last breath. It was learned afterward that he was a half blood, the stepson of the old white trader who had once rescued the boy Joseph Brown at Nickajack. He was a desperate warrior and when only twenty-two years of age had already taken six white scalps. The attack was repulsed at every point, and the assailants finally drew off, with considerable loss, carrying their dead and wounded with them, and leaving a number of hatchets, pipes, and other spoils upon the ground. Among the wounded was the chief John Watts. Not one of those in the fort was injured. It has been well said that the defense of Buchanan's station by such a handful of men against an attacking force estimated all the way at from three to seven hundred Indians is a feat of bravery which has scarcely been surpassed in the annals of border warfare. The effect upon the Indians must have been thoroughly disheartening.[2]

In the same month arrangements were made for protecting the frontier along the French Broad by means of a series of garrisoned blockhouses, with scouts to patrol regularly from one to another, North Carolina cooperating on her side of the line. The hostile inroads still continued in this section, the Creeks acting with the hostile Cherokee. One raiding party of Creeks having been traced toward Chilhowee town on Little Tennessee, the whites were about to burn that and a neighboring Cherokee town when Sevier interposed and prevented.[3] There is no reason to suppose that the people of these towns were directly concerned in the depredations along the frontier at this period,

---

[1] Ramsey, Tennessee, pp. 562–565, 1853.

[2] Blount, letter, October 2, 1792, in American State Papers: Indian Affairs, I, p. 294, 1832; Blount, letter, etc., in Ramsey, op. cit., pp. 566, 567, 599–601; see also Brown's narrative, ibid., 511, 512; Royce, Cherokee Nation, Fifth Ann. Rep. Bureau of Ethnology, p. 170, 1888.

[3] Ramsey, op. cit., 569–571.

the mischief being done by those farther to the south, in conjunction with the Creeks.

Toward the close of this year, 1792, Captain Samuel Handley, while leading a small party of men to reenforce the Cumberland settlement, was attacked by a mixed force of Cherokee, Creeks, and Shawano, near the Crab Orchard, west of the present Kingston, Tennessee. Becoming separated from his men he encountered a warrior who had lifted his hatchet to strike when Handley seized the weapon, crying out "Canaly" (for *higïna'lïï*), "friend," to which the Cherokee responded with the same word, at once lowering his arm. Handley was carried to Willstown, in Alabama, where he was adopted into the Wolf clan (29) and remained until the next spring. After having made use of his services in writing a peace letter to Governor Blount the Cherokee finally sent him home in safety to his friends under a protecting escort of eight warriors, without any demand for ransom. He afterward resided near Tellico blockhouse, near Loudon, where, after the wars were over, his Indian friends frequently came to visit and stop with him.[1]

The year 1793 began with a series of attacks all along the Tennessee frontier. As before, most of the depredation was by Chickamaugas and Creeks, with some stray Shawano from the north. The Cherokee from the towns on Little Tennessee remained peaceable, but their temper was sorely tried by a regrettable circumstance which occurred in June. While a number of friendly chiefs were assembled for a conference at Echota, on the express request of the President, a party of men under command of a Captain John Beard suddenly attacked them, killing about fifteen Indians, including several chiefs and two women, one of them being the wife of Hanging-maw (Ushwâ'li-gûtă), principal chief of the Nation, who was himself wounded. The murderers then fled, leaving others to suffer the consequences. Two hundred warriors at once took up arms to revenge their loss, and only the most earnest appeal from the deputy governor could restrain them from swift retaliation. While the chief, whose wife was thus murdered and himself wounded, forebore to revenge himself, in order not to bring war upon his people, the Secretary of War was obliged to report, "to my great pain, I find to punish Beard by law just now is out of the question." Beard was in fact arrested, but the trial was a farce and he was acquitted.[2]

Believing that the Cherokee Nation, with the exception of the Chickamaugas, was honestly trying to preserve peace, the territorial government, while making provision for the safety of the exposed settlements, had strictly prohibited any invasion of the Indian country. The frontier people were of a different opinion, and in spite of the prohibition a company of nearly two hundred mounted men under

---

[1] Ramsey, Tennessee, pp. 571–573, 1853.   [2] Ibid., pp. 574–578, 1853.

Colonels Doherty and McFarland crossed over the mountains in the summer of this year and destroyed six of the middle towns, returning with fifteen scalps and as many prisoners.[1]

Late in September a strong force estimated at one thousand warriors—seven hundred Creeks and three hundred Cherokee—under John Watts and Doublehead, crossed the Tennessee and advanced in the direction of Knoxville, where the public stores were then deposited. In their eagerness to reach Knoxville they passed quietly by one or two smaller settlements until within a short distance of the town, when, at daybreak of the 25th, they heard the garrison fire the sunrise gun and imagined that they were discovered. Differences had already broken out among the leaders, and without venturing to advance farther they contented themselves with an attack upon a small blockhouse a few miles to the west, known as Cavitts station, in which at the time were only three men with thirteen women and children. After defending themselves bravely for some time these surrendered on promise that they should be held for exchange, but as soon as they came out Doublehead's warriors fell upon them and put them all to death with the exception of a boy, who was saved by John Watts. This bloody deed was entirely the work of Doublehead, the other chiefs having done their best to prevent it.[2]

A force of seven hundred men under General Sevier was at once put upon their track, with orders this time to push the pursuit into the heart of the Indian nation. Crossing Little Tennessee and Hiwassee they penetrated to Ustanali town, near the present Calhoun, Georgia. Finding it deserted, although well filled with provision, they rested there a few days, the Indians in the meantime attempting a night attack without success. After burning the town, Sevier continued down the river to Etowah town, near the present site of Rome. Here the Indians—Cherokee and Creeks—had dug intrenchments and prepared to make a stand, but, being outflanked, were defeated with loss and compelled to retreat. This town, with several others in the neighborhood belonging to both Cherokee and Creeks, was destroyed, with all the provision of the Indians, including three hundred cattle, after which the army took up the homeward march. The Americans had lost but three men. This was the last military service of Sevier.[3]

During the absence of Sevier's force in the south the Indians made a sudden inroad on the French Broad, near the present Dandridge, killing and scalping a woman and a boy. While their friends were accompanying the remains to a neighboring burial ground for interment, two men who had incautiously gone ahead were fired upon. One

---

[1] Ramsey, Tennessee, p. 579.

[2] Ibid., pp. 580–583, 1853; Smith, letter, September 27, 1793, American State Papers: Indian Affairs, I, p. 468, 1832. Ramsey gives the Indian force 1,000 warriors; Smith says that in many places they marched in files of 28 abreast, each file being supposed to number 40 men.

[3] Ramsey, op. cit., pp. 584–588.

of them escaped, but the other one was found killed and scalped when the rest of the company came up, and was buried with the first victims. Sevier's success brought temporary respite to the Cumberland settlements. During the early part of the year the Indian attacks by small raiding parties had been so frequent and annoying that a force of men had been kept out on patrol service under officers who adopted with some success the policy of hunting the Indians in their camping places in the thickets, rather than waiting for them to come into the settlements.[1]

In February, 1794, the Territorial assembly of Tennessee met at Knoxville and, among other business transacted, addressed a strong memorial to Congress calling for more efficient protection for the frontier and demanding a declaration of war against the Creeks and Cherokee. The memorial states that since the treaty of Holston (July, 1791), these two tribes had killed in a most barbarous and inhuman manner more than two hundred citizens of Tennessee, of both sexes, had carried others into captivity, destroyed their stock, burned their houses, and laid waste their plantations, had robbed the citizens of their slaves and stolen at least two thousand horses. Special attention was directed to the two great invasions in September, 1792, and September, 1793, and the memorialists declare that there was scarcely a man of the assembly but could tell of "a dear wife or child, an aged parent or near relation, besides friends, massacred by the hands of these bloodthirsty nations in their house or fields."[2]

In the meantime the raids continued and every scattered cabin was a target for attack. In April a party of twenty warriors surrounded the house of a man named Casteel on the French Broad about nine miles above Knoxville and massacred father, mother, and four children in most brutal fashion. One child only was left alive, a girl of ten years, who was found scalped and bleeding from six tomahawk gashes, yet survived. The others were buried in one grave. The massacre roused such a storm of excitement that it required all the effort of the governor and the local officials to prevent an invasion in force of the Indian country. It was learned that Doublehead, of the Chickamauga towns, was trying to get the support of the valley towns, which, however, continued to maintain an attitude of peace. The friendly Cherokee also declared that the Spaniards were constantly instigating the lower towns to hostilities, although John Watts, one of their principal chiefs, advocated peace.[3]

In June a boat under command of William Scott, laden with pots, hardware, and other property, and containing six white men, three women, four children, and twenty negroes, left Knoxville to descend

---

[1] Ramsey, Tennessee, pp. 590, 602–605, 1853.

[2] Haywood, Civil and Political History of Tennessee, pp. 300–302; Knoxville, 1823.

[3] Ibid., pp. 303–308, 1823; Ramsey, op. cit., pp. 591–594. Haywood's history of this period is little more than a continuous record of killings and petty encounters.

Tennessee river to Natchez. As it passed the Chickamauga towns it was fired upon from Running Water and Long island without damage. The whites returned the fire, wounding two Indians. A large party of Cherokee, headed by White-man-killer (Une'ga-dihï'), then started in pursuit of the boat, which they overtook at Muscle shoals, where they killed all the white people in it, made prisoners of the negroes, and plundered the goods. Three Indians were killed and one was wounded in the action.[1] It is said that the Indian actors in this massacre fled across the Mississippi into Spanish territory and became the nucleus of the Cherokee Nation of the West, as will be noted elsewhere.

On June 26, 1794, another treaty, intended to be supplementary to that of Holston in 1791, was negotiated at Philadelphia, being signed by the Secretary of War and by thirteen principal men of the Cherokee. An arrangement was made for the proper marking of the boundary then established, and the annuity was increased to five thousand dollars, with a proviso that fifty dollars were to be deducted for every horse stolen by the Cherokee and not restored within three months.[2]

In July a man named John Ish was shot down while plowing in his field eighteen miles below Knoxville. By order of Hanging-maw, the friendly chief of Echota, a party of Cherokee took the trail and captured the murderer, who proved to be a Creek, whom they brought in to the agent at Tellico blockhouse, where he was formally tried and hanged. When asked the usual question he said that his people were at war with the whites, that he had left home to kill or be killed, that he had killed the white man and would have escaped but for the Cherokee, and that there were enough of his nation to avenge his death. A few days later a party of one hundred Creek warriors crossed Tennessee river against the settlements. The alarm was given by Hanging-maw, and fifty-three Cherokee with a few federal troops started in pursuit. On the 10th of August they came up with the Creeks, killing one and wounding another, one Cherokee being slightly wounded. The Creeks retreated and the victors returned to the Cherokee towns, where their return was announced by the death song and the firing of guns. "The night was spent in dancing the scalp dance, according to the custom of warriors after a victory over their enemies, in which the white and red people heartily joined. The Upper Cherokee had now stepped too far to go back, and their professions of friendship were now no longer to be questioned." In the same month there was an engagement between a detachment of about

---

[1] Haywood, Civil and Political History of Tennessee, p. 308,1823; Ramsey, Tennessee, p. 594. 1853; see also memorial in Putnam, Middle Tennessee, p. 502, 1859. Haywood calls the leader Unacala, which should be Une'ga-dihï', "White-man-killer." Compare Haywood's statement with that of Washburn, on page 100.

[2] Indian Treaties, pp. 39, 40, 1837; Royce, Cherokee Nation, Fifth Ann. Rep. Bureau of Ethnology, pp. 171, 172, 1888; Documents of 1797–98, American State Papers: Indian Affairs, I, pp. 628–631, 1832. The treaty is not mentioned by the Tennessee historians.

forty soldiers and a large body of Creeks near Crab Orchard, in which several of each were killed.[1] It is evident that much of the damage on both sides of the Cumberland range was due to the Creeks.

In the meantime Governor Blount was trying to negotiate peace with the whole Cherokee Nation, but with little success. The Cherokee claimed to be anxious for permanent peace, but said that it was impossible to restore the property taken by them, as it had been taken in war, and they had themselves been equal losers from the whites. They said also that they could not prevent the hostile Creeks from passing through their territory. About the end of July it was learned that a strong body of Creeks had started north against the settlements. The militia was at once ordered out along the Tennessee frontier, and the friendly Cherokees offered their services, while measures were taken to protect their women and children from the enemy. The Creeks advanced as far as Willstown, when the news came of the complete defeat of the confederated northern tribes by General Wayne (30), and fearing the same fate for themselves, they turned back and scattered to their towns.[2]

The Tennesseeans, especially those on the Cumberland, had long ago come to the conclusion that peace could be brought about only through the destruction of the Chickamauga towns. Anticipating some action of this kind, which the general government did not think necessary or advisable, orders against any such attempt had been issued by the Secretary of War to Governor Blount. The frontier people went about their preparations, however, and it is evident from the result that the local military authorities were in connivance with the undertaking. General Robertson was the chief organizer of the volunteers about Nashville, who were reenforced by a company of Kentuckians under Colonel Whitley. Major Ore had been sent by Governor Blount with a detachment of troops to protect the Cumberland settlements, and on arriving at Nashville entered as heartily into the project as if no counter orders had ever been issued, and was given chief command of the expedition, which for this reason is commonly known as "Ore's expedition."

On September 7, 1794, the army of five hundred and fifty mounted men left Nashville, and five days later crossed the Tennessee near the mouth of the Sequatchee river, their guide being the same Joseph Brown of whom the old Indian woman had said that he would one day bring the soldiers to destroy them. Having left their horses on the other side of the river, they moved up along the south bank just after daybreak of the 13th and surprised the town of Nickajack, killing several warriors and taking a number of prisoners. Some who attempted to escape in canoes were shot in the water. The warriors

---

[1] Haywood, Civil and Political History of Tennessee, pp. 309–311, 1823; Ramsey, Tennessee, pp. 594, 595, 1853.

[2] Haywood, op. cit., pp. 314–316; Ramsey, op. cit., p. 596.

in Running Water town, four miles above, heard the firing and came at once to the assistance of their friends, but were driven back after attempting to hold their ground, and the second town shared the fate of the first. More than fifty Indians had been killed, a number were prisoners, both towns and all their contents had been destroyed, with a loss to the assailants of only three men wounded. The Breath, the chief of Running Water, was among those killed. Two fresh scalps with a large quantity of plunder from the settlements were found in the towns, together with a supply of ammunition said to have been furnished by the Spaniards.[1]

Soon after the return of the expedition Robertson sent a message to John Watts, the principal leader of the hostile Cherokee, threatening a second visitation if the Indians did not very soon surrender their prisoners and give assurances of peace.[2] The destruction of their towns on Tennessee and Coosa and the utter defeat of the northern confederates had now broken the courage of the Cherokee, and on their own request Governor Blount held a conference with them at Tellico blockhouse, November 7 and 8, 1794, at which Hanging-maw, head chief of the Nation, and Colonel John Watt, principal chief of the hostile towns, with about four hundred of their warriors, attended. The result was satisfactory; all differences were arranged on a friendly basis and the long Cherokee war came to an end.[3]

Owing to the continued devastation of their towns during the Revolutionary struggle, a number of Cherokee, principally of the Chickamauga band, had removed across the Ohio about 1782 and settled on Paint creek, a branch of the Scioto river, in the vicinity of their friends and allies, the Shawano. In 1787 they were reported to number about seventy warriors. They took an active part in the hostilities along the Ohio frontier and were present in the great battle at the Maumee rapids, by which the power of the confederated northern tribes was effectually broken. As they had failed to attend the treaty conference held at Greenville in August, 1795, General Wayne sent them a special message, through their chief Long-hair, that if they refused to come in and make terms as the others had done they would be considered outside the protection of the government. Upon this a part of them came in and promised that as soon as they could gather their crops the whole band would leave Ohio forever and return to their people in the south.[4]

---

[1] Haywood, Political and Civil History of Tennessee, pp. 392–396, 1823; Ramsey, Tennessee (with Major Ore's report), pp. 608–618, 1853; Royce, Cherokee Nation, Fifth Ann. Rep. Bureau Ethnology, p. 171, 1888; Ore, Robertson, and Blount, reports, American State Papers: Indian Affairs, I, pp. 632–634, 1832.

[2] Ramsey, op. cit., p. 618.

[3] Tellico conference, November 7–8, 1794, American State Papers: Indian Affairs, I, pp. 536–538, 1832; Royce, op. cit., p. 173; Ramsey, op. cit., p. 596.

[4] Beaver's talk, 1784, Virginia State Papers, III, p. 571, 1883; McDowell, report, 1786, ibid., IV, p. 118, 1884; McDowell, report, 1787, ibid., p. 286; Todd, letter, 1787, ibid., p. 277; Tellico conference, November 7, 1794, American State Papers: Indian Affairs, I, p. 538, 1832; Greenville treaty conference, August, 1795, ibid., pp. 582–583.

The Creeks were still hostile and continued their inroads upon the western settlements. Early in January, 1795, Governor Blount held another conference with the Cherokee and endeavored to persuade them to organize a company of their young men to patrol the frontier against the Creeks, but to this proposal the chiefs refused to consent.[1]

In the next year it was discovered that a movement was on foot to take possession of certain Indian lands south of the Cumberland on pretense of authority formerly granted by North Carolina for the relief of Revolutionary soldiers. As such action would almost surely have resulted in another Indian war, Congress interposed, on the representation of President Washington, with an act for the regulation of intercourse between citizens of the United States and the various Indian tribes. Its main purpose was to prevent intrusion upon lands to which the Indian title had not been extinguished by treaty with the general government, and under its provisions a number of squatters were ejected from the Indian country and removed across the boundary. The pressure of border sentiment, however, was constantly for extending the area of white settlement and the result was an immediate agitation to procure another treaty cession.[2]

In consequence of urgent representations from the people of Tennessee, Congress took steps in 1797 for procuring a new treaty with the Cherokee by which the ejected settlers might be reinstated and the boundaries of the new state so extended as to bring about closer communication between the eastern settlements and those on the Cumberland. The Revolutionary warfare had forced the Cherokee west and south, and their capital and central gathering place was now Ustanali town, near the present Calhoun, Georgia, while Echota, their ancient capital and beloved peace town, was almost on the edge of the white settlements. The commissioners wished to have the proceedings conducted at Echota, while the Cherokee favored Ustanali. After some debate a choice was made of a convenient place near Tellico blockhouse, where the conference opened in July, but was brought to an abrupt close by the peremptory refusal of the Cherokee to sell any lands or to permit the return of the ejected settlers.

The rest of the summer was spent in negotiation along the lines already proposed, and on October 2, 1798, a treaty, commonly known as the "first treaty of Tellico," was concluded at the same place, and was signed by thirty-nine chiefs on behalf of the Cherokee. By this treaty the Indians ceded a tract between Clinch river and the Cumberland ridge, another along the northern bank of Little Tennessee extending up to Chilhowee mountain, and a third in North Carolina on the heads of French Broad and Pigeon rivers and including the sites

---

[1] Royce, Cherokee Nation, Fifth Ann. Rep. Bureau of Ethnology, p. 173, 1888.
[2] Ibid., pp. 174, 175; Ramsey, Tennessee, pp. 679-685, 1853.

of the present Waynesville and Hendersonville. These cessions included most or all of the lands from which settlers had been ejected. Permission was also given for laying out the "Cumberland road," to connect the east Tennessee settlements with those about Nashville. In consideration of the lands and rights surrendered, the United States agreed to deliver to the Cherokee five thousand dollars in goods, and to increase their existing annuity by one thousand dollars, and as usual, to "continue the guarantee of the remainder of their country forever."[1]

Wayne's victory over the northern tribes at the battle of the Maumee rapids completely broke their power and compelled them to accept the terms of peace dictated at the treaty of Greenville in the summer of 1795. The immediate result was the surrender of the Ohio river boundary by the Indians and the withdrawal of the British garrisons from the interior posts, which up to this time they had continued to hold in spite of the treaty made at the close of the Revolution. By the treaty made at Madrid in October, 1795, Spain gave up all claim on the east side of the Mississippi north of the thirty-first parallel, but on various pretexts the formal transfer of posts was delayed and a Spanish garrison continued to occupy San Fernando de Barrancas, at the present Memphis, Tennessee, until the fall of 1797, while that at Natchez, in Mississippi, was not surrendered until March, 1798. The Creeks, seeing the trend of affairs, had made peace at Colerain, Georgia, in June, 1796. With the hostile European influence thus eliminated, at least for the time, the warlike tribes on the north and on the south crushed and dispirited and the Chickamauga towns wiped out of existence, the Cherokee realized that they must accept the situation and, after nearly twenty years of continuous warfare, laid aside the tomahawk to cultivate the arts of peace and civilization.

The close of the century found them still a compact people (the westward movement having hardly yet begun) numbering probably about 20,000 souls. After repeated cessions of large tracts of land, to some of which they had but doubtful claim, they remained in recognized possession of nearly 43,000 square miles of territory, a country about equal in extent to Ohio, Virginia, or Tennessee. Of this territory about one-half was within the limits of Tennessee, the remainder being almost equally divided between Georgia and Alabama, with a small area in the extreme southwestern corner of North Carolina.[2] The old Lower towns on Savannah river had been broken up for twenty years, and the whites had so far encroached upon the Upper towns that the capital and council fire of the nation had been removed from the ancient peace town of Echota to Ustanali, in Georgia. The

---

[1] Indian Treaties, pp. 78–82, 1837; Ramsey, Tennessee, pp. 692–697, 1853; Royce, Cherokee Nation (with map and full discussion), Fifth Ann. Rep. Bureau of Ethnology, pp. 174–183, 1888.
[2] See table in Royce, op. cit., p. 378.

towns on Coosa river and in Alabama were almost all of recent establishment, peopled by refugees from the east and north. The Middle towns, in North Carolina, were still surrounded by Indian country.

Firearms had been introduced into the tribe about one hundred years before, and the Cherokee had learned well their use. Such civilized goods as hatchets, knives, clothes, and trinkets had become so common before the first Cherokee war that the Indians had declared that they could no longer live without the traders. Horses and other domestic animals had been introduced early in the century, and at the opening of the war of 1760, according to Adair, the Cherokee had "a prodigious number of excellent horses," and although hunger had compelled them to eat a great many of these during that period, they still had, in 1775, from two to a dozen each, and bid fair soon to have plenty of the best sort, as, according to the same authority, they were skilful jockeys and nice in their choice. Some of them had grown fond of cattle, and they had also an abundance of hogs and poultry, the Indian pork being esteemed better than that raised in the white settlements on account of the chestnut diet.[1] In Sevier's expedition against the towns on Coosa river, in 1793, the army killed three hundred beeves at Etowah and left their carcasses rotting on the ground. While crossing the Cherokee country in 1796 Hawkins met an Indian woman on horseback driving ten very fat cattle to the settlements for sale. Peach trees and potatoes, as well as the native corn and beans, were abundant in their fields, and some had bees and honey and did a considerable trade in beeswax. They seem to have quickly recovered from the repeated ravages of war, and there was a general air of prosperity throughout the nation. The native arts of pottery and basket-making were still the principal employment of the women, and the warriors hunted with such success that a party of traders brought down thirty wagon loads of skins on one trip.[2] In dress and house-building the Indian style was practically unchanged.

In pursuance of a civilizing policy, the government had agreed, by the treaty of 1791, to furnish the Cherokee gratuitously with farming tools and similar assistance. This policy was continued and broadened to such an extent that in 1801 Hawkins reports that "in the Cherokee agency, the wheel, the loom, and the plough is [sic] in pretty general use, farming, manufactures, and stock raising the topic of conversation among the men and women." At a conference held this year we find the chiefs of the mountain towns complaining that the people of the more western and southwestern settlements had received more than their share of spinning wheels and cards, and were consequently more advanced in making their own clothing as well as in farming, to which

---

[1] Adair, American Indians, pp. 230, 231, 1775.

[2] See Hawkins, MS journal from South Carolina to the Creeks, 1796, in library of Georgia Historical Society.

the others retorted that these things had been offered to all alike at the same time, but while the lowland people had been quick to accept, the mountaineers had hung back. "Those who complain came in late. We have got the start of them, which we are determined to keep." The progressives, under John Watts, Doublehead, and Will, threatened to secede from the rest and leave those east of Chilhowee mountain to shift for themselves.[1] We see here the germ of dissatisfaction which led ultimately to the emigration of the western band. Along with other things of civilization, negro slavery had been introduced and several of the leading men were now slaveholders (31).

Much of the advance in civilization had been due to the intermarriage among them of white men, chiefly traders of the ante-Revolutionary period, with a few Americans from the back settlements. The families that have made Cherokee history were nearly all of this mixed descent. The Doughertys, Galpins, and Adairs were from Ireland; the Rosses, Vanns, and McIntoshes, like the McGillivrays and Graysons among the Creeks, were of Scottish origin; the Waffords and others were Americans from Carolina or Georgia, and the father of Sequoya was a (Pennsylvania?) German. Most of this white blood was of good stock, very different from the "squaw man" element of the western tribes. Those of the mixed blood who could afford it usually sent their children away to be educated, while some built schoolhouses upon their own grounds and brought in private teachers from the outside. With the beginning of the present century we find influential mixed bloods in almost every town, and the civilized idea dominated even the national councils. The Middle towns, shut in from the outside world by high mountains, remained a stronghold of Cherokee conservatism.

With the exception of Priber, there seems to be no authentic record of any missionary worker among the Cherokee before 1800. There is, indeed, an incidental notice of a Presbyterian minister of North Carolina being on his way to the tribe in 1758, but nothing seems to have come of it; and we find him soon after in South Carolina and separated from his original jurisdiction.[2] The first permanent mission was established by the Moravians, those peaceful German immigrants whose teachings were so well exemplified in the lives of Zeisberger and Heckewelder. As early as 1734, while temporarily settled in Georgia, they had striven to bring some knowledge of the Christian religion to the Indians immediately about Savannah, including perhaps some stray Cherokee. Later on they established missions among the Delawares in Ohio, where their first Cherokee convert was received in 1773, being one who had been captured by the Delawares when a boy and had grown up and married in the tribe. In 1752 they had formed a settlement on the upper Yadkin, near the present Salem,

---

[1] Hawkins, Treaty Commission, 1801, manuscript No. 5, in library of Georgia Historical Society.
[2] Foote (?), in North Carolina Colonial Records, v, p. 1226, 1887.

North Carolina, where they made friendly acquaintance with the Cherokee.[1] In 1799, hearing that the Cherokee desired teachers—or perhaps by direct invitation of the chiefs—two missionaries visited the tribe to investigate the matter. Another visit was made in the next summer, and a council was held at Tellico agency, where, after a debate in which the Indians showed considerable difference of opinion, it was decided to open a mission. Permission having been obtained from the government, the work was begun in April, 1801, by Rev. Abraham Steiner and Rev. Gottlieb Byhan at the residence of David Vann, a prominent mixed-blood chief, who lodged them in his own house and gave them every assistance in building the mission, which they afterward called Spring place, where now is the village of the same name in Murray county, northwestern Georgia. They were also materially aided by the agent, Colonel Return J. Meigs (32). It was soon seen that the Cherokee wanted civilizers for their children, and not new theologies, and when they found that a school could not at once be opened the great council at Ustanali sent orders to the missionaries to organize a school within six months or leave the nation. Through Vann's help the matter was arranged and a school was opened, several sons of prominent chiefs being among the pupils. Another Moravian mission was established by Reverend J. Gambold at Oothcaloga, in the same county, in 1821. Both were in flourishing condition when broken up, with other Cherokee missions, by the State of Georgia in 1834. The work was afterward renewed beyond the Mississippi.[2]

In 1804 the Reverend Gideon Blackburn, a Presbyterian minister of Tennessee, opened a school among the Cherokee, which continued for several years until abandoned for lack of funds.[3]

Notwithstanding the promise to the Cherokee in the treaty of 1798 that the Government would "continue the guarantee of the remainder of their country forever," measures were begun almost immediately to procure another large cession of land and road privileges. In spite of the strenuous objection of the Cherokee, who sent a delegation of prominent chiefs to Washington to protest against any further sales, such pressure was brought to bear, chiefly through the efforts of the agent, Colonel Meigs, that the object of the Government was accomplished, and in 1804 and 1805 three treaties were negotiated at Tellico agency, by which the Cherokee were shorn of more than eight thousand square miles of their remaining territory.

By the first of these treaties—October 24, 1804—a purchase was made of a small tract in northeastern Georgia, known as the "Wafford

---

[1] North Carolina Colonial Records, v, p. x, 1887.

[2] Reichel, E. H., Historical Sketch of the Church and Missions of the United Brethren, pp. 65–81; Bethlehem, Pa., 1848; Holmes, John, Sketches of the Missions of the United Brethren, pp. 124, 125, 209–212; Dublin, 1818; Thompson, A. C., Moravian Missions, p. 341; New York, 1890; De Schweinitz, Edmund, Life of Zeisberger, pp. 394, 663, 696; Phila., 1870.

[3] Morse, American Geography, I, p. 577, 1819.

settlement," upon which a party led by Colonel Wafford had located some years before, under the impression that it was outside the boundary established by the Hopewell treaty.   In compensation the Cherokee were to receive an immediate payment of five thousand dollars in goods or cash with an additional annuity of one thousand dollars.   By the other treaties—October 25 and 27, 1805—a large tract was obtained in central Tennessee and Kentucky, extending between the Cumberland range and the western line of the Hopewell treaty, and from Cumberland river southwest to Duck river.   One section was also secured at Southwest point (now Kingston, Tennessee) with the design of establishing there the state capital, which, however, was located at Nashville instead seven years later.   Permission was also obtained for two mail roads through the Cherokee country into Georgia and Alabama.   In consideration of the cessions by the two treaties the United States agreed to pay fifteen thousand six hundred dollars in working implements, goods, or cash, with an additional annuity of three thousand dollars.   To secure the consent of some of the leading chiefs, the treaty commissioners resorted to the disgraceful precedent of secret articles, by which several valuable small tracts were reserved for Doublehead and Tollunteeskee, the agreement being recorded as a part of the treaty, but not embodied in the copy sent to the Senate for confirmation.[1]   In consequence of continued abuse of his official position for selfish ends Doublehead was soon afterward killed in accordance with a decree of the chiefs of the Nation, Major Ridge being selected as executioner.[2]

By the treaty of October 25, 1805, the settlements in eastern Tennessee were brought into connection with those about Nashville on the Cumberland, and the state at last assumed compact form.   The whole southern portion of the state, as defined in the charter, was still Indian country, and there was a strong and constant pressure for its opening, the prevailing sentiment being in favor of making Tennessee river the boundary between the two races.   New immigrants were constantly crowding in from the east, and, as Royce says, " the desire to settle on Indian land was as potent and insatiable with the average border settler then as it is now."   Almost within two months of the last treaties another one was concluded at Washington on January 7, 1806, by which the Cherokee ceded their claim to a large tract between Duck river and the Tennessee, embracing nearly seven thousand square miles in Tennessee and Alabama, together with the Long island (Great island) in Holston river, which up to this time they had claimed as theirs.   They were promised in compensation ten thousand dollars in five cash installments, a grist mill and cotton gin, and a life annuity

[1] Indian treaties, pp. 108, 121, 125, 1837; Royce, Cherokee Nation, Fifth Ann. Rep. Bureau of Ethnology, pp. 183 193, 1888 (map and full discussion).
[2] McKenney and Hall, Indian Tribes, II, p. 92, 1858.

of one hundred dollars for Black-fox, the aged head chief of the nation. The signers of the instrument, including Doublehead and Tollunteeskee, were accompanied to Washington by the same commissioners who had procured the previous treaty. In consequence of some misunderstanding, the boundaries of the ceded tract were still further extended in a supplementary treaty concluded at the Chickasaw Old Fields on the Tennessee, on September 11, 1807. As the country between Duck river and the Tennessee was claimed also by the Chickasaw, their title was extinguished by separate treaties.[1] The ostensible compensation for this last Cherokee cession, as shown by the treaty, was two thousand dollars, but it was secretly agreed by Agent Meigs that what he calls a " silent consideration" of one thousand dollars and some rifles should be given to the chiefs who signed it.[2]

In 1807 Colonel Elias Earle, with the consent of the Government, obtained a concession from the Cherokee for the establishment of iron works at the mouth of Chickamauga creek, on the south side of Tennessee river, to be supplied from ores mined in the Cherokee country. It was hoped that this would be a considerable step toward the civilization of the Indians, besides enabling the Government to obtain its supplies of manufactured iron at a cheaper rate, but after prolonged effort the project was finally abandoned on account of the refusal of the state of Tennessee to sanction the grant.[3] In the same year, by arrangement with the general government, the legislature of Tennessee attempted to negotiate with the Cherokee for that part of their unceded lands lying within the state limits, but without success, owing to the unwillingness of the Indians to part with any more territory, and their special dislike for the people of Tennessee.[4]

In 1810 the Cherokee national council registered a further advance in civilization by formally abolishing the custom of clan revenge, hitherto universal among the tribes. The enactment bears the signatures of Black-fox (Ina′lĭ), principal chief, and seven others, and reads as follows:

IN COUNCIL, OOSTINALEH, *April 18, 1810.*

1. Be it known this day, That the various clans or tribes which compose the Cherokee nation have unanimously passed an act of oblivion for all lives for which they may have been indebted one to the other, and have mutually agreed that after this evening the aforesaid act shall become binding upon every clan or tribe thereof.

2. The aforesaid clans or tribes have also agreed that if, in future, any life should be lost without malice intended, the innocent aggressor shall not be accounted guilty;

---

[1] Indian Treaties, pp. 132–136, 1837; Royce, Cherokee Nation, Fifth Ann. Rep. Bureau of Ethnology, pp. 193–197, 1888.

[2] Meigs, letter, September 28, 1807, American State Papers: Indian Affairs, I, p. 754, 1832; Royce, op. cit., p. 197.

[3] See treaty, December 2, 1807, and Jefferson's message, with inclosures, March 10, 1808, American State Papers: Indian Affairs, I, pp. 752–754, 1832; Royce, op. cit., pp. 199–201.

[4] Ibid., pp. 201, 202.

and, should it so happen that a brother, forgetting his natural affections, should raise his hands in anger and kill his brother, he shall be accounted guilty of murder and suffer accordingly.

3. If a man have a horse stolen, and overtake the thief, and should his anger be so great as to cause him to shed his blood, let it remain on his own conscience, but no satisfaction shall be required for his life, from his relative or clan he may have belonged to.

By order of the seven clans.[1]

Under an agreement with the Cherokee in 1813 a company composed of representatives of Tennessee, Georgia, and the Cherokee nation was organized to lay out a free public road from Tennessee river to the head of navigation on the Tugaloo branch of Savannah river, with provision for convenient stopping places along the line. The road was completed within the next three years, and became the great highway from the coast to the Tennessee settlements. Beginning on the Tugaloo or Savannah a short distance below the entrance of Toccoa creek, it crossed the upper Chattahoochee, passing through Clarkesville, Nacoochee valley, the Unicoi gap, and Hiwassee in Georgia; then entering North Carolina it descended the Hiwassee, passing through Hayesville and Murphy and over the Great Smoky range into Tennessee, until it reached the terminus at the Cherokee capital, Echota, on Little Tennessee. It was officially styled the Unicoi turn-pike,[2] but was commonly known in North Carolina as the Wachesa trail, from Watsi'sa or Wachesa, a prominent Indian who lived near the crossing-place on Beaverdam creek, below Murphy, this portion of the road being laid out along the old Indian trail which already bore that name.[3]

Passing over for the present some negotiations having for their purpose the removal of the Cherokee to the West, we arrive at the period of the Creek war.

Ever since the treaty of Greenville it had been the dream of Tecumtha, the great Shawano chief (33), to weld again the confederacy of the northern tribes as a barrier against the further aggressions of the white man. His own burning eloquence was ably seconded by the subtler persuasion of his brother, who assumed the role of a prophet with a new revelation, the burden of which was that the Indians must return to their old Indian life if they would preserve their national existence. The new doctrine spread among all the northern tribes and at last reached those of the south, where Tecumtha himself had gone to enlist the warriors in the great Indian confederacy. The prophets of the Upper Creeks eagerly accepted the doctrine and in a short time their warriors were dancing the "dance of the Indians of the lakes." In

[1] In American State Papers: Indian Affairs, II, p. 283, 1834.

[2] See contract appended to Washington treaty, 1819, Indian Treaties, pp. 269–271, 1837; Royce map, Fifth Ann. Rep. Bureau of Ethnology, 1888.

[3] Author's personal information.

anticipation of an expected war with the United States the British agents in Canada had been encouraging the hostile feeling toward the Americans by talks and presents of goods and ammunition, while the Spaniards also covertly fanned the flame of discontent.[1] At the height of the ferment war was declared between this country and England on June 28, 1812. Tecumtha, at the head of fifteen hundred warriors, at once entered the British service with a commission as general, while the Creeks began murdering and burning along the southern frontier. after having vainly attempted to secure the cooperation of the Cherokee.

From the Creeks the new revelation was brought to the Cherokee, whose priests at once began to dream dreams and to preach a return to the old life as the only hope of the Indian race. A great medicine dance was appointed at Ustanali, the national capital, where, after the dance was over, the doctrine was publicly announced and explained by a Cherokee prophet introduced by a delegation from Coosawatee. He began by saying that some of the mountain towns had abused him and refused to receive his message, but nevertheless he must continue to bear testimony of his mission whatever might happen. The Cherokee had broken the road which had been given to their fathers at the beginning of the world. They had taken the white man's clothes and trinkets, they had beds and tables and mills; some even had books and cats. All this was bad, and because of it their gods were angry and the game was leaving their country. If they would live and be happy as before they must put off the white man's dress, throw away his mills and looms, kill their cats, put on paint and buckskin, and be Indians again; otherwise swift destruction would come upon them.

His speech appealed strongly to the people, who cried out in great excitement that his talk was good. Of all those present only Major Ridge, a principal chief, had the courage to stand up and oppose it, warning his hearers that such talk would inevitably lead to war with the United States, which would end in their own destruction. The maddened followers of the prophet sprang upon Ridge and would have killed him but for the interposition of friends. As it was, he was thrown down and narrowly escaped with his life, while one of his defenders was stabbed by his side.

The prophet had threatened after a certain time to invoke a terrible storm, which should destroy all but the true believers, who were exhorted to gather for safety on one of the high peaks of the Great Smoky mountains. In full faith they abandoned their bees, their orchards, their slaves, and everything that had come to them from the white man, and took up their toilsome march for the high mountains. There they waited until the appointed day had come and passed, show-

[1] Mooney, Ghost-dance Religion, Fourteenth Ann. Rep. Bureau of Ethnology, p. 670 et passim, 1896; contemporary documents in American State Papers: Indian Affairs, I, pp. 798–801, 845–850, 1832.

ing their hopes and fears to be groundless, when they sadly returned to their homes and the great Indian revival among the Cherokee came to an end.[1]

Among the Creeks, where other hostile influences were at work, the excitement culminated in the Creek war. Several murders and outrages had already been committed, but it was not until the terrible massacre at Fort Mims (34), on August 30, 1813, that the whole American nation was aroused. Through the influence of Ridge and other prominent chiefs the Cherokee had refused to join the hostile Creeks, and on the contrary had promised to assist the whites and the friendly towns.[2] More than a year before the council had sent a friendly letter to the Creeks warning them against taking the British side in the approaching war, while several prominent chiefs had proposed to enlist a Cherokee force for the service of the United States.[3] Finding that no help was to be expected from the Cherokee, the Creeks took occasion to kill a Cherokee woman near the town of Etowah, in Georgia. With the help of a conjurer the murderers were trailed and overtaken and killed on the evening of the second day in a thicket where they had concealed themselves. After this there could be no alliance between the two tribes.[4]

At the time of the Fort Mims massacre McIntosh (35), the chief of the friendly Lower Creeks, was visiting the Cherokee, among whom he had relatives. By order of the Cherokee council he was escorted home by a delegation under the leadership of Ridge. On his return Ridge brought with him a request from the Lower Creeks that the Cherokee would join with them and the Americans in putting down the war. Ridge himself strongly urged the proposition, declaring that if the prophets were allowed to have their way the work of civilization would be destroyed. The council, however, decided not to interfere in the affairs of other tribes, whereupon Ridge called for volunteers, with the result that so many of the warriors responded that the council reversed its decision and declared war against the Creeks.[5] For a proper understanding of the situation it is necessary to state that the hostile feeling was confined almost entirely to the Upper Creek towns on the Tallapoosa, where the prophets of the new religion had their residence. The half-breed chief, Weatherford (36), was the leader of the war party. The Lower Creek towns on the Chattahoo-

---

[1] See Mooney, Ghost-dance Religion, Fourteenth Ann. Rep. Bureau of Ethnology, pp. 670–677, 1896; McKenney and Hall, Indian Tribes, II, pp. 93–95, 1858; see also contemporary letters (1813, etc.) by Hawkins, Cornells, and others in American State Papers: Indian Affairs, I, 1832.

[2] Letters of Hawkins, Pinckney, and Cussetah King, July, 1813, American State Papers: Indian Affairs, II, pp. 847–849, 1832.

[3] Meigs, letter, May 8, 1812, and Hawkins, letter, May 11, 1812, ibid., p. 809.

[4] Author's information from James D. Wafford.

[5] McKenney and Hall, Indian Tribes, II, pp. 96–97, 1858.

chee, under McIntosh, another half-breed chief, were friendly, and acted with the Cherokee and the Americans against their own brethren.

It is not our purpose to give a history of the Creek war, but only to note the part which the Cherokee had in it. The friendly Lower Creeks, under McIntosh, with a few refugees from the Upper towns, operated chiefly with the army under General Floyd which invaded the southern part of the Creek country from Georgia. Some friendly Choctaw and Chickasaw also lent their assistance in this direction. The Cherokee, with some friendly Creeks of the Upper towns, acted with the armies under Generals White and Jackson, which entered the Creek country from the Tennessee side. While some hundreds of their warriors were thus fighting in the field, the Cherokee at home were busily collecting provisions for the American troops.

As Jackson approached from the north, about the end of October, 1813, he was met by runners asking him to come to the aid of Pathkiller, a Cherokee chief, who was in danger of being cut off by the hostiles, at his village of Turkeytown, on the upper Coosa, near the present Center, Alabama. A fresh detachment on its way from east Tennessee, under General White, was ordered by Jackson to relieve the town, and successfully performed this work. White's force consisted of one thousand men, including four hundred Cherokee under Colonel Gideon Morgan and John Lowrey.[1]

As the army advanced down the Coosa the Creeks retired to Tallaseehatchee, on the creek of the same name, near the present Jacksonville, Calhoun county, Alabama. One thousand men under General Coffee, together with a company of Cherokee under Captain Richard Brown and some few Creeks, were sent against them. The Indian auxiliaries wore headdresses of white feathers and deertails. The attack was made at daybreak of November 3, 1813, and the town was taken after a desperate resistance, from which not one of the defenders escaped alive, the Creeks having been completely surrounded on all sides. Says Coffee in his official report:

They made all the resistance that an overpowered soldier could do—they fought as long as one existed, but their destruction was very soon completed. Our men rushed up to the doors of the houses and in a few minutes killed the last warrior of them. The enemy fought with savage fury and met death with all its horrors, without shrinking or complaining—not one asked to be spared, but fought as long as they could stand or sit.

Of such fighting stuff did the Creeks prove themselves, against overwhelming numbers, throughout the war. The bodies of nearly two hundred dead warriors were counted on the field, and the general reiterates that "not one of the warriors escaped." A number of women and children were taken prisoners. Nearly every man of the Creeks had a bow with a bundle of arrows, which he used after the

---

[1] Drake, Indians, pp. 395–396, 1880; Pickett, Alabama, p. 556, reprint of 1896.

first fire with his gun. The American loss was only five killed and forty-one wounded, which may not include the Indian contingent.[1]

White's advance guard, consisting chiefly of the four hundred other Cherokee under Morgan and Lowrey, reached Tallaseehatchee the same evening, only to find it already destroyed. They picked up twenty wounded Creeks, whom they brought with them to Turkeytown.[2]

The next great battle was at Talladega, on the site of the present town of the same name, in Talladega county, Alabama, on November 9, 1813. Jackson commanded in person with two thousand infantry and cavalry. Although the Cherokee are not specifically mentioned they were a part of the army and must have taken part in the engagement. The town itself was occupied by friendly Creeks, who were besieged by the hostiles, estimated at over one thousand warriors on the outside. Here again the battle was simply a slaughter, the odds being two to one, the Creeks being also without cover, although they fought so desperately that at one time the militia was driven back. They left two hundred and ninety-nine dead bodies on the field, which, according to their own statement afterwards, was only a part of their total loss. The Americans lost fifteen killed and eighty-five wounded.[3]

A day or two later the people of Hillabee town, about the site of the present village of that name in Clay county, Alabama, sent messengers to Jackson's camp to ask for peace, which that commander immediately granted. In the meantime, even while the peace messengers were on their way home with the good news, an army of one thousand men from east Tennessee under General White, who claimed to be independent of Jackson's authority, together with four hundred Cherokee under Colonel Gideon Morgan and John Lowrey, surrounded the town on November 18, 1813, taking it by surprise, the inhabitants having trusted so confidently to the success of their peace embassy that they had made no preparation for defense. Sixty warriors were killed and over two hundred and fifty prisoners taken, with no loss to the Americans, as there was practically no resistance. In White's official report of the affair he states that he had sent ahead a part of his force, together with the Cherokee under Morgan, to surround the town, and adds that "Colonel Morgan and the Cherokees under his command gave undeniable evidence that they merit the employ of their government."[4] Not knowing that the attack had been made without Jackson's sanction or knowledge, the Creeks naturally con-

[1] Coffee, report, etc., in Drake, Indians, p. 396, 1880; Lossing, Field Book of the War of 1812, pp. 762, 763 [n. d. (1869)]; Pickett, Alabama, p. 553, reprint of 1896.

[2] Ibid., p. 556.

[3] Drake, Indians, p. 396, 1880; Pickett, op. cit., pp. 554, 555.

[4] White's report, etc., in Fay and Davison, Sketches of the War, pp. 240, 241; Rutland, Vt., 1815; Low, John, Impartial History of the War, p. 199; New York, 1815; Drake, op. cit., p. 397; Pickett, op. cit., p. 557; Lossing, op. cit., p. 767. Low says White had about 1,100 mounted men, "including upward of 300 Cherokee Indians." Pickett gives White 400 Cherokee.

cluded that peace overtures were of no avail, and thenceforth until the close of the war there was no talk of surrender.

On November 29, 1813, the Georgia army under General Floyd, consisting of nine hundred and fifty American troops and four hundred friendly Indians, chiefly Lower Creeks under McIntosh, took and destroyed Autossee town on the Tallapoosa, west of the present Tuskegee, killing about two hundred warriors and burning four hundred well-built houses. On December 23 the Creeks were again defeated by General Claiborne, assisted by some friendly Choctaws, at Ecanachaca or the Holy Ground on Alabama river, near the present Benton in Lowndes county. This town and another a few miles away were also destroyed, with a great quantity of provisions and other property.[1] It is doubtful if any Cherokee were concerned in either action.

Before the close of the year Jackson's force in northern Alabama had been so far reduced by mutinies and expiration of service terms that he had but one hundred soldiers left and was obliged to employ the Cherokee to garrison Fort Armstrong, on the upper Coosa, and to protect his provision depot.[2] With the opening of the new year, 1814, having received reinforcements from Tennessee, together with about two hundred friendly Creeks and sixty-five more Cherokee, he left his camp on the Coosa and advanced against the towns on the Tallapoosa. Learning, on arriving near the river, that he was within a few miles of the main body of the enemy, he halted for a reconnoissance and camped in order of battle on Emukfaw creek, on the northern bank of the Tallapoosa, only a short distance from the famous Horseshoe bend. Here, on the morning of June 24, 1814, he was suddenly attacked by the enemy with such fury that, although the troops charged with the bayonet, the Creeks returned again to the fight and were at last broken only by the help of the friendly Indians, who came upon them from the rear. As it was, Jackson was so badly crippled that he retreated to Fort Strother on the Coosa, carrying his wounded, among them General Coffee, on horse-hide litters. The Creeks pursued and attacked him again as he was crossing Enotochopco creek on January 24, but after a severe fight were driven back with discharges of grapeshot from a six-pounder at close range. The army then continued its retreat to Fort Strother. The American loss in these two battles was about one hundred killed and wounded. The loss of the Creeks was much greater, but they had compelled a superior force, armed with bayonet and artillery, to retreat, and without the aid of the friendly Indians it is doubtful if Jackson could have saved his army from demoralization. The Creeks themselves claimed a victory and boasted afterward that they had "whipped Jackson and run him to the Coosa river."

[1] Drake, Indians, pp. 391, 398, 1880; Pickett, Alabama, pp. 557-559, 572-576, reprint of 1896.
[2] Ibid., p. 579; Lossing, Field Book of the War of 1812, p. 773.

Pickett states, on what seems good authority, that the Creeks engaged did not number more than five hundred warriors. Jackson had probably at least one thousand two hundred men, including Indians.[1]

While these events were transpiring in the north, General Floyd again advanced from Georgia with a force of about one thousand three hundred Americans and four hundred friendly Indians, but was surprised on Caleebee creek, near the present Tuskegee, Alabama, on the morning of January 27, 1814, and compelled to retreat, leaving the enemy in possession of the field.[2]

We come now to the final event of the Creek war, the terrible battle of the Horseshoe bend. Having received large reenforcements from Tennessee, Jackson left a garrison at Fort Strother, and, about the middle of March, descended the Coosa river to the mouth of Cedar creek, southeast from the present Columbiana, where he built Fort Williams. Leaving his stores here with a garrison to protect them, he began his march for the Horseshoe bend of the Tallapoosa, where the hostiles were reported to have collected in great force. At this place, known to the Creeks as Tohopki or Tohopeka, the Tallapoosa made a bend so as to inclose some eighty or a hundred acres in a narrow peninsula opening to the north. On the lower side was an island in the river, and about a mile below was Emukfaw creek, entering from the north, where Jackson had been driven back two months before Both locations were in the present Tallapoosa county, Alabama, within two miles of the present post village of Tohopeka. Across the neck of the peninsula the Creeks had built a strong breastwork of logs, behind which were their houses, and behind these were a number of canoes moored to the bank for use if retreat became necessary. The fort was defended by a thousand warriors, with whom were also about three hundred women and children. Jackson's force numbered about two thousand men, including, according to his own statement, five hundred Cherokee. He had also two small cannon. The account of the battle, or rather massacre, which occurred on the morning of March 27, 1814, is best condensed from the official reports of the principal commanders.

Having arrived in the neighborhood of the fort, Jackson disposed his men for the attack by detailing General Coffee with the mounted men and nearly the whole of the Indian force to cross the river at a ford about three miles below and surround the bend in such manner that none could escape in that direction. He himself, with the rest of his force, advanced to the front of the breastwork and planted his can-

---

[1] Fay and Davison, Sketches of the War, pp. 247–250, 1815; Pickett, Alabama, pp. 579–584, reprint of 1896; Drake, Indians, pp. 398–400, 1880. Pickett says Jackson had "767 men, with 200 friendly Indians"; Drake says he started with 930 men and was joined at Talladega by 200 friendly Indians; Jackson himself, as quoted in Fay and Davison, says that he started with 930 men, *excluding Indians*, and was joined at Talladega "by between 200 and 300 friendly Indians," 65 being Cherokee, the rest Creeks. The inference is that he already had a number of Indians with him at the start—probably the Cherokee who had been doing garrison duty.

[2] Pickett, op. cit., pp. 584–586.

non upon a slight rise within eighty yards of the fortification. He then directed a heavy cannonade upon the center of the breastwork, while the rifles and muskets kept up a galling fire upon the defenders whenever they showed themselves behind the logs. The breastwork was very strongly and compactly built, from five to eight feet high, with a double row of portholes, and so planned that no enemy could approach without being exposed to a crossfire from those on the inside. After about two hours of cannonading and rifle fire to no great purpose, "Captain Russell's company of spies and a party of the Cherokee force, headed by their gallant chieftain, Colonel Richard Brown, and conducted by the brave Colonel Morgan, crossed over to the peninsula in canoes and set fire to a few of their buildings there situated. They then advanced with great gallantry toward the breastwork and commenced firing upon the enemy, who lay behind it. Finding that this force, notwithstanding the determination they displayed, was wholly insufficient to dislodge the enemy, and that General Coffee had secured the opposite banks of the river, I now determined on taking possession of their works by storm." [1]

Coffee's official report to his commanding officer states that he had taken seven hundred mounted troops and about six hundred Indians, of whom five hundred were Cherokee and the rest friendly Creeks, and had come in behind, having directed the Indians to take position secretly along the bank of the river to prevent the enemy crossing, as already noted. This was done, but with fighting going on so near at hand the Indians could not remain quiet. Continuing, Coffee says:

> The firing of your cannon and small arms in a short time became general and heavy, which animated our Indians, and seeing about one hundred of the warriors and all the squaws and children of the enemy running about among the huts of the village, which was open to our view, they could no longer remain silent spectators. While some kept up a fire across the river to prevent the enemy's approach to the bank, others plunged into the water and swam the river for canoes that lay at the other shore in considerable numbers and brought them over, in which crafts a number of them embarked and landed on the bend with the enemy. Colonel Gideon Morgan, who commanded the Cherokees, Captain Kerr, and Captain William Russell, with a part of his company of spies, were among the first that crossed the river. They advanced into the village and very soon drove the enemy from the huts up the river bank to the fortified works from which they were fighting you. They pursued and continued to annoy during your whole action. This movement of my Indian forces left the river bank unguarded and made it necessary that I should send a part of my line to take possession of the river bank. [2]

According to the official report of Colonel Morgan, who commanded the Cherokee and who was himself severely wounded, the Cherokee took the places assigned them along the bank in such regular order

[1] Jackson's report to Governor Blount, March 31, 1814, in Fay and Davison, Sketches of the War, pp. 253, 254, 1815.

[2] General Coffee's report to General Jackson, April 1, 1814, ibid., p. 257.

that no part was left unoccupied, and the few fugitives who attempted to escape from the fort by water "fell an easy prey to their vengeance." Finally, seeing that the cannonade had no more effect upon the breastwork than to bore holes in the logs, some of the Cherokee plunged into the river, and swimming over to the town brought back a number of canoes. A part crossed in these, under cover of the guns of their companions, and sheltered themselves under the bank while the canoes were sent back for reenforcements. In this way they all crossed over and then advanced up the bank, where at once they were warmly assailed from every side except the rear, which they kept open only by hard fighting.[1]

The Creeks had been fighting the Americans in their front at such close quarters that their bullets flattened upon the bayonets thrust through the portholes. This attack from the rear by five hundred Cherokee diverted their attention and gave opportunity to the Tennesseeans, Sam Houston among them, cheering them on, to swarm over the breastwork. With death from the bullet, the bayonet and the hatchet all around them, and the smoke of their blazing homes in their eyes, not a warrior begged for his life. When more than half their number lay dead upon the ground, the rest turned and plunged into the river, only to find the banks on the opposite side lined with enemies and escape cut off in every direction. Says General Coffee:

Attempts to cross the river at all points of the bend were made by the enemy, but not one ever escaped. Very few ever reached the bank and that few was killed the instant they landed. From the report of my officers, as well as from my own observation, I feel warranted in saying that from two hundred and fifty to three hundred of the enemy was buried under water and was not numbered with the dead that were found.

Some swam for the island below the bend, but here too a detachment had been posted and "not one ever landed. They were sunk by Lieutenant Bean's command ere they reached the bank."[2]

Quoting again from Jackson—

The enemy, although many of them fought to the last with that kind of bravery which desperation inspires, were at last entirely routed and cut to pieces. The battle may be said to have continued with severity for about five hours, but the firing and slaughter continued until it was suspended by the darkness of night. The next morning it was resumed and sixteen of the enemy slain who had concealed themselves under the banks.[3]

It was supposed that the Creeks had about a thousand warriors, besides their women and children. The men sent out to count the dead found five hundred and fifty-seven warriors lying dead within the inclosure, and Coffee estimates that from two hundred and fifty to

---

[1] Colonel Morgan's report to Governor Blount, in Fay and Davison, Sketches of the War, pp. 258, 259 1815.

[2] Coffee's report to Jackson, ibid., pp. 257, 258.

[3] Jackson's report to Governor Blount, ibid., pp. 255, 256.

three hundred were shot in the water. How many more there may have been can not be known, but Jackson himself states that not more than twenty could have escaped. There is no mention of any wounded. About three hundred prisoners were taken, of whom only three were men. The defenders of the Horseshoe had been exterminated.[1]

On the other side the loss was 26 Americans killed and 107 wounded, 18 Cherokee killed and 36 wounded, 5 friendly Creeks killed and 11 wounded. It will be noted that the loss of the Cherokee was out of all proportion to their numbers, their fighting having been hand to hand work without protecting cover. In view of the fact that Jackson had only a few weeks before been compelled to retreat before this same enemy, and that two hours of artillery and rifle fire had produced no result until the Cherokee turned the rear of the enemy by their daring passage of the river, there is considerable truth in the boast of the Cherokee that they saved the day for Jackson at Horseshoe bend. In the number of men actually engaged and the immense proportion killed, this ranks as the greatest Indian battle in the history of the United States, with the possible exception of the battle of Mauvila, fought by the same Indians in De Soto's time. The result was decisive. Two weeks later Weatherford came in and surrendered, and the Creek war was at an end.

As is usual where Indians have acted as auxiliaries of white troops, it is difficult to get an accurate statement of the number of Cherokee engaged in this war or to apportion the credit among the various leaders. Coffee's official report states that five hundred Cherokee were engaged in the last great battle, and from incidental hints it seems probable that others were employed elsewhere, on garrison duty or otherwise, at the same time. McKenney and Hall state that Ridge recruited eight hundred warriors for Jackson,[2] and this may be near the truth, as the tribe had then at least six times as many fighting men. On account of the general looseness of Indian organization we com monly find the credit claimed for whichever chief may be best known to the chronicler. Thus, McKenney and Hall make Major Ridge the hero of the war, especially of the Horseshoe fight, although he is not mentioned in the official reports. Jackson speaks particularly of the Cherokee in that battle as being "headed by their gallant chieftain, Colonel Richard Brown, and conducted by the brave Colonel Morgan." Coffee says that Colonel Gideon Morgan "commanded the Cherokees," and it is Morgan who makes the official report of their part in the battle. In a Washington newspaper notice of the treaty

---

[1] Jackson's report and Colonel Morgan's report, in Fay and Davison, Sketches of the War, pp. 255, 256, 259, 1815. Pickett makes the loss of the white troops 32 killed and 99 wounded. The Houston reference is from Lossing. The battle is described also by Pickett, Alabama, pp. 588–591, reprint of 1896; Drake, Indians, pp. 391, 400, 1880; McKenney and Hall, Indian Tribes, II, pp. 98, 99, 1858.

[2] McKenney and Hall, op. cit., p. 98.

Major Ridge

From a lithograph published by McKenney and Hall in The Indian
Tribes of North America, *1836–1844, and subsequent editions. Artist of the original painting is unknown; probably painted in Washington, D.C., in 1834 or 1836.*

delegation of 1816 the six signers are mentioned as Colonel [John] Lowrey, Major [John] Walker, Major Ridge, Captain [Richard] Taylor, Adjutant [John] Ross, and Kunnesee (Tsi'yu-gûnsi'nĭ, Cheucunsene) and are described as men of cultivation, nearly all of whom had served as officers of the Cherokee forces with Jackson and distinguished themselves as well by their bravery as by their attachment to the United States.[1] Among the East Cherokee in Carolina the only name still remembered is that of their old chief, Junaluska (Tsunu'lahuñ'skĭ), who said afterward: "If I had known that Jackson would drive us from our homes I would have killed him that day at the Horseshoe."

The Cherokee returned to their homes to find them despoiled and ravaged in their absence by disorderly white troops. Two years afterward, by treaty at Washington, the Government agreed to reimburse them for the damage. Interested parties denied that they had suffered any damage or rendered any services, to which their agent indignantly replied: "It may be answered that thousands witnessed both; that in nearly all the battles with the Creeks the Cherokees rendered the most efficient service, and at the expense of the lives of many fine men, whose wives and children and brothers and sisters are mourning their fall."[2]

In the spring of 1816 a delegation of seven principal men, accompanied by Agent Meigs, visited Washington, and the result was the negotiation of two treaties at that place on the same date, March 22, 1816. By the first of these the Cherokee ceded for five thousand dollars their last remaining territory in South Carolina, a small strip in the extreme northwestern corner, adjoining Chattooga river. By the second treaty a boundary was established between the lands claimed by the Cherokee and Creeks in northern Alabama. This action was made necessary in order to determine the boundaries of the great tract which the Creeks had been compelled to surrender in punishment for their late uprising. The line was run from a point on Little Bear creek in northwestern Alabama direct to the Ten islands of the Coosa at old Fort Strother, southeast of the present Asheville. General Jackson protested strongly against this line, on the ground that all the territory south of Tennessee river and west of the Coosa belonged to the Creeks and was a part of their cession. The Chickasaw also protested against considering this tract as Cherokee territory. The treaty also granted free and unrestricted road privileges throughout the Cherokee country, this concession being the result of years of persistent effort on the part of the Government; and an appropriation of twenty-five thousand five hundred dollars was made

---

[1] Drake, Indians, p. 401, 1880.

[2] Indian Treaties, p. 187, 1837; Meigs' letter to Secretary of War, August 19, 1816, in American State Papers: Indian Affairs, II, pp. 113, 114, 1834.

for damages sustained by the Cherokee from the depredations of the troops passing through their country during the Creek war.[1]

At the last treaty the Cherokee had resisted every effort to induce them to cede more land on either side of the Tennessee, the Government being especially desirous to extinguish their claim north of that river within the limits of the state of Tennessee. Failing in this, pressure was at once begun to bring about a cession in Alabama, with the result that on September 14 of the same year a treaty was concluded at the Chickasaw council-house, and afterward ratified in general council at Turkeytown on the Coosa, by which the Cherokee ceded all their claims in that state south of Tennessee river and west of an irregular line running from Chickasaw island in that stream, below the entrance of Flint river, to the junction of Wills creek with the Coosa, at the present Gadsden. For this cession, embracing an area of nearly three thousand five hundred square miles, they were to receive sixty thousand dollars in ten annual payments, together with five thousand dollars for the improvements abandoned.[2]

We turn aside now for a time from the direct narrative to note the development of events which culminated in the forced expatriation of the Cherokee from their ancestral homes and their removal to the far western wilderness.

With a few notable exceptions the relations between the French and Spanish colonists and the native tribes, after the first occupation of the country, had been friendly and agreeable. Under the rule of France or Spain there was never any Indian boundary. Pioneer and Indian built their cabins and tilled their fields side by side, ranged the woods together, knelt before the same altar and frequently intermarried on terms of equality, so far as race was concerned. The result is seen to-day in the mixed-blood communities of Canada, and in Mexico, where a nation has been built upon an Indian foundation. Within the area of English colonization it was otherwise. From the first settlement to the recent inauguration of the allotment system it never occurred to the man of Teutonic blood that he could have for a neighbor anyone not of his own stock and color. While the English colonists recognized the native proprietorship so far as to make treaties with the Indians, it was chiefly for the purpose of fixing limits beyond which the Indian should never come after he had once parted with his title for a consideration of goods and trinkets. In an early Virginia treaty it was even stipulated that friendly Indians crossing the line should suffer death. The Indian was regarded as an incumbrance to be cleared off, like the trees and the wolves, before white men could live in the country. Intermarriages were practically

---

[1] Indian Treaties, pp. 185–187, 1837; Royce, Cherokee Nation, Fifth Ann. Rep. Bureau of Ethnology, pp. 197–209, 1888.

[2] Indian Treaties, pp. 199, 200, 1837; Royce, op. cit., pp. 209–211.

unknown, and the children of such union were usually compelled by race antipathy to cast their lot with the savage.

Under such circumstances the tribes viewed the advance of the English and their successors, the Americans, with keen distrust, and as early as the close of the French and Indian war we find some of them removing from the neighborhood of the English settlements to a safer shelter in the more remote territories still held by Spain. Soon after the French withdrew from Fort Toulouse, in 1763, a part of the Alabama, an incorporated tribe of the Creek confederacy, left their villages on the Coosa, and crossing the Mississippi, where they halted for a time on its western bank, settled on the Sabine river under Spanish protection.[1] They were followed some years later by a part of the Koasati, of the same confederacy,[2] the two tribes subsequently drifting into Texas, where they now reside. The Hichitee and others of the Lower Creeks moved down into Spanish Florida, where the Yamassee exiles from South Carolina had long before preceded them, the two combining to form the modern Seminole tribe. When the Revolution brought about a new line of division, the native tribes, almost without exception, joined sides with England as against the Americans, with the result that about one-half the Iroquois fled to Canada, where they still reside upon lands granted by the British government. A short time before Wayne's victory a part of the Shawano and Delawares, worn out by nearly twenty years of battle with the Americans, crossed the Mississippi and settled, by permission of the Spanish government, upon lands in the vicinity of Cape Girardeau, in what is now southeastern Missouri, for which they obtained a regular deed from that government in 1793.[3] Driven out by the Americans some twenty years later, they removed to Kansas and thence to Indian territory, where they are now incorporated with their old friends, the Cherokee.

When the first Cherokee crossed the Mississippi it is impossible to say, but there was probably never a time in the history of the tribe when their warriors and hunters were not accustomed to make excursions beyond the great river. According to an old tradition, the earliest emigration took place soon after the first treaty with Carolina, when a portion of the tribe, under the leadership of Yûñwĭ-usgă'sĕ'tĭ, "Dangerous-man," foreseeing the inevitable end of yielding to the demands of the colonists, refused to have any relations with the white man, and took up their long march for the unknown West. Communication was kept up with the home body until after crossing the Mississippi, when they were lost sight of and forgotten. Long years

[1] Claiborne, letter to Jefferson, November 5, 1808, American State Papers, I, p. 755, 1832; Gatschet, Creek Migration Legend, I, p. 88, 1884.

[2] Hawkins, 1799, quoted in Gatschet, op. cit., p. 89.

[3] See Treaty of St Louis, 1825, and of Castor hill, 1852, in Indian Treaties, pp. 388, 539, 1837.

afterward a rumor came from the west that they were still living near the base of the Rocky mountains.[1] In 1782 the Cherokee, who had fought faithfully on the British side throughout the long Revolutionary struggle, applied to the Spanish governor at New Orleans for permission to settle on the west side of the Mississippi, within Spanish territory. Permission was granted, and it is probable that some of them removed to the Arkansas country, although there seems to be no definite record of the matter.[2] We learn incidentally, however, that about this period the hostile Cherokee, like the Shawano and other northern tribes, were in the habit of making friendly visits to the Spanish settlements in that quarter.

According to Reverend Cephas Washburn, the pioneer misssionary of the western Cherokee, the first permanent Cherokee settlement beyond the Mississippi was the direct result of the massacre, in 1794, of the Scott party at Muscle shoals, on Tennessee river, by the hostile warriors of the Chickamauga towns, in the summer. As told by the missionary, the story differs considerably from that given by Haywood and other Tennessee historians, narrated in another place.[3] According to Washburn, the whites were the aggressors, having first made the Indians drunk and then swindled them out of the annuity money with which they were just returning from the agency at Tellico. When the Indians became sober enough to demand the return of their money the whites attacked and killed two of them, whereupon the others boarded the boat and killed every white man. They spared the women and children, however, with their negro slaves and all their personal belongings, and permitted them to continue on their way, the chief and his party personally escorting them down Tennessee, Ohio, and Mississippi rivers as far as the mouth of the St. Francis, whence the emigrants descended in safety to New Orleans, while their captors, under their chief, The Bowl, went up St. Francis river—then a part of Spanish territory—to await the outcome of the event. As soon as the news came to the Cherokee Nation the chiefs formally repudiated the action of the Bowl party and volunteered to assist in arresting those concerned. Bowl and his men were finally exonerated, but had conceived such bitterness at the conduct of their former friends, and, moreover, had found the soil so rich and the game so abundant where they were, that they refused to return to their tribe and decided to remain permanently in the West. Others joined them from time to time, attracted by the hunting prospect, until they were in sufficient number to obtain recognition from the Government.[4]

---

[1] See number 107, "The Lost Cherokee."

[2] See letter of Governor Estevan Miro to Robertson, April 20, 1783, in Roosevelt, Winning of the West, II, p. 407, 1889.

[3] See pp. 76–77.

[4] Washburn, Reminiscences, pp. 76–79, 1869; see also Royce, Cherokee Nation, Fifth Ann. Rep. Bureau of Ethnology, p. 204, 1888.

While the missionary may be pardoned for making the best showing possible for his friends, his statement contains several evident
errors, and it is probable that Haywood's account is more correct in
the main. As the Cherokee annuity at that time amounted to but
fifteen hundred dollars for the whole tribe, or somewhat less than ten
cents per head, they could hardly have had enough money from that
source to pay such extravagant prices as sixteen dollars apiece for
pocket mirrors, which it is alleged the boatmen obtained. Moreover,
as the Chickamauga warriors had refused to sign any treaties and were
notoriously hostile, they were not as yet entitled to receive payments.
Haywood's statement that the emigrant party was first attacked while
passing the Chickamauga towns and then pursued to the Muscle shoals
and there massacred is probably near the truth, although it is quite
possible that the whites may have provoked the attack in some such
way as is indicated by the missionary. As Washburn got his account
from one of the women of the party, living long afterward in New
Orleans, it is certain that some at least were spared by the Indians,
and it is probable that, as he states, only the men were killed.

The Bowl emigration may not have been the first, or even the most
important removal to the western country, as the period was one of
Indian unrest. Small bands were constantly crossing the Mississippi
into Spanish territory to avoid the advancing Americans, only to find
themselves again under American jurisdiction when the whole western
country was ceded to the United States in 1803. The persistent land-
hunger of the settler could not be restrained or satisfied, and early in
the same year President Jefferson suggested to Congress the desira-
bility of removing all the tribes to the west of the Mississippi. In
the next year, 1804, an appropriation was made for taking preliminary steps toward such a result.[1] There were probably but few Cherokee on the Arkansas at this time, as they are not mentioned in Sibley's
list of tribes south of that river in 1805.

In the summer of 1808, a Cherokee delegation being about to visit
Washington, their agent, Colonel Meigs, was instructed by the Secretary of War to use every effort to obtain their consent to an exchange
of their lands for a tract beyond the Mississippi. By this time the
government's civilizing policy, as carried out in the annual distribution
of farming tools, spinning wheels, and looms, had wrought a considerable difference of habit and sentiment between the northern and
southern Cherokee. Those on Little Tennessee and Hiwassee were
generally farmers and stock raisers, producing also a limited quantity
of cotton, which the women wove into cloth. Those farther down in
Georgia and Alabama, the old hostile element, still preferred the
hunting life and rejected all effort at innovation, although the game
had now become so scarce that it was evident a change must soon

---

[1] Royce, Cherokee Nation, Fifth Ann. Rep. Bureau of Ethnology, pp. 202, 203, 1888.

come.   Jealousies had arisen in consequence, and the delegates representing the progressive element now proposed to the government that a line be run through the nation to separate the two parties, allowing those on the north to divide their lands in severalty and become citizens of the United States, while those on the south might continue to be hunters as long as the game should last.   Taking advantage of this condition of affairs, the government authorities instructed the agent to submit to the conservatives a proposition for a cession of their share of the tribal territory in return for a tract west of the Mississippi of sufficient area to enable them to continue the hunting life.   The plan was approved by President Jefferson, and a sum was appropriated to pay the expenses of a delegation to visit and inspect the lands on Arkansas and White rivers, with a view to removal.   The visit was made in the summer of 1809, and the delegates brought back such favorable report that a large number of Cherokee signified their intention to remove at once.   As no funds were then available for their removal, the matter was held in abeyance for several years, during which period families and individuals removed to the western country at their own expense until, before the year 1817, they numbered in all two or three thousand souls.[1]   They became known as the Arkansas, or Western, Cherokee.

The emigrants soon became involved in difficulties with the native tribes, the Osage claiming all the lands north of Arkansas river, while the Quapaw claimed those on the south.   Upon complaining to the government the emigrant Cherokee were told that they had originally been permitted to remove only on condition of a cession of a portion of their eastern territory, and that nothing could be done to protect them in their new western home until such cession had been carried out.   The body of the Cherokee Nation, however, was strongly opposed to any such sale and proposed that the emigrants should be compelled to return.   After protracted negotiation a treaty was concluded at the Cherokee agency (now Calhoun, Tennessee) on July 8, 1817, by which the Cherokee Nation ceded two considerable tracts—the first in Georgia, lying east of the Chattahoochee, and the other in Tennessee, between Waldens ridge and the Little Sequatchee—as an equivalent for a tract to be assigned to those who had already removed, or intended to remove, to Arkansas.   Two smaller tracts on the north bank of the Tennessee, in the neighborhood of the Muscle shoals, were also ceded.   In return for these cessions the emigrant Cherokee were to receive a tract within the present limits of the state of Arkan-

---

[1] Royce, Cherokee Nation, Fifth Ann. Rep. Bureau of Ethnology, pp. 202–204, 1888; see also Indian Treaties, pp. 209–215, 1837.   The preamble to the treaty of 1817 says that the delegation of 1808 had desired a division of the tribal territory in order that the people of the Upper (northern) towns might "begin the establishment of fixed laws and a regular government," while those of the Lower (southern) towns desired to remove to the West.   Nothing is said of severalty allotments or citizenship.

sas, bounded on the north and south by White river and Arkansas river, respectively, on the east by a line running between those streams approximately from the present Batesville to Lewisburg, and on the west by a line to be determined later.   As afterward established, this western line ran from the junction of the Little North Fork with White river to just beyond the point where the present western Arkansas boundary strikes Arkansas river.   Provision was made for taking the census of the whole Cherokee nation east and west in order to apportion annuities and other payments properly in the future, and the two bands were still to be considered as forming one people.   The United States agreed to pay for any substantial improvements abandoned by those removing from the ceded lands, and each emigrant warrior who left no such valuable property behind was to be given as full compensation for his abandoned field and cabin a rifle and ammunition, a blanket, and a kettle or a beaver trap.   The government further agreed to furnish boats and provisions for the journey.   Provision was also made that individuals residing upon the ceded lands might retain allotments and become citizens, if they so elected, the amount of the allotment to be deducted from the total cession.

The commissioners for the treaty were General Andrew Jackson, General David Meriwether, and Governor Joseph McMinn of Tennessee.   On behalf of the Cherokee it was signed by thirty-one principal men of the eastern Nation and fifteen of the western band, who signed by proxy.[1]

The majority of the Cherokee were bitterly opposed to any cession or removal project, and before the treaty had been concluded a memorial signed by sixty-seven chiefs and headmen of the nation was presented to the commissioners, which stated that the delegates who had first broached the subject in Washington some years before had acted without any authority from the nation.   They declared that the great body of the Cherokee desired to remain in the land of their birth, where they were rapidly advancing in civilization, instead of being compelled to revert to their original savage conditions and surroundings.   They therefore prayed that the matter might not be pressed further, but that they might be allowed to remain in peaceable possession of the land of their fathers.   No attention was paid to the memorial, and the treaty was carried through and ratified.   Without waiting for the ratification, the authorities at once took steps for the removal of those who desired to go to the West.   Boats were provided at points between Little Tennessee and Sequatchee rivers, and the emigrants were collected under the direction of Governor McMinn. Within the next year a large number had emigrated, and before the

---

[1] Indian Treaties, pp. 209–215, 1837; Royce, Cherokee Nation, Fifth Ann. Rep. Bureau of Ethnology, pp. 212–217, 1888; see also maps in Royce.

end of 1819 the number of emigrants was said to have increased to six thousand. The chiefs of the nation, however, claimed that the estimate was greatly in excess of the truth.[1]

"There can be no question that a very large portion, and probably a majority, of the Cherokee nation residing east of the Mississippi had been and still continued bitterly opposed to the terms of the treaty of 1817. They viewed with jealous and aching hearts all attempts to drive them from the homes of their ancestors, for they could not but consider the constant and urgent importunities of the federal authorities in the light of an imperative demand for the cession of more territory. They felt that they were, as a nation, being slowly but surely compressed within the contracting coils of the giant anaconda of civilization; yet they held to the vain hope that a spirit of justice and mercy would be born of their helpless condition which would finally prevail in their favor. Their traditions furnished them no guide by which to judge of the results certain to follow such a conflict as that in which they were engaged. This difference of sentiment in the nation upon a subject so vital to their welfare was productive of much bitterness and violent animosities. Those who had favored the emigration scheme and had been induced, either through personal preference or by the subsidizing influences of the government agents, to favor the conclusion of the treaty, became the object of scorn and hatred to the remainder of the nation. They were made the subjects of a persecution so relentless, while they remained in the eastern country, that it was never forgotten, and when, in the natural course of events, the remainder of the nation was forced to remove to the Arkansas country and join the earlier emigrants, the old hatreds and dissensions broke out afresh, and to this day they find lodgment in some degree in the breasts of their descendants."[2]

Two months after the signing of the treaty of July 8, 1817, and three months before its ratification, a council of the nation sent a delegation to Washington to recount in detail the improper methods and influences which had been used to consummate it, and to ask that it be set aside and another agreement substituted. The mission was without result.[3]

In 1817 the American Board of Commissioners for Foreign Missions established its first station among the Cherokee at Brainerd, in Tennessee, on the west side of Chickamauga creek, two miles from the Georgia line. The mission took its name from a distinguished pioneer worker among the northern tribes (37). The government aided in the erection of the buildings, which included a schoolhouse, gristmill, and workshops, in which, besides the ordinary branches, the boys were taught simple mechanic arts while the girls learned the use of the

[1] Royce, Cherokee Nation, Fifth Ann. Rep. Bureau of Ethnology, 217–218, 1888.
[2] Ibid., pp. 218–219.   [3] Ibid., p. 219.

needle and the spinningwheel. There was also a large work farm. The mission prospered and others were established at Willstown, Hightower, and elsewhere by the same board, in which two hundred pupils were receiving instruction in 1820.[1] Among the earliest and most noted workers at the Brainerd mission were Reverend D. S. Buttrick and Reverend S. A. Worcester (38), the latter especially having done much for the mental elevation of the Cherokee, and more than once having suffered imprisonment for his zeal in defending their cause. The missions flourished until broken up by the state of Georgia at the beginning of the Removal troubles, and they were afterwards renewed in the western country. Mission ridge preserves the memory of the Brainerd establishment.

Early in 1818 a delegation of emigrant Cherokee visited Washington for the purpose of securing a more satisfactory determination of the boundaries of their new lands on the Arkansas. Measures were soon afterward taken for that purpose. They also asked recognition in the future as a separate and distinct tribe, but nothing was done in the matter. In order to remove, if possible, the hostile feeling between the emigrants and the native Osage, who regarded the former as intruders, Governor William Clark, superintendent of Indian affairs for Missouri, arranged a conference of the chiefs of the two tribes at St. Louis in October of that year, at which, after protracted effort, he succeeded in establishing friendly relations between them. Efforts were made about the same time, both by the emigrant Cherokee and by the government, to persuade the Shawano and Delawares then residing in Missouri, and the Oneida in New York, to join the western Cherokee, but nothing came of the negotiations.[2] In 1825 a delegation of western Cherokee visited the Shawano in Ohio for the same purpose, but without success. Their object in thus inviting friendly Indians to join them was to strengthen themselves against the Osage and other native tribes.

In the meantime the government, through Governor McMinn, was bringing strong pressure to bear upon the eastern Cherokee to compel their removal to the West. At a council convened by him in November, 1818, the governor represented to the chiefs that it was now no longer possible to protect them from the encroachments of the surrounding white population; that, however the government might wish to help them, their lands would be taken, their stock stolen, their women corrupted, and their men made drunkards unless they removed to the western paradise. He ended by proposing to pay them one hundred thousand dollars for their whole territory, with the expense of removal, if they would go at once. Upon their prompt and indignant refusal he offered to double the amount, but with as little success.

---

[1] Morse, Geography, I, p. 577, 1819; and p. 185, 1822.
[2] Royce, Cherokee Nation, Fifth Ann. Rep. Bureau of Ethnology, pp. 221–222, 1888.

Every point of the negotiation having failed, another course was adopted, and a delegation was selected to visit Washington under the conduct of Agent Meigs. Here the effort was renewed until, wearied and discouraged at the persistent importunity, the chiefs consented to a large cession, which was represented as necessary in order to compensate in area for the tract assigned to the emigrant Cherokee in Arkansas in accordance with the previous treaty. This estimate was based on the figures given by Governor McMinn, who reported 5,291 Cherokee enrolled as emigrants, while the eastern Cherokee claimed that not more than 3,500 had removed and that those remaining numbered 12,544, or more than three-fourths of the whole nation. The governor, however, chose to consider one-half of the nation as in favor of removal and one-third as having already removed.[1]

The treaty, concluded at Washington on February 27, 1819, recites that the greater part of the Cherokee nation, having expressed an earnest desire to remain in the East, and being anxious to begin the necessary measures for the civilization and preservation of their nation, and to settle the differences arising out of the treaty of 1817, have offered to cede to the United States a tract of country "at least as extensive" as that to which the Government is entitled under the late treaty. The cession embraces (1) a tract in Alabama and Tennessee, between Tennessee and Flint rivers; (2) a tract in Tennessee, between Tennessee river and Waldens ridge; (3) a large irregular tract in Tennessee, North Carolina, and Georgia, embracing in Tennessee nearly all the remaining Cherokee lands north of Hiwassee river, and in North Carolina and Georgia nearly everything remaining to them east of the Nantahala mountains and the upper western branch of the Chattahoochee; (4) six small pieces reserved by previous treaties. The entire cession aggregated nearly six thousand square miles, or more than one-fourth of all then held by the nation. Individual reservations of one mile square each within the ceded area were allowed to a number of families which decided to remain among the whites and become citizens rather than abandon their homes. Payment was to be made for all substantial improvements abandoned, one-third of all tribal annuities were hereafter to be paid to the western band, and the treaty was declared to be a final adjustment of all claims and differences arising from the treaty of 1817.[2]

Civilization had now progressed so far among the Cherokee that in the fall of 1820 they adopted a regular republican form of government modeled after that of the United States. Under this arrangement the nation was divided into eight districts, each of which was entitled

---

[1] Royce, Cherokee Nation, Fifth Ann. Rep. Bureau of Ethnology, pp. 222–228, 1888.
[2] Indian Treaties, pp. 265–269, 1837; Royce, op. cit., pp. 219–221 and table, p. 378.

to send four representatives to the Cherokee national legislature, which met at Newtown, or New Echota, the capital, at the junction of Conasauga and Coosawatee rivers, a few miles above the present Calhoun, Georgia. The legislature consisted of an upper and a lower house, designated, respectively (in the Cherokee language), the national committee and national council, the members being elected for limited terms by the voters of each district. The principal officer was styled president of the national council; the distinguished John Ross was the first to hold this office. There was also a clerk of the committee and two principal members to express the will of the council or lower house. For each district there were appointed a council house for meetings twice a year, a judge, and a marshal. Companies of "light horse" were organized to assist in the execution of the laws, with a "ranger" for each district to look after stray stock. Each head of a family and each single man under the age of sixty was subject to a poll tax. Laws were passed for the collection of taxes and debts, for repairs on roads, for licenses to white persons engaged in farming or other business in the nation, for the support of schools, for the regulation of the liquor traffic and the conduct of negro slaves, to punish horse stealing and theft, to compel all marriages between white men and Indian women to be according to regular legal or church form, and to discourage polygamy. By special decree the right of blood revenge or capital punishment was taken from the seven clans and vested in the constituted authorities of the nation. It was made treason, punishable with death, for any individual to negotiate the sale of lands to the whites without the consent of the national council (39). White men were not allowed to vote or to hold office in the nation.[1] The system compared favorably with that of the Federal government or of any state government then existing.

At this time there were five principal missions, besides one or two small branch establishments in the nation, viz: Spring Place, the oldest, founded by the Moravians at Spring place, Georgia, in 1801; Oothcaloga, Georgia, founded by the same denomination in 1821 on the creek of that name, near the present Calhoun; Brainerd, Tennessee, founded by the American Board of Commissioners for Foreign Missions in 1817; "Valley-towns," North Carolina, founded by the Baptists in 1820, on the site of the old Natchez town on the north side of Hiwassee river, just above Peachtree creek; Coosawatee, Georgia ("Tensawattee," by error in the State Papers), founded also by the Baptists in 1821, near the mouth of the river of that name. All were in flourishing condition, the Brainerd establishment especially, with nearly one hundred pupils, being obliged to turn away applicants for

[1] Laws of the Cherokee Nation (several documents), 1820, American State Papers: Indian Affairs, II, pp. 279-283, 1834; letter quoted by McKenney, 1825, ibid., pp. 651, 652; Drake, Indians, pp. 437, 438, ed. 1880.

lack of accommodation.   The superintendent reported that the children were apt to learn, willing to labor, and readily submissive to discipline, adding that the Cherokee were fast advancing toward civilized life and generally manifested an ardent desire for instruction.   The Valley-towns mission, established at the instance of Currahee Dick, a prominent local mixed-blood chief, was in charge of the Reverend Evan Jones, known as the translator of the New Testament into the Cherokee language, his assistant being James D. Wafford, a mixed-blood pupil, who compiled a spelling book in the same language.   Reverend S. A. Worcester, a prolific translator and the compiler of the Cherokee almanac and other works, was stationed at Brainerd, removing thence to New Echota and afterward to the Cherokee Nation in the West.[1] Since 1817 the American Board had also supported at Cornwall, Connecticut, an Indian school at which a number of young Cherokee were being educated, among them being Elias Boudinot, afterward the editor of the *Cherokee Phœnix*.

About this time occurred an event which at once placed the Cherokee in the front rank among native tribes and was destined to have profound influence on their whole future history, viz., the invention of the alphabet.

The inventor, aptly called the Cadmus of his race, was a mixed-blood known among his own people as Sikwâ'yĭ (Sequoya) and among the whites as George Gist, or less correctly Guest or Guess. As is usually the case in Indian biography much uncertainty exists in regard to his parentage and early life.   Authorities generally agree that his father was a white man, who drifted into the Cherokee Nation some years before the Revolution and formed a temporary alliance with a Cherokee girl of mixed blood, who thus became the mother of the future teacher.   A writer in the *Cherokee Phœnix*, in 1828, says that only his paternal grandfather was a white man.[2]   McKenney and Hall say that his father was a white man named Gist.[3]   Phillips asserts that his father was George Gist, an unlicensed German trader from Georgia, who came into the Cherokee Nation in 1768.[4]   By a Kentucky family it is claimed that Sequoya's father was Nathaniel Gist, son of the scout who accompanied Washington on his memorable excursion to the Ohio.   As the story goes, Nathaniel Gist was captured by the Cherokee at Braddock's defeat (1755) and remained a prisoner with them for six years, during which time he became the father of Sequoya.   On his return to civilization he married a white woman in Virginia, by whom he had other children, and afterward

---

[1] List of missions and reports of missionaries, etc., American State Papers: Indian Affairs, II, pp. 277–279, 459, 1834; personal information from James D. Wafford concerning Valley-towns mission. For notices of Worcester, Jones, and Wafford, see Pilling, Bibliography of the Iroquoian Languages, 1888.

[2] G. C., in Cherokee Phœnix; reprinted in Christian Advocate and Journal, New York, September 26, 1828.

[3] McKenney and Hall, Indian Tribes, I, p. 35, et passim, 1858.

[4] Phillips, Sequoyah, in Harper's Magazine, pp. 542–548, September, 1870.

Sequoya

From McKenney and Hall's copy of the original painting of 1828.

removed to Kentucky, where Sequoya, then a Baptist preacher, frequently visited him and was always recognized by the family as his son.[1]

Aside from the fact that the Cherokee acted as allies of the English during the war in which Braddock's defeat occurred, and that Sequoya, so far from being a preacher, was not even a Christian, the story contains other elements of improbability and appears to be one of those genealogical myths built upon a chance similarity of name. On the other hand, it is certain that Sequoya was born before the date that Phillips allows. On his mother's side he was of good family in the tribe, his uncle being a chief in Echota.[2] According to personal information of James Wafford, who knew him well, being his second cousin, Sequoya was probably born about the year 1760, and lived as a boy with his mother at Tuskegee town in Tennessee, just outside of old Fort Loudon. It is quite possible that his white father may have been a soldier of the garrison, one of those lovers for whom the Cherokee women risked their lives during the siege.[3] What became of the father is not known, but the mother lived alone with her son.

The only incident of his boyhood that has come down to us is his presence at Echota during the visit of the Iroquois peace delegation, about the year 1770.[4] His early years were spent amid the stormy alarms of the Revolution, and as he grew to manhood he developed a considerable mechanical ingenuity, especially in silver working. Like most of his tribe he was also a hunter and fur trader. Having nearly reached middle age before the first mission was established in the Nation, he never attended school and in all his life never learned to speak, read, or write the English language. Neither did he ever abandon his native religion, although from frequent visits to the Moravian mission he became imbued with a friendly feeling toward the new civilization. Of an essentially contemplative disposition, he was led by a chance conversation in 1809 to reflect upon the ability of the white men to communicate thought by means of writing, with the result that he set about devising a similar system for his own people. By a hunting accident, which rendered him a cripple for life, he was fortunately afforded more leisure for study. The presence of his name, George Guess, appended to a treaty of 1816, indicates that he was already of some prominence in the Nation, even before the perfection of his great invention. After years of patient and unremitting labor in the face of ridicule, discouragement, and repeated failure, he finally evolved the Cherokee syllabary and in 1821 submitted it to a public test by the leading men of the Nation. By this time, in consequence of repeated cessions, the Cherokee had been dispossessed of the country about Echota, and Sequoya was now living at Willstown,

---

[1] Manuscript letters by John Mason Brown, January 17, 18, 22, and February 4, 1889, in archives of the Bureau of American Ethnology.

[2] McKenney and Hall, Indian Tribes, I, p. 45, 1858.

[3] See page 43.   [4] See number 89, "The Iroquois wars."

on an upper branch of Coosa river, in Alabama. The syllabary was soon recognized as an invaluable invention for the elevation of the tribe, and within a few months thousands of hitherto illiterate Cherokee were able to read and write their own language, teaching each other in the cabins and along the roadside. The next year Sequoya visited the West, to introduce the new science among those who had emigrated to the Arkansas. In the next year, 1823, he again visited the Arkansas and took up his permanent abode with the western band, never afterward returning to his eastern kinsmen. In the autumn of the same year the Cherokee national council made public acknowledgment of his merit by sending to him, through John Ross, then president of the national committee, a silver medal with a commemorative inscription in both languages.[1] In 1828 he visited Washington as one of the delegates from the Arkansas band, attracting much attention, and the treaty made on that occasion contains a provision for the payment to him of five hundred dollars, "for the great benefits he has conferred upon the Cherokee people, in the beneficial results which they are now experiencing from the use of the alphabet discovered by him."[2] His subsequent history belongs to the West and will be treated in another place (40).[3]

The invention of the alphabet had an immediate and wonderful effect on Cherokee development. On account of the remarkable adaptation of the syllabary to the language, it was only necessary to learn the characters to be able to read at once. No schoolhouses were built and no teachers hired, but the whole Nation became an academy for the study of the system, until, "in the course of a few months, without school or expense of time or money, the Cherokee were able to read and write in their own language.[4] An active correspondence began to be carried on between the eastern and western divisions, and plans were made for a national press, with a national library and museum to be established at the capital, New Echota.[5] The missionaries, who had at first opposed the new alphabet on the ground of its Indian origin, now saw the advisability of using it to further their own work. In the fall of 1824 Atsĭ or John Arch, a young native convert, made a manuscript translation of a portion of St. John's gospel, in the syllabary, this being the first Bible translation ever given to the Cherokee. It was copied hundreds of times and was widely disseminated through

---

[1] McKenney and Hall, Indian Tribes, I, p. 46, 1858; Phillips, in Harper's Magazine, p. 547, September, 1870.

[2] Indian Treaties, p. 425, 1837.

[3] For details concerning the life and invention of Sequoya, see McKenney and Hall, Indian Tribes, I, 1858; Phillips, Sequoyah, in Harper's Magazine, September 1870; Foster, Sequoyah, 1885, and Story of the Cherokee Bible, 1899, based largely on Phillips' article; G. C., Invention of the Cherokee Alphabet, in Cherokee Phœnix, republished in Christian Advocate and Journal, New York, September 26, 1828: Pilling, Bibliography of the Iroquoian Languages, 1888.

[4] G. C., Invention of the Cherokee Alphabet, op. cit.

[5] (Unsigned) letter of David Brown, September 2, 1825, quoted in American State Papers: Indian Affairs, II, p. 652, 1834.

the Nation.[1] In September, 1825, David Brown, a prominent half-breed preacher, who had already made some attempt at translation in the Roman alphabet, completed a translation of the New Testament in the new syllabary, the work being handed about in manuscript, as there were as yet no types cast in the Sequoya characters.[2]   In the same month he forwarded to Thomas McKenney, chief of the Bureau of Indian Affairs at Washington, a manuscript table of the characters, with explanation, this being probably its first introduction to official notice.[3]

In 1827 the Cherokee council having formally resolved to establish a national paper in the Cherokee language and characters, types for that purpose were cast in Boston, under the supervision of the noted missionary, Worcester, of the American Board of Commissioners for Foreign Missions, who, in December of that year contributed to the *Missionary Herald* five verses of Genesis in the new syllabary, this seeming to be its first appearance in print.   Early in the next year the press and types arrived at New Echota, and the first number of the new paper, *Tsa'lăgĭ Tsu'lehisanuñ'hĭ*, the *Cherokee Phœnix*, printed in both languages, appeared on February 21, 1828.   The first printers were two white men, Isaac N. Harris and John F. Wheeler, with John Candy, a half-blood apprentice.   Elias Boudinot (Gălagi'na, "The Buck"), an educated Cherokee, was the editor, and Reverend S. A. Worcester was the guiding spirit who brought order out of chaos and set the work in motion.   The office was a log house.   The hand press and types, after having been shipped by water from Boston, were transported two hundred miles by wagon from Augusta to their destination. The printing paper had been overlooked and had to be brought by the same tedious process from Knoxville.   Cases and other equipments had to be devised and fashioned by the printers, neither of whom understood a word of Cherokee, but simply set up the characters, as handed to them in manuscript by Worcester and the editor.   Such was the beginning of journalism in the Cherokee nation.   After a precarious existence of about six years the *Phœnix* was suspended, owing to the hostile action of the Georgia authorities, who went so far as to throw Worcester and Wheeler into prison.   Its successor, after the removal of the Cherokee to the West, was the *Cherokee Advocate*, of which the first number appeared at Tahlequah in 1844, with William P. Ross as editor.   It is still continued under the auspices of the Nation, printed in both languages and distributed free at the expense of the Nation to those unable to read English—an example without parallel in any other government.

In addition to numerous Bible translations, hymn books, and other

[1] Foster, Sequoyah, pp. 120, 121, 1885.   [2] Pilling, Iroquoian Bibliography, p. 21, 1888.
[3] Brown letter (unsigned), in American State Papers: Indian Affairs, II, p. 652, 1834.

religious works, there have been printed in the Cherokee language and syllabary the *Cherokee Phœnix* (journal), *Cherokee Advocate* (journal), *Cherokee Messenger* (periodical), *Cherokee Almanac* (annual), Cherokee spelling books, arithmetics, and other schoolbooks for those unable to read English, several editions of the laws of the Nation, and a large body of tracts and minor publications. Space forbids even a mention of the names of the devoted workers in this connection. Besides this printed literature the syllabary is in constant and daily use among the non-English-speaking element, both in Indian Territory and in North Carolina, for letter writing, council records, personal memoranda, etc. What is perhaps strangest of all in this literary evolution is the fact that the same invention has been seized by the priests and conjurers of the conservative party for the purpose of preserving to their successors the ancient rituals and secret knowledge of the tribe, whole volumes of such occult literature in manuscript having been obtained among them by the author.[1]

In 1819 the whole Cherokee population had been estimated at 15,000, one-third of them being west of the Mississippi. In 1825 a census of the eastern Nation showed: native Cherokee, 13,563; white men married into the Nation, 147; white women married into the Nation, 73; negro slaves, 1,277. There were large herds of cattle, horses, hogs, and sheep, with large crops of every staple, including cotton, tobacco, and wheat, and some cotton was exported by boats as far as New Orleans. Apple and peach orchards were numerous, butter and cheese were in use to some extent, and both cotton and woolen cloths, especially blankets, were manufactured. Nearly all the merchants were native Cherokee. Mechanical industries flourished, the Nation was out of debt, and the population was increasing.[2] Estimating one-third beyond the Mississippi, the total number of Cherokee, exclusive of adopted white citizens and negro slaves, must then have been about 20,000.

Simultaneously with the decrees establishing a national press, the Cherokee Nation, in general convention of delegates held for the purpose at New Echota on July 26, 1827, adopted a national constitution, based on the assumption of distinct and independent nationality. John Ross, so celebrated in connection with the history of his tribe, was president of the convention which framed the instrument. Charles R. Hicks, a Moravian convert of mixed blood, and at that time the most influential man in the Nation, was elected principal chief, with John

---

[1] For extended notice of Cherokee literature and authors see numerous references in Pilling, Bibliography of the Iroquoian Languages, 1888; also Foster, Sequoyah, 1885, and Story of the Cherokee Bible, 1899. The largest body of original Cherokee manuscript material in existence, including hundreds of ancient ritual formulas, was obtained by the writer among the East Cherokee, and is now in possession of the Bureau of American Ethnology, to be translated at some future time.

[2] Brown letter (unsigned), September 2, 1825, American State Papers: Indian Affairs, II, pp. 651, 652, 1834.

The Cherokee Alphabet

A Syllabary invented by Sequoyah. From a lithograph prepared for the American Board of Foreign Missions.

Ross as assistant chief.[1] With a constitution and national press, a well-developed system of industries and home education, and a government administered by educated Christian men, the Cherokee were now justly entitled to be considered a civilized people.

The idea of a civilized Indian government was not a new one. The first treaty ever negotiated by the United States with an Indian tribe, in 1778, held out to the Delawares the hope that by a confederation of friendly tribes they might be able "to form a state, whereof the Delaware nation shall be the head and have a representation in Congress."[2] Priber, the Jesuit, had already familiarized the Cherokee with the forms of civilized government before the middle of the eighteenth century. As the gap between the conservative and progressive elements widened after the Revolution the idea grew, until in 1808 representatives of both parties visited Washington to propose an arrangement by which those who clung to the old life might be allowed to remove to the western hunting grounds, while the rest should remain to take up civilization and "begin the establishment of fixed laws and a regular government." The project received the warm encouragement of President Jefferson, and it was with this understanding that the western emigration was first officially recognized a few years later. Immediately upon the return of the delegates from Washington the Cherokee drew up their first brief written code of laws, modeled agreeably to the friendly suggestions of Jefferson.[3]

By this time the rapid strides of civilization and Christianity had alarmed the conservative element, who saw in the new order of things only the evidences of apostasy and swift national decay. In 1828 White-path (Nûñ'nâ-tsune'ga), an influential full-blood and councilor, living at Turniptown (Uʻlûñ'yĭ), near the present Ellijay, in Gilmer county, Georgia, headed a rebellion against the new code of laws, with all that it implied. He soon had a large band of followers, known to the whites as "Red-sticks," a title sometimes assumed by the more warlike element among the Creeks and other southern tribes. From the townhouse of Ellijay he preached the rejection of the new constitution, the discarding of Christianity and the white man's ways, and a return to the old tribal law and custom—the same doctrine that had more than once constituted the burden of Indian revelation in the past. It was now too late, however, to reverse the wheel of progress, and under the rule of such men as Hicks and Ross the conservative opposition gradually melted away. White-path was deposed from his seat

---

[1] See Royce, Cherokee Nation, Fifth Ann. Rep. Bureau of Ethnology, p. 241, 1888; Meredith, in The Five Civilized Tribes, Extra Census Bulletin, p. 41, 1894; Morse, American Geography, I, p. 577, 1819 (for Hicks).

[2] Fort Pitt treaty, September 17, 1778, Indian Treaties, p. 3, 1837.

[3] Cherokee Agency treaty, July 8, 1817, ibid., p. 209; Drake, Indians, p. 450, ed. 1880; Johnson in Senate Report on Territories; Cherokee Memorial, January 18, 1831; see laws of 1808, 1810, and later, in American State Papers: Indian Affairs, II, pp. 279–283, 1834. The volume of Cherokee laws, compiled in the Cherokee language by the Nation, in 1850, begins with the year 1808.

in council, but subsequently made submission and was reinstated. He was afterward one of the detachment commanders in the Removal, but died while on the march.[1]

In this year, also, John Ross became principal chief of the Nation, a position which he held until his death in 1866, thirty-eight years later.[2] In this long period, comprising the momentous episodes of the Removal and the War of the Rebellion, it may be truly said that his history is the history of the Nation.

And now, just when it seemed that civilization and enlightenment were about to accomplish their perfect work, the Cherokee began to hear the first low muttering of the coming storm that was soon to overturn their whole governmental structure and sweep them forever from the land of their birth.

By an agreement between the United States and the state of Georgia in 1802, the latter, for valuable consideration, had ceded to the general government her claims west of the present state boundary, the United States at the same time agreeing to extinguish, at its own expense, but for the benefit of the state, the Indian claims within the state limits, "as early as the same can be peaceably obtained on reasonable terms."[3] In accordance with this agreement several treaties had already been made with the Creeks and Cherokee, by which large tracts had been secured for Georgia at the expense of the general government. Notwithstanding this fact, and the terms of the proviso, Georgia accused the government of bad faith in not taking summary measures to compel the Indians at once to surrender all their remaining lands within the chartered state limits, coupling the complaint with a threat to take the matter into her own hands. In 1820 Agent Meigs had expressed the opinion that the Cherokee were now so far advanced that further government aid was unnecessary, and that their lands should be allotted and the surplus sold for their benefit, they themselves to be invested with full rights of citizenship in the several states within which they resided. This suggestion had been approved by President Monroe, but had met the most determined opposition from the states concerned. Tennessee absolutely refused to recognize individual reservations made by previous treaties, while North Carolina and Georgia bought in all such reservations with money appropriated by Congress.[4] No Indian was to be allowed to live within those states on any pretext whatsoever.

In the meantime, owing to persistent pressure from Georgia, repeated unsuccessful efforts had been made to procure from the Cherokee a cession of their lands within the chartered limits of the

---

[1] Personal information from James D. Wafford. So far as is known this rebellion of the conservatives has never hitherto been noted in print.

[2] See Resolutions of Honor, in Laws of the Cherokee Nation, pp. 137-140, 1868; Meredith, in The Five Civilized Tribes, Extra Census Bulletin, p. 41, 1894; Appleton, Cyclopedia of American Biography.

[3] See fourth article of "Articles of agreement and cession," April 24, 1802, in American State Papers: class VIII, Public Lands, I, quoted also by Greeley, American Conflict, I, p. 103, 1864.

[4] Royce, Cherokee Nation, Fifth Ann. Rep. Bureau of Ethnology, pp. 231-233, 1888.

state. Every effort met with a firm refusal, the Indians declaring that having already made cession after cession from a territory once extensive, their remaining lands were no more than were needed for themselves and their children, more especially as experience had shown that each concession would be followed by a further demand. They conclude: "It is the fixed and unalterable determination of this nation never again to cede one foot more of land." Soon afterward they addressed to the President a memorial of similar tenor, to which Calhoun, as Secretary of War, returned answer that as Georgia objected to their presence either as a tribe or as individual owners or citizens, they must prepare their minds for removal beyond the Mississippi.[1]

In reply, the Cherokee, by their delegates—John Ross, George Lowrey, Major Ridge, and Elijah Hicks—sent a strong letter calling attention to the fact that by the very wording of the 1802 agreement the compact was a conditional one which could not be carried out without their own voluntary consent, and suggesting that Georgia might be satisfied from the adjoining government lands in Florida. Continuing, they remind the Secretary that the Cherokee are not foreigners, but original inhabitants of America, inhabiting and standing now upon the soil of their own territory, with limits defined by treaties with the United States, and that, confiding in the good faith of the government to respect its treaty stipulations, they do not hesitate to say that their true interest, prosperity, and happiness demand their permanency where they are and the retention of their lands.[2]

A copy of this letter was sent by the Secretary to Governor Troup of Georgia, who returned a reply in which he blamed the missionaries for the refusal of the Indians, declared that the state would not permit them to become citizens, and that the Secretary must either assist the state in taking possession of the Cherokee lands, or, in resisting that occupancy, make war upon and shed the blood of brothers and friends. The Georgia delegation in Congress addressed a similar letter to President Monroe, in which the government was censured for having instructed the Indians in the arts of civilized life and having thereby imbued them with a desire to acquire property.[3]

For answer the President submitted a report by Secretary Calhoun showing that since the agreement had been made with Georgia in 1802 the government had, at its own expense, extinguished the Indian claim to 24,600 square miles within the limits of that state, or more than three-fifths of the whole Indian claim, and had paid on that and other accounts connected with the agreement nearly seven and a half million

[1] Cherokee correspondence, 1823 and 1824, American State Papers: Indian Affairs, II, pp. 468–473, 1834; Royce, Cherokee Nation, Fifth Ann. Rep. Bureau of Ethnology, pp. 236–237, 1888.
[2] Cherokee memorial, February 11, 1824, in American State Papers: Indian Affairs, II, pp. 473, 494, 1834; Royce, op. cit., p. 237.
[3] Letters of Governor Troup of Georgia, February 28, 1824, and of Georgia delegates, March 10, 1824, American State Papers: Indian Affairs, II, pp. 475, 477, 1834; Royce, op. cit., pp. 237, 238.

George Lowrey

Probably painted by John Mix Stanley, 1844.

dollars, of which by far the greater part had gone to Georgia or her citizens. In regard to the other criticism the report states that the civilizing policy was as old as the government itself, and that in performing the high duties of humanity to the Indians, it had never been conceived that the stipulation of the convention was contravened. In handing in the report the President again called attention to the conditional nature of the agreement and declared it as his opinion that the title of the Indians was not in the slightest degree affected by it and that there was no obligation on the United States to remove them by force.[1]

Further efforts, even to the employment of secret methods, were made in 1827 and 1828 to induce a cession or emigration, but without avail. On July 26, 1827, as already noted, the Cherokee adopted a constitution as a distinct and sovereign Nation. Upon this the Georgia legislature passed resolutions affirming that that state "had the power and the right to possess herself, by any means she might choose, of the lands in dispute, and to extend over them her authority and laws," and recommending that this be done by the next legislature, if the lands were not already acquired by successful negotiation of the general government in the meantime. The government was warned that the lands belonged to Georgia, and she must and would have them. It was suggested, however, that the United States might be permitted to make a certain number of reservations to individual Indians.[2]

Passing over for the present some important negotiations with the western Cherokee, we come to the events leading to the final act in the drama. Up to this time the pressure had been for land only, but now a stronger motive was added. About the year 1815 a little Cherokee boy playing along Chestatee river, in upper Georgia, had brought in to his mother a shining yellow pebble hardly larger than the end of his thumb. On being washed it proved to be a nugget of gold, and on her next trip to the settlements the woman carried it with her and sold it to a white man. The news spread, and although she probably concealed the knowledge of the exact spot of its origin, it was soon known that the golden dreams of De Soto had been realized in the Cherokee country of Georgia. Within four years the whole territory east of the Chestatee had passed from the possession of the Cherokee. They still held the western bank, but the prospector was abroad in the mountains and it could not be for long.[3] About 1828 gold was found on Ward's creek, a western branch of Chestatee, near the present Dahlonega,[4] and the doom of the nation was sealed (41).

[1] Monroe, message to the Senate, with Calhoun's report, March 30, 1824, American State Papers: Indian Affairs, II, pp. 460, 462, 1834.

[2] Royce, Cherokee Nation, Fifth Ann. Rep. Bureau of Ethnology, pp. 241, 242, 1888.

[3] Personal information from J. D. Wafford.

[4] Nitze, H. B. C., in Twentieth Annual Report United States Geological Survey, part 6 (Mineral Resources), p. 112, 1899.

In November, 1828, Andrew Jackson was elected to succeed John Quincy Adams as President. He was a frontiersman and Indian hater, and the change boded no good to the Cherokee. His position was well understood, and there is good ground for believing that the action at once taken by Georgia was at his own suggestion.[1] On December 20, 1828, a month after his election, Georgia passed an act annexing that part of the Cherokee country within her chartered limits and extending over it her jurisdiction; all laws and customs established among the Cherokee were declared null and void, and no person of Indian blood or descent residing within the Indian country was henceforth to be allowed as a witness or party in any suit where a white man should be defendant. The act was to take effect June 1, 1830 (42). The whole territory was soon after mapped out into counties and surveyed by state surveyors into "land lots" of 160 acres each, and "gold lots" of 40 acres, which were put up and distributed among the white citizens of Georgia by public lottery, each white citizen receiving a ticket. Every Cherokee head of a family was, indeed, allowed a reservation of 160 acres, but no deed was given, and his continuance depended solely on the pleasure of the legislature. Provision was made for the settlement of contested lottery claims among the white citizens, but by the most stringent enactments, in addition to the sweeping law which forbade anyone of Indian blood to bring suit or to testify against a white man, it was made impossible for the Indian owner to defend his right in any court or to resist the seizure of his homestead, or even his own dwelling house, and anyone so resisting was made subject to imprisonment at the discretion of a Georgia court. Other laws directed to the same end quickly followed, one of which made invalid any contract between a white man and an Indian unless established by the testimony of two white witnesses—thus practically canceling all debts due from white men to Indians—while another obliged all white men residing in the Cherokee country to take a special oath of allegiance to the state of Georgia, on penalty of four years' imprisonment in the penitentiary, this act being intended to drive out all the missionaries, teachers, and other educators who refused to countenance the spoliation. About the same time the Cherokee were forbidden to hold councils, or to assemble for any public purpose,[2] or to. dig for gold upon their own lands.

---

[1] See Butler letter, quoted in Royce, Cherokee Nation, Fifth Ann. Rep. Bureau of Ethnology, p. 297, 1888; see also Everett, speech in the House of Representatives on May 31, 1838, pp. 16–17, 32–33, 1839.

[2] For extracts and synopses of these acts see Royce, op. cit., pp. 259–264; Drake, Indians, pp. 438–456, 1880; Greeley, American Conflict, I, pp. 105, 106, 1864; Edward Everett, speech in the House of Representatives, February 14, 1831 (lottery law). The gold lottery is also noted incidentally by Lanman, Charles, Letters from the Alleghany Mountains, p. 10; New York, 1849, and by Nitze, in his report on the Georgia gold fields, in the Twentieth Annual Report of the United States Geological Survey, part 6 (Mineral Resources), p. 112, 1899. The author has himself seen in a mountain village in Georgia an old book titled "The Cherokee Land and Gold Lottery," containing maps and plats covering the whole Cherokee country of Georgia, with each lot numbered, and descriptions of the water courses, soil, and supposed mineral veins.

The purpose of this legislation was to render life in their own country intolerable to the Cherokee by depriving them of all legal protection and friendly counsel, and the effect was precisely as intended. In an eloquent address upon the subject before the House of Representatives the distinguished Edward Everett clearly pointed out the encouragement which it gave to lawless men: " They have but to cross the Cherokee line; they have but to choose the time and the place where the eye of no white man can rest upon them, and they may burn the dwelling, waste the farm, plunder the property, assault the person, murder the children of the Cherokee subject of Georgia, and though hundreds of the tribe may be looking on, there is not one of them that can be permitted to bear witness against the spoiler."[1] Senator Sprague, of Maine, said of the law that it devoted the property of the Cherokee to the cupidity of their neighbors, leaving them exposed to every outrage which lawless persons could inflict, so that even robbery and murder might be committed with impunity at noonday, if not in the presence of whites who would testify against it.[2]

The prediction was fulfilled to the letter. Bands of armed men invaded the Cherokee country, forcibly seizing horses and cattle, taking possession of houses from which they had ejected the occupants, and assaulting the owners who dared to make resistance.[3] In one instance, near the present Dahlonega, two white men, who had been hospitably received and entertained at supper by an educated Cherokee citizen of nearly pure white blood, later in the evening, during the temporary absence of the parents, drove out the children and their nurse and deliberately set fire to the house, which was burned to the ground with all its contents. They were pursued and brought to trial, but the case was dismissed by the judge on the ground that no Indian could testify against a white man.[4] Cherokee miners upon their own ground were arrested, fined, and imprisoned, and their tools and machinery destroyed, while thousands of white intruders were allowed to dig in the same places unmolested.[5] A Cherokee on trial in his own nation for killing another Indian was seized by the state authorities, tried and condemned to death, although, not understanding English, he was unable to speak in his own defense. A United States court forbade the execution, but the judge who had conducted the trial defied the writ, went to the place of execution, and stood beside the sheriff while the Indian was being hanged.[6]

---

[1] Speech of May 19, 1830, Washington; printed by Gales & Seaton, 1830.

[2] Speech in the Senate of the United States, April 16, 1830; Washington, Peter Force, printer, 1830.

[3] See Cherokee Memorial to Congress, January 18, 1831.

[4] Personal information from Prof. Clinton Duncan, of Tahlequah, Cherokee Nation, whose father's house was the one thus burned.

[5] Cherokee Memorial to Congress January 18, 1831.

[6] Ibid.; see also speech of Edward Everett in House of Representatives February 14, 1831; report of the select committee of the senate of Massachusetts upon the Georgia resolutions, Boston, 1831; Greeley, American Conflict, I, p. 106, 1864; Abbott, Cherokee Indians in Georgia; Atlanta Constitution, October 27, 1889.

Immediately on the passage of the first act the Cherokee appealed to President Jackson, but were told that no protection would be afforded them.   Other efforts were then made—in 1829—to persuade them to removal, or to procure another cession—this time of all their lands in North Carolina—but the Cherokee remained firm.   The Georgia law was declared in force on June 3, 1830, whereupon the President directed that the annuity payment due the Cherokee Nation under previous treaties should no longer be paid to their national treasurer, as hitherto, but distributed per capita by the agent.   As a national fund it had been used for the maintenance of their schools and national press.   As a per capita payment it amounted to forty-two cents to each individual.   Several years afterward it still remained unpaid.   Federal troops were also sent into the Cherokee country with orders to prevent all mining by either whites or Indians unless authorized by the state of Georgia.   All these measures served only to render the Cherokee more bitter in their determination.   In September, 1830, another proposition was made for the removal of the tribe, but the national council emphatically refused to consider the subject.[1]

In January, 1831, the Cherokee Nation, by John Ross as principal chief, brought a test suit of injunction against Georgia, in the United States Supreme Court.   The majority of the court dismissed the suit on the ground that the Cherokee were not a foreign nation within the meaning of the Constitution, two justices dissenting from this opinion.[2]

Shortly afterward, under the law which forbade any white man to reside in the Cherokee Nation without taking an oath of allegiance to Georgia, a number of arrests were made, including Wheeler, the printer of the *Cherokee Phœnix*, and the missionaries, Worcester, Butler, Thompson, and Proctor, who, being there by permission of the agent and feeling that plain American citizenship should hold good in any part of the United States, refused to take the oath.   Some of those arrested took the oath and were released, but Worcester and Butler, still refusing, were dressed in prison garb and put at hard labor among felons.   Worcester had plead in his defense that he was a citizen of Vermont, and had entered the Cherokee country by permission of the President of the United States and approval of the Cherokee Nation; and that as the United States by several treaties had acknowledged the Cherokee to be a nation with a guaranteed and definite territory, the state had no right to interfere with him.   He was sentenced to four years in the penitentiary.   On March 3, 1832, the matter was appealed as a test case to the Supreme Court of the United States, which rendered a decision in favor of Worcester and the Cherokee Nation and ordered his release.   Georgia, however, through her governor, had defied the summons with a threat of opposition, even to the

---

[1] Royce, Cherokee Nation, Fifth Ann. Rep. Bureau of Ethnology, pp. 261, 262, 1888.
[2] Ibid., p. 262.

annihilation of the Union, and now ignored the decision, refusing to release the missionary, who remained in prison until set free by the will of the governor nearly a year later. A remark attributed to President Jackson, on hearing of the result in the Supreme Court, may throw some light on the whole proceeding: "John Marshall has made his decision, now let him enforce it."[1]

On the 19th of July, 1832, a public fast was observed throughout the Cherokee Nation. In the proclamation recommending it, Chief Ross observes that "Whereas the crisis in the affairs of the Nation exhibits the day of tribulation and sorrow, and the time appears to be fast hastening when the destiny of this people must be sealed; whether it has been directed by the wonted depravity and wickedness of man, or by the unsearchable and mysterious will of an allwise Being, it equally becomes us, as a rational and Christian community, humbly to bow in humiliation," etc.[2]

Further attempts were made to induce the Cherokee to remove to the West, but met the same firm refusal as before. It was learned that in view of the harrassing conditions to which they were subjected the Cherokee were now seriously considering the project of emigrating to the Pacific Coast, at the mouth of the Columbia, a territory then claimed by England and held by the posts of the British Hudson Bay Company. The Secretary of War at once took steps to discourage the movement.[3] A suggestion from the Cherokee that the government satisfy those who had taken possession of Cherokee lands under the lottery drawing by giving them instead an equivalent from the unoccupied government lands was rejected by the President.

In the spring of 1834 the Cherokee submitted a memorial which, after asserting that they would never voluntarily consent to abandon their homes, proposed to satisfy Georgia by ceding to her a portion of their territory, they to be protected in possession of the remainder until the end of a definite period to be fixed by the United States, at the expiration of which, after disposing of their surplus lands, they should become citizens of the various states within which they resided. They were told that their difficulties could be remedied only by their removal to the west of the Mississippi. In the meantime a removal treaty was being negotiated with a self-styled committee of some fifteen or twenty Cherokee called together at the agency. It was carried through in spite of the protest of John Ross and the Cherokee Nation, as embodied in a paper said to contain the signatures of 13,000 Cherokee, but failed of ratification.[4]

Despairing of any help from the President, the Cherokee delega-

[1] Royce, Cherokee Nation, Fifth Ann. Rep. Bureau of Ethnology, pp. 264–266, 1888; Drake, Indians, pp. 454–457, 1880; Greeley, American Conflict, I, 106, 1864.

[2] Drake, Indians, p. 458, 1880.

[3] Royce, op. cit.. pp. 262–264, 272, 273.

[4] Ibid., pp. 274, 275.

tion, headed by John Ross, addressed another earnest memorial to Congress on May 17, 1834. Royce quotes the document at length, with the remark, "Without affecting to pass judgment on the merits of the controversy, the writer thinks this memorial well deserving of reproduction here as evidencing the devoted and pathetic attachment with which the Cherokee clung to the land of their fathers, and, remembering the wrongs and humiliations of the past, refused to be convinced that justice, prosperity, and happiness awaited them beyond the Mississippi."[1]

In August of this year another council was held at Red Clay, southeastward from Chattanooga and just within the Georgia line, where the question of removal was again debated in what is officially described as a tumultuous and excited meeting. One of the principal advocates of the emigration scheme, a prominent mixed-blood named John Walker, jr., was assassinated from ambush while returning from the council to his home a few miles north of the present Cleveland, Tennessee. On account of his superior education and influential connections, his wife being a niece of former agent Return J. Meigs, the affair created intense excitement at the time. The assassination has been considered the first of the long series of political murders growing out of the removal agitation, but, according to the testimony of old Cherokee acquainted with the facts, the killing was due to a more personal motive.[2]

The Cherokee were now nearly worn out by constant battle against a fate from which they could see no escape. In February, 1835, two rival delegations arrived in Washington, One, the national party, headed by John Ross, came prepared still to fight to the end for home and national existence. The other, headed by Major John Ridge, a prominent subchief, despairing of further successful resistance, was prepared to negotiate for removal. Reverend J. F. Schermerhorn was appointed commissioner to arrange with the Ridge party a treaty to be confirmed later by the Cherokee people in general council. On this basis a treaty was negotiated with the Ridge party by which the Cherokee were to cede their whole eastern territory and remove to the West in consideration of the sum of $3,250,000 with some additional acreage in the West and a small sum for depredations committed upon them by the whites. Finding that these negotiations were proceeding, the Ross party filed a counter proposition for $20,000,000, which was rejected by the Senate as excessive. The Schermerhorn compact with the Ridge party, with the consideration changed to $4,500,000, was thereupon completed and signed on March 14, 1835, but with the express stipulation that it should receive the approval of

---

[1] Royce, Cherokee Nation, Fifth Ann. Report Bureau of Ethnology, p. 276, 1888.

[2] Commissioner Elbert Herring, November 25, Report of Indian Commissioner, p. 240, 1834; author's personal information from Major R. C. Jackson and J. D. Wafford.

the Cherokee nation in full council assembled before being considered of any binding force.   This much accomplished, Mr. Schermerhorn departed for the Cherokee country, armed with an address from President Jackson in which the great benefits of removal were set forth to the Cherokee.   Having exhausted the summer and fall in fruitless effort to secure favorable action, the reverend gentleman notified the President, proposing either to obtain the signatures of the leading Cherokee by promising them payment for their improvements at their own valuation, if in any degree reasonable, or to conclude a treaty with a part of the Nation and compel its acceptance by the rest.   He was promptly informed by the Secretary of War, Lewis Cass, on behalf of the President, that the treaty, if concluded at all, must be procured upon fair and open terms, with no particular promise to any individual, high or low, to gain his aid or influence, and without sacrificing the interest of the whole to the cupidity of a few.   He was also informed that, as it would probably be contrary to his wish, his letter would not be put on file.[1]

In October, 1835, the Ridge treaty was rejected by the Cherokee Nation in full council at Red Clay, even its main supporters, Ridge himself and Elias Boudinot, going over to the majority, most unexpectedly to Schermerhorn, who reports the result, piously adding, "but the Lord is able to overrule all things for good."   During the session of this council notice was served on the Cherokee to meet commissioners at New Echota in December following for the purpose of negotiating a treaty.   The notice was also printed in the Cherokee language and circulated throughout the Nation, with a statement that those who failed to attend would be counted as assenting to any treaty that might be made.[2]

The council had authorized the regular delegation, headed by John Ross, to conclude a treaty either there or at Washington, but, finding that Schermerhorn had no authority to treat on any other basis than the one rejected by the Nation, the delegates proceeded to Washington.[3]   Before their departure John Ross, who had removed to Tennessee to escape persecution in his own state, was arrested at his home by the Georgia guard, all his private papers and the proceedings of the council being taken at the same time, and conveyed across the line into Georgia, where he was held for some time without charge against him, and at last released without apology or explanation.   The poet, John Howard Payne, who was then stopping with Ross, engaged in the work of collecting historical and ethnologic material relating to the Cherokee, was seized at the same time, with all his letters and scien-

---

[1] Royce, Cherokee Nation, Fifth Ann. Rep. Bureau of Ethnology, pp. 278–280, 1888; Everett speech in House of Representatives, May 31, 1838, pp. 28, 29, 1839, in which the Secretary's reply is given in full.

[2] Royce, op. cit., pp. 280–281.   [3] Ibid., p. 281.

tific manuscripts.   The national paper, the *Cherokee Phœnix*, had been suppressed and its office plant seized by the same guard a few days before.[1]   Thus in their greatest need the Cherokee were deprived of the help and counsel of their teachers, their national press, and their chief.

Although for two months threats and inducements had been held out to secure a full attendance at the December conference at New Echota, there were present when the proceedings opened, according to the report of Schermerhorn himself, only from three hundred to five hundred men, women, and children, out of a population of over 17,000.   Notwithstanding the paucity of attendance and the absence of the principal officers of the Nation, a committee was appointed to arrange the details of a treaty, which was finally drawn up and signed on December 29, 1835.[2]

Briefly stated, by this treaty of New Echota, Georgia, the Cherokee Nation ceded to the United States its whole remaining territory east of the Mississippi for the sum of five million dollars and a common joint interest in the territory already occupied by the western Cherokee, in what is now Indian Territory, with an additional smaller tract adjoining on the northeast, in what is now Kansas.   Improvements were to be paid for, and the Indians were to be removed at the expense of the United States and subsisted at the expense of the Government for one year after their arrival in the new country.   The removal was to take place within two years from the ratification of the treaty.

On the strong representations of the Cherokee signers, who would probably not have signed otherwise even then, it was agreed that a limited number of Cherokee who should desire to remain behind in North Carolina, Tennessee, and Alabama, and become citizens, having first been adjudged "qualified or calculated to become useful citizens," might so remain, together with a few holding individual reservations under former treaties.   This provision was allowed by the commissioners, but was afterward struck out on the announcement by President Jackson of his determination "not to allow any preemptions or reservations, his desire being that the whole Cherokee people should remove together."

Provision was made also for the payment of debts due by the Indians out of any moneys coming to them under the treaty; for the reestablishment of the missions in the West; for pensions to Cherokee wounded in the service of the government in the war of 1812 and the Creek war; for permission to establish in the new country such military posts and roads for the use of the United States as should be deemed necessary; for satisfying Osage claims in the western territory and

---

[1] Royce, Cherokee Nation, op. cit. (Ross arrest), p. 281; Drake, Indians (Ross, Payne, Phœnix), p. 459, 1880; see also Everett speech of May 31, 1838, op. cit.

[2] Royce, op. cit., pp. 281, 282; see also Everett speech, 1838.

for bringing about a friendly understanding between the two tribes; and for the commutation of all annuities and other sums due from the United States into a permanent national fund, the interest to be placed at the disposal of the officers of the Cherokee Nation and by them disbursed, according to the will of their own people, for the care of schools and orphans, and for general national purposes.

The western territory assigned the Cherokee under this treaty was in two adjoining tracts, viz, (1) a tract of seven million acres, together with a "perpetual outlet west," already assigned to the western Cherokee under treaty of 1833, as will hereafter be noted,[1] being identical with the present area occupied by the Cherokee Nation in Indian Territory, together with the former "Cherokee strip," with the exception of a two-mile strip along the northern boundary, now included within the limits of Kansas; (2) a smaller additional tract of eight hundred thousand acres, running fifty miles north and south and twenty-five miles east and west, in what is now the southeastern corner of Kansas. For this second tract the Cherokee themselves were to pay the United States five hundred thousand dollars.

The treaty of 1833, assigning the first described tract to the western Cherokee, states that the United States agrees to "guaranty it to them forever, and that guarantee is hereby pledged." By the same treaty, "in addition to the seven millions of acres of land thus provided for and bounded, the United States further guaranty to the Cherokee nation a perpetual outlet west and a free and unmolested use of all the country lying west of the western boundary of said seven millions of acres, as far west as the sovereignty of the United States and their right of soil extend . . . and letters patent shall be issued by the United States as soon as practicable for the land hereby guaranteed." All this was reiterated by the present treaty, and made to include also the smaller (second) tract, in these words:

ART. 3. The United States also agree that the lands above ceded by the treaty of February 14, 1833, including the outlet, and those ceded by this treaty, shall all be included in one patent, executed to the Cherokee nation of Indians by the President of the United States, according to the provisions of the act of May 28, 1830. . . .

ART. 5. The United States hereby covenant and agree that the lands ceded to the Cherokee nation in the foregoing article shall in no future time, without their consent, be included within the territorial limits or jurisdiction of any state or territory. But they shall secure to the Cherokee nation the right of their national councils to make and carry into effect all such laws as they may deem necessary for the government and protection of the persons and property within their own country belonging to their people or such persons as have connected themselves with them: Provided always, that they shall not be inconsistent with the Constitution of the United States and such acts of Congress as have been or may be passed regulating trade and intercourse with the Indians; and also that they shall not be considered as extending to such citizens and army of the United States as may travel or reside in the Indian

---

[1] See Fort Gibson treaty, 1833, p. 142.

country by permission, according to the laws and regulations established by the government of the same. . . .

ART. 6. Perpetual peace and friendship shall exist between the citizens of the United States and the Cherokee Indians. The United States agree to protect the Cherokee nation from domestic strife and foreign enemies and against intestine wars between the several tribes. The Cherokees shall endeavor to preserve and maintain the peace of the country, and not make war upon their neighbors; they shall also be protected against interruption and intrusion from citizens of the United States who may attempt to settle in the country without their consent; and all such persons shall be removed from the same by order of the President of the United States. But this is not intended to prevent the residence among them of useful farmers, mechanics, and teachers for the instruction of the Indians according to treaty stipulations.

ARTICLE 7. The Cherokee nation having already made great progress in civilization, and deeming it important that every proper and laudable inducement should be offered to their people to improve their condition, as well as to guard and secure in the most effectual manner the rights guaranteed to them in this treaty, and with a view to illustrate the liberal and enlarged policy of the government of the United States toward the Indians in their removal beyond the territorial limits of the states, it is stipulated that they shall be entitled to a Delegate in the House of Representatives of the United States whenever Congress shall make provision for the same.

The instrument was signed by (Governor) William Carroll of Tennessee and (Reverend) J. F. Schermerhorn as commissioners—the former, however, having been unable to attend by reason of illness—and by twenty Cherokee, among whom the most prominent were Major Ridge and Elias Boudinot, former editor of the *Phœnix*. Neither John Ross nor any one of the officers of the Cherokee Nation was present or represented. After some changes by the Senate, it was ratified May 23, 1836.[1]

Upon the treaty of New Echota and the treaty previously made with the western Cherokee at Fort Gibson in 1833, the united Cherokee Nation based its claim to the present territory held by the tribe in Indian Territory and to the Cherokee outlet, and to national self-government, with protection from outside intrusion.

An official census taken in 1835 showed the whole number of Cherokee in Georgia, North Carolina, Alabama, and Tennessee to be 16,542, exclusive of 1,592 negro slaves and 201 whites intermarried with Cherokee. The Cherokee were distributed as follows: Georgia, 8,946; North Carolina, 3,644; Tennessee, 2,528; Alabama, 1,424.[2]

Despite the efforts of Ross and the national delegates, who presented protests with signatures representing nearly 16,000 Cherokee, the treaty

---

[1] See New Echota treaty, 1835, and Fort Gibson treaty, 1833, Indian Treaties, pp. 633–648 and 561–565, 1837; also, for full discussion of both treaties, Royce, Cherokee Nation, Fifth Ann. Rep. Bureau of Ethnology, pp. 249–298. For a summary of all the measures of pressure brought to bear upon the Cherokee up to the final removal see also Everett, speech in the House of Representatives, May 31, 1838; the chapters on "Expatriation of the Cherokees," Drake, Indians, 1880; and the chapter on "State Rights—Nullification," in Greeley, American Conflict, I, 1864. The Georgia side of the controversy is presented in E. J. Harden's Life of (Governor) George M. Troup, 1849.

[2] Royce, op. cit., p. 289. The Indian total is also given in the Report of the Indian Commissioner, p. 369, 1836.

had been ratified by a majority of one vote over the necessary number, and preliminary steps were at once taken to carry it into execution. Councils were held in opposition all over the Cherokee Nation, and resolutions denouncing the methods used and declaring the treaty absolutely null and void were drawn up and submitted to General Wool, in command of the troops in the Cherokee country, by whom they were forwarded to Washington. The President in reply expressed his surprise that an officer of the army should have received or transmitted a paper so disrespectful to the Executive, the Senate, and the American people; declared his settled determination that the treaty should be carried out without modification and with all consistent dispatch, and directed that after a copy of the letter had been delivered to Ross, no further communication, by mouth or writing, should be held with him concerning the treaty. It was further directed that no council should be permitted to assemble to discuss the treaty. Ross had already been informed that the President had ceased to recognize any existing government among the eastern Cherokee, and that any further effort by him to prevent the consummation of the treaty would be suppressed.[1]

Notwithstanding this suppression of opinion, the feeling of the Nation was soon made plain through other sources. Before the ratification of the treaty Major W. M. Davis had been appointed to enroll the Cherokee for removal and to appraise the value of their improvements. He soon learned the true condition of affairs, and, although holding his office by the good will of President Jackson, he addressed to the Secretary of War a strong letter upon the subject, from which the following extract is made:

I conceive that my duty to the President, to yourself, and to my country reluctantly compels me to make a statement of facts in relation to a meeting of a small number of Cherokees at New Echota last December, who were met by Mr. Schermerhorn and articles of a general treaty entered into between them for the whole Cherokee nation. . . . Sir, that paper, . . . called a treaty, is no treaty at all, because not sanctioned by the great body of the Cherokee and made without their participation or assent. I solemnly declare to you that upon its reference to the Cherokee people it would be instantly rejected by nine-tenths of them, and I believe by nineteen-twentieths of them. There were not present at the conclusion of the treaty more than one hundred Cherokee voters, and not more than three hundred, including women and children, although the weather was everything that could be desired. The Indians had long been notified of the meeting, and blankets were promised to all who would come and vote for the treaty. The most cunning and artful means were resorted to to conceal the paucity of numbers present at the treaty. No enumeration of them was made by Schermerhorn. The business of making the treaty was transacted with a committee appointed by the Indians present, so as not to expose their numbers. The power of attorney under which the committee acted was signed only by the president and secretary of the meeting, so as not to disclose their weakness. . . . Mr. Schermerhorn's apparent design was to conceal the real number present and to impose on the public and the government upon this point.

[1] Royce, Cherokee Nation, op. cit., pp. 283, 284; Report of Indian Commissioner, pp. 285, 286, 1836.

The delegation taken to Washington by Mr. Schermerhorn had no more authority to make a treaty than any other dozen Cherokee accidentally picked up for the purpose. I now warn you and the President that if this paper of Schermerhorn's called a treaty is sent to the Senate and ratified you will bring trouble upon the government and eventually destroy this [the Cherokee] Nation. The Cherokee are a peaceable, harmless people, but you may drive them to desperation, and this treaty can not be carried into effect except by the strong arm of force.[1]

General Wool, who had been placed in command of the troops concentrated in the Cherokee country to prevent opposition to the enforcement of the treaty, reported on February 18, 1837, that he had called them together and made them an address, but "it is, however, vain to talk to a people almost universally opposed to the treaty and who maintain that they never made such a treaty. So determined are they in their opposition that not one of all those who were present and voted at the council held but a day or two since, however poor or destitute, would receive either rations or clothing from the United States lest they might compromise themselves in regard to the treaty. These same people, as well as those in the mountains of North Carolina, during the summer past, preferred living upon the roots and sap of trees rather than receive provisions from the United States, and thousands, as I have been informed, had no other food for weeks. Many have said they will die before they will leave the country."[2]

Other letters from General Wool while engaged in the work of disarming and overawing the Cherokee show how very disagreeable that duty was to him and how strongly his sympathies were with the Indians, who were practically unanimous in repudiating the treaty. In one letter he says:

The whole scene since I have been in this country has been nothing but a heart-rending one, and such a one as I would be glad to get rid of as soon as circumstances will permit. Because I am firm and decided, do not believe I would be unjust. If I could, and I could not do them a greater kindness, I would remove every Indian to-morrow beyond the reach of the white men, who, like vultures, are watching, ready to pounce upon their prey and strip them of everything they have or expect from the government of the United States. Yes, sir, nineteen-twentieths, if not ninety-nine out of every hundred, will go penniless to the West.[3]

How it was to be brought about is explained in part by a letter addressed to the President by Major Ridge himself, the principal signer of the treaty:

We now come to address you on the subject of our griefs and afflictions from the acts of the white people. They have got our lands and now they are preparing to fleece us of the money accruing from the treaty. We found our plantations taken either in whole or in part by the Georgians—suits instituted against us for back rents for our own farms. These suits are commenced in the inferior courts, with the

---

[1] Quoted by Royce, Cherokee Nation, op. cit., pp. 284–285; quoted also, with some verbal differences, by Everett, speech in House of Representatives on May 31, 1838.

[2] Quoted in Royce, op. cit., p. 286.

[3] Letter of General Wool, September 10, 1836, in Everett, speech in House of Representatives, May 31, 1838.

evident design that, when we are ready to remove, to arrest our people, and on these vile claims to induce us to compromise for our own release, to travel with our families. Thus our funds will be filched from our people, and we shall be compelled to leave our country as beggars and in want.

Even the Georgia laws, which deny us our oaths, are thrown aside, and notwithstanding the cries of our people, and protestation of our innocence and peace, the lowest classes of the white people are flogging the Cherokees with cowhides, hickories, and clubs. We are not safe in our houses—our people are assailed by day and night by the rabble. Even justices of the peace and constables are concerned in this business. This barbarous treatment is not confined to men, but the women are stripped also and whipped without law or mercy. . . . Send regular troops to protect us from these lawless assaults, and to protect our people as they depart for the West. If it is not done, we shall carry off nothing but the scars of the lash on our backs, and our oppressors will get all the money. We talk plainly, as chiefs having property and life in danger, and we appeal to you for protection. . . .[1]

General Dunlap, in command of the Tennessee troops called out to prevent the alleged contemplated Cherokee uprising, having learned for himself the true situation, delivered an indignant address to his men in which he declared that he would never dishonor the Tennessee arms by aiding to carry into execution at the point of the bayonet a treaty made by a lean minority against the will and authority of the Cherokee people. He stated further that he had given the Cherokee all the protection in his power, the whites needing none.[2]

A confidential agent sent to report upon the situation wrote in September, 1837, that opposition to the treaty was unanimous and irreconcilable, the Cherokee declaring that it could not bind them because they did not make it, that it was the work of a few unauthorized individuals and that the Nation was not a party to it. They had retained the forms of their government, although no election had been held since 1830, having continued the officers then in charge until their government could again be reestablished regularly. Under this arrangement John Ross was principal chief, with influence unbounded and unquestioned. "The whole Nation of eighteen thousand persons is with him, the few—about three hundred—who made the treaty having left the country, with the exception of a small number of prominent individuals—as Ridge, Boudinot, and others—who remained to assist in carrying it into execution. It is evident, therefore, that Ross and his party are in fact the Cherokee Nation. . . . I believe that the mass of the Nation, particularly the mountain Indians, will stand or fall with Ross. . . ."[3]

So intense was public feeling on the subject of this treaty that it became to some extent a party question, the Democrats supporting President Jackson while the Whigs bitterly opposed him. Among

---

[1] Letter of June 30, 1836, to President Jackson, in Everett, speech in the House of Representatives, May 31, 1838.

[2] Quoted by Everett, ibid.; also by Royce, Cherokee Nation, op. cit., p. 286.

[3] Letter of J. M. Mason, jr., to Secretary of War, September 25, 1837, in Everett, speech in House of Representatives, May 31, 1838; also quoted in extract by Royce, op. cit., pp. 286-287.

notable leaders of the opposition were Henry Clay, Daniel Webster, Edward Everett, Wise of Virginia, and David Crockett.   The speeches in Congress upon the subject "were characterized by a depth and bitterness of feeling such as had never been exceeded even on the slavery question."[1]   It was considered not simply an Indian question, but an issue between state rights on the one hand and federal jurisdiction and the Constitution on the other.

In spite of threats of arrest and punishment, Ross still continued active effort in behalf of his people.   Again, in the spring of 1838, two months before the time fixed for the removal, he presented to Congress another protest and memorial, which, like the others, was tabled by the Senate.   Van Buren had now succeeded Jackson and was disposed to allow the Cherokee a longer time to prepare for emigration, but was met by the declaration from Governor Gilmer of Georgia that any delay would be a violation of the rights of that state and in opposition to the rights of *the owners of the soil*, and that if trouble came from any protection afforded by the government troops to the Cherokee a direct collision must ensue between the authorities of the state and general government.[2]

Up to the last moment the Cherokee still believed that the treaty would not be consummated, and with all the pressure brought to bear upon them only about 2,000 of the 17,000 in the eastern Nation had removed at the expiration of the time fixed for their departure, May 26, 1838.   As it was evident that the removal could only be accomplished by force, General Winfield Scott was now appointed to that duty with instructions to start the Indians for the West at the earliest possible moment.   For that purpose he was ordered to take command of the troops already in the Cherokee country, together with additional reenforcements of infantry, cavalry, and artillery, with authority to call upon the governors of the adjoining states for as many as 4,000 militia and volunteers.   The whole force employed numbered about 7,000 men—regulars, militia, and volunteers.[3]   The Indians had already been disarmed by General Wool.

On arriving in the Cherokee country Scott established headquarters at the capital, New Echota, whence, on May 10, he issued a proclamation to the Cherokee, warning them that the emigration must be commenced in haste and that before another moon had passed every Cherokee man, woman, and child must be in motion to join his brethren in the far West, according to the determination of the President, which he, the general, had come to enforce.   The proclamation concludes: " My troops already occupy many positions . . . and

---

[1] Royce, Cherokee Nation, op. cit. pp. 287, 289.

[2] Ibid., pp. 289, 290.

[3] Ibid., p. 291.   The statement of the total number of troops employed is from the speech of Everett in the House of Representatives, May 31, 1838, covering the whole question of the treaty.

thousands and thousands are approaching from every quarter to render resistance and escape alike hopeless. . . . Will you, then, by resistance compel us to resort to arms . . . or will you by flight seek to hide yourselves in mountains and forests and thus oblige us to hunt you down?"—reminding them that pursuit might result in conflict and bloodshed, ending in a general war.[1]

Even after this Ross endeavored, on behalf of his people, to secure some slight modification of the terms of the treaty, but without avail.[2]

THE REMOVAL—1838-39

The history of this Cherokee removal of 1838, as gleaned by the author from the lips of actors in the tragedy, may well exceed in weight of grief and pathos any other passage in American history. Even the much-sung exile of the Acadians falls far behind it in its sum of death and misery. Under Scott's orders the troops were disposed at various points throughout the Cherokee country, where stockade forts were erected for gathering in and holding the Indians preparatory to removal (43). From these, squads of troops were sent to search out with rifle and bayonet every small cabin hidden away in the coves or by the sides of mountain streams, to seize and bring in as prisoners all the occupants, however or wherever they might be found. Families at dinner were startled by the sudden gleam of bayonets in the doorway and rose up to be driven with blows and oaths along the weary miles of trail that led to the stockade. Men were seized in their fields or going along the road, women were taken from their wheels and children from their play. In many cases, on turning for one last look as they crossed the ridge, they saw their homes in flames, fired by the lawless rabble that followed on the heels of the soldiers to loot and pillage. So keen were these outlaws on the scent that in some instances they were driving off the cattle and other stock of the Indians almost before the soldiers had fairly started their owners in the other direction. Systematic hunts were made by the same men for Indian graves, to rob them of the silver pendants and other valuables deposited with the dead. A Georgia volunteer, afterward a colonel in the Confederate service, said: "I fought through the civil war and have seen men shot to pieces and slaughtered by thousands, but the Cherokee removal was the cruelest work I ever knew."

To prevent escape the soldiers had been ordered to approach and surround each house, so far as possible, so as to come upon the occupants without warning. One old patriarch, when thus surprised, calmly called his children and grandchildren around him, and, kneeling down, bid them pray with him in their own language, while the astonished soldiers looked on in silence. Then rising he led the way into

---

[1] Royce, Cherokee Nation, op. cit., p. 291,   [2] Ibid, p. 291.

exile. A woman, on finding the house surrounded, went to the door and called up the chickens to be fed for the last time, after which, taking her infant on her back and her two other children by the hand, she followed her husband with the soldiers.

All were not thus submissive. One old man named Tsalĭ, "Charley," was seized with his wife, his brother, his three sons and their families. Exasperated at the brutality accorded his wife, who, being unable to travel fast, was prodded with bayonets to hasten her steps, he urged the other men to join with him in a dash for liberty. As he spoke in Cherokee the soldiers, although they heard, understood nothing until each warrior suddenly sprang upon the one nearest and endeavored to wrench his gun from him. The attack was so sudden and unexpected that one soldier was killed and the rest fled, while the Indians escaped to the mountains. Hundreds of others, some of them from the various stockades, managed also to escape to the mountains from time to time, where those who did not die of starvation subsisted on roots and wild berries until the hunt was over. Finding it impracticable to secure these fugitives, General Scott finally tendered them a proposition, through (Colonel) W. H. Thomas, their most trusted friend, that if they would surrender Charley and his party for punishment, the rest would be allowed to remain until their case could be adjusted by the government. On hearing of the proposition, Charley voluntarily came in with his sons, offering himself as a sacrifice for his people. By command of General Scott, Charley, his brother, and the two elder sons were shot near the mouth of Tuckasegee, a detachment of Cherokee prisoners being compelled to do the shooting in order to impress upon the Indians the fact of their utter helplessness. From those fugitives thus permitted to remain originated the present eastern band of Cherokee.[1]

When nearly seventeen thousand Cherokee had thus been gathered into the various stockades the work of removal began. Early in June several parties, aggregating about five thousand persons, were brought down by the troops to the old agency, on Hiwassee, at the present Calhoun, Tennessee, and to Ross's landing (now Chattanooga), and Gunter's landing (now Guntersville, Alabama), lower down on the Tennessee, where they were put upon steamers and transported down the Tennessee and Ohio to the farther side of the Mississippi, when the journey was continued by land to Indian Territory. This removal,

---

[1] The notes on the Cherokee round-up and Removal are almost entirely from author's information as furnished by actors in the events, both Cherokee and white, among whom may be named the late Colonel W. H. Thomas; the late Colonel Z. A. Zile, of Atlanta, of the Georgia volunteers; the late James Bryson, of Dillsboro, North Carolina, also a volunteer; James D. Wafford, of the western Cherokee Nation, who commanded one of the emigrant detachments; and old Indians, both east and west, who remembered the Removal and had heard the story from their parents. Charley's story is a matter of common note among the East Cherokee, and was heard in full detail from Colonel Thomas and from Wasitûna ("Washington"), Charley's youngest son, who alone was spared by General Scott on account of his youth. The incident is also noted, with some slight inaccuracies, in Lanman, Letters from the Alleghany Mountains. See p. 157.

in the hottest part of the year, was attended with so great sickness and mortality that, by resolution of the Cherokee national council, Ross and the other chiefs submitted to General Scott a proposition that the Cherokee be allowed to remove themselves in the fall, after the sickly season had ended. This was granted on condition that all should have started by the 20th of October, excepting the sick and aged who might not be able to move so rapidly. Accordingly, officers were appointed by the Cherokee council to take charge of the emigration; the Indians being organized into detachments averaging one thousand each, with two leaders in charge of each detachment, and a sufficient number of wagons and horses for the purpose. In this way the remainder, enrolled at about 13,000 (including negro slaves), started on the long march overland late in the fall (44).

Those who thus emigrated under the management of their own officers assembled at Rattlesnake springs, about two miles south of Hiwassee river, near the present Charleston, Tennessee, where a final council was held, in which it was decided to continue their old constitution and laws in their new home. Then, in October, 1838, the long procession of exiles was set in motion. A very few went by the river route; the rest, nearly all of the 13,000, went overland. Crossing to the north side of the Hiwassee at a ferry above Gunstocker creek, they proceeded down along the river, the sick, the old people, and the smaller children, with the blankets, cooking pots, and other belongings in wagons, the rest on foot or on horses. The number of wagons was 645.

It was like the march of an army, regiment after regiment, the wagons in the center, the officers along the line and the horsemen on the flanks and at the rear. Tennessee river was crossed at Tuckers (?) ferry, a short distance above Jollys island, at the mouth of Hiwassee. Thence the route lay south of Pikeville, through McMinnville and on to Nashville, where the Cumberland was crossed. Then they went on to Hopkinsville, Kentucky, where the noted chief White-path, in charge of a detachment, sickened and died. His people buried him by the roadside, with a box over the grave and poles with streamers around it, that the others coming on behind might note the spot and remember him. Somewhere also along that march of death—for the exiles died by tens and twenties every day of the journey—the devoted wife of John Ross sank down, leaving him to go on with the bitter pain of bereavement added to heartbreak at the ruin of his nation. The Ohio was crossed at a ferry near the mouth of the Cumberland, and the army passed on through southern Illinois until the great Mississippi was reached opposite Cape Girardeau, Missouri. It was now the middle of winter, with the river running full of ice, so that several detachments were obliged to wait some time on the eastern bank for the channel to become clear. In talking with old men and women at Tahlequah the author found that the lapse of over half a century had not sufficed to wipe out the memory of the miseries of that halt beside the frozen river, with hundreds of sick and dying penned up in wagons or stretched upon the ground, with only a blanket overhead to keep out the January blast. The crossing was made at last in two divisions, at Cape Girardeau and at Green's ferry, a short distance below, whence the march was on through Missouri to Indian Territory, the later detachments making a northerly circuit by Springfield, because those who had gone before had killed off all the game along the direct route. At last their destination was reached. They had started in October, 1838, and it was now March, 1839, the journey having occupied nearly six months of the hardest part of the year.[1]

It is difficult to arrive at any accurate statement of the number of Cherokee who died as the result of the Removal. According to the official figures those who removed under the direction of Ross lost over 1,600 on the journey.[2] The proportionate mortality among those previously removed under military supervision was probably greater, as it was their suffering that led to the proposition of the Cherokee national officers to take charge of the emigration. Hundreds died in the stockades and the waiting camps, chiefly by reason of the rations furnished, which were of flour and other provisions to which they were unaccustomed and which they did not know how to prepare properly. Hundreds of others died soon after their arrival in Indian territory, from sickness and exposure on the journey. Altogether it is asserted, probably with reason, that over 4,000 Cherokee died as the direct result of the removal.

On their arrival in Indian Territory the emigrants at once set about building houses and planting crops, the government having agreed under the treaty to furnish them with rations for one year after arrival. They were welcomed by their kindred, the "Arkansas Cherokee"—hereafter to be known for distinction as the "Old Settlers"—who held the country under previous treaties in 1828 and 1833. These, however, being already regularly organized under a government and chiefs of their own, were by no means disposed to be swallowed by the governmental authority of the newcomers. Jealousies developed in which the minority or treaty party of the emigrants, headed by Ridge, took sides with the Old Settlers against the Ross or national party, which outnumbered both the others nearly three to one.

While these differences were at their height the Nation was thrown into a fever of excitement by the news that Major Ridge, his son John Ridge, and Elias Boudinot—all leaders of the treaty party—had been killed by adherents of the national party, immediately after the close

[1] Author's personal information, as before cited.

[2] As quoted in Royce, Cherokee Nation, Fifth Ann. Rep. Bureau of Ethnology, p. 292, 1888, the disbursing agent makes the number unaccounted for 1,428; the receiving agent, who took charge of them on their arrival, makes it 1,645.

of a general council, which had adjourned after nearly two weeks of debate without having been able to bring about harmonious action. Major Ridge was waylaid and shot close to the Arkansas line, his son was taken from bed and cut to pieces with hatchets, while Boudinot was treacherously killed at his home at Park Hill, Indian territory, all three being killed upon the same day, June 22, 1839.

The agent's report to the Secretary of War, two days later, says of the affair:

The murder of Boudinot was treacherous and cruel. He was assisting some workmen in building a new house. Three men called upon him and asked for medicine. He went off with them in the direction of Wooster's, the missionary, who keeps medicine, about three hundred yards from Boudinot's. When they got about half way two of the men seized Boudinot and the other stabbed him, after which the three cut him to pieces with their knives and tomahawks. This murder taking place within two miles of the residence of John Ross, his friends were apprehensive it might be charged to his connivance; and at this moment I am writing there are six hundred armed Cherokee around the dwelling of Ross, assembled for his protection. The murderers of the two Ridges and Boudinot are certainly of the late Cherokee emigrants, and, of course, adherents of Ross, but I can not yet believe that Ross has encouraged the outrage. He is a man of too much good sense to embroil his nation at this critical time; and besides, his character, since I have known him, which is now twenty-five years, has been pacific. . . . Boudinot's wife is a white woman, a native of New Jersey, as I understand. He has six children. The wife of John Ridge, jr., is a white woman, but from whence, or what family left, I am not informed. Boudinot was in moderate circumstances. The Ridges, both father and son, were rich. . . .[1]

While all the evidence shows that Ross was in no way a party to the affair, there can be no question that the men were killed in accordance with the law of the Nation—three times formulated, and still in existence—which made it treason, punishable with death, to cede away lands except by act of the general council of the Nation. It was for violating a similar law among the Creeks that the chief, McIntosh, lost his life in 1825, and a party led by Major Ridge himself had killed Doublehead years before on suspicion of accepting a bribe for his part in a treaty.

On hearing of the death of the Ridges and Boudinot several other signers of the repudiated treaty, among whom were John Bell, Archilla Smith, and James Starr, fled for safety to the protection of the garrison at Fort Gibson. Boudinot's brother, Stand Watie, vowed vengeance against Ross, who was urged to flee, but refused, declaring his entire innocence. His friends rallied to his support, stationing a guard around his house until the first excitement had subsided. About three weeks afterward the national council passed decrees declaring that the men killed and their principal confederates

---

[1] Agent Stokes to Secretary of War, June 24, 1839, in Report Indian Commissioner, p. 355, 1839; Royce, Cherokee Nation, Fifth Ann. Rep. Bureau of Ethnology, p. 293, 1888; Drake, Indians, pp. 459–460, 1880; author's personal information. The agent's report incorrectly makes the killings occur on three different days.

Colonel E. C. Boudinot, Jr.

By Charles M. Bell, Washington, D.C., date not recorded, ca. 1880's.

had rendered themselves outlaws by their own conduct, extending amnesty on certain stringent conditions to their confederates, and declaring the slayers guiltless of murder and fully restored to the confidence and favor of the community. This was followed in August by another council decree declaring the New Echota treaty void and reasserting the title of the Cherokee to their old country, and three weeks later another decree summoned the signers of the treaty to appear and answer for their conduct under penalty of outlawry. At this point the United States interfered by threatening to arrest Ross as accessory to the killing of the Ridges.[1] In the meantime the national party and the Old Settlers had been coming together, and a few of the latter who had sided with the Ridge faction and endeavored to perpetuate a division in the Nation were denounced in a council of the Old Settlers, which declared that "in identifying themselves with those individuals known as the Ridge party, who by their conduct had rendered themselves odious to the Cherokee people, they have acted in opposition to the known sentiments and feelings of that portion of this Nation known as Old Settlers, frequently and variously and publicly expressed." The offending chiefs were at the same time deposed from all authority. Among the names of over two hundred signers attached that of "George Guess" (Sequoya) comes second as vice-president.[2]

On July 12, 1839, a general convention of the eastern and western Cherokee, held at the Illinois camp ground, Indian territory, passed an act of union, by which the two were declared "one body politic, under the style and title of the Cherokee Nation." On behalf of the eastern Cherokee the instrument bears the signature of John Ross, principal chief, George Lowrey, president of the council, and Goingsnake (I'nadû-na'ï), speaker of the council, with thirteen others. For the western Cherokee it was signed by John Looney, acting principal chief, George Guess (Sequoya), president of the council, and fifteen others. On September 6, 1839, a convention composed chiefly of eastern Cherokee assembled at Tahlequah, Indian territory—then first officially adopted as the national capital—adopted a new constitution, which was accepted by a convention of the Old Settlers at Fort Gibson, Indian Territory, on June 26, 1840, an act which completed the reunion of the Nation.[3]

THE ARKANSAS BAND—1817–1838

Having followed the fortunes of the main body of the Nation to their final destination in the West, we now turn to review briefly

---

[1] Royce, Cherokee Nation, op. cit., pp. 294, 295.

[2] Council resolutions, August 23, 1839, in Report Indian Commissioner, p. 387, 1839; Royce, op. cit., p. 294.

[3] See "Act of Union" and "Constitution" in Constitution and Laws of the Cherokee Nation, 1875; General Arbuckle's letter to the Secretary of War, June 28, 1840, in Report of Indian Commissioner, p. 46, 1840; also Royce, op. cit., pp. 294, 295.

the history of the earlier emigrants, the Arkansas or Old Settler Cherokee.

The events leading to the first westward migration and the subsequent negotiations which resulted in the assignment of a territory in Arkansas to the western Cherokee, by the treaty of 1817, have been already noted. The great majority of those thus voluntarily removing belonged to the conservative hunter element, who desired to reestablish in the western wilderness the old Indian life from which, through the influence of schools and intelligent leadership, the body of the Cherokee was rapidly drifting away. As the lands upon which the emigrants had settled belonged to the Osage, whose claim had not yet been extinguished by the United States, the latter objected to their presence, and the Cherokee were compelled to fight to maintain their own position, so that for the first twenty years or more the history of the western band is a mere petty chronicle of Osage raids and Cherokee retaliations, emphasized from time to time by a massacre on a larger scale. By the treaty of 1817 the western Cherokee acquired title to a definite territory and official standing under Government protection and supervision, the lands assigned them having been acquired by treaty from the Osage. The great body of the Cherokee in the East were strongly opposed to any recognition of the western band, seeing in such action only the beginning of an effort looking toward the ultimate removal of the whole tribe. The Government lent support to the scheme, however, and a steady emigration set in until, in 1819, the emigrants were said to number several thousands. Unsuccessful endeavors were made to increase the number by inducing the Shawano and Delawares of Missouri and the Oneida of New York to join them.[1]

In 1818 Tollunteeskee (Ata'lûñti'skĭ), principal chief of the Arkansas Cherokee, while on a visit to old friends in the East, had become acquainted with one of the officers of the American Board of Commissioners for Foreign Missions, and had asked for the establishment of a mission among his people in the West. In response to the invitation the Reverend Cephas Washburn and his assistant, Reverend Alfred Finney, with their families, set out the next year from the old Nation, and after a long and exhausting journey reached the Arkansas country, where, in the spring of 1820, they established Dwight mission, adjoining the agency at the mouth of Illinois creek, on the northern bank of the Arkansas, in what is now Pope county, Arkansas. The name was bestowed in remembrance of Timothy Dwight, a Yale president and pioneer organizer of the American Board. Tollunteeskee having died in the meantime was succeeded as principal chief by his brother, John Jolly,[2] the friend and adopted father of Samuel Houston. Jolly

---

[1] See ante, pp. 105–106; Nuttall, who was on the ground, gives them only 1,500.

[2] Washburn, Cephas, Reminiscences of the Indians, pp. 81, 103; Richmond, 1869.

Dwight Mission Cherokee School. First Cherokee Mission west of the Mississippi. Photographer and date not recorded.

had removed from his old home at the mouth of Hiwassee, in Tennessee, in 1818.[1]

In the spring of 1819 Thomas Nuttall, the naturalist, ascended the Arkansas, and he gives an interesting account of the western Cherokee as he found them at the time.   In going up the stream, "both banks of the river, as we proceeded, were lined with the houses and farms of the Cherokee, and though their dress was a mixture of indigenous and European taste, yet in their houses, which are decently furnished, and in their farms, which were well fenced and stocked with cattle, we perceive a happy approach toward civilization.   Their numerous families, also, well fed and clothed, argue a propitious progress in their population.   Their superior industry either as hunters or farmers proves the value of property among them, and they are no longer strangers to avarice and the distinctions created by wealth.   Some of them are possessed of property to the amount of many thousands of dollars, have houses handsomely and conveniently furnished, and their tables spread with our dainties and luxuries."   He mentions an engagement some time before between them and the Osage, in which the Cherokee had killed nearly one hundred of the Osage, besides taking a number of prisoners.   He estimates them at about fifteen hundred, being about half the number estimated by the eastern Nation as having emigrated to the West, and only one-fourth of the official estimate. A few Delawares were living with them.[2]

The Osage troubles continued in spite of a treaty of peace between the two tribes made at a council held under the direction of Governor Clark at St. Louis, in October, 1818.[3]   Warriors from the eastern Cherokee were accustomed to make the long journey to the Arkansas to assist their western brethren, and returned with scalps and captives.[4]

In the summer of 1820 a second effort for peace was made by Governor Miller of Arkansas territory.   In reply to his talk the Osage complained that the Cherokee had failed to deliver their Osage captives as stipulated in the previous agreement at St. Louis.   This, it appears, was due in part to the fact that some of these captives had been carried to the eastern Cherokee, and a messenger was accordingly dispatched to secure and bring them back.   Another peace conference was held soon afterward at Fort Smith, but to very little purpose, as hostilities were soon resumed and continued until the United States actively interposed in the fall of 1822.[5]

In this year also Sequoya visited the western Cherokee to introduce

---

[1] Nuttall, Journal of Travels into the Arkansas Territory, etc., p. 129; Philadelphia, 1821.

[2] Ibid., pp. 123–136.   The battle mentioned seems to be the same noted somewhat differently by Washburn, Reminiscences, p. 120, 1869.

[3] Royce, Cherokee Nation, op. cit., p. 222.

[4] Washburn, op. cit., p. 160, and personal information from J. D. Wafford.

[5] Royce, op. cit., pp. 242, 243; Washburn, op. cit., pp. 112–122 et passim; see also sketches of Tahcheɔ and Tooantuh or Spring-frog, in McKenney and Hall, Indian Tribes, I and II, 1858.

to them the knowledge of his great invention, which was at once taken up through the influence of Takatoka (Degatâ'ga), a prominent chief who had hitherto opposed every effort of the missionaries to introduce their own schools and religion. In consequence perhaps of this encouragement Sequoya removed permanently to the West in the following year and became henceforth a member of the western Nation.[1]

Like other Indians, the western Cherokee held a firm belief in witchcraft, which led to frequent tragedies of punishment or retaliation. In 1824 a step forward was marked by the enactment of a law making it murder to kill any one for witchcraft, and an offense punishable with whipping to accuse another of witchcraft.[2] This law may have been the result of the silent working of missionary influence, supported by such enlightened men as Sequoya.

The treaty which assigned the Arkansas lands to the western Cherokee had stipulated that a census should be made of the eastern and western divisions of the Nation, separately, and an apportionment of the national annuity forthwith made on that basis. The western line of the Arkansas tract had also been left open, until according to another stipulation of the same treaty, the whole amount of land ceded through it to the United States by the Cherokee Nation in the East could be ascertained in order that an equal quantity might be included within the boundaries of the western tract.[3] These promises had not yet been fulfilled, partly because of the efforts of the Government to bring about a larger emigration or a further cession, partly on account of delay in the state surveys, and partly also because the Osage objected to the running of a line which should make the Cherokee their next door neighbors.[4] With their boundaries unadjusted and their annuities withheld, distress and dissatisfaction overcame the western Cherokee, many of whom, feeling themselves absolved from territorial restrictions, spread over the country on the southern side of Arkansas river,[5] while others, under the lead of a chief named The Bowl (Diwa'lĭ), crossed Red river into Texas—then a portion of Mexico—in a vain attempt to escape American jurisdiction.[6]

A provisional western boundary having been run, which proved unsatisfactory both to the western Cherokee and to the people of Arkansas, an effort was made to settle the difficulty by arranging an exchange of the Arkansas tract for a new country west of the Arkansas line. So strongly opposed, however, were the western Cherokee to this project that their council, in 1825, passed a law, as the eastern Cherokee and the Creeks had already done, fixing the death penalty

---

[1] Washburn, Reminiscences, p. 178, 1869; see also ante p. 206.
[2] Ibid, p. 138.
[3] See Treaty of 1817, Indian Treaties, 1837.
[4] Royce, Cherokee Nation, Fifth Report Bureau of Ethnology, pp. 243, 244, 1888.
[5] Ibid, p. 243.
[6] Author's personal information; see p. 143.

for anyone of the tribe who should undertake to cede or exchange land belonging to the Nation.[1]

After a long series of negotiations such pressure was brought to bear upon a delegation which visited Washington in 1828 that consent was at last obtained to an exchange of the Arkansas tract for another piece of seven million acres lying farther west, together with "a perpetual outlet west" of the tract thus assigned, as far west as the sovereignty of the United States might extend.[2] The boundaries given for this seven-million-acre tract and the adjoining western outlet were modified by treaty at Fort Gibson five years later so as to be practically equivalent to the present territory of the Cherokee Nation in Indian Territory, with the Cherokee strip recently ceded.

The preamble of the Washington treaty of May 6, 1828, recites that "Whereas, it being the anxious desire of the Government of the United States to secure to the Cherokee nation of Indians, as well those now living within the limits of the territory of Arkansas as those of their friends and brothers who reside in states east of the Mississippi, and who may wish to join their brothers of the West, *a permanent home*, and which shall, under the most solemn guarantee of the United States, be and remain theirs forever—a home that shall never, in all future time, be embarrassed by having extended around it the lines or placed over it the jurisdiction of a territory or state, nor be pressed upon by the extension in any way of any of the limits of any existing territory or state; and whereas the present location of the Cherokees in Arkansas being unfavorable to their present repose, and tending, as the past demonstrates, to their future degradation and misery, and the Cherokees being anxious to avoid such consequences," etc.—therefore, they cede everything confirmed to them in 1817.

Article 2 defines the boundaries of the new tract and the western outlet to be given in exchange, lying immediately west of the present Arkansas line, while the next article provides for the removal of all whites and others residing within the said boundaries, "so that no obstacles arising out of the presence of a white population, or any population of any other sort, shall exist to annoy the Cherokees, and also to keep all such from the west of said line in future."

Other articles provide for payment for improvements left behind; for a cash sum of $50,000 to pay for trouble and expense of removal and to compensate for the inferior quality of the lands in the new tract; for $6,000 to pay for recovering stock which may stray away "in quest of the pastures from which they may be driven;" $8,760 for spoliations committed by Osage and whites; $500 to George Guess (Sequoya)—who was himself one of the signers—in consideration of the beneficial results to his tribe from the alphabet invented by him; $20,000 in ten annual payments for education; $1,000 for a printing

---

[1] Royce, Cherokee Nation, op. cit., p. 245.　　[2] Ibid., pp. 247, 248.

press and type to aid in the enlightenment of the people "in their own and our language"; a personal indemnity for false imprisonment; and for the removal and reestablishment of the Dwight mission.

In article 6 "it is moreover agreed by the United States, whenever the Cherokee may desire it, to give them a set of plain laws, suited to their condition; also, when they wish to lay off their lands and own them individually, a surveyor shall be sent to make the surveys at the cost of the United States." This article was annulled in 1833 by request of the Cherokee.

Article 9 provides for the Fort Gibson military reservation within the new tract, while article 7 binds the Cherokee to surrender and remove from all their lands in Arkansas within fourteen months.

Article 8 shows that all this was intended to be only preliminary to the removal of the whole Cherokee Nation from the east of the Mississippi, a consummation toward which the Jackson administration and the state of Georgia immediately began to bend every effort. It is as follows:

ARTICLE 8. The Cherokee nation, west of the Mississippi, having by this agreement freed themselves from the harassing and ruinous effects consequent upon a location amidst a white population, and secured to themselves and their posterity, under the solemn sanction of the guarantee of the United States as contained in this agreement, a large extent of unembarrassed country; and that their brothers yet remaining in the states may be induced to join them and enjoy the repose and blessings of such a state in the future, it is further agreed on the part of the United States that to each head of a Cherokee family now residing within the chartered limits of Georgia, or of either of the states east of the Mississippi, who may desire to remove west, shall be given, on enrolling himself for emigration, a good rifle, a blanket, a kettle, and five pounds of tobacco; (and to each member of his family one blanket), also a just compensation for the property he may abandon, to be assessed by persons to be appointed by the President of the United States. The cost of the emigration of all such shall also be borne by the United States, and good and suitable ways opened and procured for their comfort, accommodation, and support by the way, and provisions for twelve months after their arrival at the agency; and to each person, or head of a family, if he take along with him four persons, shall be paid immediately on his arriving at the agency and reporting himself and his family or followers as emigrants or permanent settlers, in addition to the above, *provided he and they shall have emigrated from within the chartered limits of the State of Georgia*, the sum of fifty dollars, and this sum in proportion to any greater or less number that may accompany him from within the aforesaid chartered limits of the State of Georgia.

A Senate amendment, defining the limits of the western outlet, was afterward found to be impracticable in its restrictions and was canceled by the treaty made at Fort Gibson in 1833.[1]

The Washington treaty was signed by several delegates, including Sequoya, four of them signing in Cherokee characters. As the laws

[1] Treaty of Washington, May 6, 1828, Indian Treaties, pp. 423–428, 1837; treaty of Fort Gibson, 1833, ibid., pp. 561–565; see also for synopsis, Royce, Cherokee Nation, Fifth Ann. Rep. Bureau of Ethnology, pp. 229, 230, 1888.

of the western Cherokee made it a capital offense to negotiate any sale or exchange of land excepting by authority of council, and the delegates had acted without such authority, they were so doubtful as to what might happen on their return that the Secretary of War sent with them a letter of explanation assuring the Cherokee that their representatives had acted with integrity and earnest zeal for their people and had done the best that could be done with regard to the treaty. Notwithstanding this, they found the whole tribe so strongly opposed to the treaty that their own lives and property were unsafe. The national council pronounced them guilty of fraud and deception and declared the treaty null and void, as having been made without authority, and asked permission to send on a delegation authorized to arrange all differences.[1] In the meantime, however, the treaty had been ratified within three weeks of its conclusion, and thus, hardly ten years after they had cleared their fields on the Arkansas, the western Cherokee were forced to abandon their cabins and plantations and move once more into the wilderness.

A considerable number, refusing to submit to the treaty or to trust longer to guarantees and promises, crossed Red river into Texas and joined the Cherokee colony already located there by The Bowl, under Mexican jurisdiction. Among those thus removing was the noted chief Tahchee (Tătsĭ') or "Dutch," who had been one of the earliest emigrants to the Arkansas country. After several years in Texas, during which he led war parties against the wilder tribes, he recrossed Red river and soon made himself so conspicuous in raids upon the Osage that a reward of five hundred dollars was offered by General Arbuckle for his capture. To show his defiance of the proclamation, he deliberately journeyed to Fort Gibson, attacked a party of Osage at a trading post near by, and scalped one of them within hearing of the drums of the fort. With rifle in one hand and the bleeding scalp in the other, he leaped a precipice and made his escape, although a bullet grazed his cheek. On promise of amnesty and the withdrawal of the reward, he afterward returned and settled, with his followers, on the Canadian, southwest of Fort Gibson, establishing a reputation among army officers as a valuable scout and guide.[2]

By treaties made in 1826 and 1827 the Creeks had ceded all their remaining lands in Georgia and agreed to remove to Indian Territory. Some of these emigrants had settled along the northern bank of the Arkansas and on Verdigris river, on lands later found to be within the limits of the territory assigned to the western Cherokee by the treaty of 1828. This led to jealousies and collisions between

---

[1] Royce, Cherokee Nation, Fifth Ann. Rep. Bureau of Ethnology, p. 248, 1888.

[2] For a sketch of Tahchee, with portraits, see McKenney and Hall, I, pp. 251–260, 1858; Catlin, North American Indians, II, pp. 121, 122, 1844. Washburn also mentions the emigration to Texas consequent upon the treaty of 1828 (Reminiscences, p. 217, 1869).

the two tribes, and in order to settle the difficulty the United States convened a joint council of Creeks and Cherokee at Fort Gibson, with the result that separate treaties were concluded with each on February 14, 1833, defining their respective bounds to the satisfaction of all concerned. By this arrangement the upper Verdigris was confirmed to the Cherokee, and the Creeks who had settled along that portion of the stream agreed to remove to Creek territory immediately adjoining on the south.[1]

By the treaty made on this occasion with the Cherokee the boundaries of the tract of seven million acres granted by the treaty of 1828 are defined so as to correspond with the present boundaries of the Cherokee country in Indian territory, together with a strip two miles wide along the northern border, which was afterward annexed to the state of Kansas by the treaty of 1866. A tract in the northeastern corner, between Neosho or Grand river and the Missouri line, was set apart for the use of the Seneca and several other remnants of tribes removed from their original territories. The western outlet established by the treaty of 1828 was reestablished as a western extension from the seven-million-acre tract thus bounded, being what was afterward known as the Cherokee strip or outlet plus the two-mile strip extending westward along the south line of Kansas.

After describing the boundaries of the main residence tract, the first article continues:

In addition to the seven millions of acres of land thus provided for and bounded the United States further guarantee to the Cherokee nation a perpetual outlet west and a free and unmolested use of all the country lying west of the western boundary of said seven millions of acres, as far west as the sovereignty of the United States and their right of soil extend—provided, however, that if the saline or salt plain on the great western prairie shall fall within said limits prescribed for said outlet the right is reserved to the United States to permit other tribes of red men to get salt on said plain in common with the Cherokees—and letters patent shall be issued by the United States as soon as practicable for the lands hereby guaranteed.

The third article cancels, at the particular request of the Cherokee, that article of the treaty of 1828 by which the government was to give to the Cherokee a set of laws and a surveyor to survey lands for individuals, when so desired by the Cherokee.[2]

Their differences with the Creeks having been thus adjusted, the Arkansas Cherokee proceeded to occupy the territory guaranteed to them, where they were joined a few years later by their expatriated kinsmen from the east. By tacit agreement some of the Creeks who had settled within the Cherokee bounds were permitted to remain. Among these were several families of Uchee—an incorporated tribe

---

[1] Treaties at Fort Gibson, February 14, 1833, with Creeks and Cherokee, in Indian Treaties, pp. 561–569, 1837.

[2] Treaty of 1833, Indian Treaties, pp. 561–565, 1837; Royce, Cherokee Nation, Fifth Ann. Rep. Bureau of Ethnology, pp. 249–253, 1888; see also Treaty of New Echota, 1835, ante, pp. 123–125.

Tooantuh or Spring Frog, a Cherokee Chief

From a lithograph published by McKenney and Hall in The Indian Tribes of North America, *1836–44, and subsequent editions.*

of the Creek confederacy—who had fixed their residence at the spot
where the town of Tahlequah was afterward established. They
remained here until swept off by smallpox some sixty years ago. [1]

THE TEXAS BAND—1817–1900

As already stated, a band of western Cherokee under Chief Bowl,
dissatisfied with the delay in fulfilling the terms of the treaty of 1817,
had left Arkansas and crossed Red river into Texas, then under
Mexican jurisdiction, where they were joined a few years later by
Tahchee and others of the western band who were opposed to the
treaty of 1828. Here they united with other refugee Indians from
the United States, forming together a loose confederacy known afterward as "the Cherokee and their associated bands," consisting of
Cherokee, Shawano, Delaware, Kickapoo, Quapaw, Choctaw, Biloxi,
"Iawanie" (Heyowani, Yowani), "Unataqua" (Nada'ko or Ana-
darko, another Caddo subtribe), "Tahookatookie" (?), Alabama (a
Creek subtribe), and "Cooshatta" (Koasa'ti, another Creek subtribe).
The Cherokee being the largest and most important band, their chief,
Bowl—known to the whites as Colonel Bowles—was regarded as the
chief and principal man of them all.

The refugees settled chiefly along Angelina, Neches, and Trinity
rivers in eastern Texas, where Bowl endeavored to obtain a grant of
land for their use from the Mexican government. According to the
Texan historians they were tacitly permitted to occupy the country
and hopes were held out that a grant would be issued, but the papers
had not been perfected when the Texas revolution began.[2] According
to the Cherokee statement the grant was actually issued and the Spanish document inclosed in a tin box was on the person of Bowl when he
was killed.[3] On complaint of some of the American colonists in Texas
President Jackson issued a proclamation forbidding any Indians to
cross the Sabine river from the United States.[4]

In 1826–27 a dissatisfied American colony in eastern Texas, under the
leadership of Hayden Edwards, organized what was known as the
"Fredonia rebellion" against the Mexican government. To secure
the alliance of the Cherokee and their confederates the Americans
entered into a treaty by which the Indians were guaranteed the lands

---

[1] Author's personal information. In 1891 the author opened two Uchee graves on the grounds of
Cornelius Boudinot, at Tahlequah, finding with one body a number of French, Spanish, and American silver coins wrapped in cloth and deposited in two packages on each side of the head. They are
now in the National Museum at Washington.

[2] Bonnell, Topographic Description of Texas, p. 141; Austin, 1840; Thrall, History of Texas, p. 58;
New York, 1876.

[3] Author's personal information from J. D. Wafford and other old Cherokee residents and from recent
Cherokee delegates. Bancroft agrees with Bonnell and Thrall that no grant was formally issued,
but states that the Cherokee chief established his people in Texas "confiding in promises made to
him, and a conditional agreement in 1822" with the Spanish governor (History of the North Mexican
States and Texas, II, p. 103, 1889). It is probable that the paper carried by Bowl was the later
Houston treaty. See next page.   [4] Thrall, op. cit.,s, p. 58.

occupied by them, but without specification as to boundaries. The Fredonia movement soon collapsed and nothing tangible seems to have come of the negotiations.[1]

In the fall of 1835 the Texan revolution began, resulting in the secession of Texas from Mexico and her establishment as an independent republic until annexed later to the United States. General Samuel Houston, a leading member of the revolutionary body, was an old friend of the Cherokee, and set forth so strongly the claims of them and their confederates that an act was passed by the convention pledging to these tribes all the lands which they had held under the Mexican government. In accordance with this act General Houston and John Forbes were appointed to hold a treaty with the Cherokee and their associated bands. They met the chiefs, including Bowl and Big-mush (Gatûñ'wa'lǐ, "Hard-mush"), of the Cherokee, at Bowl's village on February 23, 1836, and concluded a formal treaty by which the Cherokee and their allies received a fee simple title to all the land lying " west of the San Antonio road and beginning on the west at a point where the said road crosses the river Angelina, and running up said river until it reaches the mouth of the first large creek below the great Shawnee village, emptying into the said river from the northeast, thence running with said creek to its main source and from thence a due north line to the Sabine and with said river west. Then starting where the San Antonio road crosses the Angelina and with said road to where it crosses the Neches and thence running up the east side of said river in a northwest direction." The historian remarks that the description is somewhat vague, but is a literal transcription from the treaty.[2] The territory thus assigned was about equivalent to the present Cherokee county, Texas.

The treaty provoked such general dissatisfaction among the Texans that it was not presented to the convention for ratification. General Houston became President of Texas in November, 1836, but notwithstanding all his efforts in behalf of the Cherokee, the treaty was rejected by the Texas senate in secret session on December 16, 1837.[3] Texas having in the meantime achieved victorious independence was now in position to repudiate her engagements with the Indians, which she did, not only with the Cherokee, but with the Comanche and other wild tribes, which had been induced to remain neutral during the struggle on assurance of being secured in possession of their lands.

In the meantime President Houston was unremitting in his effort to secure the ratification of the Cherokee treaty, but without success. On the other hand the Cherokee were accused of various depredations, and it was asserted that they had entered into an agreement with

---

[1] Thrall, Texas, p. 46, 1879.   [3] Ibid., p. 143, 1840.
[2] Bonnell, Texas, pp. 142, 143, 1840.

Mexico by which they were to be secured in the territory in question on condition of assisting to drive out the Americans.[1] The charge came rather late in the day, and it was evident that President Houston put no faith in it, as he still continued his efforts in behalf of the Cherokee, even so far as to order the boundary line to be run, according to the terms of the treaty (45).[2]

In December, 1838, Houston was succeeded as President by Mirabeau B. Lamar, who at once announced his intention to expel every Indian tribe from Texas, declaring in his inaugural message that "the sword should mark the boundaries of the republic." At this time the Indians in eastern Texas, including the Cherokee and their twelve confederated bands and some others, were estimated at 1,800 warriors, or perhaps 8,000 persons.[3]

A small force of troops sent to take possession of the salt springs in the Indian country at the head of the Neches was notified by Bowl that such action would be resisted. The Indians were then informed that they must prepare to leave the country in the fall, but that they would be paid for the improvements abandoned. In the meantime the neighboring Mexicans made an effort to free themselves from Texan rule and sent overtures to the Indians to make common cause with them. This being discovered, the crisis was precipitated, and a commission consisting of General Albert Sidney Johnston (secretary of war of the republic), Vice-President Burnet, and some other officials, backed up by several regiments of troops, was sent to the Cherokee village on Angelina river to demand of the Indians that they remove at once across the border. The Indians refused and were attacked and defeated on July 15, 1839, by the Texan troops under command of General Douglas. They were pursued and a second engagement took place the next morning, resulting in the death of Bowl himself and his assistant chief Gatûñ'wa'lĭ, "Hard-mush," and the dispersion of the Indian forces, with a loss in the two engagements of about 55 killed and 80 wounded, the Texan loss being comparatively trifling. The first fight took place at a hill close to the main Cherokee village on the Angelina, where the Indians made a stand and defended their position well for some time. The second occurred at a ravine near Neches river, where they were intercepted in their retreat. Says Thrall, "After this fight the Indians abandoned Texas, leaving their fine lands in possession of the whites."[4]

By these two defeats the forces of the Cherokee and their confederates were completely broken up. A part of the Cherokee recrossed Red river and rejoined their kinsmen in Indian territory, bringing with them the blood-stained canister containing the patent for their

[1] Bonnell, Texas, pp. 143, 144.
[2] Ibid., pp. 144, 146.
[3] Thrall, Texas, pp. 116–168, 1876.
[4] Bonnell, op. cit., pp. 146–150; Thrall, op. cit., pp. 118–120.

Texas land, which Bowl had carried about with him since the treaty with Houston and which he had upon his person when shot. It is still kept in the Nation.[1] Others, with the Kickapoo, Delawares, and Caddo, scattered in small bands along the western Texas frontier, where they were occasionally heard from afterward. On Christmas day of the same year a fight occurred on Cherokee creek, San Saba county, in which several Indians were killed and a number of women and children captured, including the wife and family of the dead chief Bowl.[2] Those of the Cherokee who did not return to Indian territory gradually drifted down into Mexico, where some hundreds of them are now permanently and prosperously domiciled far south in the neighborhood of Guadalajara and Lake Chapala, communication being still kept up through occasional visits from their kinsmen in the territory.[3]

THE CHEROKEE NATION IN THE WEST—1840–1900

With the final removal of the Cherokee from their native country and their reunion and reorganization under new conditions in Indian Territory in 1840 their aboriginal period properly comes to a close and the rest may be dismissed in a few paragraphs as of concern rather to the local historian than to the ethnologist. Having traced for three full centuries their gradual evolution from a savage tribe to a civilized Christian nation, with a national constitution and national press printed in their own national alphabet, we can afford to leave the rest to others, the principal materials being readily accessible in the Cherokee national archives at Tahlequah, in the files of the *Cherokee Advocate* and other newspapers published in the Nation, and in the annual reports and other documents of the Indian office.

For many years the hunter and warrior had been giving place to the farmer and mechanic, and the forced expatriation made the change complete and final. Torn from their native streams and mountains, their council fires extinguished and their townhouses burned behind them, and transported bodily to a far distant country where everything was new and strange, they were obliged perforce to forego the old life and adjust themselves to changed surroundings. The ballplay was neglected and the green-corn dance proscribed, while the heroic tradition of former days became a fading memory or a tale to amuse a child. Instead of ceremonials and peace councils we hear now of railroad deals and contracts with cattle syndicates, and instead of the old warrior chiefs who had made the Cherokee name a terror—Oconostota, Hanging-maw, Doublehead, and Pathkiller—we find the destinies of the

---

[1] Author's personal information from J. D. Wafford and other old western Cherokee, and recent Cherokee delegates; by some this is said to have been a Mexican patent, but it is probably the one given by Texas. See ante, p. 143.

[2] Thrall, Texas, p. 120, 1876.

[3] Author's personal information from Mexican and Cherokee sources.

Group listening to the inaugural address of their chief, W. C. Rogers. Large brick building in the photograph is the Cherokee capitol. Photographer not recorded, 1903.

nation guided henceforth by shrewd mixed-blood politicians, bearing white men's names and speaking the white man's language, and frequently with hardly enough Indian blood to show itself in the features.

The change was not instantaneous, nor is it even yet complete, for although the tendency is constantly away from the old things, and although frequent intermarriages are rapidly bleaching out the brown of the Indian skin, there are still several thousand full-blood Cherokee—enough to constitute a large tribe if set off by themselves—who speak only their native language and in secret bow down to the nature-gods of their fathers. Here, as in other lands, the conservative elément has taken refuge in the mountain districts, while the mixed-bloods and the adopted whites are chiefly on the richer low grounds and in the railroad towns.

On the reorganization of the united Nation the council ground at Tahlequah was designated as the seat of government, and the present town was soon afterward laid out upon the spot, taking its name from the old Cherokee town of Tălikwă', or Tellico, in Tennessee. The missions were reestablished, the *Advocate* was revived, and the work of civilization was again taken up, though under great difficulties, as continued removals and persecutions, with the awful suffering and mortality of the last great emigration, had impoverished and more than decimated the Nation and worn out the courage even of the bravest. The bitterness engendered by the New Echota treaty led to a series of murders and assassinations and other acts of outlawry, amounting almost to civil war between the Ross and Ridge factions, until the Government was at last obliged to interfere. The Old Settlers also had their grievances and complaints against the newcomers, so that the history of the Cherokee Nation for the next twenty years is largely a chronicle of factional quarrels, through which civilization and every good work actually retrograded behind the condition of a generation earlier.

Sequoya, who had occupied a prominent position in the affairs of the Old Settlers and assisted much in the reorganization of the Nation, had become seized with a desire to make linguistic investigations among the remote tribes, very probably with a view of devising a universal Indian alphabet. His mind dwelt also on the old tradition of a lost band of Cherokee living somewhere toward the western mountains. In 1841 and 1842, with a few Cherokee companions and with his provisions and papers loaded in an ox cart, he made several journeys into the West, received everywhere with kindness by even the wildest tribes. Disappointed in his philologic results, he started out in 1843 in quest of the lost Cherokee, who were believed to be somewhere in northern Mexico, but, being now an old man and worn out by hardship, he sank under the effort and died—alone and unattended, it is said—near the village of San Fernando, Mexico, in August of that year. Rumors having come of his helpless condition, a party had been sent out from the Nation to bring him back, but arrived too late to find him alive. A pension of three hundred dollars, previously voted to him by the Nation, was continued to his widow—the only literary pension in the United States. Besides a wife he left two sons and a daughter.[1] Sequoyah district of the Cherokee Nation was named in his honor, and the great trees of California (*Sequoia gigantea*) also preserve his memory.

In 1846 a treaty was concluded at Washington by which the conflicting claims of the Old Settlers and later emigrants were adjusted, reimbursement was promised for sums unjustly deducted from the five-million-dollar payment guaranteed under the treaty of 1835, and a general amnesty was proclaimed for all past offenses within the Nation.[2] Final settlement of the treaty claims has not yet been made, and the matter is still a subject of litigation, including all the treaties and agreements up to the present date.

In 1859 the devoted missionary Samuel Worcester, author of numerous translations and first organizer of the *Advocate*, died at Park Hill mission, in the Cherokee Nation, after thirty-five years spent in the service of the Cherokee, having suffered chains, imprisonment, and exile for their sake.[3]

The breaking out of the civil war in 1861 found the Cherokee divided in sentiment. Being slave owners, like the other Indians removed from the southern states, and surrounded by southern influences, the agents in charge being themselves southern sympathizers, a considerable party in each of the tribes was disposed to take active part with the Confederacy. The old Ridge party, headed by Stand Watie and supported by the secret secession organization known as the Knights of the Golden Circle, declared for the Confederacy. The National party, headed by John Ross and supported by the patriotic organization known as the Kitoowah society—whose members were afterward known as Pin Indians—declared for strict neutrality. At last, however, the pressure became too strong to be resisted, and on October 7, 1861, a treaty was concluded at Tahlequah, with General Albert Pike, commissioner for the Confederate states, by which the Cherokee Nation cast its lot with the Confederacy, as the Creeks, Choctaw, Chickasaw, Seminole, Osage, Comanche, and several smaller tribes had already done.[4]

---

[1] W. A. Phillips, Sequoyah, in Harper's Magazine, September, 1870; Foster, Sequoyah, 1885; Royce, Cherokee Nation, Fifth Ann. Rep. Bureau of Ethnology, p. 302, 1888; letter of William P. Ross, former editor of Cherokee Advocate, March 11, 1889, in archives of Bureau of American Ethnology; Cherokee Advocate, October 19, 1844, November 2, 1844, and March 6, 1845; author's personal information. San Fernando seems to have been a small village in Chihuahua, but is not shown on the maps.

[2] For full discussion see Royce, op. cit., pp. 298–312.

[3] Pilling, Bibliography of the Iroquoian Languages (bulletin of the Bureau of Ethnology), p. 174, 1888.

[4] See treaties with Cherokee, October 7, 1861, and with other tribes, in Confederate States Statutes at Large, 1864; Royce, op. cit., pp. 324–328; Greeley, American Conflict, II, pp. 30–34, 1866; Reports of Indian Commissioner for 1860 to 1862.

Two Cherokee regiments were raised for the Confederate service, under command of Stand Watie and Colonel Drew, respectively, the former being commissioned as brigadier-general. They participated in several engagements, chief among them being the battle of Pea Ridge, Arkansas, on March 7, 1862.[1] In the following summer the Union forces entered the Cherokee country and sent a proposition to Ross, urging him to repudiate the treaty with the Confederate states, but the offer was indignantly declined. Shortly afterward, however, the men of Drew's regiment, finding themselves unpaid and generally neglected by their allies, went over almost in a body to the Union side, thus compelling Ross to make an arrangement with the Union commander, Colonel Weir. Leaving the Cherokee country, Ross retired to Philadelphia, from which he did not return until the close of the war.[2] In the meantime Indian Territory was ravaged alternately by contending factions and armed bodies, and thousands of loyal fugitives were obliged to take refuge in Kansas, where they were cared for by the government. Among these, at the close of 1862, were two thousand Cherokee. In the following spring they were sent back to their homes under armed escort to give them an opportunity to put in a crop, seeds and tools being furnished for the purpose, but had hardly begun work when they were forced to retire by the approach of Stand Watie and his regiment of Confederate Cherokee, estimated at seven hundred men. Stand Watie and his men, with the Confederate Creeks and others, scoured the country at will, destroying or carrying off everything belonging to the loyal Cherokee, who had now, to the number of nearly seven thousand, taken refuge at Fort Gibson. Refusing to take sides against a government which was still unable to protect them, they were forced to see all the prosperous accumulations of twenty years of industry swept off in this guerrilla warfare. In stock alone their losses were estimated at more than 300,000 head.[3]

"The events of the war brought to them more of desolation and ruin than perhaps to any other community. Raided and sacked alternately, not only by the Confederate and Union forces, but by the vindictive ferocity and hate of their own factional divisions, their country became a blackened and desolate waste. Driven from comfortable homes, exposed to want, misery, and the elements, they perished like sheep in a snow storm. Their houses, fences, and other improvements were burned, their orchards destroyed, their flocks and herds slaughtered or driven off, their schools broken up, their schoolhouses given to the flames, and their churches and public buildings subjected to a similar fate; and that entire portion of their country which

---

[1] In this battle the Confederates were assisted by from 4,000 to 5,000 Indians of the southern tribes, including the Cherokee, under command of General Albert Pike.
[2] Royce, Cherokee Nation, Fifth Ann. Rep. Bureau of Ethnology, pp. 329, 330, 1888.
[3] Ibid, p. 331.

Major John Drew

During the Civil War, Drew was in command of a regiment of Cherokees on the side of the Confederates. This is a greatly retouched version of a photograph copied from an old tin type. Photographer and date of original tin type not recorded.

had been occupied by their settlements was distinguishable from the virgin prairie only by the scorched and blackened chimneys and the plowed but now neglected fields."[1]

After five years of desolation the Cherokee emerged from the war with their numbers reduced from 21,000 to 14,000,[2] and their whole country in ashes.   On July 19, 1866, by a treaty concluded at Tahlequah, the nation was received back into the protection of the United States, a general amnesty was proclaimed, and all confiscations on account of the war prohibited; slavery was abolished without compensation to former owners, and all negroes residing within the Nation were admitted to full Cherokee citizenship.   By articles 15 and 16 permission was given the United States to settle friendly Indians within the Cherokee home country or the Cherokee strip by consent and purchase from the Nation.   By article 17 the Cherokee sold the 800,000-acre tract in Kansas secured by the treaty of 1835, together with a two-mile strip running along the southern border of Kansas, and thereafter to be included within the limits of that state, thus leaving the Cherokee country as it was before the recent cession of the Cherokee strip.   Payment was promised for spoliations by United States troops during the war; and $3,000 were to be paid out of the Cherokee funds to the Reverend Evan Jones, then disabled and in poverty, as a reward for forty years of faithful missionary labors. By article 26 "the United States guarantee to the Cherokees the quiet and peaceable possession of their country and protection against domestic feuds and insurrection as well as hostilities of other tribes. They shall also be protected from intrusion by all unauthorized citizens of the United States attempting to settle on their lands or reside in their territory."[3]

The missionary, Reverend Evan Jones, who had followed the Cherokee into exile, and his son, John B. Jones, had been admitted to Cherokee citizenship the year before by vote of the Nation.   The act conferring this recognition recites that "we do bear witness that they have done their work well."[4]

John Ross, now an old man, had been unable to attend this treaty, being present at the time in Washington on business for his people. Before its ratification he died in that city on August 1, 1866, at the age of seventy-seven years, fifty-seven of which had been given to the service of his Nation.   No finer panegyric was ever pronounced than the memorial resolution passed by the Cherokee Nation on learning of his death.[5]   Notwithstanding repeated attempts to subvert his authority, his people had remained steadfast in their fidelity to him,

---

[1] Royce, Cherokee Nation, op. cit., p. 376.

[2] Ibid., p. 376.   A census of 1867 gives them 13,566 (ibid., p. 351).

[3] See synopsis and full discussion in Royce, op. cit., pp. 334–340.

[4] Act of Citizenship, November 7, 1865, Laws of the Cherokee Nation, p. 119; St. Louis, 1868.

[5] See Resolutions of Honor, ibid., pp. 137–140.

John Ross, 1790–1866

From a lithograph published by McKenney and Hall in The Indian
Tribes of North America, *1836–44, and subsequent editions. Based
on a painting made in 1835, artist unknown.*

and he died, as he had lived for nearly forty years, the officially recognized chief of the Nation. With repeated opportunities to enrich himself at the expense of his tribe, he died a poor man. His body was brought back and interred in the territory of the Nation. In remembrance of the great chief one of the nine districts of the Cherokee Nation has been called by his Indian name, Cooweescoowee (46).

Under the provisions of the late treaty the Delawares in Kansas, to the number of 985, removed to Indian territory in 1867 and became incorporated as citizens of the Cherokee Nation. They were followed in 1870 by the Shawano, chiefly also from Kansas, to the number of 770.[1] These immigrants settled chiefly along the Verdigris, in the northwestern part of the Nation. Under the same treaty the Osage, Kaw, Pawnee, Ponca, Oto and Missouri, and Tonkawa were afterward settled on the western extension known then as the Cherokee strip. The captive Nez Percés of Joseph's band were also temporarily located there, but have since been removed to the states of Washington and Idaho.

In 1870 the Missouri, Kansas and Texas railway, a branch of the Union Pacific system, was constructed through the lands of the Cherokee Nation under an agreement ratified by the Government, it being the first railroad to enter that country.[2] Several others have since been constructed or projected.

The same year saw a Cherokee literary revival. The publication of the *Advocate*, which had been suspended since some years before the war, was resumed, and by authority of the Nation John B. Jones began the preparation of a series of schoolbooks in the Cherokee language and alphabet for the benefit of those children who knew no English.[3]

In the spring of 1881 a delegation from the Cherokee Nation visited the East Cherokee still remaining in the mountains of North Carolina and extended to them a cordial and urgent invitation to remove and incorporate upon equal terms with the Cherokee Nation in the Indian territory. In consequence several parties of East Cherokee, numbering in all 161 persons, removed during the year to the western Nation, the expense being paid by the Federal government. Others afterwards applied for assistance to remove, but as no further appropriation was made for the purpose nothing more was done.[4] In 1883 the East Cherokee brought suit for a proportionate division of the Cherokee funds and other interests under previous treaties,[5] but their claim was

[1] Royce, Cherokee Nation, Fifth Ann. Rep. Bureau of Ethnology, pp. 356–358, 1888; Constitution and Laws of the Cherokee Nation, pp. 277–284; St. Louis, 1875.

[2] Royce, op. cit., p. 367.

[3] Foster, Sequoyah, pp. 147, 148, 1885; Pilling, Iroquoian Bibliography, 1888, articles "Cherokee Advocate" and "John B. Jones." The schoolbook series seems to have ended with the arithmetic—cause, as the Cherokee national superintendent of schools explained to the author, "too much white man."

[4] Commissioner H. Price, Report of Indian Commissioner, p. lxv, 1881, and p. lxx, 1882; see also p. 175.

[5] Report of Indian Commissioner, p. lxv, 1883.

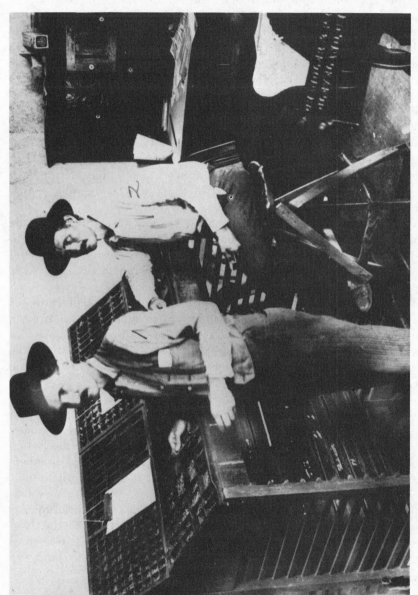

Printing office of the "Cherokee Advocate." Photographer and date not recorded.

finally decided adversely three years later on appeal to the Supreme Court.[1]

In 1889 the Cherokee female seminary was completed at Tahlequah at a cost of over $60,000, supplementing the work of the male seminary, built some years before at a cost of $90,000. The Cherokee Nation was now appropriating annually over $80,000 for school purposes, including the support of the two seminaries, an orphan asylum, and over one hundred primary schools, besides which there were a number of mission schools.[2]

For a number of years the pressure for the opening of Indian territory to white settlement had been growing in strength. Thousands of intruders had settled themselves upon the lands of each of the five civilized tribes, where they remained upon various pretexts in spite of urgent and repeated appeals to the government by the Indians for their removal. Under treaties with the five civilized tribes, the right to decide citizenship or residence claims belonged to the tribes concerned, but the intruders had at last become so numerous and strong that they had formed an organization among themselves to pass upon their own claims, and others that might be submitted to them, with attorneys and ample funds to defend each claim in outside courts against the decision of the tribe. At the same time the Government policy was steadily toward the reduction or complete breaking up of Indian reservations and the allotment of lands to the Indians in severalty, with a view to their final citizenship, and the opening of the surplus lands to white settlement. As a part of the same policy the jurisdiction of the United States courts was gradually being extended over the Indian country, taking cognizance of many things hitherto considered by the Indian courts under former treaties with the United States. Against all this the Cherokee and other civilized tribes protested, but without avail. To add to the irritation, companies of armed "boomers" were organized for the express purpose of invading and seizing the Cherokee outlet and other unoccupied portions of the Indian territory—reserved by treaty for future Indian settlement—in defiance of the civil and military power of the Government.

We come now to what seems the beginning of the end of Indian autonomy. In 1889 a commission, afterward known as the Cherokee Commission, was appointed, under act of Congress, to "negotiate with the Cherokee Indians, and with all other Indians owning or claiming lands lying west of the ninety-sixth degree of longitude in the Indian territory, for the cession to the United States of all their title, claim, or interest of every kind or character in and to said lands." In August of that year the commission made a proposition to

---

[1] Commissioner J. D. C. Atkins, Report of Indian Commissioner, p. xlv, 1886, and p. lxxvii, 1887.
[2] Agent L. E. Bennett, in Report of Indian Commissioner, p. 93, 1890.

Cherokee National Female Seminary. Photographer and date not recorded.

Chief J. B. Mayes for the cession of all the Cherokee lands thus described, being that portion known as the Cherokee outlet or strip. The proposition was declined on the ground that the Cherokee constitution forbade its consideration.[1] Other tribes were approached for a similar purpose, and the commission was continued, with changing personnel from year to year, until agreements for cession and the taking of allotments had been made with nearly all the wilder tribes in what is now Oklahoma.

In the meantime the Attorney-General had rendered a decision denying the right of Indian tribes to lease their lands without permission of the Government. At this time the Cherokee were deriving an annual income of $150,000 from the lease of grazing privileges upon the strip, but by a proclamation of President Harrison on February 17, 1890, ordering the cattlemen to vacate before the end of the year, this income was cut off and the strip was rendered practically valueless to them.[2] The Cherokee were now forced to come to terms, and a second proposition for the cession of the Cherokee strip was finally accepted by the national council on January 4, 1892. "It was known to the Cherokees that for some time would-be settlers on the lands of the outlet had been encamped in the southern end of Kansas, and by every influence at their command had been urging the Government to open the country to settlement and to negotiate with the Cherokees afterwards, and that a bill for that purpose had been introduced in Congress." The consideration was nearly $8,600,000, or about $1.25 per acre, for something over 6,000,000 acres of land. One article of the agreement stipulates for "the reaffirmation to the Cherokee Nation of the right of local self-government."[3] The agreement having been ratified by Congress, the Cherokee strip was opened by Presidential proclamation on September 16, 1893.[4]

The movement for the abolition of the Indian governments and the allotment and opening of the Indian country had now gained such force that by act of Congress approved March 3, 1893, the President was authorized to appoint a commission of three—known later as the Dawes Commission, from its distinguished chairman, Senator Henry L. Dawes of Massachusetts—to negotiate with the five civilized tribes of Indian territory, viz, the Cherokee, Choctaw, Chickasaw, Creek, and Seminole, for "the extinguishment of tribal titles to any lands within that territory, now held by any and all of such nations and tribes, either by cession of the same or some part thereof to the United States, or by the allotment and division of the same in severalty among the Indians of such nations or tribes respectively as may be

---

[1] Report of Indian Commissioner, p. 22, 1889.

[2] See proclamation by President Harrison and order from Indian Commissioner in Report of Indian Commissioner, pp. lxxii–lxxiii, 421–422, 1890. The lease figures are from personal information.

[3] Commissioner T. J. Morgan, Report of Indian Commissioner, pp. 79–80, 1892.

[4] Commissioner D. M. Browning, Report of Indian Commissioner, pp. 33–34, 1893.

entitled to the same, or by such other method as may be agreed upon
. . .   to enable the ultimate creation of a state or states of the
Union, which shall embrace the land within the said Indian territory."[1]
The commission appointed arrived in the Indian territory in January,
1894, and at once began negotiations.[2]

At this time the noncitizen element in Indian Territory was officially
reported to number at least 200,000 souls, while those having rights
as citizens of the five civilized tribes, including full-blood and mixed-
blood Indians, adopted whites, and negroes, numbered but 70,500.[3]
Not all of the noncitizens were intruders, many being there by permission of the Indian governments or on official or other legitimate
business, but the great body of them were illegal squatters or unrecognized claimants to Indian rights, against whose presence the Indians
themselves had never ceased to protest.   A test case brought this year
in the Cherokee Nation was decided by the Interior Department against
the claimants and in favor of the Cherokee.   Commenting upon threats
made in consequence by the rejected claimants, the agent for the five
tribes remarks: "It is not probable that Congress will establish a
court to nullify and vacate a formal decision of the Interior Department."[4]   A year later he says of these intruders that "so long as they
have a foothold—a residence, legal or not—in the Indian country they
will be disturbers of peace and promoters of discord, and while they
cry aloud, and spare not, for allotment and statehood, they are but
stumbling blocks and obstacles to that mutual good will and fraternal
feeling which must be cultivated and secured before allotment is practicable and statehood desirable."[5]   The removal of the intruders was
still delayed, and in 1896 the decision of citizenship claims was taken
from the Indian government and relegated to the Dawes Commission.[6]

In 1895 the commission was increased to five members, with enlarged
powers.   In the meantime a survey of Indian Territory had been
ordered and begun.   In September the agent wrote: "The Indians
now know that a survey of their lands is being made, and whether
with or without their consent, the survey is going on.   The meaning
of such survey is too plain to be disregarded, and it is justly considered as the initial step, solemn and authoritative, toward the over-
throw of their present communal holdings.   At this writing surveying
corps are at work in the Creek, Choctaw, and Chickasaw Nations, and
therefore each one of these tribes has an ocular demonstration of the
actual intent and ultimate purpose of the government of the United
States."[7]

---

[1] Quotation from act, etc., Report of Indian Commissioner for 1894, p. 27, 1895.
[2] Report of Agent D. M. Wisdom, ibid., p. 141.
[3] Ibid., and statistical table, p. 570.
[4] Report of Agent D. M. Wisdom, ibid., p. 145.
[5] Agent D. M. Wisdom, in Report Indian Commissioner for 1895, p. 155, 1896.
[6] Commissioner D. M. Browning, Report of Indian Commissioner, p. 81, 1896.
[7] Report of Agent D. M. Wisdom, Report of Indian Commissioner for 1895, pp. 159, 160, 1896.

The general prosperity and advancement of the Cherokee Nation at this time may be judged from the report of the secretary of the Cherokee national board of education to Agent Wisdom. He reports 4,800 children attending two seminaries, male and female, two high schools, and one hundred primary schools, teachers being paid from $35 to $100 per month for nine months in the year. Fourteen primary schools were for the use of the negro citizens of the Nation, besides which they had a fine high school, kept up, like all the others, at the expense of the Cherokee goverment. Besides the national schools there were twelve mission schools helping to do splendid work for children of both citizens and noncitizens. Children of noncitizens were not allowed to attend the Cherokee national schools, but had their own subscription schools. The orphan asylum ranked as a high school, in which 150 orphans were boarded and educated, with graduates every year. It was a large brick building of three stories, 80 by 240 feet. The male seminary, accommodating 200 pupils, and the female seminary, accommodating 225 pupils, were also large brick structures, three stories in height and 150 by 240 feet on the ground. Three members, all Cherokee by blood, constituted a board of education. The secretary adds that the Cherokee are proud of their schools and educational institutions, and that no other country under the sun is so blessed with educational advantages at large.[1]

At this time the Cherokee Nation numbered something over 25,000 Indian, white, and negro citizens; the total citizen population of the three races in the five civilized tribes numbered about 70,000, while the noncitizens had increased to 250,000 and their number was being rapidly augmented.[2] Realizing that the swift, inevitable end must be the destruction of their national governments, the Cherokee began once more to consider the question of removal from the United States. The scheme is outlined in a letter written by a brother of the principal chief of the Cherokee Nation under date of May 31, 1895, from which we quote.

After prefacing that the government of the United States seems determined to break up the tribal autonomy of the five civilized tribes and to divide their lands, thus bringing about conditions under which the Cherokee could not exist, he continues:

Then for a remedy that will lead us out of it, away from it, and one that promises our preservation as a distinct race of people in the enjoyment of customs, social and political, that have been handed down to us from remote generations of the past. My plan is for the Cherokees to sell their entire landed possessions to the United States, divide the proceeds thereof per capita, then such as desire to do so unite in the formation of an Indian colony, and with their funds jointly purchase in Mexico

[1] Letter of A. E. Ivy, Secretary of the Board of Education, in Report of Indian Commissioner for 1895, p. 161, 1896. The author can add personal testimony as to the completeness of the seminary establishment.

[2] Report of Agent Wisdom, ibid., p. 162.

or South America a body of land sufficient for all their purposes, to be forever their joint home. . . . I believe also that for such Indians as did not desire to join the colony and leave the country provision should be made for them to repurchase their old homes, or such other lands in the country here as they might desire, and they could remain here and meet such fate as awaits them. I believe this presents the most feasible and equitable solution of the questions that we must decide in the near future, and will prove absolutely just and fair to all classes and conditions of our citizens. I also believe that the same could be acted upon by any or all of the five civilized tribes. . . .[1]

The final chapter is nearly written. By successive enactments within the last ten years the jurisdiction of the Indian courts has been steadily narrowed and the authority of the Federal courts proportionately extended; the right to determine Indian citizenship has been taken from the Indians and vested in a Government commission; the lands of the five tribes have been surveyed and sectionized by Government surveyors; and by the sweeping provisions of the Curtis act of June 28, 1898, "for the protection of the people of the Indian Territory," the entire control of tribal revenues is taken from the five Indian tribes and vested with a resident supervising inspector, the tribal courts are abolished, allotments are made compulsory, and authority is given to incorporate white men's towns in the Indian tribes.[2] By this act the five civilized tribes are reduced to the condition of ordinary reservation tribes under government agents with white communities planted in their midst. In the meantime the Dawes commission, continued up to the present, has by unremitting effort broken down the opposition of the Choctaw and Chickasaw, who have consented to allotment, while the Creeks and the Seminole are now wavering.[3] The Cherokee still hold out, the Ketoowah secret society (47) especially being strong in its resistance, and when the end comes it is possible that the protest will take shape in a wholesale emigration to Mexico. Late in 1897 the agent for the five tribes reports that "there seems a determined purpose on the part of many fullbloods . . . to emigrate to either Mexico or South America and there purchase new homes for themselves and families. Such individual action may grow to the proportion of a colony, and it is understood that liberal grants of land can be secured from the countries mentioned.[4] Mexican agents are now (1901) among the Cherokee advocating the scheme, which may develop to include a large proportion of the five civilized tribes.[5]

By the census of 1898, the most recent taken, as reported by Agent

[1] Letter of Bird Harris, May 31, 1895, in Report of Indian Commissioner for 1895, p. 160, 1896.

[2] Synopsis of Curtis act, pp. 75–79, and Curtis act in full, p. 425 et seq., in Report of Indian Commissioner for 1898; noted also in Report of Indian Commissioner, p. 84 et seq., 1899.

[3] Commissioner W. A. Jones, ibid., pp. i, 84 et seq. (Curtis act and Dawes commission).

[4] Report of Agent D. M. Wisdom, Report of Indian Commissioner, pp. 141–144, 1897.

[5] Author's personal information; see also House bill No. 1165 " for the relief of certain Indians in Indian Territory," etc., Fifty-sixth Congress, first session, 1900.

The last Grand Jury in the Cherokee Nation. Date not given.

Wisdom, the Cherokee Nation numbered 34,461 persons, as follows: Cherokee by blood (including all degrees of admixture), 26,500; intermarried whites, 2,300; negro freedmen, 4,000; Delaware, 871; Shawnee, 790. The total acreage of the Nation was 5,031,351 acres, which, if divided per capita under the provisions of the Curtis bill, after deducting 60,000 acres reserved for town-site and other purposes, would give to each Cherokee citizen 144 acres.[1] It must be noted that the official rolls include a large number of persons whose claims are disputed by the Cherokee authorities.

THE EASTERN BAND

It remains to speak of the eastern band of Cherokee—the remnant which still clings to the woods and waters of the old home country. As has been said, a considerable number had eluded the troops in the general round-up of 1838 and had fled to the fastnesses of the high mountains. Here they were joined by others who had managed to break through the guard at Calhoun and other collecting stations, until the whole number of fugitives in hiding amounted to a thousand or more, principally of the mountain Cherokee of North Carolina, the purest-blooded and most conservative of the Nation. About one-half the refugee warriors had put themselves under command of a noted leader named U'tsălă, " Lichen, " who made his headquarters amid the lofty peaks at the head of Oconaluftee, from which secure hiding place, although reduced to extremity of suffering from starvation and exposure, they defied every effort to effect their capture.

The work of running down these fugitives proved to be so difficult an undertaking and so well-nigh barren of result that when Charley and his sons made their bold stroke for freedom[2] General Scott eagerly seized the incident as an opportunity for compromise. To this end he engaged the services of William H. Thomas, a trader who for more than twenty years had been closely identified with the mountain Cherokee and possessed their full confidence, and authorized him to submit to U'tsălă a proposition that if the latter would seize Charley and the others who had been concerned in the attack upon the soldiers and surrender them for punishment, the pursuit would be called off and the fugitives allowed to stay unmolested until an effort could be made to secure permission from the general government for them to remain.

Thomas accepted the commission, and taking with him one or two Indians made his way over secret paths to U'tsălă's hiding place. He presented Scott's proposition and represented to the chief that by aiding in bringing Charley's party to punishment according to the rules of war he could secure respite for his sorely pressed followers, with the ultimate hope that they might be allowed to remain in their

---

[1] Report of Agent D. M. Wisdom, Report of Indian Commissioner, p. 159, 1898.
[2] See page 131.

own country, whereas if he rejected the offer the whole force of the seven thousand troops which had now completed the work of gathering up and deporting the rest of the tribe would be set loose upon his own small band until the last refugee had been either taken or killed.

U'tsălă turned the proposition in his mind long and seriously. His heart was bitter, for his wife and little son had starved to death on the mountain side, but he thought of the thousands who were already on their long march into exile and then he looked round upon his little band of followers. If only they might stay, even though a few must be sacrificed, it was better than that all should die—for they had sworn never to leave their country. He consented and Thomas returned to report to General Scott.

Now occurred a remarkable incident which shows the character of Thomas and the masterly influence which he already had over the Indians, although as yet he was hardly more than thirty years old. It was known that Charley and his party were in hiding in a cave of the Great Smokies, at the head of Deep creek, but it was not thought likely that he could be taken without bloodshed and a further delay which might prejudice the whole undertaking. Thomas determined to go to him and try to persuade him to come in and surrender. Declining Scott's offer of an escort, he went alone to the cave, and, getting between the Indians and their guns as they were sitting around the fire near the entrance, he walked up to Charley and announced his message. The old man listened in silence and then said simply, "I will come in. I don't want to be hunted down by my own people." They came in voluntarily and were shot, as has been already narrated, one only, a mere boy, being spared on account of his youth. This boy, now an old man, is still living, Wasitû'na, better known to the whites as Washington.[1]

A respite having thus been obtained for the fugitives, Thomas next went to Washington to endeavor to make some arrangement for their permanent settlement. Under the treaty of New Echota, in 1835, the Cherokee were entitled, besides the lump sum of five million dollars for the lands ceded, to an additional compensation for the improvements which they were forced to abandon and for spoliations by white citizens, together with a per capita allowance to cover the cost of removal and subsistence for one year in the new country. The twelfth article had also provided that such Indians as chose to remain in the East and become citizens there might do so under certain conditions,

---

[1] Charley's story as here given is from the author's personal information, derived chiefly from conversations with Colonel Thomas and with Wasitû'na and other old Indians. An ornate but somewhat inaccurate account is given also in Lanman's Letters from the Alleghany Mountains, written on the ground ten years after the events described. The leading facts are noted in General Scott's official dispatches.

each head of a family thus remaining to be confirmed in a preemption right to 160 acres.   In consequence of the settled purpose of President Jackson to deport every Indian, this permission was canceled and supplementary articles substituted by which some additional compensation was allowed in lieu of the promised preemptions and all individual reservations granted under previous treaties.[1]   Every Cherokee was thus made a landless alien in his original country.

The last party of emigrant Cherokee had started for the West in December, 1838.   Nine months afterwards the refugees still scattered about in the mountains of North Carolina and Tennessee were reported to number 1,046.[2]   By persistent effort at Washington from 1836 to 1842, including one continuous stay of three years at the capital city, Thomas finally obtained governmental permission for these to remain, and their share of the moneys due for improvements and reservations confiscated was placed at his disposal, as their agent and trustee, for the purpose of buying lands upon which they could be permanently settled. Under this authority he bought for them, at various times up to the year 1861, a number of contiguous tracts of land upon Oconaluftee river and Soco creek, within the present Swain and Jackson counties of North Carolina, together with several detached tracts in the more western counties of the same state.   The main body, upon the waters of Oconaluftee, which was chiefly within the limits of the cession of 1819, came afterward to be known as the Qualla boundary, or Qualla reservation, taking the name from Thomas' principal trading store and agency headquarters.   The detached western tracts were within the final cession of 1835, but all alike were bought by Thomas from white owners.   As North Carolina refused to recognize Indians as landowners within the state, and persisted in this refusal until 1866,[3] Thomas, as their authorized agent under the Government, held the deeds in his own name.   Before it was legally possible under the state laws to transfer the title to the Indians, his own affairs had become involved and his health impaired by age and the hardships of military service so that his mind gave way, thus leaving the whole question of the Indian title a subject of litigation until its adjudication by the United States in 1875, supplemented by further decisions in 1894.

To Colonel William Holland Thomas the East Cherokee of to-day owe their existence as a people, and for half a century he was as intimately connected with their history as was John Ross with that of the main Cherokee Nation.   Singularly enough, their connection with Cherokee affairs extended over nearly the same period, but while Ross participated in their national matters Thomas gave his effort to

---

[1] See New Echota treaty, December 29, 1835, and supplementary articles, March 1, 1836, in Indian Treaties, pp. 633–648, 1837: also full discussion of same treaty in Royce, Cherokee Nation, Fifth Ann. Rep. Bureau of Ethnology, 1888.

[1] Royce, op. cit., p. 292.   [1] Ibid., p. 314.

a neglected band hardly known in the councils of the tribe. In his many-sided capacity he strikingly resembles another white man prominent in Cherokee history, General Sam Houston.

Thomas was born in the year 1805 on Raccoon creek, about two miles from Waynesville in North Carolina. His father, who was related to President Zachary Taylor, came of a Welsh family which had immigrated to Virginia at an early period, while on his mother's side he was descended from a Maryland family of Revolutionary stock. He was an only and posthumous child, his father having been accidentally drowned a short time before the boy was born. Being unusually bright for his age, he was engaged when only twelve years old to tend an Indian trading store on Soco creek, in the present Jackson county, owned by Felix Walker, son of the Congressman of the same name who made a national reputation by "talking for Buncombe." The store was on the south side of the creek, about a mile above the now abandoned Macedonia mission, within the present reservation, and was a branch of a larger establishment which Walker himself kept at Waynesville. The trade was chiefly in skins and ginseng, or "sang," the latter for shipment to China, where it was said to be worth its weight in silver. This trade was very profitable, as the price to the Indians was but ten cents per pound in merchandise for the green root, whereas it now brings seventy-five cents in cash upon the reservation, the supply steadily diminishing with every year. The contract was for three years' service for a total compensation of one hundred dollars and expenses, but Walker devoted so much of his attention to law studies that the Waynesville store was finally closed for debt, and at the end of his contract term young Thomas was obliged to accept a lot of second-hand law books in lieu of other payment. How well he made use of them is evident from his subsequent service in the state senate and in other official capacities.

Soon after entering upon his duties he attracted the notice of Yonaguska, or Drowning-bear (Yâ'na-gûñ'skĭ, "Bear-drowning-him"), the acknowledged chief of all the Cherokee then living on the waters of Tuckasegee and Oconaluftee—the old Kituhwa country. On learning that the boy had neither father nor brother, the old chief formally adopted him as his son, and as such he was thenceforth recognized in the tribe under the name of Wil-Usdi', or "Little Will," he being of small stature even in mature age. From his Indian friends, particularly a boy of the same age who was his companion in the store, he learned the language as well as a white man has ever learned it, so that in his declining years it dwelt in memory more strongly than his mother tongue. After the invention of the Cherokee alphabet, he learned also to read and write the language.

In 1819 the lands on Tuckasegee and its branches were sold by the

Colonel William Holland Thomas or Wil-usdi' (1805–1893)

A white man who was adopted as the son of the Cherokee Chief Yonaguska. After the death of Yonaguska in April 1839, Colonel Thomas became chief of the tribe. Photographer not recorded, 1858.

Indians, and Thomas's mother soon after removed from Waynesville to a farm which she purchased on the west bank of Oconaluftee, opposite the mouth of Soco, where her son went to live with her, having now set up in business for himself at Qualla. Yonaguska and his immediate connection continued to reside on a small reservation in the same neighborhood, while the rest of the Cherokee retired to the west of the Nantahala mountains, though still visiting and trading on Soco. After several shiftings Thomas finally, soon after the removal in 1838, bought a farm on the northern bank of Tuckasegee, just above the present town of Whittier in Swain county, and built there a homestead which he called Stekoa, after an Indian town destroyed by Rutherford which had occupied the same site. At the time of the removal he was the proprietor of five trading stores in or adjoining the Cherokee country, viz, at Qualla town, near the mouth of Soco creek; on Scott's creek, near Webster; on Cheowa, near the present Robbinsville; at the junction of Valley river and Hiwassee, now Murphy; and at the Cherokee agency at Calhoun (now Charleston), Tennessee. Besides carrying on a successful trading business he was also studying law and taking an active interest in local politics.

In his capacity as agent for the eastern Cherokee he laid off the lands purchased for them into five districts or "towns," which he named Bird town, Paint town, Wolf town, Yellow hill, and Big cove, the names which they still retain, the first three being those of Cherokee clans.[1] He also drew up for them a simple form of government, the execution of which was in his own and Yonaguska's hands until the death of the latter, after which the band knew no other chief than Thomas until his retirement from active life. In 1848 he was elected to the state senate and continued to serve in that capacity until the outbreak of the civil war. As state senator he inaugurated a system of road improvements for western North Carolina and was also the father of the Western North Carolina Railroad (now a part of the Southern system), originally projected to develop the copper mines of Ducktown, Tennessee.

With his colleagues in the state senate he voted for secession in 1861, and at once resigned to recruit troops for the Confederacy, to which, until the close of the war, he gave his whole time, thought, and effort. In 1862 he organized the Thomas Legion, consisting of two regiments of infantry, a battalion of cavalry, a company of engineers, and a field battery, he himself commanding as colonel, although then nearly sixty years of age. Four companies were made up principally of his own Cherokee. The Thomas Legion operated chiefly as a frontier guard

---

[1] In the Cherokee language Tsiskwâ'hĭ, "Bird place," Aniʹ-Wâ'dihĭ, "Paint place," Wa'yâ'hĭ, "Wolf place," Eʹlawâ'di, "Red earth" (now Cherokee post-office and agency), and Kâlänûñ'yĭ, "Raven place." There was also, for a time, a "Pretty-woman town" (Aniʹ-Gĭlâ'hĭ?).

for the Confederacy along the mountain region southward from Cumberland gap.

After the close of the conflict he returned to his home at Stekoa and again took charge, unofficially, of the affairs of the Cherokee, whom he attended during the smallpox epidemic of 1866 and assisted through the unsettled conditions of the reconstruction period. His own resources had been swept away by the war, and all his hopes had gone down with the lost cause. This, added to the effects of three years of hardship and anxiety in the field when already almost past the age limit, soon after brought about a physical and mental collapse, from which he never afterward rallied except at intervals, when for a short time the old spirit would flash out in all its brightness. He died in 1893 at the advanced age of nearly ninety, retaining to the last the courteous manner of a gentleman by nature and training, with an exact memory and the clear-cut statement of a lawyer and man of affairs. To his work in the state senate the people of western North Carolina owe more than to that of any other man, while among the older Cherokee the name of Wil-Usdi' is still revered as that of a father and a great chief.[1]

Yonaguska, properly Yâ'nû-gûñ'skĭ, the adopted father of Thomas, is the most prominent chief in the history of the East Cherokee, although, singularly enough, his name does not occur in connection with any of the early wars or treaties. This is due partly to the fact that he was a peace chief and counselor rather than a war leader, and in part to the fact that the isolated position of the mountain Cherokee kept them aloof in a great measure from the tribal councils of those living to the west and south. In person he was strikingly handsome, being six feet three inches in height and strongly built, with a faint tinge of red, due to a slight strain of white blood on his father's side, relieving the brown of his cheek. In power of oratory he is said to have surpassed any other chief of his day. When the Cherokee lands on Tuckasegee were sold by the treaty of 1819, Yonaguska continued to reside on a reservation of 640 acres in a bend of the river a short distance above the present Bryson City, on the site of the ancient Kituhwa. He afterward moved over to Oconaluftee, and finally, after the Removal, gathered his people about him and settled with them on Soco creek on lands purchased for them by Thomas.

[1] The facts concerning Colonel Thomas's career are derived chiefly from the author's conversations with Thomas himself, supplemented by information from his former assistant, Capt. James W. Terrell, and others who knew him, together with an admirable sketch in the North Carolina University Magazine for May 1899, by Mrs. A. C. Avery, his daughter. He is also frequently noticed, in connection with East Cherokee matters, in the annual reports of the Commissioner of Indian Affairs; in the North Carolina Confederate Roster; in Lanman's Letters from the Alleghany Mountains; and in Zeigler and Grosscup's Heart of the Alleghanies, etc. Some manuscript contributions to the library of the Georgia Historical Society in Savannah—now unfortunately mislaid—show his interest in Cherokee linguistics.

He was a prophet and reformer as well as a chief. When about sixty years of age he had a severe sickness, terminating in a trance, during which his people mourned him as dead. At the end of twenty-four hours, however, he awoke to consciousness and announced that he had been to the spirit world, where he had talked with friends who had gone before, and with God, who had sent him back with a message to the Indians, promising to call him again at a later time. From that day until his death his words were listened to as those of one inspired. He had been somewhat addicted to liquor, but now, on the recommendation of Thomas, not only quit drinking himself, but organized his tribe into a temperance society. To accomplish this he called his people together in council, and, after clearly pointing out to them the serious effect of intemperance, in an eloquent speech that moved some of his audience to tears, he declared that God had permitted him to return to earth especially that he might thus warn his people and banish whisky from among them. He then had Thomas write out a pledge, which was signed first by the chief and then by each one of the council, and from that time until after his death whisky was unknown among the East Cherokee.

Although frequent pressure was brought to bear to induce him and his people to remove to the West, he firmly resisted every persuasion, declaring that the Indians were safer from aggression among their rocks and mountains than they could ever be in a land which the white man could find profitable, and that the Cherokee could be happy only in the country where nature had planted him. While counseling peace and friendship with the white man, he held always to his Indian faith and was extremely suspicious of missionaries. On one occasion, after the first Bible translation into the Cherokee language and alphabet, some one brought a copy of Matthew from New Echota, but Yonaguska would not allow it to be read to his people until it had first been read to himself. After listening to one or two chapters the old chief dryly remarked: "Well, it seems to be a good book—strange that the white people are not better, after having had it so long."

He died, aged about eighty, in April, 1839, within a year after the Removal. Shortly before the end he had himself carried into the townhouse on Soco, of which he had supervised the building, where, extended on a couch, he made a last talk to his people, commending Thomas to them as their chief and again warning them earnestly against ever leaving their own country. Then wrapping his blanket around him, he quietly lay back and died. He was buried beside Soco, about a mile below the old Macedonia mission, with a rude mound of stones to mark the spot. He left two wives and considerable property, including an old negro slave named Cudjo, who was devotedly attached to him. One of his daughters, Katâ′lsta, still survives, and is the last conservator of the potter's art among the East Cherokee.[1]

Yonaguska had succeeded in authority to Yane'gwa, "Big-bear," who appears to have been of considerable local prominence in his time, but whose name, even with the oldest of the band, is now but a memory. He was among the signers of the treaties of 1798 and 1805, and by the treaty of 1819 was confirmed in a reservation of 640 acres as one of those living within the ceded territory who were "believed to be persons of industry and capable of managing their property with discretion," and who had made considerable improvements on the tracts reserved. This reservation, still known as the Big-bear farm, was on the western bank of Oconaluftee, a few miles above its mouth, and appears to have been the same afterward occupied by Yonaguska.[2]

Another of the old notables among the East Cherokee was Tsunu'lă-hûñ'skĭ, corrupted by the whites to Junaluska, a great warrior, from whom the ridge west of Waynesville takes its name. In early life he was known as Gûl'ʻkăla'skĭ.[3] On the outbreak of the Creek war in 1813 he raised a party of warriors to go down, as he boasted, "to exterminate the Creeks." Not meeting with complete success, he announced the result, according to the Cherokee custom, at the next dance after his return in a single word, *detsinu'lăhûñgû'*, "I tried, but could not," given out as a cue to the song leader, who at once took it as the burden of his song. Thenceforth the disappointed warrior was known as Tsunu'lăhûñ'skĭ, "One who tries, but fails." He distinguished himself at the Horseshoe bend, where the action of the Cherokee decided the battle in favor of Jackson's army, and was often heard to say after the removal: "If I had known that Jackson would drive us from our homes, I would have killed him that day at the Horseshoe." He accompanied the exiles of 1838, but afterward returned to his old home; he was allowed to remain, and in recognition of his services the state legislature, by special act, in 1847 conferred upon him the right of citizenship and granted to him a tract of land in fee simple, but without power of alienation.[4] This reservation was in the Cheowa Indian settlement, near the present Robbinsville, in Graham county, where he died about the year 1858. His grave is still to be seen just outside of Robbinsville.

---

[1] The facts concerning Yonaguska are based on the author's personal information obtained from Colonel Thomas, supplemented from conversations with old Indians. The date of his death and his approximate age are taken from the Terrell roll. He is also noticed at length in Lanman's Letters from the Alleghany Mountains, 1848, and in Zeigler and Grosscup's Heart of the Alleghanies, 1883. The trance which, according to Thomas and Lanman, lasted about one day, is stretched by the last-named authors to fifteen days, with the whole 1,200 Indians marching and countermarching around the sleeping body!

[2] The name in the treaties occurs as Yonahequah (1798), Yohanaqua (1805), and Yonah (1819).—Indian Treaties, pp. 82, 123, 268; Washington, 1837.

[3] The name refers to something habitually falling from a leaning position.

[4] Act quoted in Report of Indian Commissioner for 1895, p. 636, 1896.

As illustrative of his shrewdness it is told that he once tracked a little Indian girl to Charleston, South Carolina, where she had been carried by kidnappers and sold as a slave, and regained her freedom by proving, from expert microscopic examination, that her hair had none of the negro characteristics.[1]

Christianity was introduced among the Kituhwa Cherokee shortly before the Removal through Worcester and Boudinot's translation of Matthew, first published at New Echota in 1829. In the absence of missionaries the book was read by the Indians from house to house. After the Removal a Methodist minister, Reverend Ulrich Keener, began to make visits for preaching at irregular intervals, and was followed several years later by Baptist workers.[2]

In the fall of 1839 the Commissioner of Indian Affairs reported that the East Cherokee had recently expressed a desire to join their brethren in the West, but had been deterred from so doing by the unsettled condition of affairs in the Territory. He states that "they have a right to remain or to go," but that as the interests of others are involved in their decision they should decide without delay.[3]

In 1840 about one hundred Catawba, nearly all that were left of the tribe, being dissatisfied with their condition in South Carolina, moved up in a body and took up their residence with the Cherokee. Latent tribal jealousies broke out, however, and at their own request negotiations were begun in 1848, through Thomas and others, for their removal to Indian Territory. The effort being without result, they soon after began to drift back to their own homes, until, in 1852, there were only about a dozen remaining among the Cherokee. In 1890 only one was left, an old woman, the widow of a Cherokee husband. She and her daughter, both of whom spoke the language, were expert potters according to the Catawba method, which differs markedly from that of the Cherokee. There are now two Catawba women, both married to Cherokee husbands, living with the tribe, and practicing their native potter's art. While residing among the Cherokee, the Catawba acquired a reputation as doctors and leaders of the dance.[4]

On August 6, 1846, a treaty was concluded at Washington with the representatives of the Cherokee Nation west by which the rights of the East Cherokee to a participation in the benefits of the New Echota treaty of 1835 were distinctly recognized, and provision was made for a final adjustment of all unpaid and pending claims due under that treaty. The right claimed by the East Cherokee to participate in the

[1] The facts concerning Junaluska are from the author's information obtained from Colonel Thomas, Captain James Terrell, and Cherokee informants.

[2] Author's information from Colonel Thomas.

[3] Commissioner Crawford, November 25, Report of Indian Commissioner, p. 333, 1839.

[4] Author's information from Colonel Thomas, Captain Terrell, and Indian sources; Commissioner W. Medill, Report of Indian Commissioner, p. 399, 1848; Commissioner Orlando Brown, Report of Indian Commissioner for 1849, p. 14, 1850.

benefits of the New Echota treaty, although not denied by the government, had been held to be conditional upon their removal to the West.[1]

In the spring of 1848 the author, Lanman, visited the East Cherokee and has left an interesting account of their condition at the time, together with a description of their ballplays, dances, and customs generally, having been the guest of Colonel Thomas, of whom he speaks as the guide, counselor, and friend of the Indians, as well as their business agent and chief, so that the connection was like that existing between a father and his children. He puts the number of Indians at about 800 Cherokee and 100 Catawba on the "Qualla town" reservation—the name being in use thus early—with 200 more Indians residing in the more westerly portion of the state. Of their general condition he says:

About three-fourths of the entire population can read in their own language, and, though the majority of them understand English, a very few can speak the language. They practice, to a considerable extent, the science of agriculture, and have acquired such a knowledge of the mechanic arts as answers them for all ordinary purposes, for they manufacture their own clothing, their own ploughs, and other farming utensils, their own axes, and even their own guns. Their women are no longer treated as slaves, but as equals; the men labor in the fields and their wives are devoted entirely to household employments. They keep the same domestic animals that are kept by their white neighbors, and cultivate all the common grains of the country. They are probably as temperate as any other class of people on the face of the earth, honest in their business intercourse, moral in their thoughts, words, and deeds, and distinguished for their faithfulness in performing the duties of religion. They are chiefly Methodists and Baptists, and have regularly ordained ministers, who preach to them on every Sabbath, and they have also abandoned many of their mere senseless superstitions. They have their own court and try their criminals by a regular jury. Their judges and lawyers are chosen from among themselves. They keep in order the public roads leading through their settlement. By a law of the state they have a right to vote, but seldom exercise that right, as they do not like the idea of being identified with any of the political parties. Excepting on festive days, they dress after the manner of the white man, but far more picturesquely. They live in small log houses of their own construction, and have everything they need or desire in the way of food. They are, in fact, the happiest community that I have yet met with in this southern country.[2]

Among the other notables Lanman speaks thus of Salâ'lĭ, "Squirrel," a born mechanic of the band, who died only a few years since:

He is quite a young man and has a remarkably thoughtful face. He is the blacksmith of his nation, and with some assistance supplies the whole of Qualla town with all their axes and plows; but what is more, he has manufactured a number of very superior rifles and pistols, including stock, barrel, and lock, and he is also the builder of grist mills, which grind all the corn which his people eat. A specimen of his workmanship in the way of a rifle may be seen at the Patent Office in Washington, where it was deposited by Mr. Thomas; and I believe Salola is the first Indian who

---

[1] Synopsis of the treaty, etc., in Royce, Cherokee Nation, Fifth Ann. Rep. Bureau of Ethnology, pp. 300–313, 1888; see also ante, p. 148.

[2] Lanman, Letters from the Alleghany Mountains, pp. 94–95, 1849.

ever manufactured an entire gun. But when it is remembered that he never received a particle of education in any of the mechanic arts but is entirely self-taught, his attainments must be considered truly remarkable.[1]

On July 29, 1848, Congress approved an act for taking a census of all those Cherokee who had remained in North Carolina after the Removal, and who still resided east of the Mississippi, in order that their share of the "removal and subsistence fund" under the New Echota treaty might be set aside for them. A sum equivalent to $53.33⅓ was at the same time appropriated for each one, or his representative, to be available for defraying the expenses of his removal to the Cherokee Nation west and subsistence there for one year whenever he should elect so to remove. Any surplus over such expense was to be paid to him in cash after his arrival in the west. The whole amount thus expended was to be reimbursed to the Government from the general fund to the credit of the Cherokee Nation under the terms of the treaty of New Echota. In the meantime it was ordered that to each individual thus entitled should be paid the accrued interest on this per capita sum from the date of the ratification of the New Echota treaty (May 23, 1836), payment of interest at the same rate to continue annually thereafter.[2] In accordance with this act a census of the Cherokee then residing in North Carolina, Tennessee, and Georgia, was completed in the fall of 1848 by J. C. Mullay, making the whole number 2,133. On the basis of this enrollment, several payments were made to them by special agents within the next ten years, one being a per-capita payment by Alfred Chapman in 1851–52 of unpaid claims arising under the treaty of New Echota and amounting in the aggregate to $197,534.50, the others being payments of the annual interest upon the "removal and subsistence fund" set apart to their credit in 1848. In the accomplishment of these payments two other enrollments were made by D. W. Siler in 1851 and by Chapman in 1852, the last being simply a corrected revision of the Siler roll, and neither varying greatly from the Mullay roll.[3]

Upon the appointment of Chapman to make the per capita payment above mentioned, the Cherokee Nation west had filed a protest against the payment, upon the double ground that the East Cherokee had forfeited their right to participation, and furthermore that their census was believed to be enormously exaggerated. As a matter of fact the number first reported by Mullay was only 1,517, to which so many

---

[1] Lanman, Letters from the Alleghany Mountains, p. 111.

[2] See act quoted in "The United States of America v. William H, Thomas et al."; also Royce, Cherokee Nation, Fifth Ann. Rep. Bureau of Ethnology, p. 313, 1888. In the earlier notices the terms "North Carolina Cherokee" and "Eastern Cherokee" are used synonymously, as the original fugitives were all in North Carolina.

[3] See Royce, op. cit., pp. 313–314; Commissioner H. Price, Report of Indian Commissioner, p. li, 1884; Report of Indian Commissioner, p. 495, 1898; also references by Commissioner W. Medill, Report of Indian Commissioner, p. 399, 1848; and Report of Indian Commissioner for 1855, p. 255, 1856.

were subsequently added as to increase the number by more than 600.[1]
A census taken by their agent, Colonel Thomas, in 1841, gave the
number of East Cherokee (possibly only those in North Carolina
intended) as 1,220,[2] while a year later the whole number residing in
North Carolina, Tennessee, Alabama, and Georgia was officially estimated at from 1,000 to 1,200.[3] It is not the only time a per capita
payment has resulted in a sudden increase of the census population.

In 1852 (Capt.) James W. Terrell was engaged by Thomas, then in
the state senate, to take charge of his store at Qualla, and remained
associated with him and in close contact with the Indians from then until
after the close of the war, assisting, as special United States agent, in
the disbursement of the interest payments, and afterward as a Confederate officer in the organization of the Indian companies, holding a
commission as captain of Company A, Sixty-ninth North Carolina
Confederate infantry. Being of an investigating bent, Captain Terrell
was led to give attention to the customs and mythology of the Cherokee, and to accumulate a fund of information on the subject seldom
possessed by a white man. He still resides at Webster, a few miles
from the reservation, and is now seventy-one years of age.

In 1855 Congress directed the per capita payment to the East Cherokee of the removal fund established for them in 1848, provided that
North Carolina should first give assurance that they would be allowed
to remain permanently in that state. This assurance, however, was
not given until 1866, and the money was therefore not distributed,
but remained in the treasury until 1875, when it was made applicable
to the purchase of lands and the quieting of titles for the benefit of
the Indians.[4]

From 1855 until after the civil war we find no official notice of the
East Cherokee, and our information must be obtained from other
sources. It was, however, a most momentous period in their history.
At the outbreak of the war Thomas was serving his seventh consec-
utive term in the state senate. Being an ardent Confederate sym-
pathizer, he was elected a delegate to the convention which passed the
secession ordinance, and immediately after voting in favor of that
measure resigned from the senate in order to work for the southern
cause. As he was already well advanced in years it is doubtful if his
effort would have gone beyond the raising of funds and other supplies
but for the fact that at this juncture an effort was made by the Confederate General Kirby Smith to enlist the East Cherokee for active
service.

The agent sent for this purpose was Washington Morgan, known to
the Indians as Â'ganstâ'ta, son of that Colonel Gideon Morgan who

---

[1] Royce, Cherokee Nation, op. cit., p. 313 and note.
[2] Report of the Indian Commissioner, pp. 459–460, 1845.
[3] Commissioner Crawford, Report of Indian Commissioner, p. 3, 1842.
[4] Royce, op. cit., p. 314.

had commanded the Cherokee at the Horseshoe bend. By virtue of his Indian blood and historic ancestry he was deemed the most fitting emissary for the purpose. Early in 1862 he arrived among the Cherokee, and by appealing to old-time memories so aroused the war spirit among them that a large number declared themselves ready to follow wherever he led. Conceiving the question at issue in the war to be one that did not concern the Indians, Thomas had discouraged their participation in it and advised them to remain at home in quiet neutrality. Now, however, knowing Morgan's reputation for reckless daring, he became alarmed at the possible result to them of such leadership. Forced either to see them go from his own protection or to lead them himself, he chose the latter alternative and proposed to them to enlist in the Confederate legion which he was about to organize. His object, as he himself has stated, was to keep them out of danger so far as possible by utilizing them as scouts and home guards through the mountains, away from the path of the large armies. Nothing of this was said to the Indians, who might not have been satisfied with such an arrangement. Morgan went back alone and the Cherokee enrolled under the command of their white chief. [1]

The "Thomas Legion," recruited in 1862 by William H. Thomas for the Confederate service and commanded by him as colonel, consisted originally of one infantry regiment of ten companies (Sixty-ninth North Carolina Infantry), one infantry battalion of six companies, one cavalry battalion of eight companies (First North Carolina Cavalry Battalion), one field battery (Light Battery) of 103 officers and men, and one company of engineers; in all about 2,800 men. The infantry battalion was recruited toward the close of the war to a full regiment of ten companies. Companies A and B of the Sixty-ninth regiment and two other companies of the infantry regiment recruited later were composed almost entirely of East Cherokee Indians, most of the commissioned officers being white men. The whole number of Cherokee thus enlisted was nearly four hundred, or about every able-bodied man in the tribe. [2]

In accordance with Thomas's plan the Indians were employed chiefly as scouts and home guards in the mountain region along the Tennessee-Carolina border, where, according to the testimony of Colonel String-

[1] The history of the events leading to the organization of the "Thomas Legion" is chiefly from the author's conversations with Colonel Thomas himself, corroborated and supplemented from other sources. In the words of Thomas, "If it had not been for the Indians I would not have been in the war."

[2] This is believed to be a correct statement of the strength and make-up of the Thomas Legion. Owing to the imperfection of the records and the absence of reliable memoranda among the surviving officers, no two accounts exactly coincide. The roll given in the North Carolina Confederate Roster, handed in by Captain Terrell, assistant quartermaster, was compiled early in the war and contains no notice of the engineer company or of the second infantry regiment, which included two other Indian companies. The information therein contained is supplemented from conversations and personal letters of Captain Terrell, and from letters and newspaper articles by Lieutenant-Colonel Stringfield of the Sixty-ninth. Another statement is given in Mrs Avery's sketch of Colonel Thomas in the North Carolina University Magazine for May, 1899.

field, "they did good work and service for the South." The most important engagement in which they were concerned occurred at Baptist gap, Tennessee, September 15, 1862, where Lieutenant Astu'-gatâ'ga, "a splendid specimen of Indian manhood," was killed in a charge. The Indians were furious at his death, and before they could be restrained they scalped one or two of the Federal dead. For this action ample apologies were afterward given by their superior officers. The war, in fact, brought out all the latent Indian in their nature. Before starting to the front every man consulted an oracle stone to learn whether or not he might hope to return in safety. The start was celebrated with a grand old-time war dance at the townhouse on Soco, and the same dance was repeated at frequent intervals there-after, the Indians being "painted and feathered in good old style," Thomas himself frequently assisting as master of ceremonies. The ballplay, too, was not forgotten, and on one occasion a detachment of Cherokee, left to guard a bridge, became so engrossed in the excite-ment of the game as to narrowly escape capture by a sudden dash of the Federals. Owing to Thomas's care for their welfare, they suffered but slightly in actual battle, although a number died of hardship and disease. When the Confederates evacuated eastern Tennessee, in the winter of 1863–64, some of the white troops of the legion, with one or two of the Cherokee companies, were shifted to western Virginia, and by assignment to other regiments a few of the Cherokee were present at the final siege and surrender of Richmond. The main body of the Indians, with the rest of the Thomas Legion, crossed over into North Carolina and did service protecting the western border until the close of the war, when they surrendered on parole at Waynesville, North Carolina, in May, 1865, all those of the command being allowed to keep their guns. It is claimed by their officers that they were the last of the Confederate forces to surrender. About fifty of the Cher-okee veterans still survive, nearly half of whom, under conduct of Colonel Stringfield, attended the Confederate reunion at Louisville, Kentucky, in 1900, where they attracted much attention.[1]

In 1863, by resolution of February 12, the Confederate House of Representatives called for information as to the number and condition of the East Cherokee, and their pending relations with the Federal government at the beginning of the war, with a view to continuing these relations under Confederate auspices. In response to this inquiry a report was submitted by the Confederate commissioner of Indian affairs, S. S. Scott, based on information furnished by Colonel Thomas and Captain James W. Terrell, their former disbursing agent, showing that interest upon the " removal and subsistence fund " estab-

---

[1] Personal Information from Colonel W. H. Thomas, Lieutenant-Colonel W. W. Stringfield, Captain James W. Terrell, Chief N. J. Smith (first sergeant Company B), and others, with other details from Moore's (Confederate) Roster of North Carolina Troops, IV; Raleigh, 1882; also list of survivors in 1890, by Carrington, in Eastern Band of Cherokees, Extra Bulletin of Eleventh Census, p. 21, 1892.

lished in 1848 had been paid annually up to and including the year 1859, at the rate of $3.20 per capita, or an aggregate, exclusive of disbursing agent's commission, of $4,838.40 annually, based upon the original Mullay enumeration of 1,517.

Upon receipt of this report it was enacted by the Confederate congress that the sum of $19,352.36 be paid the East Cherokee to cover the interest period of four years from May 23, 1860, to May 23, 1864. In this connection the Confederate commissioner suggested that the payment be made in provisions, of which the Indians were then greatly in need, and which, if the payment were made in cash, they would be unable to purchase, on account of the general scarcity. He adds that, according to his information, almost every Cherokee capable of bearing arms was then in the Confederate service. The roll furnished by Captain Terrell is the original Mullay roll corrected to May, 1860, no reference being made to the later Mullay enumeration (2,133), already alluded to. There is no record to show that the payment thus authorized was made, and as the Confederate government was then in hard straits it is probable that nothing further was done in the matter.

In submitting his statement of previous payments, Colonel Thomas, their former agent, adds:

As the North Carolina Cherokees have, like their brethren west, taken up arms against the Lincoln government, it is not probable that any further advances of interest will be made by that government to any portion of the Cherokee tribe. I also enclose a copy of the act of July 29, 1848, so far as relates to the North Carolina Cherokees, and a printed explanation of their rights, prepared by me in 1851, and submitted to the attorney-general, and his opinion thereon, which may not be altogether uninteresting to those who feel an interest in knowing something of the history of the Cherokee tribe of Indians, whose destiny is so closely identified with that of the Southern Confederacy.[1]

In a skirmish near Bryson City (then Charleston), Swain county, North Carolina, about a year after enlistment, a small party of Cherokee—perhaps a dozen in number—was captured by a detachment of Union troops and carried to Knoxville, where, having become dissatisfied with their experience in the Confederate service, they were easily persuaded to go over to the Union side. Through the influence of their principal man, Digăne'skĭ, several others were induced to desert to the Union army, making about thirty in all. As a part of the Third North Carolina Mounted Volunteer Infantry, they served with the Union forces in the same region until the close of the war, when they returned to their homes to find their tribesmen so bitterly incensed against them that for some time their lives were in danger. Eight of these are still alive in 1900.[2]

One of these Union Cherokee had brought back with him the small-

---

[1] Thomas-Terrell manuscript East Cherokee roll, with accompanying letters, 1864 (Bur. Am. Eth. archives).

[2] Personal information from Colonel W. H. Thomas, Captain J. W. Terrell, Chief N. J. Smith, and others; see also Carrington, Eastern Band of Cherokees, Extra Bulletin of Eleventh Census, p. 21, 1892.

pox from an infected camp near Knoxville. Shortly after his return
he became sick and soon died. As the characteristic pustules had not
appeared, the disease seeming to work inwardly, the nature of his
sickness was not at first suspected—smallpox having been an unknown
disease among the Cherokee for nearly a century—and his funeral was
largely attended. A week later a number of those who had been present became sick, and the disease was recognized by Colonel Thomas as
smallpox in all its virulence. It spread throughout the tribe, this
being in the early spring of 1866, and in spite of all the efforts of
Thomas, who brought a doctor from Tennessee to wait upon them,
more than one hundred of the small community died in consequence.
The fatal result was largely due to the ignorance of the Indians, who,
finding their own remedies of no avail, used the heroic aboriginal
treatment of the plunge bath in the river and the cold-water douche,
which resulted in death in almost every case. Thus did the war bring
its harvest of death, misery, and civil feud to the East Cherokee.[1]

Shortly after this event Colonel Thomas was compelled by physical
and mental infirmity to retire from further active participation in the
affairs of the East Cherokee, after more than half a century spent in
intimate connection with them, during the greater portion of which
time he had been their most trusted friend and adviser. Their affairs
at once became the prey of confusion and factional strife, which continued until the United States stepped in as arbiter.

In 1868 Congress ordered another census of the East Cherokee, to
serve as a guide in future payments, the roll to include only those
persons whose names had appeared upon the Mullay roll of 1848 and
their legal heirs and representatives. The work was completed in the
following year by S. H. Sweatland, and a payment of interest then
due under former enactment was made by him on this basis.[2] "In
accordance with their earnestly expressed desire to be brought under
the immediate charge of the government as its wards," the Congress
which ordered this last census directed that the Commissioner of Indian
Affairs should assume the same charge over the East Cherokee as over
other tribes, but as no extra funds were made available for the purpose the matter was held in abeyance.[3] An unratified treaty made
this year with the Cherokee Nation west contained a stipulation that
any Cherokee east of the Mississippi who should remove to the Cherokee nation within three years should be entitled to full citizenship and
privileges therein, but after that date could be admitted only by act
of the Cherokee national council.[4]

After the retirement of Thomas, in the absence of any active

[1] Author's information from Colonel Thomas and others. Various informants have magnified the
number of deaths to several hundred, but the estimate here given, obtained from Thomas, is probably more reliable.

[2] Royce, Cherokee Nation, Fifth Ann. Rep. Bureau of Ethnology, p. 314, 1888.

[3] Commissioner F. A. Walker, Report of Indian Commissioner, p. 25, 1872.

[4] Royce, op. cit., p. 353.

governmental supervision, need was felt of some central authority. On December 9, 1868, a general council of the East Cherokee assembled at Cheowa, in Graham county, North Carolina, took preliminary steps toward the adoption of a regular form of tribal government under a constitution. N. J. Smith, afterward principal chief, was clerk of the council. The new government was formally inaugurated on December 1, 1870. It provided for a first and a second chief to serve for a term of two years, minor officers to serve one year, and an annual council representing each Cherokee settlement within the state of North Carolina. Kâ′lahû′, "All-bones," commonly known to the whites as Flying-squirrel or Sawnook (Sawănu′gĭ), was elected chief. A new constitution was adopted five years later, by which the chief's term of office was fixed at four years.[1]

The status of the lands held by the Indians had now become a matter of serious concern, As has been stated, the deeds had been made out by Thomas in his own name, as the state laws at that time forbade Indian ownership of real estate. In consequence of his losses during the war and his subsequent disability, the Thomas properties, of which the Cherokee lands were technically a part, had become involved, so that the entire estate had passed into the hands of creditors, the most important of whom, William Johnston, had obtained sheriff's deeds in 1869 for all of these Indian lands under three several judgments against Thomas, aggregating $33,887.11. To adjust the matter so as to secure title and possession to the Indians, Congress in 1870 authorized suit to be brought in their name for the recovery of their interest. This suit was begun in May, 1873, in the United States circuit court for western North Carolina. A year later the matters in dispute were submitted by agreement to a board of arbitrators, whose award was confirmed by the court in November, 1874.

The award finds that Thomas had purchased with Indian funds a tract estimated to contain 50,000 acres on Oconaluftee river and Soco creek, and known as the Qualla boundary, together with a number of individual tracts outside the boundary; that the Indians were still indebted to Thomas toward the purchase of the Qualla boundary lands for the sum of $18,250, from which should be deducted $6,500 paid by them to Johnston to release titles, with interest to date of award, making an aggregate of $8,486, together with a further sum of $2,478, which had been intrusted to Terrell, the business clerk and assistant of Thomas, and by him turned over to Thomas, as creditor of the Indians, under power of attorney, this latter sum, with interest to date of award, aggregating $2,697.89; thus leaving a balance due from the Indians to Thomas or his legal creditor, Johnston, of $7,066.11. The award declares that on account of the questionable manner in

---

[1] Constitution, etc., quoted in Carrington, Eastern Band of Cherokees, Extra Bulletin Eleventh Census, pp. 18–20, 1892; author's personal information.

Cabin home on the Qualla Reservation, North Carolina. Photograph by James Mooney of the Bureau of American Ethnology 1888.

which the disputed lands had been bought in by Johnston, he should be allowed to hold them only as security for the balance due him until paid, and that on the payment of the said balance of $7,066.11, with interest at 6 per cent from the date of the award, the Indians should be entitled to a clear conveyance from him of the legal title to all the lands embraced within the Qualla boundary.[1]

To enable the Indians to clear off this lien on their lands and for other purposes, Congress in 1875 directed that as much as remained of the "removal and subsistence fund" set apart for their benefit in 1848 should be used "in perfecting the titles to the lands awarded to them, and to pay the costs, expenses, and liabilities attending their recent litigations, also to purchase and extinguish the titles of any white persons to lands within the general boundaries allotted to them by the court, and for the education, improvement, and civilization of their people." In accordance with this authority the unpaid balance and interest due Johnston, amounting to $7,242.76, was paid him in the same year, and shortly afterward there was purchased on behalf of the Indians some fifteen thousand acres additional, the Commissioner of Indian Affairs being constituted trustee for the Indians. For the better protection of the Indians the lands were made inalienable except by assent of the council and upon approval of the President of the United States. The deeds for the Qualla boundary and the 15,000 acre purchase were executed respectively on October 9, 1876, and August 14, 1880.[2] As the boundaries of the different purchases were but vaguely defined, a new survey of the whole Qualla boundary and adjoining tracts was authorized. The work was intrusted to M. S. Temple, deputy United States surveyor, who completed it in 1876, his survey maps of the reservation being accepted as the official standard.[3]

The titles and boundaries having been adjusted, the Indian Office assumed regular supervision of East Cherokee affairs, and in June, 1875, the first agent since the retirement of Thomas was sent out in the person of W. C. McCarthy. He found the Indians, according to his report, destitute and discouraged, almost without stock or farming tools. There were no schools, and very few full-bloods could speak English, although to their credit nearly all could read and write their own language, the parents teaching the children. Under his authority a distribution was made of stock animals, seed wheat, and farming tools, and several schools were started. In the next year, however,

---

[1] See award of arbitrators, Rufus Barringer, John H. Dillard, and T. Ruffin, with full statement, in Eastern Band of Cherokee Indians against W. T. Thomas et al. H. R. Ex. Doc. 128, 53d Cong., 2d sess., 1894; summary in Royce, Cherokee Nation, Fifth Ann. Rep. Bureau of Ethnology, pp. 315–318, 1888.

[2] See Royce, op. cit., pp. 315–318; Commissioner T. J. Morgan, Report of Indian Commissioner, p. xxix, 1890. The final settlement, under the laws of North Carolina, was not completed until 1894.

[3] Royce, op. cit., pp. 315–318; Carrington, Eastern Band of Cherokees, with map of Temple survey, Extra Bulletin of Eleventh Census, 1892.

the agency was discontinued and the educational interests of the band turned over to the state school superintendent.[1]

In the meantime Kâ'lahû' had been succeeded as chief by Lloyd R. Welch (Da'si͡ giya'gĭ), an educated mixed-blood of Cheowa, who served about five years, dying shortly after his reelection to a second term (48). He made a good record by his work in reconciling the various factions which had sprung up after the withdrawal of the guiding influence of Thomas, and in defeating the intrigues of fraudulent white claimants and mischief makers. Shortly before his death the Government, through Special Agent John A. Sibbald, recognized his authority as principal chief, together with the constitution which had been adopted by the band under his auspices in 1875. N. J. Smith (Tsa'lădihĭ'), who had previously served as clerk of the council, was elected to his unexpired term and continued to serve until the fall of 1890.[2]

We find no further official notice of the East Cherokee until 1881, when Commissioner Price reported that they were still without agent or superintendent, and that so far as the Indian Office was concerned their affairs were in an anomalous and unsatisfactory condition, while factional feuds were adding to the difficulties and retarding the progress of the band. In the spring of that year a visiting delegation from the Cherokee Nation west had extended to them an urgent invitation to remove to Indian Territory and the Indian Office had encouraged the project, with the result that 161 persons of the band removed during the year to Indian Territory, the expense being borne by the Government. Others were represented as being desirous to remove, and the Commissioner recommended an appropriation for the purpose, but as Congress failed to act the matter was dropped.[3]

The neglected condition of the East Cherokee having been brought to the attention of those old-time friends of the Indian, the Quakers, through an appeal made in their behalf by members of that society residing in North Carolina, the Western Yearly Meeting, of Indiana, volunteered to undertake the work of civilization and education. On May 31, 1881, representatives of the Friends entered into a contract with the Indians, subject to approval by the Government, to establish and continue among them for ten years an industrial school and other common schools, to be supported in part from the annual interest of the trust fund held by the Government to the credit of the East Cherokee and in part by funds furnished by the Friends themselves. Through the efforts of Barnabas C. Hobbs, of the Western Yearly Meeting, a yearly contract to the same effect was entered into with the Commis-

---

[1] Report of Agent W. C. McCarthy, Report of Indian Commissioner, pp. 343–344, 1875; and Report of Indian Commissione, pp. 118–119, 1876.

[2] Author's personal information; see also Carrington, Eastern Band of Cherokees; Zeigler and Grosscup, Heart of the Alleghanies, pp. 35–36, 1883.

[3] Commissioner H. Price, Report of Indian Commissioner, pp. lxiv–lxv, 1881, and Report of Indian Commissioner, pp. lxix–lxx, 1882; see also ante, p. 151.

sioner of Indian Affairs later in the same year, and was renewed by successive commissioners to cover the period of ten years ending June 30, 1892, when the contract system was terminated and the Government assumed direct control.   Under the joint arrangement, with some aid at the outset from the North Carolina Meeting, work was begun in 1881 by Thomas Brown with several teachers sent out by the Indiana Friends, who established a small training school at the agency headquarters at Cherokee, and several day schools in the outlying settlements.   He was succeeded three years later by H. W. Spray, an experienced educator, who, with a corps of efficient assistants and greatly enlarged facilities, continued to do good work for the elevation of the Indians until the close of the contract system eight years later.[1] After an interregnum, during which the schools suffered from frequent changes, he was reappointed as government agent and superintendent in 1898, a position which he still holds in 1901.   To the work conducted under his auspices the East Cherokee owe much of what they have to-day of civilization and enlightenment.

From some travelers who visited the reservation about this time we have a pleasant account of a trip along Soco and a day with Chief Smith at Yellow Hill.   They describe the Indians as being so nearly like the whites in their manner of living that a stranger could rarely distinguish an Indian's cabin or little cove farm from that of a white man.   Their principal crop was corn, which they ground for themselves, and they had also an abundance of apples, peaches, and plums, and a few small herds of ponies and cattle.   Their wants were so few that they had but little use for money.   Their primitive costume had long been obsolete, and their dress was like that of the whites, excepting that moccasins took the place of shoes, and they manufactured their own clothing by the aid of spinning-wheels and looms.   Finely cut pipes and well-made baskets were also produced, and the good influence of the schools recently established was already manifest in the children.[2]

In 1882 the agency was reestablished and provision was made for taking a new census of all Cherokee east of the Mississippi, Joseph G. Hester being appointed to the work.[3]   The census was submitted as complete in June, 1884, and contained the names of 1,881 persons in North Carolina, 758 in Georgia, 213 in Tennessee, 71 in Alabama, and 33 scattering, a total of 2,956.[4]   Although this census received the approval and certificate of the East Cherokee council, a large portion of the band still refuse to recognize it as authoritative, claiming that a large number of persons therein enrolled have no Cherokee blood.

[1] See Commissioner T. J. Morgan, Report of Indian Commissioner, pp. 141-145, 1892; author's personal information from B. C. Hobbs, Chief N. J. Smith, and others. For further notice of school growth see also Report of Indian Commissioner, pp. 426-427, 1897.

[2] Zeigler and Grosscup, Heart of the Alleghanies, pp. 36-42, 1883.

[3] Commissioner H. Price, Report of Indian Commissioner, pp. lxix-lxx, 1882.

[4] Report of Indian Commissioner, pp. li-lii, 1884.

The East Cherokee had never ceased to contend for a participation in the rights and privileges accruing to the western Nation under treaties with the Government. In 1882 a special agent had been appointed to investigate their claims, and in the following year, under authority of Congress, the eastern band of Cherokee brought suit in the Court of Claims against the United States and the Cherokee Nation west to determine its rights in the permanent annuity fund and other trust funds held by the United States for the Cherokee Indians.[1] The case was decided adversely to the eastern band, first by the Court of Claims in 1885,[2] and finally, on appeal, by the Supreme Court on March 1, 1886, that court holding in its decision that the Cherokee in North Carolina had dissolved their connection with the Cherokee Nation and ceased to be a part of it when they refused to accompany the main body at the Removal, and that if Indians in North Carolina or in any state east of the Mississippi wished to enjoy the benefits of the common property of the Cherokee Nation in any form whatever they must be readmitted to citizenship in the Cherokee Nation and comply with its constitution and laws. In accordance with this decision the agent in the Indian territory was instructed to issue no more residence permits to claimants for Cherokee citizenship, and it was officially announced that all persons thereafter entering that country without consent of the Cherokee authorities would be treated as intruders.[3] This decision, cutting off the East Cherokee from all hope of sharing in any of the treaty benefits enjoyed by their western kinsmen, was a sore disappointment to them all, especially to Chief Smith, who had worked unceasingly in their behalf from the institution of the proceedings. In view of the result, Commissioner Atkins strongly recommended, as the best method of settling them in permanent homes, secure from white intrusion and from anxiety on account of their uncertain tenure and legal status in North Carolina, that negotiations be opened through government channels for their readmission to citizenship in the Cherokee Nation, to be followed, if successful, by the sale of their lands in North Carolina and their removal to Indian Territory.[4]

In order to acquire a more definite legal status, the Cherokee residing in North Carolina—being practically all those of the eastern band having genuine Indian interests—became a corporate body under the laws of the state in 1889. The act, ratified on March 11, declares in its first section "That the North Carolina or Eastern Cherokee Indians, resident or domiciled in the counties of Jackson, Swain, Graham, and Cherokee, be and at the same time are hereby

[1] Commissioner H. Price, Report of Indian Commissioner, pp. lxix-lxxi, 1882, also "Indian legislation," ibid., p. 214; Commissioner H. Price, Report of Indian Commissioner, pp. lxv-lxvi, 1883.
[2] Commissioner J. D. C. Atkins, Report of Indian Commissioner, p. lxx, 1885.
[3] Same commissioner, Report of the Indian Commissioner, p. xlv, 1886; decision quoted by same commissioner, Report of Indian Commissioner, p. lxxvii, 1887.
[4] Same commissioner, Report of the Indian Commissioner, p. li, 1886; reiterated by him in Report for 1887, p. lxxvii.

created and constituted a body politic and corporate under the name, style, and title of the Eastern Band of Cherokee Indians, with all the rights, franchises, privileges and powers incident and belonging to corporations under the laws of the state of North Carolina.[1]

On August 2, 1893, ex-Chief Smith died at Cherokee, in the fifty-seventh year of his life, more than twenty of which had been given to the service of his people. Nimrod Jarrett Smith, known to the Cherokee as Tsa'lădihĭ', was the son of a halfbreed father by an Indian mother, and was born near the present Murphy, Cherokee county, North Carolina, on January 3, 1837. His earliest recollections were thus of the miseries that attended the flight of the refugees to the mountains during the Removal period. His mother spoke very little English, but his father was a man of considerable intelligence, having acted as interpreter and translator for Reverend Evan Jones at the old Valleytown mission. As the boy grew to manhood he acquired a fair education, which, aided by a commanding presence, made him a person of influence among his fellows. At twenty-five years of age he enlisted in the Thomas Legion as first sergeant of Company B, Sixty-ninth North Carolina (Confederate) Infantry, and served in that capacity till the close of the war. He was clerk of the council that drafted the first East Cherokee constitution in 1868, and on the death of Principal Chief Lloyd Welch in 1880 was elected to fill the unexpired term, continuing in office by successive reelections until the close of 1891, a period of about twelve years, the longest term yet filled by an incumbent. As principal chief he signed the contract under which the school work was inaugurated in 1881. For several years thereafter his duties, particularly in connection with the suit against the western Cherokee, required his presence much of the time at Washington, while at home his time was almost as constantly occupied in attending to the wants of a dependent people. Although he was entitled under the constitution of the band to a salary of five hundred dollars per year, no part of this salary was ever paid, because of the limited resources of his people, and only partial reimbursement was made to him, shortly before his death, for expenses incurred in official visits to Washington. With frequent opportunities to enrich himself at the expense of his people, he maintained his honor and died a poor man.

In person Chief Smith was a splendid specimen of physical manhood, being six feet four inches in height and built in proportion, erect in figure, with flowing black hair curling down over his shoulders, a deep musical voice, and a kindly spirit and natural dignity that never failed to impress the stranger. His widow—a white woman—and several children survive him.[2]

---

[1] See act in full, Report of Indian Commissioner, vol. I, pp. 680–681, 1891.

[2] From author's personal acquaintance; see also Zeigler and Grosscup, Heart of the Alleghanies, pp. 38–39, 1883; Agent J. L. Holmes, in Report of Indian Commissioner, p. 160, 1885; Commissioner T. J. Morgan, Report of Indian Commissioner, p. 142, 1892; Moore, Roster of the North Carolina Troops, IV, 1882.

Tsaladihi' or Chief Nimrod Jarrett Smith

Photographer not recorded, 1886.

In 1894 the long-standing litigation between the East Cherokee and a number of creditors and claimants to Indian lands within and adjoining the Qualla boundary was finally settled by a compromise by which the several white tenants and claimants within the boundary agreed to execute a quitclaim and vacate on payment to them by the Indians of sums aggregating $24,552, while for another disputed adjoining tract of 33,000 acres the United States agreed to pay, for the Indians, at the rate of $1.25 per acre. The necessary Government approval having been obtained, Congress appropriated a sufficient amount for carrying into effect the agreement, thus at last completing a perfect and unincumbered title to all the lands claimed by the Indians, with the exception of a few outlying tracts of comparative unimportance.[1]

In 1895 the Cherokee residing in North Carolina upon the reservation and in the outlying settlements were officially reported to number 1,479.[2] A year later an epidemic of grippe spread through the band, with the result that the census of 1897 shows but 1,312,[3] among those who died at this time being Big-witch (Tskĭl-e′gwa), the oldest man of the band, who distinctly remembered the Creek war, and Wadi′yăhĭ, the last old woman who preserved the art of making double-walled baskets. In the next year the population had recovered to 1,351. The description of the mode of living then common to most of the Indians will apply nearly as well to-day:

While they are industrious, these people are not progressive farmers and have learned nothing of modern methods. The same crops are raised continuously until the soil will yield no more or is washed away, when new ground is cleared or broken. The value of rotation and fertilizing has not yet been discovered or taught. . . .

That these people can live at all upon the products of their small farms is due to the extreme simplicity of their food, dress, and manner of living. The typical house is of logs, is about fourteen by sixteen feet, of one room, just high enough for the occupants to stand erect, with perhaps a small loft for the storage of extras. The roof is of split shingles or shakes. There is no window, the open door furnishing what light is required. At one end of the house is the fireplace, with outside chimney of stones or sticks chinked with clay. The furniture is simple and cheap. An iron pot, a bake kettle, a coffeepot and mill, small table, and a few cups, knives, and spoons are all that is needed. These, with one or two bedsteads, homemade, a few pillows and quilts, with feather mattresses for winter covering, as well as for the usual purpose, constitute the principal house possessions. For outdoor work there is an ax, hoe, and shovel plow. A wagon or cart may be owned, but is not essential. The outfit is inexpensive and answers every purpose. The usual food is bean bread, with coffee. In the fall chestnut bread is also used. Beef is seldom eaten, but pork is highly esteemed, and a considerable number of hogs are kept, running wild and untended in summer.[4]

By the most recent official count, in 1900, the East Cherokee residing in North Carolina under direct charge of the agent and included

[1] Commissioner D. M. Browning, Report of Indian Commissioner for 1894, pp. 81–82, 1895; also Agent T. W. Potter, ibid., p. 398.

[2] Agent T. W. Potter, Report of Indian Commissioner for 1895, p. 387, 1896.

[3] Agent J. C. Hart, Report of Indian Commissioner, p. 208, 1897.

[4] Agent J. C. Hart, Report of Indian Commissioner, pp. 218–219, 1898.

Family in front of a dwelling. Photograph probably by James Mooney, Qualla Reservation, North Carolina, 1912.

within the act of incorporation number 1,376, of whom about 1,100 are on the reservation, the rest living farther to the west, on Nanta-hala, Cheowa, and Hiwassee rivers. This does not include mixed-bloods in adjoining states and some hundreds of unrecognized claim-ants. Those enumerated own approximately 100,000 acres of land, of which 83,000 are included within the Qualla reservation and a contiguous tract in Jackson and Swain counties. They receive no rations or annuities and are entirely self-supporting, the annual interest on their trust fund established in 1848, which has dwindled to about $23,000, being applied to the payment of taxes upon their unoc-cupied common lands. From time to time they have made leases of timber, gold-washing, and grazing privileges, but without any great profit to themselves. By special appropriation the government sup-ports an industrial training school at Cherokee, the agency head-quarters, in which 170 pupils are now being boarded, clothed, and educated in the practical duties of life. This school, which in its work-ings is a model of its kind, owes much of its usefulness and high standing to the efficient management of Prof. H. W. Spray (Wĭlsĭnĭ'), already mentioned, who combines the duties of superintendent and agent for the band. His chief clerk, Mr James Blythe (Diskwa''nĭ, "Chestnut-bread"), a Cherokee by blood, at one time filled the posi-tion of agent, being perhaps the only Indian who has ever served in such capacity.

The exact legal status of the East Cherokee is still a matter of dis-pute, they being at once wards of the government, citizens of the United States, and (in North Carolina) a corporate body under state laws. They pay real estate taxes and road service, exercise the voting privilege,[1] and are amenable to the local courts, but do not pay poll tax or receive any pauper assistance from the counties; neither can they make free contracts or alienate their lands (49). Under their tribal constitution they are governed by a principal and an assistant chief, elected for a term of four years, with an executive council appointed by the chief, and sixteen councilors elected by the various settlements for a term of two years. The annual council is held in October at Cherokee, on the reservation, the proceedings being in the Cherokee language and recorded by their clerk in the Cherokee alphabet, as well as in English. The present chief is Jesse Reid (Tsĕ'si-Ska'tsĭ, "Scotch Jesse"), an intelligent mixed-blood, who fills the office with dignity and ability. As a people they are peaceable and law-abiding, kind and hospitable, providing for their simple wants by their own industry without asking or expecting outside assistance. Their fields, orchards, and fish traps, with some few domestic animals and occasional hunting, supply them with food, while by the sale of

---

[1] At the recent election in November, 1900, they were debarred by the local polling officers from either registering or voting, and the matter is now being contested.

Cherokee Payment, 1894. Photographer not recorded.

ginseng and other medicinal plants gathered in the mountains, with fruit and honey of their own raising, they procure what additional supplies they need from the traders. The majority are fairly comfortable, far above the condition of most Indian tribes, and but little, if any, behind their white neighbors. In literary ability they may even be said to surpass them, as in addition to the result of nearly twenty years of school work among the younger people, nearly all the men and some of the women can read and write their own language. All wear civilized costumes, though an occasional pair of moccasins is seen, while the women find means to gratify the racial love of color in the wearing of red bandanna kerchiefs in place of bonnets. The older people still cling to their ancient rites and sacred traditions, but the dance and the ballplay wither and the Indian day is nearly spent.

III—NOTES TO THE HISTORICAL SKETCH

(1) TRIBAL SYNONYMY (page 15): Very few Indian tribes are known to us under the names by which they call themselves. One reason for this is the fact that the whites have usually heard of a tribe from its neighbors, speaking other languages, before coming upon the tribe itself. Many of the popular tribal names were originally nicknames bestowed by neighboring tribes, frequently referring to some peculiar custom, and in a large number of cases would be strongly repudiated by the people designated by them. As a rule each tribe had a different name in every surrounding Indian language, besides those given by Spanish, French, Dutch, or English settlers.

Yûñ'wiyǎ'—This word is compounded from *yûñwǐ* (person) and *yǎ* (real or principal). The assumption of superiority is much in evidence in Indian tribal names; thus, the Iroquois, Delawares, and Pawnee call themselves, respectively, Oñwe-hoñwe, Leni-lenape', and Tsariksi-tsa'riks, all of which may be rendered "men of men," "men surpassing other men," or "real men."

Kǐtu'hwagǐ—This word, which can not be analyzed, is derived from Kǐtu'hwǎ, the name of an ancient Cherokee settlement formerly on Tuckasegee river, just above the present Bryson City, in Swain county, North Carolina. It is noted in 1730 as one of the "seven mother towns" of the tribe. Its inhabitants were called Ani'-Kǐtu'hwagǐ (people of Kituhwa), and seem to have exercised a controlling influence over those of all the towns on the waters of Tuckasegee and the upper part of Little Tennessee, the whole body being frequently classed together as Ani'-Kǐtu'hwagǐ. The dialect of these towns held a middle place linguistically between those spoken to the east, on the heads of Savannah, and to the west, on Hiwassee, Cheowah, and the lower course of Little Tennessee. In various forms the word was adopted by the Delawares, Shawano, and other northern Algonquian tribes as a synonym for Cherokee, probably from the fact that the Kituhwa people guarded the Cherokee northern frontier. In the form Cuttawa it appears on the French map of Vaugondy in 1755. From a similarity of spelling, Schoolcraft incorrectly makes it a synonym for Catawba, while Brinton incorrectly asserts that it is an Algonquian term, fancifully rendered, "inhabitants of the great wilderness." Among the western Cherokee it is now the name of a powerful secret society, which had its origin shortly before the War of the Rebellion.

Cherokee—This name occurs in fully fifty different spellings. In the standard recognized form, which dates back at least to 1708, it has given name to counties in North Carolina, South Carolina, Georgia, and Alabama, within the ancient territory of the tribe, and to as many as twenty other geographic locations within the United States. In the Eastern or Lower dialect, with which the English settlers first became familiar, the form is Tsa'rǎgǐ', whence we get Cherokee. In the other dialects the form is Tsa'lǎgǐ'. It is evidently foreign to the tribe, as is frequently the case in tribal names, and in all probability is of Choctaw origin, having come up from the south through the medium of the Mobilian trade jargon. It will be noted that De Soto, whose chroniclers first use the word, in the form Chalaque, obtained his interpreters from the Gulf coast of Florida. Fontanedo, writing about the year 1575, mentions other inland tribes known to the natives of Florida under names which seem to be of Choctaw origin; for instance, the Canogacole, interpreted "wicked people," the final part being apparently the Choctaw word *okla* or *ogula*, "people", which appears also in Pascagoula, Bayou Goula, and Pensacola. Shetimasha, Atakapa, and probably Biloxi, are also Choctaw names, although the tribes themselves are of other origins. As the Choctaw held much of the Gulf coast and were the principal traders of that region, it was natural that explorers landing among them should adopt their names for the more remote tribes.

The name seems to refer to the fact that the tribe occupied a cave country. In the "Choctaw Leksikon" of Allen Wright, 1880, page 87, we find *choluk*, a noun, signifying a hole, cavity, pit, chasm, etc., and as an adjective signifying hollow. In the manuscript Choctaw dictionary of Cyrus Byington, in the library of the Bureau of American Ethnology, we find *chiluk*, noun, a hole, cavity, hollow, pit, etc., with a statement that in its usual application it means a cavity or hollow, and not a hole through anything. As an adjective, the same form is given as signifying hollow, having a hole, as *iti chiluk*, a hollow tree; *aboha chiluk*, an empty house; *chiluk chukoa*, to enter a hole. Other noun forms given are *chuluk* and *achiluk* in the singular and *chilukoa* in the plural, all signifying hole, pit, or cavity. Verbal forms are *chilukikbi*, to make a hole, and *chilukba*, to open and form a fissure.

In agreement with the genius of the Cherokee language the root form of the tribal name takes nominal or verbal prefixes according to its connection with the rest of the sentence, and is declined, or rather conjugated, as follows: SINGULAR—first person, *tsi-Tsa′lăgĭ*, I (am) a Cherokee; second person, *hi-Tsa′lăgĭ*, thou art a Cherokee; third person, *a-Tsa′lăgĭ*, he is a Cherokee. DUAL—first person, *ăsti-Tsa′lăgĭ*, we two are Cherokee; second person, *sti-Tsa′lăgĭ*, you two are Cherokee; third person, *ani′-Tsa′lăgĭ*, they two are Cherokee. PLURAL—first person, *atsi-Tsa′lăgĭ*, we (several) are Cherokee; second person, *hitsi-Tsa′lăgĭ*, you (several) are Cherokee; third person, *ani′-Tsa′lăgĭ*, they (several) are Cherokee. It will be noticed that the third person dual and plural are alike.

Oyata′ge′ronoñ′, etc.—The Iroquois (Mohawk) form is given by Hewitt as O-yata′-ge′ronoñ′, of which the root is *yata′*, cave, *o* is the assertive prefix, *ge* is the locative at, and *ronoñ′* is the tribal suffix, equivalent to (English) *-ites* or people. The word, which has several dialectic forms, signifies "inhabitants of the cave country," or "cave-country people," rather than "people who dwell in caves," as rendered by Schoolcraft. The same radix *yata′* occurs also in the Iroquois name for the opossum, which is a burrowing animal. As is well known, the Allegheny region is peculiarly a cave country, the caves having been used by the Indians for burial and shelter purposes, as is proved by numerous remains found in them. It is probable that the Iroquois simply translated the name (Chalaque) current in the South, as we find is the case in the West, where the principal plains tribes are known under translations of the same names in all the different languages. The Wyandot name for the Cherokee, Wataiyo-ronoñ′, and their Catawba name, Mañterañ′, both seem to refer to coming out of the ground, and may have been originally intended to convey the same idea of cave people.

Rickahockan—This name is used by the German explorer, Lederer, in 1670, as the name of the people inhabiting the mountains to the southwest of the Virginia settlements. On his map he puts them in the mountains on the southern head streams of Roanoke river, in western North Carolina. He states that, according to his Indian informants, the Rickahockan lived beyond the mountains in a land of great waves, which he interpreted to mean the sea shore (!), but it is more likely that the Indians were trying to convey, by means of the sign language, the idea of a succession of mountain ridges. The name was probably of Powhatan origin, and is evidently identical with Rechahecrian of the Virginia chronicles of about the same period, the *r* in the latter form being perhaps a misprint. It may be connected with Righka-hauk, indicated on Smith's map of Virginia, in 1607, as the name of a town within the

Powhatan territory, and still preserved in Rockahock, the name of an estate on lower Pamunkey river. We have too little material of the Powhatan language to hazard an interpretation, but it may possibly contain the root of the word for sand, which appears as *lekawa*, *nikawa*, *negaw*, *rigawa*, *rekwa*, etc, in various eastern Algonquian dialects, whence Rockaway (sand), and Recgawawank (sandy place). The Powhatan form, as given by Strachey, is *racawh* (sand). He gives also *rocoyhook* (otter), *reihcahahcoik*, hidden under a cloud, overcast, *rickahone* or *reihcoan* (a comb), and *rickewh* (to divide in halves).

Talligewi—As Brinton well says: "No name in the Lenape' legends has given rise to more extensive discussion than this." On Colden's map in his "History of the Five Nations," 1727, we find the "Alleghens" indicated upon Allegheny river. Heckewelder, who recorded the Delaware tradition in 1819, says: "Those people, as I was told, called themselves Talligeu or Talligewi. Colonel John Gibson, however, a gentleman who has a thorough knowledge of the Indians, and speaks several of their languages, is of the opinion that they were not called Talligewi, but Alligewi; and it would seem that he is right from the traces of their name which still remain in the country, the Allegheny river and mountains having indubitably been named after them. The Delawares still call the former Alligewi Sipu (the river of the Alligewi)"—Indian Nations, p. 48, ed. 1876. Loskiel, writing on the authority of Zeisberger, says that the Delawares knew the whole country drained by the Ohio under the name of Alligewinengk, meaning "the land in which they arrived from distant places," basing his interpretation upon an etymology compounded from *talli* or *alli*, there, *icku*, to that place, and *ewak*, they go, with a locative final. Ettwein, another Moravian writer, says the Delawares called "the western country" Alligewenork, meaning a warpath, and called the river Alligewi Sipo. This definition would make the word come from *palliton* or *alliton*, to fight, to make war, *ewak*, they go, and a locative, i. e., "they go there to fight." Trumbull, an authority on Algonquian languages, derives the river name from *wulik*, good, best, *hanne*, rapid stream, and *sipu*, river, of which rendering its Iroquois name, *Ohio*, is nearly an equivalent. Rafinesque renders Talligewi as "there found," from *talli*, there, and some other root, not given (Brinton, Walam Olum, pp. 229–230, 1885).

It must be noted that the names Ohio and Alligewi (or Allegheny) were not applied by the Indians, as with us, to different parts of the same river, but to the whole stream, or at least the greater portion of it from its head downward. Although Brinton sees no necessary connection between the river name and the traditional tribal name, the statement of Heckewelder, generally a competent authority on Delaware matters, makes them identical.

In the traditional tribal name, Talligewi or Alligewi, *wi* is an assertive verbal suffix, so that the form properly means "he is a Tallige," or "they are Tallige." This comes very near to Tsa′lăgĭ′, the name by which the Cherokee call themselves, and it may have been an early corruption of that name. In Zeisberger's Delaware dictionary, however, we find *waloh* or *walok*, signifying a cave or hole, while in the "Walam Olum" we have *oligonunk* rendered "at the place of caves," the region being further described as a buffalo land on a pleasant plain, where the Lenape', advancing seaward from a less abundant northern region, at last found food (Walam Olum, pp. 194–195). Unfortunately, like other aboriginal productions of its kind among the northern tribes, the Lenape chronicle is suggestive rather than complete and connected. With more light it may be that seeming discrepancies would disappear and we should find at last that the Cherokee, in ancient times as in the historic period, were always the southern vanguard of the Iroquoian race, always primarily a mountain people, but with their flank resting upon the Ohio and its great tributaries, following the trend of the Blue ridge and the Cumberland as they slowly gave way before the pressure from the north until they were finally cut off from the parent stock by the wedge of Algonquian invasion, but always, whether in the north or in the south, keeping their distinctive title among the tribes as the "people of the cave country."

As the Cherokee have occupied a prominent place in history for so long a period their name appears in many synonyms and diverse spellings. The following are among the principal of these:

SYNONYMS

Tsaʹlăgĭʹ (plural, *Aniʹ-Tsaʹlăgĭʹ*). Proper form in the Middle and Western Cherokee dialects.

Tsaʹrăgĭʹ. Proper form in the Eastern or Lower Cherokee dialect.

Achalaque. Schoolcraft, Notes on Iroquois, 1847 (incorrectly quoting Garcilaso).

Chalakee. Nuttall, Travels, 124, 1821.

Chalaque. Gentleman of Elvas, 1557; Publications of Hakluyt Society, IX, 60, 1851.

Chalaquies. Barcia, Ensayo, 335, 1723.

Charakeys. Homann heirs' map, about 1730.

Charikees. Document of 1718, *fide* Rivers, South Carolina, 55, 1856.

Charokees. Governor Johnson, 1720, *fide* Rivers, Early History South Carolina, 93, 1874.

Cheelake. Barton, New Views, xliv, 1798.

Cheerake. Adair, American Indians, 226, 1775.

Cheerakee. Ibid., 137.

Cheeraque's. Moore, 1704, in Carroll, Hist. Colls. South Carolina, II, 576, 1836.

Cheerokee. Ross (?), 1776, in Historical Magazine, 2d series, II, 218, 1867.

Chel-a-ke. Long, Expedition to Rocky Mountains, II, lxx, 1823.

Chelakees. Gallatin, Trans. Am. Antiq. Soc., II, 90, 1836.

Chelaques. Nuttall, Travels, 247, 1821.

Chelekee. Keane, in Stanford's Compendium, 506, 1878.

Chellokee. Schoolcraft, Indian Tribes, II, 204, 1852.

Cheloculgee. White, Statistics of Georgia, 28, 1849 (given as plural form of Creek name).

Chelokees. Gallatin, Trans. Am. Antiq. Soc., II, 104, 1836.

Cheokees. Johnson, 1772, in New York Doc. Col. Hist., VIII, 314, 1857 (misprint for *Cherokees*).

Cheraguees. Coxe, Carolina, II, 1741.

Cherakees. Ibid., map, 1741.

Cherakis. Chauvignerie, 1736, *fide* Schoolcraft, Indian Tribes, III, 555, 1853.

Cheraquees. Coxe, Carolana, 13, 1741.

Cheraquis. Penicaut, 1699, in Margry, V, 404, 1883.

Cherickees. Clarke, 1739, in New York Doc. Col. Hist., VI, 148, 1855.

Cherikee. Albany conference, 1742, ibid., 218.

CHEROKEE. Governor Johnson, 1708, in Rivers, South Carolina, 238, 1856.

Cherookees. Croghan, 1760, in Mass. Hist. Soc. Colls., 4th series, IX, 372, 1871.

Cheroquees. Campbell, 1761, ibid., 416.

Cherrackees. Evans, 1755, in Gregg, Old Cheraws, 15, 1867.

Cherrokees. Treaty of 1722, *fide* Drake, Book of Indians, bk. 4, 32, 1848.

Cherrykees. Weiser, 1748, *fide* Kauffman, Western Pennsylvania, appendix, 18, 1851.

Chirakues. Randolph, 1699, in Rivers, South Carolina, 449, 1856.

Chirokys. Writer about 1825, Annales de la Prop. de la Foi, II, 384, 1841.

Chorakis. Document of 1748, New York Doc. Col. Hist., x, 143, 1858.

Chreokees. Piké, Travels, 173, 1811 (misprint, transposed).

Shanaki. Gatschet, Caddo MS, Bureau Am. Ethn., 1882 (Caddo name).

Shan-nack. Marcy, Red River, 273, 1854 (Wichita name).

Shannaki. Gatschet, Fox MS, Bureau Am. Ethn., 1882 (Fox name: plural form, *Shannakiak*).

Shayage. Gatschet, Kaw MS, Bur. Am. Ethn., 1878 (Kaw name).

Sulluggoes. Coxe, Carolana, 22, 1741.

Tcalke. Gatschet, Tonkawa MS, Bur. Am. Ethn., 1882 (Tonkawa name, *Chal-ke*).

Tcerokiec. Gatschet, Wichita MS, Bur. Am. Ethn., 1882 (Wichita name, *Cherokish*).

Tchatakes. La Salle, 1682, in Margry, II, 197, 1877 (misprint).

Tsalakies. Gallatin, Trans. Am. Antiq. Soc., II, 90, 1836.

Tsallakee. Schoolcraft, Notes on Iroquois, 310, 1847.

Tsä-ló-kee. Morgan, Ancient Society, 113, 1878.

Tschirokesen. Wrangell, Ethn. Nachrichten, XIII, 1839 (German form).

Tsúlahki. Grayson, Creek MS, Bur. Am. Ethn., 1885 (Creek name; plural form, *Tsălgăl'gi* or *Tsŭlgŭl'gi*—Mooney).

Tzerrickey. Urlsperger, *fide* Gatschet, Creek Migration Legend, I, 26, 1884.

Tzulukis. Rafinesque, Am. Nations, I, 123, 1836.

Zolucans.
Zulocans. } Rafinesque, in Marshall, Kentucky, I, 23, 1824.

TALLIGEU.
TALLIGEWI. } Heckewelder, 1819, Indian Nations, 48, reprint of 1876 (traditional Dela-
ALLIGEWI. } ware name; singular, *Tallige'* or *Allige'* (see preceding explanation).

Alleg. Schoolcraft, Indian Tribes, V, 133, 1855.

Allegans. Colden, map, 1727, *fide* Schoolcraft, ibid., III, 525, 1853.

Allegewi. Schoolcraft, ibid., V, 133, 1855.

Alleghans. Colden, 1727, quoted in Schoolcraft, Notes on Iroquois, 147, 1847.

Alleghanys. Rafinesque, in Marshall, Kentucky, I, 34, 1824.

Alleghens. Colden, map, 1727, *fide* Schoolcraft, Notes on Iroquois, 305, 1847.

Allegwi. Squier, in Beach, Indian Miscellany, 26, 1877.

Alli. Schoolcraft, Indian Tribes, V, 133, 1855.

Allighewis. Keane, in Stanford's Compendium, 500, 1878.

Talagans. Rafinesque, in Marshall, Kentucky, I, 28, 1824.

Talega. Brinton, Walam Olum, 201, 1885.

Tallagewy. Schoolcraft, Indian Tribes, II, 36, 1852.

Tallegwi. Rafinesque, *fide* Mercer, Lenape Stone, 90, 1885.

Talligwee. Schoolcraft, Notes on Iroquois, 310, 1847.

Tallike. Brinton, Walam Olum, 230, 1885.

KĬTU'HWAGĬ (plural, *Ani'-Kĭtu'hwagĭ.* See preceding explanation).

Cuttawa. Vaugondy, map, Partie de l'Amérique, Septentrionale 1755.

Gatohua.
Gattochwa. } Gatschet, Creek Migration Legend, I, 28, 1884.
Katowa (plural, *Katowagi*).

Ketawaugas. Haywood, Natural and Aboriginal Tennessee, 233, 1823.

Kittuwa. Brinton, Walam Olum, 16, 1885 (Delaware name).

Kuttoowauw. Aupaumut, 1791, *fide* Brinton, ibid., 16 (Mahican name).

OYATA'GE'RONOÑ'. Hewitt, oral information (Iroquois (Mohawk) name. See preceding explanation).

Ojadagochroene. Livingston, 1720, in New York Doc. Col. Hist., V, 567, 1855.

Ondadeonwas. Bleeker, 1701, ibid., IV, 918, 1854.

Oyadackuchraono. Weiser, 1753, ibid., VI, 795, 1855.

Oyadagahroenes. Letter of 1713, ibid., V, 386, 1855 (incorrectly stated to be the Flatheads, i. e., either Catawbas or Choctaws).

Oyadage'ono. Gatschet, Seneca MS, 1882, Bur. Am. Ethn. (Seneca name).

O-ya-dä'-go-o-no. Morgan, League of Iroquois, 337, 1851.

Oyaudah. Schoolcraft, Notes on Iroquois, 448, 1847 (Seneca name).

Uwata'-yo-ro'-no. Gatschet, Creek Migration Legend, 28, 1884 (Wyandot name).

Uyada. Ibid. (Seneca name).

We-yau-dah. Schoolcraft, Notes on Iroquois, 253, 1847.

Wu-tai-yo-ro-noñ'. Hewitt, Wyandot MS, 1893, Bur. Am. Ethn. (Wyandot name).

RICKAHOCKANS. Lederer, 1672, Discoveries, 26, reprint of 1891 (see preceding explanation).

Rickohockans. Map, ibid.

Rechahecrians. Drake, Book of Indians, book 4, 22, 1848 (from old Virginia documents).

Rechehecrians. Rafinesque, in Marshall, Kentucky, I, 36, 1824.

MÂÑTERÂÑ'. Gatschet, Catawba MS, 1881, Bur. Am. Ethn. (Catawba name. See preceding explanation).

ENTARIRONNON.
OCHIE'TARIRONNON. } Potier, Racines Huronnes et Grammaire, MS, 1751 (Wyandot names. The first, according to Hewitt, is equivalent to "ridge, or mountain, people").

T'KWE^n-TAH-E-U-HA-NE. Beauchamp, in Journal Am. Folklore, v, 225, 1892 (given as the Onondaga name and rendered, "people of a beautiful red color").

C ᴜGACOLE(?). Fontanedo, about 1575, Memoir, translated in French Hist. Colls., II, 257, 1875 (rendered "wicked people").

(2) MOBILIAN TRADE LANGUAGE (page 16): This trade jargon, based upon Choctaw, but borrowing also from all the neighboring dialects and even from the more northern Algonquian languages, was spoken and understood among all the tribes of the Gulf states, probably as far west as Matagorda bay and northward along both banks of the Mississippi to the Algonquian frontier about the entrance of the Ohio. It was called Mobilienne by the French, from Mobile, the great trading center of the Gulf region. Along the Mississippi it was sometimes known also as the Chickasaw trade language, the Chickasaw being a dialect of the Choctaw language proper. Jeffreys, in 1761, compares this jargon in its uses to the lingua franca of the Levant, and it was evidently by the aid of this intertribal medium that De Soto's interpreter from Tampa bay could converse with all the tribes they met until they reached the Mississippi. Some of the names used by Fontanedo about 1575 for the tribes northward from Appalachee bay seem to be derived from this source, as in later times were the names of the other tribes of the Gulf region, without regard to linguistic affinities, including among others the Taensa, Tunica, Atakapa, and Shetimasha, representing as many different linguistic stocks. In his report upon the southwestern tribes in 1805, Sibley says that the "Mobilian" was spoken in addition to their native languages by all the Indians who had come from the east side of the Mississippi. Among those so using it he names the Alabama, Apalachi, Biloxi, Chactoo, Pacana, Pascagula, Taensa, and Tunica. Woodward, writing from Louisiana more than fifty years later, says: "There is yet a language the Texas Indians call the Mobilian tongue, that has been the trading language of almost all the tribes that have inhabited the country. I know white men that now speak it. There is a man now living near me that is fifty years of age, raised in Texas, that speaks the language well. It is a mixture of Creek, Choctaw, Chickasay, Netches [Natchez], and Apelash [Apalachi]"—Reminiscences, 79. For further information see also Gatschet, Creek Migration Legend, and Sibley, Report.

The Mobilian trade jargon was not unique of its kind. In America, as in other parts of the world, the common necessities of intercommunication have resulted in the formation of several such mongrel dialects, prevailing sometimes over wide areas. In some cases, also, the language of a predominant tribe serves as the common medium for all the tribes of a particular region. In South America we find the lingoa geral, based upon the Tupi' language, understood for everyday purposes by all the tribes of the immense central region from Guiana to Paraguay, including almost the whole Amazon basin. On the northwest coast we find the well-known "Chinook jargon," which takes its name from a small tribe formerly residing at the mouth of the Columbia, in common use among all the tribes from California far up into Alaska, and eastward to the great divide of the Rocky mountains. In the southwest the Navaho-Apache language is understood by nearly all the Indians of Arizona and New Mexico, while on the plains the Sioux language in the north and the Comanche in the south hold almost the same position. In addition to these we have also the noted "sign language," a gesture system used and perfectly understood as a fluent means of communication among all the hunting tribes of the plains from the Saskatchewan to the Rio Grande.

(3) DIALECTS (page 17): The linguistic affinity of the Cherokee and northern Iroquoian dialects, although now well established, is not usually obvious on the surface, but requires a close analysis of words, with a knowledge of the laws of phonetic changes, to make it appear. The superficial agreement is perhaps most apparent between the Mohawk and the Eastern (Lower) Cherokee dialects, as both of these lack the labials entirely and use *r* instead of *l*. In the short table given below the Iroquois words are taken, with slight changes in the alphabet used, from Hewitt's manuscripts, the Cherokee from those of the author:

	Mohawk	Cherokee (Eastern)
person	oñgwe'	yûñwĭ
fire	otsi'ra'	atsi'ra (atsi'la)
water	awĕñ'	ăwä' (ămä')
stone	onĕñya'	nûñyû'
arrow	ka'noñ'	kûnĭ'
pipe	kanoñnäwĕñ'	känûñ'näwû
hand (arm)	owe'ya'	uwâ'yĭ
milk	unĕñ'ta'	unûñ'tĭ
five	wĭsk	hĭskĭ
tobacco	[tcärhû', Tuscarora]	tsârû (tsâlû)
fish	otcoñ'ta'	û'tsûtĭ'
ghost	o'skĕñna'	asgi'na
snake	ĕñnätûñ	i'nädû'

Comparison of Cherokee dialects

	Eastern (Lower)	Middle	Western (Upper)
fire	atsi'ra	atsi'la	atsi'la
water	ăwä'	ămä'	ămä'
dog	gi'rĭ'	gi'lĭ'	gi'lĭ'
hair	gitsû'	gitsû'	gitlû'
hawk	tsä'nuwă'	tsä'nuwă'	tlä'nuwä'
leech	tsanu'sĭ'	tsanu'sĭ'	tlanu'sĭ'
bat	tsa'wehă'	tsa'mehă'	tlä'mehă'
panther	tsûñtû'tsĭ	tsûñtû'tsĭ	tlûñtû'tsĭ
jay	tsay'kû'	tsay'kû'	tlay'kû'
martin (bird)	tsutsû'	tsutsû'	tlutlû'
war-club	atäsû'	atäsû'	atäsĭ'
heart	unähû'	unähû'	unähwĭ'
where?	ga'tsû	ga'tsû	ha'tlû
how much?	hûñgû'	hûñgû'	hila'gû
key	stugi'stĭ	stugi'stĭ	stui'stĭ
I pick it up (long)	tsĭnigi'û	tsĭnigi'û	tsĭne'û
my father	agidâ'tă	agidâ'tă	edä'tă
my mother	a'gitsĭ'	a'gitsĭ'	etsĭ'
my father's father	agini'sĭ	agini'sĭ	eni'sĭ
my mother's father	agidu'tû	agidu'tû	edu'tû

It will be noted that the Eastern and Middle dialects are about the same, excepting for the change of l to r, and the entire absence of the labial m from the Eastern dialect, while the Western differs considerably from the others, particularly in the greater frequency of the liquid l and the softening of the guttural g, the changes tending to render it the most musical of all the Cherokee dialects. It is also the standard literary dialect. In addition to these three principal dialects there are some peculiar forms and expressions in use by a few individuals which indicate the former existence of one or more other dialects now too far extinct to be reconstructed. As in most other tribes, the ceremonial forms used by the priesthood are so filled with archaic and figurative expressions as to be almost unintelligible to the laity.

(4) IROQUOIAN TRIBES AND MIGRATIONS (p. 17): The Iroquoian stock, taking its name from the celebrated Iroquois confederacy, consisted formerly of from fifteen to twenty tribes, speaking nearly as many different dialects, and including, among others, the following:

Wyandot, or Huron.
Tionontati, or Tobacco nation.
Attiwan'daron, or Neutral nation. } Ontario, Canada.
Tohotaenrat.
Wenrorono.
Mohawk.
Oneida.
Onondaga. } Iroquois, or Five Nations, New York.
Cayuga.
Seneca.
Erie. Northern Ohio, etc.
Conestoga, or Susquehanna. Southern Pennsylvania and Maryland.
Nottoway.
Meherrin?. } Southern Virginia.
Tuscarora. Eastern North Carolina.
Cherokee. Western Carolina, etc.

Tradition and history alike point to the St. Lawrence region as the early home of this stock. Upon this point all authorities concur. Says Hale, in his paper on Indian Migrations (p. 4): "The constant tradition of the Iroquois represents their ancestors as emigrants from the region north of the Great lakes, where they dwelt in early times with their Huron brethren. This tradition is recorded with much particularity by Cadwallader Colden, surveyor-general of New York, who in the early part of the last century composed his well known 'History of the Five Nations.' It is told in a somewhat different form by David Cusick, the Tuscarora historian, in his 'Sketches of Ancient History of the Six Nations,' and it is repeated by Mr. L. H. Morgan in his now classical work, 'The League of the Iroquois,' for which he procured his information chiefly among the Senecas. Finally, as we learn from the narrative of the Wyandot Indian, Peter Clarke, in his book entitled 'Origin and Traditional History of the Wyandotts,' the belief of the Hurons accords in this respect with that of the Iroquois. Both point alike to the country immediately north of the St. Lawrence, and especially to that portion of it lying east of Lake Ontario, as the early home of the Huron-Iroquois nations." Nothing is known of the traditions of the Conestoga or the Nottoway, but the tradition of the Tuscarora, as given by Cusick and other authorities, makes them a direct offshoot from the northern Iroquois, with whom they afterward reunited. The traditions of the Cherokee also, as we have seen, bring them from the north, thus completing the cycle. "The striking fact has become evident that the course of migration of the Huron-Cherokee family has been from the northeast to the southwest—that is, from eastern Canada, on the Lower St. Lawrence, to the mountains of northern Alabama."—Hale, Indian Migrations, p. 11.

The retirement of the northern Iroquoian tribes from the St. Lawrence region was due to the hostility of their Algonquian neighbors, by whom the Hurons and their allies were forced to take refuge about Georgian bay and the head of Lake Ontario, while the Iroquois proper retreated to central New York. In 1535 Cartier found the shores of the river from Quebec to Montreal occupied by an Iroquoian people, but on the settlement of the country seventy years later the same region was found in possession of Algonquian tribes. The confederation of the five Iroquois nations, probably about the year 1540, enabled them to check the Algonquian invasion and to assume the offensive. Linguistic and other evidence shows that the separation of the Cherokee from the parent stock must have far antedated this period.

(5) WALAM OLUM (p. 18): The name signifies "red score," from the Delaware *walam*, "painted," more particularly "painted red," and *olum*, "a score, tally-mark." The Walam Olum was first published in 1836 in a work entitled "The American Nations," by Constantine Samuel Rafinesque, a versatile and voluminous, but very erratic, French scholar, who spent the latter half of his life in this country, dying in Philadelphia in 1840. He asserted that it was a translation of a manuscript in the Delaware language, which was an interpretation of an ancient sacred metrical legend of the Delawares, recorded in pictographs cut upon wood, obtained in 1820 by a medical friend of his among the Delawares then living in central Indiana. He says himself: "These actual *olum* were first obtained in 1820 as a reward for a medical cure, deemed a curiosity, and were unexplicable. In 1822 were obtained from another individual the songs annexed thereto in the original language, but no one could be found by me able to translate them. I had therefore to learn the language since, by the help of Zeisberger, Heckewelder, and a manuscript dictionary, on purpose to translate them, which I only accomplished in 1833." On account of the unique character of the alleged Indian record and Rafinesque's own lack of standing among his scientific contemporaries, but little attention was paid to the discovery until Brinton took up the subject a few years ago. After a critical sifting of the evidence from every point of view he arrived at the conclusion that the work is a genuine native production, although the manuscript rendering is faulty, partly from the white scribe's ignorance of the language and partly from the Indian narrator's ignorance of the meaning of the archaic forms. Brinton's edition (q. v.), published from Rafinesque's manuscript, gives the legend in triplicate form—pictograph, Delaware, and English translation, with notes and glossary, and a valuable ethnologic introduction by Brinton himself.

It is not known that any of the original woodcut pictographs of the Walam Olum are now in existence, although a statement of Rafinesque implies that he had seen them. As evidence of the truth of his statement, however, we have the fact that precisely similar pictographic series cut upon birch bark, each pictograph representing a line or couplet of a sacred metrical recitation, are now known to be common among the Ojibwa, Menomini, and other northern tribes. In 1762 a Delaware prophet recorded his visions in hieroglyphics cut upon a wooden stick, and about the year 1827 a Kickapoo reformer adopted the same method to propagate a new religion among the tribes. One of these "prayer sticks" is now in the National Museum, being all that remains of a large basketful delivered to a missionary in Indiana by a party of Kickapoo Indians in 1830 (see plate and description, pp. 665, 697 et seq. in the author's Ghost-dance Religion, Fourteenth Annual Report of the Bureau of Ethnology).

(6) FISH RIVER (p. 18): Namæsi Sipu (Heckewelder, Indian Nations, 49), or Namassipi (Walam Olum, p. 198). Deceived by a slight similarity of sound, Heckewelder makes this river identical with the Mississippi, but as Schoolcraft shows (Notes on Iroquois, p. 316) the true name of the Mississippi is simply Misi-sipi, "great river," and "fish river" would be a most inappropriate name for such a turbulent current, where only the coarser species can live. The mere fact that there can be a question of identity among experts familiar with Indian nomenclature would indicate that it

was not one of the larger streams. Although Heckewelder makes the Alligewi, as ne prefers to call them, flee down the Mississippi after their final defeat, the Walam Olum chronicle says only "all the Talega go south." It was probably a gradual withdrawal, rather than a sudden and concerted flight (see Hale, Indian Migrations, pp. 19–22).

(7) FIRST APPEARANCE OF WHITES (p. 19): It is possible that this may refer to one of the earlier adventurers who coasted along the North Atlantic in the first decades after the discovery of America, among whom were Sebastian Cabot, in 1498; Verrazano, in 1524; and Gomez, in 1525. As these voyages were not followed up by permanent occupation of the country it is doubtful if they made any lasting impression upon Indian tradition. The author has chosen to assume, with Brinton and Rafinesque, that the Walam Olum reference is to the settlement of the Dutch at New York and the English in Virginia soon after 1600.

(8) DE SOTO'S ROUTE (p. 26): On May 30, 1539, Hernando de Soto, of Spain, with 600 armed men and 213 horses, landed at Tampa bay, on the west coast of Florida, in search of gold. After more than four years of hardship and disappointed wandering from Florida to the great plains of the West and back again to the Mississippi, where De Soto died and his body was consigned to the great river, 311 men, all that were left of the expedition, arrived finally at Pánuco, in Mexico, on September 10, 1543.

For the history of this expedition, the most important ever undertaken by Spain within eastern United States, we have four original authorities. First is the very brief, but evidently truthful (Spanish) report of Biedma, an officer of the expedition, presented to the King in 1544, immediately after the return to Spain. Next in order, but of first importance for detail and general appearance of reliability, is the narrative of an anonymous Portuguese cavalier of the expedition, commonly known as the Gentleman of Elvas, originally published in the Portuguese language in 1557. Next comes the (Spanish) narrative of Garcilaso, written, but not published, in 1587. Unlike the others, the author was not an eyewitness of what he describes, but made up his account chiefly from the oral recollections of an old soldier of the expedition more than forty years after the event, this information being supplemented from papers written by two other soldiers of De Soto. As might be expected, the Garcilaso narrative, although written in flowery style, abounds in exaggeration and trivial incident, and compares unfavorably with the other accounts, while probably giving more of the minor happenings. The fourth original account is an unfinished (Spanish) report by Ranjel, secretary of the expedition, written soon after reaching Mexico, and afterward incorporated with considerable change by Oviedo, in his "Historia natural y general de las Indias." As this fourth narrative remained unpublished until 1851 and has never been translated, it has hitherto been entirely overlooked by the commentators, excepting Winsor, who notes it incidentally. In general it agrees well with the Elvas narrative and throws valuable light upon the history of the expedition.

The principal authorities, while preserving a general unity of narrative, differ greatly in detail, especially in estimates of numbers and distances, frequently to such an extent that it is useless to attempt to reconcile their different statements. In general the Gentleman of Elvas is most moderate in his expression, while Biedma takes a middle ground and Garcilaso exaggerates greatly. Thus the first named gives De Soto 600 men, Biedma makes the number 620, while Garcilaso says 1,000. At a certain stage of the journey the Portuguese Gentleman gives De Soto 700 Indians as escort, Biedma says 800, while Garcilaso makes it 8,000. At the battle of Mavilla the Elvas account gives 18 Spaniards and 2,500 Indians killed, Biedma says 20 Spaniards killed, without giving an estimate of the Indians, while Garcilaso has 82 Spaniards and over 11,000 Indians killed. In distances there is as great discrepancy. Thus Biedma makes the distance from Guaxule to Chiaha four days, Garcilaso has it six days, and Elvas seven days. As to the length of an average day's march we find it estimated all the way from "four leagues, more or less" (Garcilaso) to "every day seven or eight leagues" (Elvas). In another place the Elvas chronicler states that they usually made five or six leagues a day through inhabited territories, but that in crossing uninhabited regions—as that between Canasagua and Chiaha, they marched every day as far as possible for fear of running out of provisions. One of the most glaring discrepancies appears in regard to the distance between Chiaha and Coste. Both the Portuguese writer and Garcilaso put Chiaha upon an island—a statement which in itself is at variance with any present conditions,—but while the former makes the island a fraction over a league in length the latter says that it was five leagues long. The next town was Coste, which Garcilaso puts immediately at the lower end of the same island while the Portuguese Gentleman represents it as seven days distant, although he himself has given the island the shorter length.

Notwithstanding a deceptive appearance of exactness, especially in the Elvas and Ranjel narratives, which have the form of a daily journal, the conclusion is irresistible that much of the record was made after dates had been forgotten, and the sequence of events had become confused. Considering all the difficulties, dangers, and uncertainties that constantly beset the expedition, it would be too much to expect the regularity of a ledger, and it is more probable that the entries were made, not from day to day, but at irregular intervals as opportunity presented at the several resting places. The story must be interpreted in the light of our later knowledge of the geography and ethnology of the country traversed.

Each of the three principal narratives has passed through translations and later editions of more or less doubtful fidelity to the original, the English edition in some cases being itself a translation from an earlier French or Dutch translation. English speaking historians of the expedition have usually drawn their material from one or the other of these translations, without knowledge of the original language, of the etymologies of the Indian names or the relations of the various tribes mentioned, or of the general system of Indian geographic nomenclature. One of the greatest errors has been the attempt to give in every case a fixed local habitation to a name which in some instances is not a proper name at all, and in others is merely a descriptive term or a duplicate name occurring at several places in the same tribal territory. Thus Tali is simply the Creek word *talua*, town, and not a definite place name as represented by a mistake natural in dealing through interpreters with an unknown Indian language. Tallise and Tallimuchase are respectively "Old town" and "New town" in Creek, and there can be no certainty that the same names were applied to the same places a century later. Canasagua is a corruption of a Cherokee name which occurs in at least three other places in the old Cherokee country in addition to the one mentioned in the narrative, and almost every old Indian local name was thus repeated several times, as in the case of such common names as Short creek, Whitewater, Richmond, or Lexington among ourselves. The fact that only one name of the set has been retained on the map does not prove its identity with the town of the old chronicle. Again such loose terms as "a large river," "a beautiful valley," have been assumed to mean something more definitely localized than the wording warrants. The most common error in translation has been the rendering of the Spanish "despoblado" as "desert." There are no deserts in the Gulf states, and the word means simply an uninhabited region, usually the debatable strip between two tribes.

There have been many attempts to trace De Soto's route. As nearly every historian who has written of the southern states has given attention to this subject it is unnecessary to enumerate them all. Of some thirty works consulted by the author, in addition to the original narratives already mentioned, not more than two or three can be considered as speaking with any authority, the rest simply copying from these without investigation. The first attempt to locate the route definitely was made by Meek (Romantic Passages, etc.) in 1839 (reprinted in 1857), his conclusions being based upon his general knowledge of the geography of the region. In 1851 Pickett tried to locate the route, chiefly, he asserts, from Indian tradition as related by mixed-bloods. How much dependence can be placed upon Indian tradition as thus interpreted three centuries after the event it is unnecessary to say. Both these writers have brought De Soto down the Coosa river, in which they have been followed without investigation by Irving, Shea and others, but none of these was aware of the existence of a Suwali tribe or correctly acquainted with the Indian nomenclature of the upper country, or of the Creek country as so well summarized by Gatschet in his Creek Migration Legend. They are also mistaken in assuming that only De Soto passed through the country, whereas we now know that several Spanish explorers and numerous French adventurers traversed the same territory, the latest expeditions of course being freshest in Indian memory. Jones in his "De Soto's March Through Georgia" simply dresses up the earlier statements in more literary style, sometimes changing surmises to positive assertions, without mentioning his authorities. Maps of the supposed route, all bringing De Soto down the Coosa instead of the Chattahoochee, have been published in Irving's Conquest of Florida, the Hakluyt Society's edition of the Gentleman of Elva's account, and in Buckingham Smith's translation of the same narrative, as well as in several other works. For the eastern portion, with which we have to deal, all of these are practically duplicates of one another. On several old Spanish and French maps the names mentioned in the narrative seem to have been set down merely to fill space, without much reference to the text of the chronicle. For a list and notices of principal writers who have touched upon this subject see the appendix to Shea's chapter on "Ancient Florida" in Winsor's Narrative and Critical History of America, II; Boston, 1886. We shall speak only of that part of the route which lay near the Cherokee mountains.

The first location which concerns us in the narrative is Cofitachiqui, the town from which De Soto set out for the Cherokee country. The name appears variously as Cofitachequi (Ranjel), Cofitachique (Biedma), Cofachiqui (Garcilaso), Cutifa-Chiqui (by transposition, Elvas), Cofetaçque (Vandera), Catafachique (Williams) and Cosatachiqui (misprint, Brooks MSS), and the Spaniards first heard of the region as Yupaha from a tribe farther to the south. The correct form appears to be that first given, which Gatschet, from later information than that quoted in his Creek Migration Legend, makes a Hitchitee word about equivalent to "Dogwood town," from cofi, "dogwood," cofita, "dogwood thicket," and chiki, "house," or collectively "town." McCulloch puts the town upon the headwaters of the Ocmulgee; Williams locates it on the Chattahoochee; Gallatin on the Oconee or the Savannah; Meek and Monette, following him, probably in the fork of the Savannah and the Broad; Pickett, with Jones and others following him, at Silver bluff on the east (north) bank of the Savannah, in Barnwell county, South Carolina, about 25 miles by water below the present Augusta. It will thus be seen that at the very outset of our inquiry the commentators differ by a distance equal to more than half the width of the state of Georgia. It will suffice here to say, without going into the argument, that the author is inclined to believe that the Indian town was on or near Silver bluff, which was noted for its extensive ancient remains as far back as Bartram's time (Travels, 313), and where the noted George Galphin established a trading post in 1736. The original site has since been almost entirely worn away by the river. According to the Indians of Cofitachiqui, the town, which was on the farther (north) bank of the stream, was two day's journey from the sea, probably by canoe, and the sailors with the expedition believed the river to be the same one that entered at St. Helena, which was a very close guess. The Spaniards were shown here European articles which they were told had been obtained from white men who had entered the river's mouth many years before. These they conjectured to have been the men with Ayllon, who had landed on that coast in 1520 and again in 1524. The town was probably the ancient capital of the Uchee Indians, who, before their absorption by the Creeks, held or claimed most of the territory on both banks of Savannah river from the Cherokee border to within about forty miles of Savannah and westward to the Ogeechee and Cannouchee rivers (see Gatschet, Creek Migration Legend, I, 17–24). The country was already on the decline in 1540 from a recent fatal epidemic, but was yet populous and wealthy, and was ruled by a woman chief whose authority extended for a considerable distance.   The town was visited also by Pardo in 1567 and again by Torres in 1628, when it was still a principal settlement, as rich in pearls as in De Soto's time (Brooks MSS, in the archives of the Bureau of American Ethnology).

Somewhere in southern Georgia De Soto had been told of a rich province called Coça (Coosa, the Creek country) toward the northwest.   At Cofitachiqui he again heard of it and of one of its principal towns called Chiaha (Chehaw) as being twelve days inland.   Although on first hearing of it he had kept on in the other direction in order to reach Cofitachiqui, he now determined to go there, and made the queen a prisoner to compel her to accompany him a part of the way as guide.   Coça province was, though he did not know it, almost due west, and he was in haste to reach it in order to obtain corn, as his men and horses were almost worn out from hunger.   It is apparent, however, that the unwilling queen, afraid of being carried beyond her own territories, led the Spaniards by a roundabout route in the hope of making her escape, as she finally did, or perhaps of leaving them to starve and die in the mountains, precisely the trick attempted by the Indians upon another Spanish adventurer, Coronado, entering the great plains from the Pacific coast in search of golden treasure in the same year.

Instead therefore of recrossing the river to the westward, the Spaniards, guided by the captive queen, took the direction of the north ("la vuelta del norte"— Biedma), and, after passing through several towns subject to the queen, came in seven days to "the province of Chalaque" (Elvas).   Elvas, Garcilaso, and Ranjel agree upon the spelling, but the last named makes the distance only two days from Cofitachiqui.   Biedma does not mention the country at all.   The trifling difference in statement of five days in seven need not trouble us, as Biedma makes the whole distance from Cofitachiqui to Xuala eight days, and from Guaxule to Chiaha four days, where Elvas makes it, respectively, twelve and seven days.   Chalaque is, of course, Cherokee, as all writers agree, and De Soto was now probably on the waters of Keowee river, the eastern head stream of Savannah river, where the Lower Cherokee had their towns.   Finding the country bare of corn, he made no stay.

Proceeding six days farther they came next to Guaquili, where they were kindly received.   This name occurs only in the Ranjel narrative, the other three being entirely silent in regard to such a halting place.   The name has a Cherokee sound (Wakili), but if we allow for a dialectic substitution of *l* for *r* it may be connected with such Catawba names as Congaree, Wateree, and Sugeree.   It was probably a village of minor importance.

They came next to the province of Xuala, or Xualla, as the Elvas narrative more often has it.   In a French edition it appears as Chouala.   Ranjel makes it three days from Guaquili or five from Chalaque.   Elvas also makes it five days from Chalaque, while Biedma makes it eight days from Cofitachiqui, a total discrepancy of four days from the last-named place.   Biedma describes it as a rough mountain country, thinly populated, but with a few Indian houses, and thinks that in these mountains the great river of Espiritu Santo (the Mississippi) had its birth.   Ranjel describes the town as situated in a plain in the vicinity of rivers and in a country with greater appearance of gold mines than any they had yet seen.   The Portuguese gentleman describes it as having very little corn, and says that they reached it from Cofitachiqui over a hilly country.   In his final chapter he states that the course from Cofitachiqui to this place was from south to north, thus agreeing with Biedma. According to Garcilaso (pp. 136–137) it was fifty leagues by the road along which the Spaniards had come from Cofitachiqui to the first valley of the province of Xuala, with but few mountains on the way, and the town itself was situated close under a mountain ("a la falda de una sierra") beside a small but rapid stream which formed the boundary of the territory of Cofitachiqui in this direction. From Ranjel we learn that on the same day after leaving this place for the next "province" the Spaniards crossed a very high mountain ridge ("una sierra muy alta").

Without mentioning the name, Pickett (1851) refers to Xuala as "a town in the present Habersham county, Georgia," but gives no reason for this opinion. Rye and Irving, of the same date, arguing from a slight similarity of name, think it may have been on the site of a former Cherokee town, Qualatchee, on the head of Chattahoochee river in Georgia. The resemblance, however, is rather farfetched, and moreover this same name is found on Keowee river in South Carolina. Jones (De Soto in Georgia, 1880) interprets Garcilaso's description to refer to "Nacoochee valley, Habersham county"—which should be White county—and the neighboring Mount Yonah, overlooking the fact that the same description of mountain, valley, and swift flowing stream might apply equally well to any one of twenty other localities in this southern mountain country. With direct contradiction Garcilaso says that the Spaniards rested here fifteen days because they found provisions plentiful, while the Portuguese Gentleman says that they stopped but two days because they found so little corn! Ranjel makes them stop four days and says they found abundant provisions and assistance.

However that may have been, there can be no question of the identity of the name. As the province of Chalaque is the country of the Cherokee, so the province of Xuala is the territory of the Suwali or Sara Indians, better known later as Cheraw, who lived in early times in the piedmont country about the head of Broad river in North Carolina, adjoining the Cherokee, who still remember them under the name of Ani′-Suwa′li. A principal trail to their country from the west led up Swannanoa river and across the gap which, for this reason, was known to the Cherokee as Suwa′li-nuñnâ, "Suwali trail," corrupted by the whites to Swannanoa. Lederer, who found them in the same general region in 1670, calls this gap the "Suala pass" and the neighboring mountains the Sara mountains, "which," he says, "The Spaniards make Suala." They afterward shifted to the north and finally returned and were incorporated with the Catawba (see Mooney, Siouan Tribes of the East, bulletin of the Bureau of Ethnology, 1894).

Up to this point the Spaniards had followed a north course from Cofitachiqui (Biedma and Elvas), but they now turned to the west (Elvas, final chapter). On the same day on which they left Xuala they crossed "a very high mountain ridge," and descended the next day to a wide meadow bottom ("savana"), through which flowed a river which they concluded was a part of the Espiritu Santo, the Mississippi (Ranjel). Biedma speaks of crossing a mountain country and mentions the river, which he also says they thought to be a tributary of the Mississippi. Garcilaso says that this portion of their route was through a mountain country without inhabitants ("despoblado") and the Portuguese gentleman describes it as being over "very rough and high ridges." In five days of such travel—for here, for a wonder, all the narratives agree—they came to Guaxule. This is the form given by Garcilaso and the Gentleman of Elvas; Biedma has Guasula, and Ranjel Guasili or Guasuli. The translators and commentators have given us such forms as Guachoule, Quaxule, Quaxulla, and Quexale. According to the Spanish method of writing Indian words the name was pronounced Washulé or Wasuli, which has a Cherokee sound, although it can not be translated. Buckingham Smith (Narratives, p. 222) hints that the Spaniards may have changed Guasili to Guasule, because of the similarity of the latter form to a town name in southern Spain. Such corruptions of Indian names are of frequent occurrence. Garcilaso speaks of it as a "province and town," while Biedma and Ranjel call it simply a town ("pueblo"). Before reaching this place the Indian queen had managed to make her escape. All the chroniclers tell of the kind reception which the Spaniards met here, but the only description of the town itself is from Garcilaso, who says that it was situated in the midst of many small streams which came down from the mountains round about, that it consisted of three hundred houses, which is probably an exaggeration, though it goes to show that the village was of considerable size, and that the chief's house, in which the principal officers were lodged, was upon a high hill ("un cerro alto"), around which was a roadway ("paseadero") wide enough for six men to walk abreast. By the "chief's house" we are to understand the town-house, while from various similar references in other parts of the narrative there can be no doubt that the "hill" upon which it stood was an artificial mound. In modern Spanish writing such artificial elevations are more often called *lomas*, but these early adventurers may be excused for not noting the distinction. Issuing from the mountains round about the town were numerous small streams, which united to form the river which the Spaniards henceforth followed from here down to Chiaha, where it was as large as the Guadalquivir at Sevilla (Garcilaso).

Deceived by the occurrence, in the Portuguese narrative, of the name Canasagua, which they assumed could belong in but one place, earlier commentators have identified this river with the Coosa, Pickett putting Guaxule somewhere upon its upper waters, while Jones improves upon this by making the site "identical, or very nearly so, with Coosawattee Old town, in the southeastern corner of Murray county," Georgia. As we shall show, however, the name in question was duplicated in several states, and a careful study of the narratives, in the light of present knowledge of the country, makes it evident that the river was not the Coosa, but the Chattahoochee.

Turning our attention once more to Xuala, the most northern point reached by De Soto, we have seen that this was the territory of the Suwala or Sara Indians, in the eastern foothills of the Alleghenies, about the head waters of Broad and Catawba rivers, in North Carolina. As the Spaniards turned here to the west they probably did not penetrate far beyond the present South Carolina boundary. The "very high mountain ridge" which they crossed immediately after leaving the town was in all probability the main chain of the Blue ridge, while the river which they found after descending to the savanna on the other side, and which they guessed to be a branch of the Mississippi, was almost as certainly the upper part of the French Broad, the first stream flowing in an opposite direction from those which they had previously encountered. They may have struck it in the neighborhood of Hendersonville or Brevard, there being two gaps, passable for vehicles, in the main ridge eastward from the first-named town. The uninhabited mountains through which they struggled for several days on their way to Chiaha and Coça (the Creek country) in the southwest were the broken ridges in which the Savannah and the Little Tennessee have their sources, and if they followed an Indian trail they may have passed through the Rabun gap, near the present Clayton, Georgia. Guaxule, and not Xuala, as Jones supposes, was in Nacoochee valley, in the present White county, Georgia, and the small streams which united to form the river down which the Spaniards proceeded to Chiaha were the headwaters of the Chattahoochee. The hill upon which the townhouse was built must have been the great Nacoochee mound, the most prominent landmark in the valley, on the east bank of Sautee creek, in White county, about twelve miles northwest of Clarkesville. This is the largest mound in upper Georgia, with the exception of the noted Etowah mound near Cartersville, and is the only one which can fill the requirements of the case. There are but two considerable mounds in western North Carolina, that at Franklin and a smaller one on Oconaluftee river, on the present East Cherokee reservation, and as both of these are on streams flowing away from the Creek country, this fact alone would bar them from consideration. The only large mounds in upper Georgia are this one at Nacoochee and the group on the Etowah river, near Cartersville. The largest of the Etowah group is some fifty feet in height and is ascended on one side by means of a roadway about fifty feet wide at the base and narrowing gradually to the top. Had this been the mound of the narrative it is hardly possible that the chronicler would have failed to notice also the two other mounds of the group or the other one on the opposite side of the river, each of these being from twenty to twenty-five feet in height, to say nothing of the great ditch a quarter of a mile in length which encircles the group. Moreover, Cartersville is at some distance from the mountains, and the Etowah river at this point does not answer the description of a small rushing mountain stream. There is no considerable mound at Coosawatee or in any of the three counties adjoining.

The Nacoochee mound has been cleared and cultivated for many years and does not now show any appearance of a roadway up the side, but from its great height we may be reasonably sure that some such means of easy ascent existed in ancient times. In other respects it is the only mound in the whole upper country which fills the conditions. The valley is one of the most fertile spots in Georgia and numerous ancient remains give evidence that it was a favorite center of settlement in early days. At the beginning of the modern historic period it was held by the Cherokee, who had there a town called Nacoochee, but their claim was disputed by the Creeks. The Gentleman of Elvas states that Guaxule was subject to the queen of Cofitachiqui, but this may mean only that the people of the two towns or tribes were in friendly alliance. The modern name is pronounced *Nagu'tsĭ'* by the Cherokee, who say, however, that it is not of their language. The terminal may be the Creek *udshi*, "small," or it may have a connection with the name of the Uchee Indians.

From Guaxule the Spaniards advanced to Canasoga (Ranjel) or Canasagua (Elvas), one or two days' march from Guaxule, according to one or the other authority. Garcilaso and Biedma do not mention the name. As Garcilaso states that from Guaxule to Chiaha the march was down the bank of the same river, which we identify with the Chattahoochee, the town may have been in the neighborhood of the present Gainesville. As we have seen, however, it is unsafe to trust the estimates of distance. Arguing from the name, Meek infers that the town was about Conasauga river in Murray county, and that the river down which they marched to reach it was "no doubt the Etowah," although to reach the first named river from the Etowah it would be necessary to make another sharp turn to the north. From the same coincidence Pickett puts it on the Conasauga, "in the modern county of Murray, Georgia," while Jones, on the same theory, locates it "at or near the junction of the Connasauga and Coosawattee rivers, in originally Cass, now Gordon county." Here his modern geography as well as his ancient is at fault, as the original Cass county is now Bartow, the name having been changed in consequence of a local dislike for General Cass. The whole theory of a march down the Coosa river rests upon this coincidence of the name. The same name however, pronounced *Gänsä'gĭ* by the Cherokee, was applied by them to at least three different locations within their old territory, while the one mentioned in the narrative would make the fourth. The others were (1) on Oostanaula river, opposite the mouth of the Conasauga, where afterward was New Echota, in Gordon county, Georgia; (2) on Canasauga creek, in McMinn county, Tennessee; (3) on Tuckasegee river, about two miles above Webster, in Jackson county, North Carolina. At each of these places are remains of ancient settlement. It is possible that the name of Kenesaw mountain, near Marietta, in Cobb county, Georgia, may be a corruption of Gänsâgĭ, and if so, the Canasagua of the narrative may have been somewhere in this vicinity on the Chattahoochee. The meaning of the name is lost.

On leaving Canasagua they continued down the same river which they had followed from Guaxule (Garcilaso), and after traveling several days through an uninhabited ("despoblado") country (Elvas) arrived at Chiaha, which was subject to the great chief of Coça (Elvas). The name is spelled Chiaha by Ranjel and the Gentleman of Elvas, Chiha by Biedma in the Documentos, China by a misprint in an English rendering, and Ychiaha by Garcilaso. It appears as Chiha on an English map of 1762 reproduced in Winsor, Westward Movement, page 31, 1897. Gallatin spells it Ichiaha, while Williams and Fairbanks, by misprint, make it Chiapa. According to both Ranjel and Elvas the army entered it on the 5th of June, although the former makes it four days from Canasagua, while the other makes it five. Biedma says it was four days from Guaxule, and, finally, Garcilaso says it was six days and thirty leagues from Guaxule and on the same river, which was, here at Chiaha, as large as the Guadalquivir at Sevilla. As we have seen, there is a great discrepancy in the statements of the distance from Cofitachiqui to this point. All four authorities agree that the town was on an island in the river, along which they had been marching for some time (Garcilaso, Ranjel), but while the Elvas narrative makes the island "two crossbow shot" in length above the town and one league in length below it, Garcilaso calls it a "great island more than five leagues long." On both sides of the island the stream was very broad and easily waded (Elvas). Finding welcome and food for men and horses the Spaniards rested here nearly a month (June 5–28, Ranjel; twenty-six or twenty-seven days, Biedma; thirty days, Elvas). In spite of the danger from attack De Soto allowed his men to sleep under trees in the open air, "because it was very hot and the people should have suffered great extremity if it had not been so" (Elvas). This in itself is evidence that the place was pretty far to the south, as it was yet only the first week in June. The town was subject to the chief of the great province of Coça, farther to the west. From here onward they began to meet palisaded towns.

On the theory that the march was down Coosa river, every commentator hitherto has located Chiaha at some point upon this stream, either in Alabama or Georgia. Gallatin (1836) says that it "must have been on the Coosa, probably some distance below the site of New Echota." He notes a similarity of sound between Ichiaha and "Echoy" (Itseyĭ), a Cherokee town name. Williams (1837) says that it was on Mobile (i. e., the Alabama or lower Coosa river). Meek (1839) says "there can be little doubt that Chiaha was situated but a short distance above the junction of the Coosa and Chattooga rivers," i. e., not far within the Alabama line. He notes the occurrence of a "Chiaha" (Chehawhaw) creek near Talladega, Alabama. In regard to the island upon which the town was said to have been situated he says: "There is no such island now in the Coosa. It is probable that the Spaniards either mistook the peninsula formed by the junction of two rivers, the Coosa and Chattooga, for an island, or that those two rivers were originally united so as to form an island near their present confluence. We have heard this latter supposition asserted by persons well acquainted with the country."—Romantic Passages, p. 222, 1857. Monette (1846) puts it on Etowah branch of the Coosa, probably in Floyd county, Georgia. Pickett (1851), followed in turn by Irving, Jones, and Shea, locates it at "the site of the modern Rome." The "island" is interpreted to mean the space between the two streams above the confluence.

Pickett, as has been stated, bases his statements chiefly or entirely upon Indian traditions as obtained from halfbreeds or traders. How much information can be gathered from such sources in regard to events that transpired three centuries before may be estimated by considering how much an illiterate mountaineer of the same region might be able to tell concerning the founding of the Georgia colony. Pickett himself seems to have been entirely unaware of the later Spanish expeditions of Pardo and De Luna through the same country, as he makes no mention of them in his history of Alabama, but ascribes everything to De Soto. Concerning Chiaha he says:

"The most ancient Cherokee Indians, whose tradition has been handed down to us through old Indian traders, disagree as to the precise place [!] where De Soto crossed the Oostanaula to get over into the town of Chiaha—some asserting that he passed over that river seven miles above its junction with the Etowah, and that he marched from thence down to Chiaha, which, all contend, lay immediately at the confluence of the two rivers; while other ancient Indians asserted that he crossed, with his army, immediately opposite the town. But this is not very important. Coupling the Indian traditions with the account by Garcellasso and that by the Portuguese eyewitness, we are inclined to believe the latter tradition that the expedition continued to advance down the western side of the Oostanaula until they halted in view of the mouth of the Etowah. De Soto, having arrived immediately opposite the great town of Chiaha, now the site of Rome, crossed the Oostanaula," etc. (History of Alabama, p. 23, reprint, 1896). He overlooks the fact that Chiaha was not a Cherokee town, but belonged to the province of Coça—i. e., the territory of the Creek Indians.

A careful study of the four original narratives makes it plain that the expedition did not descend either the Oostanaula or the Etowah, and that consequently Chiaha could not have been at their junction, the present site of Rome. On the other hand the conclusion is irresistible that the march was down the Chattahoochee from its extreme head springs in the mountains, and that the Chiaha of the narrative was the Lower Creek town of the same name, more commonly known as Chehaw, formerly on this river in the neighborhood of the modern city of Columbus, Georgia, while Coste, in the narrative the next adjacent town, was Kasi'ta, or Cusseta, of the same group of villages. The falls at this point mark the geologic break line where the river changes from a clear, swift current to a broad, slow-moving stream of the lower country. Attracted by the fisheries and the fertile bottom lands the Lower Creeks established here their settlement nucleus, and here, up to the beginning of the present century, they had within easy distance of each other on both sides of the river some fifteen towns, among which were Chiaha (Chehaw), Chiahudshi (Little Chehaw), and Kasi'ta (Cusseta). Most of these settlements were within what are now Muscogee and Chattahoochee counties, Georgia, and Lee and Russell counties, Alabama (see town list and map in Gatschet, Creek Migration Legend). Large mounds and other earthworks on both sides of the river in the vicinity of Columbus attest the importance of the site in ancient days, while the general appearance indicates that at times the adjacent low grounds were submerged or cut off by overflows from the main stream. A principal trail crossed here from the Ocmulgee, passing by Tuskegee to the Upper Creek towns about the junction of the Coosa and Tallapoosa in Alabama. At the beginning of the present century this trail was known to the traders as "De Soto's trace" (Woodward, Reminiscences, p. 76). As the Indian towns frequently shift their position within a limited range on account of epidemics, freshets, or impoverishment of the soil, it is not necessary to assume that they occupied exactly the same sites in 1540 as in 1800, but only that as a group they were in the same general vicinity. Thus Kasi'ta itself was at one period above the falls and at a later period some eight miles below them. Both Kasi'ta and Chiaha were principal towns, with several branch villages.

The time given as occupied on the march from Canasagua to Chiaha would seem too little for the actual distance, but as we have seen, the chroniclers do not agree among themselves. We can easily believe that the Spaniards, buoyed up by the certainty of finding food and rest at their next halting place, made better progress along the smooth river trail than while blundering helplessly through the mountains at the direction of a most unwilling guide. If Canasagua was anywhere in the neighborhood of Kenesaw, in Cobb county, the time mentioned in the Elvas or Garcilaso narrative would probably have been sufficient for reaching Chiaha at the falls. The uninhabited country between the two towns was the neutral ground between the two hostile tribes, the Cherokee and the Creeks, and it is worth noting that Kenesaw mountain was made a point on the boundary line afterward established between the two tribes through the mediation of the United States government.

There is no large island in either the Coosa or the Chattahoochee, and we are forced to the conclusion that what the chronicle describes as an island was really a portion of the bottom land temporarily cut off by back water from a freshet. In a similar way "The Slue," east of Flint river in Mitchell county, may have been formed by a shifting of the river channel. Two months later, in Alabama, the Spaniards reached a river so swollen by rains that they were obliged to wait six days before they could cross (Elvas). Lederer, while crossing South Carolina in 1670, found his farther progress barred by a "great lake," which he puts on his map as "Ushery lake," although there is no such lake in the state; but the mystery is explained by Lawson, who, in going over the same ground thirty years later, found all the bottom lands under water from a great flood, the Santee in particular being 36 feet above its normal level. As Lawson was a surveyor his figures may be considered reliable. The "Ushery lake" of Lederer was simply an overflow of Catawba river. Flood water in the streams of upper Georgia and Alabama would quickly be carried off, but would be apt to remain for some time on the more level country below the falls.

According to information supplied by Mr Thomas Robinson, an expert engineering authority familiar with the lower Chattahoochee, there was formerly a large mound, now almost entirely washed away, on the eastern bank of the river, about nine miles below Columbus, while on the western or Alabama bank, a mile or two farther down, there is still to be seen another of nearly equal size. "At extreme freshets both of these mounds were partly submerged. To the east of the former, known as the Indian mound, the flood plain is a mile or two wide, and along the eastern side of the plain stretches a series of swamps or wooded sloughs, indicating an old river bed. All the plain between the present river and the sloughs is river-made land. The river bluff along by the mound on the Georgia side is from twenty to thirty feet above the present low-water surface of the stream. About a mile above the mound are the remains of what was known as Jennies island. At ordinary stages of the river no island is there. The eastern channel was blocked by government works some years ago, and the whole is filled up and now used as a cornfield. The island remains can be traced now, I think, for a length of half a mile, with a possible extreme width of 300 feet. . . . This whole country, on both sides of the river, is full of Indian lore. I have mentioned both mounds simply to indicate that this portion of the river was an Indian locality, and have also stated the facts about the remains of Jennies island in order to give a possible clew to a professional who might study the ground."—Letter, April 22, 1900.

Chiaha was the first town of the "province of Coça," the territory of the Coosa or Creek Indians. The next town mentioned, Coste (Elvas and Ranjel), Costehe (Biedma) or Acoste (Garcilaso), was Kasi′ta, or Cusseta, as it was afterward known to the whites. While Garcilaso puts it at the lower end of the same island upon which Chiaha was situated, the Elvas narrative makes it seven days distant! The modern towns of Chehaw and Cusseta were within a few miles of each other on the Chattahoochee, the former being on the western or Alabama side, while Cusseta, in 1799, was on the east or Georgia side about eight miles below the falls at Columbus, and in Chattahoochee county, which has given its capital the same name, Cusseta. From the general tone of the narrative it is evident that the two towns were near together in De Soto's time, and it may be that the Elvas chronicle confounded Kasi′ta with Koasati, a principal Upper Creek town, a short distance below the junction of the Coosa and Tallapoosa. At Coste they crossed the river and continued westward "through many towns subject to the cacique of Coça" (Elvas) until they came to the great town of Coça itself. This was Kusa or Coosa, the ancient capital of the Upper Creeks. There were two towns of this name at different periods. One, described by Adair in 1775 as "the great and old beloved town of refuge, Koosah," was on the east bank of Coosa river, a few miles southwest of the present Talladega, Alabama. The other, known as "Old Coosa," and probably of more ancient origin, was on the west side of Alabama river, near the present site of Montgomery (see Gatschet, Creek Migration Legend). It was probably the latter which was visited by De Soto, and later on by De Luna, in 1559. Beyond Coça they passed through another Creek town, apparently lower down on the Alabama, the name of which is variously spelled Ytaua (Elvas, Force translation), Ytava (Elvas, Hakluyt Society translation), or Itaba (Ranjel), and which may be connected with I'tăwă', Etowah or "Hightower," the name of a former Cherokee settlement near the head of Etowah river in Georgia. The Cherokee regard this as a foreign name, and its occurrence in upper Georgia, as well as in central Alabama, may help to support the tradition that the southern Cherokee border was formerly held by the Creeks.

De Soto's route beyond the Cherokee country does not concern us except as it throws light upon his previous progress. In the seventeenth chapter the Elvas narrative summarizes that portion from the landing at Tampa bay to a point in southern Alabama as follows: "From the Port de Spirito Santo to Apalache, which is about an hundred leagues, the governor went from east to west; and from Apalache to Cutifachiqui, which are 430 leagues, from the southwest to the northeast; and from Cutifachiqui to Xualla, which are about 250 leagues, from the south to the north; and from Xualla to Tascaluca, which are 250 leagues more, an hundred and ninety of them he traveled from east to west, to wit, to the province of Coça; and the other 60, from Coça to Tascaluca, from the north to the south."

Chisca (Elvas and Ranjel), the mountainous northern region in search of which men were sent from Chiaha to look for copper and gold, was somewhere in the Cherokee country of upper Georgia or Alabama. The precise location is not material, as it is now known that native copper, in such condition as to have been easily workable by the Indians, occurs throughout the whole southern Allegheny region from about Anniston, Alabama, into Virginia. Notable finds of native copper have been made on the upper Tallapoosa, in Cleburne county, Alabama; about Ducktown, in Polk county, Tennessee, and in southwestern Virginia, one nugget from Virginia weighing several pounds. From the appearance of ancient soapstone vessels which have been found in the same region there is even a possibility that the Indians had some knowledge of smelting, as the Spanish explorers surmised (oral information from Mr W. H. Weed, U. S. Geological Survey). We hear again of this "province" after De Soto had reached the Mississippi, and in one place Garcilaso seems to confound it with another province called Quizqui (Ranjel) or Quizquiz (Elvas and Biedma). The name has some resemblance to the Cherokee word tsiskwa, "bird."

(9) DE LUNA AND ROGEL (p. 27): Jones, in his De Soto's March through Georgia, incorrectly ascribes certain traces of ancient mining operations in the Cherokee country, particularly on Valley river in North Carolina, to the followers of De Luna, "who, in 1560 . . . came with 300 Spanish soldiers into this region, and spent the summer in eager and laborious search for gold." Don Tristan de Luna, with fifteen hundred men, landed somewhere about Mobile bay in 1559 with the design of establishing a permanent Spanish settlement in the interior, but owing to a succession of unfortunate happenings the attempt was abandoned the next year. In the course of his wanderings he traversed the country of the Choctaw, Chickasaw, and Upper Creeks, as is shown by the names and other data in the narrative, but returned without entering the mountains or doing any digging (see Barcia, Ensayo Cronologico, pp. 32–41, 1723; Winsor, Narrative and Critical History, II, pp. 257–259).

In 1569 the Jesuit Rogel—called Father John Roger by Shea—began mission work among the South Carolina tribes inland from Santa Elena (about Port Royal). The mission, which at first promised well, was abandoned next year, owing to the unwillingness of the Indians to give up their old habits and beliefs. Shea, in his "Catholic Missions," supposes that these Indians were probably a part of the

Cherokee, but a study of the Spanish record in Barcia (Ensayo, pp. 138–141) shows that Rogel penetrated only a short distance from the coast.

(10) DAVIES' HISTORY OF THE CARRIBBY ISLANDS (p. 29): The fraudulent character of this work, which is itself an altered translation of a fictitious history by Rochefort, is noted by Buckingham Smith (Letter of Hernando de Soto, p. 36, 1854), Winsor (Narrative and Critical History, II, p. 289), and Field (Indian Bibliography, p. 95). Says Field: "This book is an example of the most unblushing effrontery. The pseudo author assumes the credit of the performance, with but the faintest allusion to its previous existence. It is a nearly faithful translation of Rochefort's 'Histoire des Antilles.' There is, however, a gratifying retribution in Davies' treatment of Rochefort, for the work of the latter was fictitious in every part which was not purloined from authors whose knowledge furnished him with all in his treatise which was true."

(11) ANCIENT SPANISH MINES (pp. 29, 31): As the existence of the precious metals in the southern Alleghenies was known to the Spaniards from a very early period, it is probable that more thorough exploration of that region will bring to light many evidences of their mining operations. In his "Antiquities of the Southern Indians," Jones describes a sort of subterranean village discovered in 1834 on Dukes creek, White county, Georgia, consisting of a row of small log cabins extending along the creek, but imbedded several feet below the surface of the ground, upon which large trees were growing, the inference being that the houses had been thus covered by successive freshets. The logs had been notched and shaped apparently with sharp metallic tools. Shafts have been discovered on Valley river, North Carolina, at the bottom of one of which was found, in 1854, a well-preserved windlass of hewn oak timbers, showing traces of having once been banded with iron. Another shaft, passing through hard rock, showed the marks of sharp tools used in the boring. The casing and other timbers were still sound (Jones, pp. 48, 49). Similar ancient shafts have been found in other places in upper Georgia and western North Carolina, together with some remarkable stone-built fortifications or corrals, notably at Fort mountain, in Murray county, Georgia, and on Silver creek, a few miles from Rome, Georgia.

Very recently remains of an early white settlement, traditionally ascribed to the Spaniards, have been reported from Lincolnton, North Carolina, on the edge of the ancient country of the Sara, among whom the Spaniards built a fort in 1566. The works include a dam of cut stone, a series of low pillars of cut stone, arranged in squares as though intended for foundations, a stone-walled well, a quarry from which the stone had been procured, a fire pit, and a series of sinks, extending along the stream, in which were found remains of timbers suggesting the subterranean cabins on Dukes creek. All these antedated the first settlement of that region, about the year 1750. Ancient mining indications are also reported from Kings mountain, about twenty miles distant (Reinhardt MS, 1900, in Bureau of American Ethnology archives). The Spanish miners of whom Lederer heard in 1670 and Moore in 1690 were probably at work in this neighborhood.

(12) SIR WILLIAM JOHNSON (p. 38): This great soldier, whose history is so inseparably connected with that of the Six Nations, was born in the county Meath, Ireland, in 1715, and died at Johnstown, New York, in 1774. The younger son of an Irish gentleman, he left his native country in 1738 in consequence of a disappointment in love, and emigrated to America, where he undertook the settlement of a large tract of wild land belonging to his uncle, which lay along the south side of the Mohawk river in what was then the wilderness of New York. This brought him into close contact with the Six Nations, particularly the Mohawks, in whom he became so much interested as to learn their language and in some degree to accommodate himself to their customs, sometimes even to the wearing of the native costume. This interest, together with his natural kindness and dignity, completely won the hearts of the Six

Nations, over whom he acquired a greater influence than has ever been exercised by any other white man before or since. He was formally adopted as a chief by the Mohawk tribe. In 1744, being still a very young man, he was placed in charge of British affairs with the Six Nations, and in 1755 was regularly commissioned at their own urgent request as superintendent for the Six Nations and their dependent and allied tribes, a position which he held for the rest of his life. In 1748 he was also placed in command of the New York colonial forces, and two years later was appointed to the governor's council. At the beginning of the French and Indian war he was commissioned a major-general. He defeated Dieskau at the battle of Lake George, where he was severely wounded early in the action, but refused to leave the field. For this service he received the thanks of Parliament, a grant of £5,000, and a baronetcy. He also distinguished himself at Ticonderoga and Fort Niagara, taking the latter after routing the French army sent to its relief. At the head of his Indian and colonial forces he took part in other actions and expeditions, and was present at the surrender of Montreal. For his services throughout the war he received a grant of 100,000 acres of land north of the Mohawk river. Here he built "Johnson Hall," which still stands, near the village of Johnstown, which was laid out by him with stores, church, and other buildings, at his own expense. At Johnson Hall he lived in the style of an old country baron, dividing his attention between Indian affairs and the raising of blooded stock, and dispensing a princely hospitality to all comers. His influence alone prevented the Six Nations joining Pontiac's great confederacy against the English. In 1768 he concluded the treaty of Fort Stanwix, which fixed the Ohio as the boundary between the northern colonies and the western tribes, the boundary for which the Indians afterward contended against the Americans until 1795. In 1739 he married a German girl of the Mohawk valley, who died after bearing him three children. Later in life he formed a connection with the sister of Brant, the Mohawk chief. He died from over-exertion at an Indian council. His son, Sir John Johnson, succeeded to his title and estates, and on the breaking out of the Revolution espoused the British side, drawing with him the Mohawks and a great part of the other Six Nations, who abandoned their homes and fled with him to Canada (see W. L. Stone, Life of Sir William Johnson).

(13) CAPTAIN JOHN STUART (p. 44): This distinguished officer was contemporaneous with Sir William Johnson, and sprang from the same adventurous Keltic stock which has furnished so many men conspicuous in our early Indian history. Born in Scotland about the year 1700, he came to America in 1733, was appointed to a subordinate command in the British service, and soon became a favorite with the Indians. When Fort Loudon was taken by the Cherokee in 1760, he was second in command, and his rescue by Ata-kullakulla is one of the romantic episodes of that period. In 1763 he was appointed superintendent for the southern tribes, a position which he continued to hold until his death. In 1768 he negotiated with the Cherokee the treaty of Hard Labor by which the Kanawha was fixed as the western boundary of Virginia, Sir William Johnson at the same time concluding a treaty with the northern tribes by which the boundary was continued northward along the Ohio. At the outbreak of the Revolution he organized the Cherokee and other southern tribes, with the white loyalists, against the Americans, and was largely responsible for the Indian outrages along the southern border. He planned a general invasion by the southern tribes along the whole frontier, in cooperation with a British force to be landed in western Florida, while a British fleet should occupy the attention of the Americans on the coast side and the Tories should rise in the interior. On the discovery of the plot and the subsequent defeat of the Cherokee by the Americans, he fled to Florida and soon afterward sailed for England, where he died in 1779.

(14) NANCY WARD (p. 47): A noted halfbreed Cherokee woman, the date and place of whose birth and death are alike unknown. It is said that her father was a

British officer named Ward and her mother a sister of Ata-kullakulla, principal chief of the Nation at the time of the first Cherokee war. She was probably related to Brian Ward, an oldtime trader among the Cherokee, mentioned elsewhere in connection with the battle of Tali'wă.   During the Revolutionary period she resided at Echota, the national capital, where she held the office of "Beloved Woman," or "Pretty Woman," by virtue of which she was entitled to speak in councils and to decide the fate of captives. She distinguished herself by her constant friendship for the Americans, always using her best effort to bring about peace between them and her own people, and frequently giving timely warning of projected Indian raids, notably on the occasion of the great invasion of the Watauga and Holston settlements in 1776. A Mrs Bean, captured during this incursion, was saved by her interposition after having been condemned to death and already bound to the stake. In 1780, on occasion of another Cherokee outbreak, she assisted a number of traders to escape, and the next year was sent by the chiefs to make peace with Sevier and Campbell, who were advancing against the Cherokee towns. Campbell speaks of her in his report as "the famous Indian woman, Nancy Ward." Although peace was not then granted, her relatives, when brought in later with other prisoners, were treated with the consideration due in return for her good offices. She is described by Robertson, who visited her about this time, as "queenly and commanding" in appearance and manner, and her house as furnished in accordance with her high dignity. When among the Arkansas Cherokee in 1819, Nuttall was told that she had introduced the first cows into the Nation, and that by her own and her children's influence the condition of the Cherokee had been greatly elevated. He was told also that her advice and counsel bordered on supreme, and that her interference was allowed to be decisive even in affairs of life and death. Although he speaks in the present tense, it is hardly probable that she was then still alive, and he does not claim to have met her. Her descendants are still found in the Nation. See Haywood, Natural and Aboriginal Tennessee; Ramsey, Tennessee; Nuttall, Travels, p. 130, 1821; Campbell letter, 1781, and Springstone deposition, 1781, in Virginia State Papers I, pp. 435, 436, 447, 1875; Appleton's Cyclopædia of American Biography.

(15) GENERAL JAMES ROBERTSON (p. 48): This distinguished pioneer and founder of Nashville was born in Brunswick county, Virginia, in 1742, and died at the Chickasaw agency in west Tennessee in 1814. Like most of the men prominent in the early history of Tennessee, he was of Scotch-Irish ancestry. His father having removed about 1750 to western North Carolina, the boy grew up without education, but with a strong love for adventure, which he gratified by making exploring expeditions across the mountains. After his marriage his wife taught him to read and write. In 1771 he led a colony to the Watauga river and established the settlement which became the nucleus of the future state of Tennessee. He took a leading part in the organization of the Watauga Association, the earliest organized government within the state, and afterward served in Dunmore's war, taking part in the bloody battle of Point Pleasant in 1774. He participated in the earlier Revolutionary campaigns against the Cherokee, and in 1777 was appointed agent to reside at their capital, Echota, and act as a medium in their correspondence with the state governments of North Carolina (including Tennessee) and Virginia. In this capacity he gave timely warning of a contemplated invasion by the hostile portion of the tribe early in 1779. Soon after in the same year he led a preliminary exploration from Watauga to the Cumberland. He brought out a larger party late in the fall, and in the spring of 1780 built the first stockades on the site which he named Nashborough, now Nashville. Only his force of character was able to hold the infant settlement together in the face of hardships and Indian hostilities, but by his tact and firmness he was finally able to make peace with the surrounding tribes, and established the Cumberland settlement upon a secure basis. The Spanish government at one time unsuccessfully attempted to engage him in a plot to cut off the western territory from the

United States, but met a patriotic refusal.   Having been commissioned a brigadier-general in 1790, he continued to organize campaigns, resist invasions, and negotiate treaties until the final close of the Indian wars in Tennessee.   He afterward held the appointment of Indian commissioner to the Chickasaw and Choctaw.   See Ramsey, Tennessee; Roosevelt, Winning of the West; Appleton's Cyclopædia of American Biography.

(16) GENERAL GRIFFITH RUTHERFORD (p. 48): Although this Revolutionary officer commanded the greatest expedition ever sent against the Cherokee, with such distinguished success that both North Carolina and Tennessee have named counties in his honor, little appears to be definitely known of his history.   He was born in Ireland about 1731, and, emigrating to America, settled near Salisbury, North Carolina.   On the opening of the Revolutionary struggle he became a member of the Provincial Congress and Council of Safety.   In June, 1776, he was commissioned a brigadier-general in the American army, and a few months later led his celebrated expedition against the Cherokee, as elsewhere narrated.   He rendered other important service in the Revolution, in one battle being taken prisoner by the British and held by them nearly a year.   He afterward served in the state senate of North Carolina, and, subsequently removing to Tennessee, was for some time a member of its territorial council.   He died in Tennessee about 1800.

(17) RUTHERFORD'S ROUTE (p. 49): The various North Carolina detachments which combined to form Rutherford's expedition against the Cherokee in the autumn of 1776 organized at different points about the upper Catawba and probably concentrated at Davidson's fort, now Old fort, in McDowell county.   Thence, advancing westward closely upon the line of the present Southern railroad and its Western North Carolina branch, the army crossed the Blue ridge over the Swannanoa gap and went down the Swannanoa to its junction with the French Broad, crossing the latter at the Warrior ford, below the present Asheville; thence up Hominy creek and across the ridge to Pigeon river, crossing it a few miles below the junction of the East and West forks; thence to Richland creek, crossing it just above the present Waynesville; and over the dividing ridge between the present Haywood and Jackson counties to the head of Scott's creek; thence down that creek by "a blind path through a very mountainous bad way," as Moore's old narrative has it, to its junction with the Tuckasegee river just below the present Webster; thence, crossing to the west (south) side of the river, the troops followed a main trail down the stream for a few miles until they came to the first Cherokee town, Stekoa, on the site of the farm formerly owned by Colonel William H. Thomas, just above the present railroad village of Whittier, Swain county, North Carolina.   After destroying the town a detachment left the main body and pursued the fugitives northward on the other side of the river to Oconaluftee river and Soco creek, getting back afterward to the settlements by steering an easterly course across the mountains to Richland creek (Moore narrative).   The main army, under Rutherford, crossed the dividing ridge to the southward of Whittier and descended Cowee creek to the waters of Little Tennessee, in the present Macon county.   After destroying the towns in this vicinity the army ascended Cartoogaja creek, west from the present Franklin, and crossed the Nantahala mountains at Waya gap—where a fight took place—to Nantahala river, probably at the town of the same name, about the present Jarretts station.   From here the march was west across the mountain into the present Cherokee county and down Valley river to its junction with the Hiwassee, at the present Murphy. *Authorities:* Moore narrative and Wilson letter in North Carolina University Magazine, February, 1888; Ramsey, Tennessee, p. 164; Roosevelt, Winning of the West, I, pp. 300–302; Royce, Cherokee map; personal information from Colonel William H. Thomas, Major James Bryson, whose grandfather was with Rutherford, and Cherokee informants.

(18) COLONEL WILLIAM CHRISTIAN (p. 50): Colonel William Christian, some-

times incorrectly called Christy, was born in Berkeley county, Virginia, in 1732. Accustomed to frontier warfare almost from boyhood, he served in the French and Indian war with the rank of captain, and was afterward in command of the Tennessee and North Carolina forces which participated in the great battle of Point Pleasant in 1774, although he himself arrived too late for the fight. He organized a regiment at the opening of the Revolutionary war, and in 1776 led an expedition from Virginia against the Upper Cherokee and compelled them to sue for peace. In 1782, while upon an expedition against the Ohio tribes, he was captured and burned at the stake.

(19) THE GREAT INDIAN WAR PATH (p. 50): This noted Indian thoroughfare from Virginia through Kentucky and Tennessee to the Creek country in Alabama and Georgia is frequently mentioned in the early narrative of that section, and is indicated on the maps accompanying Ramsey's Annals of Tennessee and Royce's Cherokee Nation, in the Fifth Annual Report of the Bureau of Ethnology. Royce's map shows it in more correct detail. It was the great trading and war path between the northern and southern tribes, and along the same path Christian, Sevier, and others of the old Indian fighters led their men to the destruction of the towns on Little Tennessee, Hiwassee, and southward.

According to Ramsey (p. 88), one branch of it ran nearly on the line of the later stage road from Harpers ferry to Knoxville, passing the Big lick in Botetourt county, Virginia, crossing New river near old Fort Chiswell (which stood on the south bank of Reed creek of New river, about nine miles east from Wytheville, Virginia) crossing Holston at the Seven-mile ford, thence to the left of the stage road near the river to the north fork of Holston, "crossing as at present"; thence to Big creek, and, crossing the Holston at Dodson's ford, to the Grassy springs near the former residence of Micajah Lea; thence down the Nolichucky to Long creek, up it to its head, and down Dumplin creek nearly to its mouth, where the path bent to the left and crossed French Broad near Buckinghams island. Here a branch left it and went up the West fork of Little Pigeon and across the mountains to the Middle towns on Tuckasegee and the upper Little Tennessee. The main trail continued up Boyd's creek to its head, and down Ellejoy creek to Little river, crossing near Henry's place; thence by the present Maryville to the mouth of Tellico, and, passing through the Cherokee towns of Tellico, Echota, and Hiwassee, down the Coosa, connecting with the great war path of the Creeks. Near the Wolf hills, now Abingdon, Virginia, another path came in from Kentucky, passing through the Cumberland gap. It was along this latter road that the early explorers entered Kentucky, and along it also the Shawano and other Ohio tribes often penetrated to raid upon the Holston and New river settlements.

On Royce's map the trail is indicated from Virginia southward. Starting from the junction of Moccasin creek with the North fork of Holston, just above the Tennessee state line, it crosses the latter river from the east side at its mouth or junction with the South fork, just below Kingsport or the Long island; then follows down along the west side of the Holston, crossing Big creek at its mouth, and crossing to the south (east) side of Holston at Dodson's creek; thence up along the east side of Dodson's creek and across Big Gap creek, following it for a short distance and continuing southwest, just touching Nolichucky, passing up the west side of Long creek of that stream and down the same side of Dumplin creek, and crossing French Broad just below the mouth of the creek; thence up along the west side of Boyd's creek to its head and down the west side of Ellejoy creek to and across Little river; thence through the present Maryville to cross Little Tennessee at the entrance of Tellico river, where old Fort Loudon was built; thence turning up along the south side of Little Tennessee river to Echota, the ancient capital, and then southwest across Tellico river along the ridge between Chestua and Canasauga creeks, and crossing the latter near its mouth to strike Hiwassee river at the town of the same name;

thence southwest, crossing Ocoee river near its mouth, passing south of Cleveland, through the present Ooltewah and across Chickamauga creek into Georgia and Alabama.

According to Timberlake (Memoirs, with map, 1765), the trail crossed Little Tennessee from Echota, northward, in two places, just above and below Four-mile creek, the first camping place being at the junction of Ellejoy creek and Little river, at the old town site. It crossed Holston within a mile of Fort Robinson.

According to Hutchins (Topographical Description of America, p. 24, 1778), the road which went through Cumberland gap was the one taken by the northern Indians in their incursions into the "Cuttawa" country, and went from Sandusky, on Lake Erie, by a direct path to the mouth of Scioto (where Portsmouth now is) and thence across Kentucky to the gap.

(20) PEACE TOWNS AND TOWNS OF REFUGE (p. 51): Towns of refuge existed among the Cherokee, the Creeks, and probably other Indian tribes, as well as among the ancient Hebrews, the institution being a merciful provision for softening the harshness of the primitive law, which required a life for a life. We learn from Deuteronomy that Moses appointed three cities on the east side of Jordan "that the slayer might flee thither which should kill his neighbor unawares and hated him not in times past, and that fleeing into one of these cities he might live." It was also ordained that as more territory was conquered from the heathen three additional cities should be thus set aside as havens of refuge for those who should accidentally take human life, and where they should be safe until the matter could be adjusted. The wilful murderer, however, was not to be sheltered, but delivered up to punishment without pity (Deut. IV, 41–43, and XIX, 1–11).

Echota, the ancient Cherokee capital near the mouth of Little Tennessee, was the Cherokee town of refuge, commonly designated as the "white town" or "peace town." According to Adair, the Cherokee in his time, although extremely degenerate in other things, still observed the law so strictly in this regard that even a wilful murderer who might succeed in making his escape to that town was safe so long as he remained there, although, unless the matter was compounded in the meantime, the friends of the slain person would seldom allow him to reach home alive after leaving it. He tells how a trader who had killed an Indian to protect his own property took refuge in Echota, and after having been there for some months prepared to return to his trading store, which was but a short distance away, but was assured by the chiefs that he would be killed if he ventured outside the town. He was accordingly obliged to stay a longer time until the tears of the bereaved relatives had been wiped away with presents. In another place the same author tells how a Cherokee, having killed a trader, was pursued and attempted to take refuge in the town, but was driven off into the river as soon as he came in sight by the inhabitants, who feared either to have their town polluted by the shedding of blood or to provoke the English by giving him sanctuary (Adair, American Indians, p. 158, 1775). In 1768 Oconostota, speaking on behalf of the Cherokee delegates who had come to Johnson Hall to make peace with the Iroquois, said: "We come from Chotte, where the wise [white?] house, the house of peace is erected" (treaty record, 1768, New York Colonial Documents, VIII, p. 42, 1857). In 1786 the friendly Cherokee made "Chota" the watchword by which the Americans might be able to distinguish them from the hostile Creeks (Ramsey, Tennessee, p. 343). From conversation with old Cherokee it seems probable that in cases where no satisfaction was made by the relatives of the man-slayer he continued to reside close within the limits of the town until the next recurrence of the annual Green-corn dance, when a general amnesty was proclaimed.

Among the Creeks the ancient town of Kusa or Coosa, on Coosa river in Alabama, was a town of refuge. In Adair's time, although then almost deserted and in ruins, it was still a place of safety for one who had taken human life without design. Certain towns were also known as peace towns, from their prominence in peace ceremonials and treaty making. Upon this Adair says: "In almost every Indian nation there are several *peaceable towns*, which are called 'old beloved, ancient, holy, or white towns.' They seem to have been formerly towns of refuge, for it is not in the memory of their oldest people that ever human blood was shed in them, although they often force persons from thence and put them to death elsewhere."—Adair, American Indians, 159. A closely parallel institution seems to have existed among the Seneca. "The Seneca nation, ever the largest, and guarding the western door of the 'long house,' which was threatened alike from the north, west, and south, had traditions peculiarly their own, besides those common to the other members of the confederacy. The stronghold or fort, Gau-stra-yea, on the mountain ridge, four miles east of Lewiston, had a peculiar character as the residence of a virgin queen known as the 'Peacemaker.' When the Iroquois confederacy was first formed the prime factors were mutual protection and domestic peace, and this fort was designed to afford comfort and relieve the distress incident to war. It was a true 'city of refuge,' to which fugitives from battle, whatever their nationality, might flee for safety and find generous entertainment. Curtains of deerskin separated pursuer and pursued while they were being lodged and fed. At parting, the curtains were withdrawn, and the hostile parties, having shared the hospitality of the queen, could neither renew hostility or pursuit without the queen's consent. According to tradition, no virgin had for many generations been counted worthy to fill the place or possessed the genius and gifts to honor the position. In 1878 the Tonawanda band proposed to revive the office and conferred upon Caroline Parker the title."—Carrington, in Six Nations of New York, Extra Bulletin Eleventh Census, p. 73, 1892.

(21) SCALPING BY WHITES (p. 53): To the student, aware how easily the civilized man reverts to his original savagery when brought in close contact with its conditions, it will be no surprise to learn that every barbarous practice of Indian warfare was quickly adopted by the white pioneer and soldier and frequently legalized and encouraged by local authority. Scalping, while the most common, was probably the least savage and cruel of them all, being usually performed after the victim was already dead, with the primary purpose of securing a trophy of the victory. The tortures, mutilations, and nameless deviltries inflicted upon Indians by their white conquerors in the early days could hardly be paralleled even in civilized Europe, when burning at the stake was the punishment for holding original opinions and sawing into two pieces the penalty for desertion. Actual torture of Indians by legal sanction was rare within the English colonies, but mutilation was common and scalping was the rule down to the end of the war of 1812, and has been practiced more or less in almost every Indian war down to the latest. Captain Church, who commanded in King Philip's war in 1676, states that his men received thirty shillings a head for every Indian killed or taken, and Philip's head, after it was cut off, "went at the same price." When the chief was killed one of his hands was cut off and given to his Indian slayer, "to show to such gentlemen as would bestow gratuities upon him, and accordingly he got many a penny by it." His other hand was chopped off and sent to Boston for exhibition, his head was sent to Plymouth and exposed upon a scaffold there for twenty years, while the rest of his body was quartered and the pieces left hanging upon four trees. Fifty years later Massachusetts offered a bounty of one hundred pounds for every Indian scalp, and scalp hunting thus became a regular and usually a profitable business. On one occasion a certain Lovewell, having recruited a company of forty men for this purpose, discovered ten Indians lying asleep by their fire and killed the whole party. After scalping them they stretched the scalps upon hoops and marched thus into Boston, where the scalps were paraded and the bounty of one thousand pounds paid for them. By a few other scalps sold from time to time at the regular market rate, Lovewell was gradually acquiring a competency when in May, 1725, his company

met disaster. He discovered and shot a solitary hunter, who was afterward scalped by the chaplain of the party, but the Indian managed to kill Lovewell before being overpowered, on which the whites withdrew, but were pursued by the tribesmen of the slain hunter, with the result that but sixteen of them got home alive. A famous old ballad of the time tells how

"Our worthy Captain Lovewell among them there did die.
They killed Lieutenant Robbins and wounded good young Frye,
Who was our English chaplain; he many Indians slew,
And some of them he scalped when bullets round him flew."

When the mission village of Norridgewock was attacked by the New England men about the same time, women and children were made to suffer the fate of the warriors. The scholarly missionary, Rasles, author of the Abnaki Dictionary, was shot down at the foot of the cross, where he was afterward found with his body riddled with balls, his skull crushed and scalped, his mouth and eyes filled with earth, his limbs broken, and all his members mutilated—and this by white men. The border men of the Revolutionary period and later invariably scalped slain Indians as often as opportunity permitted, and, as has already been shown, both British and American officials encouraged the practice by offers of bounties and rewards, even, in the case of the former, when the scalps were those of white people. Our difficulties with the Apache date from a treacherous massacre of them in 1836 by a party of American scalp hunters in the pay of the governor of Sonora. The bounty offered was one ounce of gold per scalp. In 1864 the Colorado militia under Colonel Chivington attacked a party of Cheyennes camped under the protection of the United States flag, and killed, mutilated, and scalped 170 men, women, and children, bringing the scalps into Denver, where they were paraded in a public hall. One Lieutenant Richmond killed and scalped three women and five children. Scalps were taken by American troops in the Modoc war of 1873, and there is now living in the Comanche tribe a woman who was scalped, though not mortally wounded, by white soldiers in one of the later Indian encounters in Texas. *Authorities:* Drake, Indians (for New England wars); Roosevelt, Virginia State Papers, etc. (Revolution, etc.); Bancroft, Pacific States (Apache); Official Report on the Condition of the Indian Tribes, 1867 (for Chivington episode); author's personal information.

(22) LOWER CHEROKEE REFUGEES (p. 55): "In every hut I have visited I find the children exceedingly alarmed at the sight of white men, and here [at Willstown] a little boy of eight years old was excessively alarmed and could not be kept from screaming out until he got out of the door, and then he ran and hid himself; but as soon as I can converse with them and they are informed who I am they execute any order I give them with eagerness. I inquired particularly of the mothers what could be the reason for this. They said, this town was the remains of several towns who [*sic*] formerly resided on Tugalo and Keowee, and had been much harassed by the whites; that the old people remembered their former situation and suffering, and frequently spoke of them; that these tales were listened to by the children, and made an impression which showed itself in the manner I had observed. The women told me, who I saw gathering nuts, that they had sensations upon my coming to the camp, in the highest degree alarming to them, and when I lit from my horse, took them by the hand, and spoke to them, they at first could not reply, although one of them understood and spoke English very well."—Hawkins, manuscript journal, 1796, in library of Georgia Historical Society.

(23) GENERAL ALEXANDER McGILLIVRAY (p. 56): This famous Creek chieftain, like so many distinguished men of the southern tribes, was of mixed blood, being the son of a Scotch trader, Lachlan McGillivray, by a halfbreed woman of influential family, whose father was a French officer of Fort Toulouse. The future chief was born in the Creek Nation about 1740, and died at Pensacola, Florida, in 1793. He

was educated at Charleston, studying Latin in addition to the ordinary branches, and after leaving school was placed by his father with a mercantile firm in Savannah. He remained but a short time, when he returned to the Creek country, where he soon began to attract attention, becoming a partner in the firm of Panton, Forbes & Leslie, of Pensacola, which had almost a monopoly of the Creek trade. He succeeded to the chieftainship on the death of his mother, who came of ruling stock, but refused to accept the position until called to it by a formal council, when he assumed the title of emperor of the Creek Nation. His paternal estates having been confiscated by Georgia at the outbreak of the Revolution, he joined the British side with all his warriors, and continued to be a leading instigator in the border hostilities until 1790, when he visited New York with a large retinue and made a treaty of peace with the United States on behalf of his people. President Washington's instructions to the treaty commissioners, in anticipation of this visit, state that he was said to possess great abilities and an unlimited influence over the Creeks and part of the Cherokee, and that it was an object worthy of considerable effort to attach him warmly to the United States. In pursuance of this policy the Creek chiefs were entertained by the Tammany society, all the members being in full Indian dress, at which the visitors were much delighted and responded with an Indian dance, while McGillivray was induced to resign his commission as colonel in the Spanish service for a commission of higher grade in the service of the United States. Soon afterward, on account of some opposition, excited by Bowles, a renegade white man, he absented himself from his tribe for a time, but was soon recalled, and continued to rule over the Nation until his death.

McGillivray appears to have had a curious mixture of Scotch shrewdness, French love of display, and Indian secretiveness. He fixed his residence at Little Talassee, on the Coosa, a few miles above the present Wetumpka, Alabama, where he lived in a handsome house with extensive quarters for his negro slaves, so that his place had the appearance of a small town. He entertained with magnificence and traveled always in state, as became one who styled himself emperor. Throughout the Indian wars he strove, so far as possible, to prevent unnecessary cruelties, being noted for his kindness to captives; and his last years were spent in an effort to bring teachers among his people. On the other hand, he conformed much to the Indian customs; and he managed his negotiations with England, Spain, and the United States with such adroitness that he was able to play off one against the other, holding commissions by turn in the service of all three. Woodward, who knew of him by later reputation, asserts positively that McGillivray's mother was of pure Indian blood and that he himself was without education, his letters having been written for him by Leslie, of the trading firm with which he was connected. The balance of testimony, however, seems to leave no doubt that he was an educated as well as an able man, whatever may have been his origin. *Authorities:* Drake, American Indians; documents in American State Papers, Indian Affairs, I, 1832; Pickett, Alabama, 1896; Appleton's Cyclopædia of American Biography; Woodward, Reminiscences, p. 59 et passim, 1859.

(24) GOVERNOR JOHN SEVIER (p. 57): This noted leader and statesman in the pioneer history of Tennessee was born in Rockingham county, Virginia, in 1745, and died at the Creek town of Tukabatchee, in Alabama, in 1815. His father was a French immigrant of good birth and education, the original name of the family being Xavier. The son received a good education, and being naturally remarkably handsome and of polished manner, fine courage, and generous temperament, soon acquired a remarkable influence over the rough border men with whom his lot was cast and among whom he was afterward affectionately known as "Chucky Jack." To the Cherokee he was known as Tsan-usdi', "Little John." After some service against the Indians on the Virginia frontier he removed to the new Watauga settlement in Tennessee, in 1772, and at once became prominently identified with its affairs. He took

part in Dunmore's war in 1774 and, afterward, from the opening of the Revolution in 1775 until the close of the Indian wars in Tennessee—a period extending over nearly twenty years—was the acknowledged leader or organizer in every important Indian campaign along the Tennessee border. His services in this connection have been already noted. He also commanded one wing of the American forces at the battle of King's mountain in 1780, and in 1783 led a body of mountain men to the assistance of the patriots under Marion. At one time during the Revolution a Tory plot to assassinate him was revealed by the wife of the principal conspirator. In 1779 he had been commissioned as commander of the militia of Washington county, North Carolina—the nucleus of the present state of Tennessee—a position which he had already held by common consent. Shortly after the close of the Revolution he held for a short time the office of governor of the seceding "state of Franklin," for which he was arrested and brought to trial by the government of North Carolina, but made his escape, when the matter was allowed to drop. The question of jurisdiction was finally settled in 1790, when North Carolina ceded the disputed territory to the general government. Before this Sevier had been commissioned as brigadier-general. When Tennessee was admitted as a state in 1796 he was elected its first (state) governor, serving three terms, or six years. In 1803 he was again reelected, serving three more terms. In 1811 he was elected to Congress, where he served two terms and was reelected to a third, but died before he could take his seat, having contracted a fever while on duty as a boundary commissioner among the Creeks, being then in his seventy-first year. For more than forty years he had been continuously in the service of his country, and no man of his state was ever more loved and respected. In the prime of his manhood he was reputed the handsomest man and the best Indian fighter in Tennessee.

(25) HOPEWELL, SOUTH CAROLINA (p. 61): This place, designated in early treaties and also in Hawkins's manuscript journal as "Hopewell on the Keowee," was the plantation seat of General Andrew Pickens, who resided there from the close of the Revolution until his death in 1817. It was situated on the northern edge of the present Anderson county, on the east side of Keowee river, opposite and a short distance below the entrance of Little river, and about three miles from the present Pendleton. In sight of it, on the opposite side of Keowee, was the old Cherokee town of Seneca, destroyed by the Americans in 1776. Important treaties were made here with the Cherokee in 1785, and with the Chickasaw in 1786.

(26) COLONEL BENJAMIN HAWKINS (p. 61): This distinguished soldier, statesman, and author, was born in Warren county, North Carolina, in 1754, and died at Hawkinsville, Georgia, in 1816. His father, Colonel Philemon Hawkins, organized and commanded a regiment in the Revolutionary war, and was a member of the convention that ratified the national constitution. At the outbreak of the Revolution young Hawkins was a student at Princeton, but offered his services to the American cause, and on account of his knowledge of French and other modern languages was appointed by Washington his staff interpreter for communicating with the French officers cooperating with the American army. He took part in several engagements and was afterward appointed commissioner for procuring war supplies abroad. After the close of the war he was elected to Congress, and in 1785 was appointed on the commission which negotiated at Hopewell the first federal treaty with the Cherokee. He served a second term in the House and another in the Senate, and in 1796 was appointed superintendent for all the Indians south of the Ohio. He thereupon removed to the Creek country and established himself in the wilderness at what is now Hawkinsville, Georgia, where he remained in the continuance of his office until his death. As Senator he signed the deed by which North Carolina ceded Tennessee to the United States in 1790, and as Indian superintendent helped to negotiate seven different treaties with the southern tribes. He had an extensive knowledge of the customs and language of the Creeks, and his "Sketch of the Creek

Country," written in 1799 and published by the Historical Society of Georgia in 1848, remains a standard. His journal and other manuscripts are in possession of the same society, while a manuscript Cherokee vocabulary is in possession of the American Philosophical Society in Philadelphia. *Authorities:* Hawkins's manuscripts, with Georgia Historical Society; Indian Treaties, 1837; American State Papers: Indian Affairs, I, 1832; II, 1834; Gatschet, Creek Migration Legend; Appleton, Cyclopædia of American Biography.

(27) GOVERNOR WILLIAM BLOUNT (p. 68): William Blount, territorial governor of Tennessee, was born in North Carolina in 1744 and died at Knoxville, Tennessee, in 1800. He held several important offices in his native state, including two terms in the assembly and two others as delegate to the old congress, in which latter capacity he was one of the signers of the Federal constitution in 1787. On the organization of a territorial government for Tennessee in 1790, he was appointed territorial governor and also superintendent for the southern tribes, fixing his headquarters at Knoxville. In 1791 he negotiated an important treaty with the Cherokee, and had much to do with directing the operations against the Indians until the close of the Indian war. He was president of the convention which organized the state of Tennessee in 1796, and was elected to the national senate, but was expelled on the charge of having entered into a treasonable conspiracy to assist the British in conquering Louisiana from Spain. A United States officer was sent to arrest him, but returned without executing his mission on being warned by Blount's friends that they would not allow him to be taken from the state. The impeachment proceedings against him were afterward dismissed on technical grounds. In the meantime the people of his own state had shown their confidence in him by electing him to the state senate, of which he was chosen president. He died at the early age of fifty-three, the most popular man in the state next to Sevier. His younger brother, Willie Blount, who had been his secretary, was afterward governor of Tennessee, 1809–1815.

(28) ST CLAIR'S DEFEAT, 1791 (p. 72): Early in 1791 Major-General Arthur St Clair, a veteran officer in two wars and governor of the Northwestern Territory, was appointed to the chief command of the army operating against the Ohio tribes. On November 4 of that year, while advancing upon the Miami villages with an army of 1,400 men, he was surprised by an Indian force of about the same number under Little-turtle, the Miami chief, in what is now southwestern Mercer county, Ohio, adjoining the Indiana line. Because of the cowardly conduct of the militia he was totally defeated, with the loss of 632 officers and men killed and missing, and 263 wounded, many of whom afterward died. The artillery was abandoned, not a horse being left alive to draw it off, and so great was the panic that the men threw away their arms and fled for miles, even after the pursuit had ceased. It was afterward learned that the Indians lost 150 killed, besides many wounded. Two years later General Wayne built Fort Recovery upon the same spot. The detachment sent to do the work found within a space of 350 yards 500 skulls, while for several miles along the line of pursuit the woods were strewn with skeletons and muskets. The two cannon lost were found in the adjacent stream. *Authorities:* St Clair's report and related documents, 1791; American State Papers, Indian Affairs, I, 1832; Drake, Indians 570, 571, 1880; Appleton's Cyclopædia of American Biography.

(29) CHEROKEE CLANS, (p. 74): The Cherokee have seven clans, viz: Ani′-Wa′ya, Wolf; Ani′-Kawĭ′, Deer; Ani′-Tsi′skwa, Bird; Ani′-Wâ′dĭ, Paint; Ani′-Sahâ′nĭ; Ani′-Ga′tâge′wĭ; Ani′-Gilâ′hĭ. The names of the last three can not be translated with certainty. The Wolf clan is the largest and most important in the tribe. It is probable that, in accordance with the general system in other tribes, each clan had formerly certain hereditary duties and privileges, but no trace of these now remains. Children belong to the clan of the mother, and the law forbidding marriage between persons of the same clan is still enforced among the conservative

full-bloods. The "seven clans" are frequently mentioned in the sacred formulas, and even in some of the tribal laws promulgated within the century. There is evidence that originally there were fourteen, which by extinction or absorption have been reduced to seven; thus, the ancient Turtle-dove and Raven clans now constitute a single Bird clan. The subject will be discussed more fully in a future Cherokee paper.

(30) WAYNE'S VICTORY, 1794 (p. 78): After the successive failures of Harmar and St Clair in their efforts against the Ohio tribes the chief command was assigned, in 1793, to Major-General Anthony Wayne, who had already distinguished himself by his fighting qualities during the Revolution. Having built Fort Recovery on the site of St Clair's defeat, he made that post his headquarters through the winter of 1793–94. In the summer of 1794 he advanced down the Maumee with an army of 3,000 men, two-thirds of whom were regulars. On August 20 he encountered the confederated Indian forces near the head of the Maumee rapids at a point known as the Fallen Timbers and defeated them with great slaughter, the pursuit being followed up by the cavalry until the Indians took refuge under the guns of the British garrison at Fort Miami, just below the rapids. His own loss was only 33 killed and 100 wounded, of whom 11 afterward died of their wounds. The loss of the Indians and their white auxiliaries was believed to be more than double this. The Indian force was supposed to number 2,000, while, on account of the impetuosity of Wayne's charge, the number of his troops actually engaged did not exceed 900. On account of this defeat and the subsequent devastation of their towns and fields by the victorious army the Indians were compelled to sue for peace, which was granted by the treaty concluded at Greenville, Ohio, August 3, 1795, by which the tribes represented ceded away nearly their whole territory in Ohio. *Authorities:* Wayne's report and related documents, 1794, American State Papers: Indian Affairs, I, 1832; Drake, Indians, 571–577, 1880; Greenville treaty, in Indian Treaties, 1837; Appleton's Cyclopædia of American Biography.

(31) FIRST THINGS OF CIVILIZATION (p. 83): We usually find that the first things adopted by the Indian from his white neighbor are improved weapons and cutting tools, with trinkets and articles of personal adornment. After a regular trade has been established certain traders marry Indian wives, and, taking up their permanent residence in the Indian country, engage in farming and stock raising according to civilized methods, thus, even without intention, constituting themselves industrial teachers for the tribe.

From data furnished by Haywood, guns appear to have been first introduced among the Cherokee about the year 1700 or 1710, although he himself puts the date much earlier. Horses were probably not owned in any great number before the marking out of the horse-path for traders from Augusta about 1740. The Cherokee, however, took kindly to the animal, and before the beginning of the war of 1760 had a "prodigious number." In spite of their great losses at that time they had so far recovered in 1775 that almost every man then had from two to a dozen (Adair, p. 231). In the border wars following the Revolution companies of hundreds of mounted Cherokee and Creeks sometimes invaded the settlements. The cow is called *wa'ka* by the Cherokee and *waga* by the Creeks, indicating that their first knowledge of it came through the Spaniards. Nuttall states that it was first introduced among the Cherokee by the celebrated Nancy Ward (Travels, p. 130). It was not in such favor as the horse, being valuable chiefly for food, of which at that time there was an abundant supply from the wild game. A potent reason for its avoidance was the Indian belief that the eating of the flesh of a slow-moving animal breeds a corresponding sluggishness in the eater. The same argument applied even more strongly to the hog, and to this day a few of the old conservatives among the East Cherokee will have nothing to do with beef, pork, milk, or butter. Nevertheless, Bartram tells of a trader in the Cherokee country as early as 1775 who had a stock of cattle, and whose Indian wife had learned to make butter and cheese (Travels, p. 347). In 1796 Hawkins mentions meeting two Cherokee women driving ten very fat cattle to market in the white settlements (manuscript journal, 1796). Bees, if not native, as the Indians claim, were introduced at so early a period that the Indians have forgotten their foreign origin. The De Soto narrative mentions the finding of a pot of honey in an Indian village in Georgia in 1540. The peach was cultivated in orchards a century before the Revolution, and one variety, known as early as 1700 as the Indian peach, the Indians claimed as their own, asserting that they had had it before the whites came to America (Lawson, Carolina, p. 182, ed. 1860). Potatoes were introduced early and were so much esteemed that, according to one old informant, the Indians in Georgia, before the Removal, "lived on them." Coffee came later, and the same informant remembered when the full-bloods still considered it poison, in spite of the efforts of the chief, Charles Hicks, to introduce it among them.

Spinning wheels and looms were introduced shortly before the Revolution. According to the Wahnenauhi manuscript the first among the Cherokee were brought over from England by an Englishman named Edward Graves, who taught his Cherokee wife to spin and weave. The anonymous writer may have confounded this early civilizer with a young Englishman who was employed by Agent Hawkins in 1801 to make wheels and looms for the Creeks (Hawkins, 1801, in American State Papers: Indian Affairs, I, p. 647). Wafford, in his boyhood, say about 1815, knew an old man named Tsĭ′nawĭ on Young-cane creek of Nottely river, in upper Georgia, who was known as a wheelwright and was reputed to have made the first spinning wheel and loom ever made among the mountain Cherokee, or perhaps in the Nation, long before Wafford's time, or "about the time the Cherokee began to drop their silver ornaments and go to work." In 1785 the commissioners for the Hopewell treaty reported that some of the Cherokee women had lately learned to spin, and many were very desirous of instruction in the raising, spinning, and weaving of flax, cotton, and wool (Hopewell Commissioners' Report, 1785, American State Papers: Indian Affairs, I, p. 39). In accordance with their recommendation the next treaty made with the tribe, in 1791, contained a provision for supplying the Cherokee with farming tools (Holston treaty, 1791, Indian Treaties, p. 36, 1837), and this civilizing policy was continued and broadened until, in 1801, their agent reported that at the Cherokee agency the wheel, the loom, and the plow were in pretty general use, and farming, manufacturing, and stock raising were the principal topics of conversation among men and women (Hawkins manuscripts, Treaty Commission of 1801).

(32) COLONEL RETURN J. MEIGS (p. 84): Return Jonathan Meigs was born in Middletown, Connecticut, December 17, 1734, and died at the Cherokee agency in Tennessee, January 28, 1823. He was the first-born son of his parents, who gave him the somewhat peculiar name of Return Jonathan to commemorate a romantic incident in their own courtship, when his mother, a young Quakeress, called back her lover as he was mounting his horse to leave the house forever after what he had supposed was a final refusal. The name has been handed down through five generations, every one of which has produced some man distinguished in the public service. The subject of this sketch volunteered immediately after the opening engagement of the Revolution at Lexington, and was assigned to duty under Arnold, with rank of major. He accompanied Arnold in the disastrous march through the wilderness against Quebec, and was captured in the assault upon the citadel and held until exchanged the next year. In 1777 he raised a regiment and was promoted to the rank of colonel. For a gallant and successful attack upon the enemy at Sag harbor, Long island, he received a sword and a vote of thanks from Congress, and by his conduct at the head of his regiment at Stony point won the favorable notice of Washington. After the close of the Revolution he removed to Ohio, where, as a member of the territorial legislature, he drew up the earliest code of regula-

tions for the pioneer settlers. In 1801 he was appointed agent for the Cherokee and took up his residence at the agency at Tellico blockhouse, opposite the mouth of Tellico river, in Tennessee, continuing to serve in that capacity until his death. He was succeeded as agent by Governor McMinn, of Tennessee. In the course of twenty-two years he negotiated several treaties with the Cherokee and did much to further the work of civilization among them and to defend them against unjust aggression. He also wrote a journal of the expedition to Quebec. His grandson of the same name was special agent for the Cherokee and Creeks in 1834, afterward achieving a reputation in the legal profession both in Tennesssee and in the District of Columbia. *Authorities:* Appleton, Cyclopædia of American Biography, 1894; Royce, Cherokee Nation, in Fifth Annual Report Bureau of Ethnology, 1888; documents in American State Papers, Indian Affairs, ɪ and ɪɪ.

(33) Tecumtha (p. 87): This great chief of the Shawano and commander of the allied northern tribes in the British service was born near the present Chillicothe, in western Ohio, about 1770, and fell in the battle of the Thames, in Ontario, October 5, 1813. His name signifies a "flying panther"—i. e., a meteor. He came of fighting stock good even in a tribe distinguished for its warlike qualities, his father and elder brother having been killed in battle with the whites. His mother is said to have died among the Cherokee. Tecumtha is first heard of as taking part in an engagement with the Kentuckians when about twenty years old, and in a few years he had secured recognition as the ablest leader among the allied tribes. It is said that he took part in every important engagement with the Americans from the time of Harmar's defeat in 1790 until the battle in which he lost his life. When about thirty years of age he conceived the idea of uniting the tribes northwest of the Ohio, as Pontiac had united them before, in a great confederacy to resist the further advance of the Americans, taking the stand that the whole territory between the Ohio and the Mississippi belonged to all these tribes in common and that no one tribe had the right to sell any portion of it without the consent of the others. The refusal of the government to admit this principle led him to take active steps to unite the tribes upon that basis, in which he was seconded by his brother, the Prophet, who supplemented Tecumtha's eloquence with his own claims to supernatural revelation. In the summer of 1810 Tecumtha held a conference with Governor Harrison at Vincennes to protest against a recent treaty cession, and finding after exhausting his arguments that the effort was fruitless, he closed the debate with the words: "The President is far off and may sit in his town and drink his wine, but you and I will have to fight it out." Both sides at once prepared for war, Tecumtha going south to enlist the aid of the Creek, Choctaw, and other southern tribes, while Harrison took advantage of his absence to force the issue by marching against the Prophet's town on the Tippecanoe river, where the hostile warriors from a dozen tribes had gathered. A battle fought before daybreak of November 6, 1811, resulted in the defeat of the Indians and the scattering of their forces. Tecumtha returned to find his plans brought to naught for the time, but the opening of the war between the United States and England a few months later enabled him to rally the confederated tribes once more to the support of the British against the Americans. As a commissioned brigadier-general in the British service he commanded 2,000 warriors in the war of 1812, distinguishing himself no less by his bravery than by his humanity in preventing outrages and protecting prisoners from massacre, at one time saving the lives of four hundred American prisoners who had been taken in ambush near Fort Meigs and were unable to make longer resistance. He was wounded at Maguagua, where nearly four hundred were killed and wounded on both sides. He covered the British retreat after the battle of Lake Erie, and, refusing to retreat farther, compelled the British General Proctor to make a stand at the Thames river. Almost the whole force of the American attack fell on Tecumtha's division. Early in the

engagement he was shot through the arm, but continued to fight desperately until he received a bullet in the head and fell dead, surrounded by the bodies of 120 of his slain warriors. The services of Tecumtha and his Indians to the British cause have been recognized by an English historian, who says, "but for them it is probable we should not now have a Canada." *Authorities:* Drake, Indians, ed. 1880; Appleton's Cyclopædia of American Biography, 1894; Eggleston, Tecumseh and the Shawnee Prophet.

(34) FORT MIMS MASSACRE, 1813 (p. 89): Fort Mims, so called from an old Indian trader on whose lands it was built, was a stockade fort erected in the summer of 1813 for the protection of the settlers in what was known as the Tensaw district, and was situated on Tensaw lake, Alabama, one mile east of Alabama river and about forty miles above Mobile. It was garrisoned by about 200 volunteer troops under Major Daniel Beasley, with refugees from the neighboring settlement, making a total at the time of its destruction of 553 men, women, and children. Being carelessly guarded, it was surprised on the morning of August 30 by about 1,000 Creek warriors led by the mixed-blood chief, William Weatherford, who rushed in at the open gate, and, after a stout but hopeless resistance by the garrison, massacred all within, with the exception of the few negroes and halfbreeds, whom they spared, and about a dozen whites who made their escape. The Indian loss is unknown, but was very heavy, as the fight continued at close quarters until the buildings were fired over the heads of the defenders. The unfortunate tragedy was due entirely to the carelessness of the commanding officer, who had been repeatedly warned that the Indians were about, and at the very moment of the attack a negro was tied up waiting to be flogged for reporting that he had the day before seen a number of painted warriors lurking a short distance outside the stockade. *Authorities:* Pickett, Alabama, ed. 1896; Hamilton and Owen, note, p. 170, in Transactions Alabama Historical Society, II, 1898; Agent Hawkins's report, 1813, American State Papers: Indian Affairs, I, p. 853; Drake, Indians, ed. 1880. The figures given are those of Pickett, which in this instance seem most correct, while Drake's are evidently exaggerated.

(35) GENERAL WILLIAM McINTOSH (p. 98): This noted halfbreed chief of the Lower Creeks was the son of a Scotch officer in the British army by an Indian mother, and was born at the Creek town of Coweta in Alabama, on the lower Chattahoochee, nearly opposite the present city of Columbus, Georgia, and killed at the same place by order of the Creek national council on April 30, 1825. Having sufficient education to keep up an official correspondence, he brought himself to public notice and came to be regarded as the principal chief of the Lower Creeks. In the Creek war of 1813–14 he led his warriors to the support of the Americans against his brethren of the Upper towns, and acted a leading part in the terrible slaughters at Autossee and the Horseshoe bend. In 1817 he again headed his warriors on the government side against the Seminole and was commissioned as major. His common title of general belonged to him only by courtesy. In 1821 he was the principal supporter of the treaty of Indian springs, by which a large tract between the Flint and Chattahoochee rivers was ceded. The treaty was repudiated by the Creek Nation as being the act of a small faction. Two other attempts were made to carry through the treaty, in which the interested motives of McIntosh became so apparent that he was branded as a traitor to his Nation and condemned to death, together with his principal underlings, in accordance with a Creek law making death the penalty for undertaking to sell lands without the consent of the national council. About the same time he was publicly exposed and denounced in the Cherokee council for an attempt to bribe John Ross and other chiefs of the Cherokee in the same fashion. At daylight of April 30, 1825, a hundred or more warriors sent by the Creek national council surrounded his house and, after allowing the women and children to come out, set fire to it and shot McIntosh and another chief

as they tried to escape. He left three wives, one of whom was a Cherokee. *Authorities:* Drake, Indians, ed. 1880; Letters from McIntosh's son and widows, 1825, in American State Papers: Indian Affairs, II, pp. 764 and 768.

(36) WILLIAM WEATHERFORD (p. 89): This leader of the hostiles in the Creek war was the son of a white father and a halfbreed woman of Tuskegee town whose father had been a Scotchman. Weatherford was born in the Creek Nation about 1780 and died on Little river, in Monroe county, Alabama, in 1826. He came first into prominence by leading the attack upon Fort Mims, August 30, 1813, which resulted in the destruction of the fort and the massacre of over five hundred inmates. It is maintained, with apparent truth, that he did his best to prevent the excesses which followed the victory, and left the scene rather than witness the atrocities when he found that he could not restrain his followers. The fact that Jackson allowed him to go home unmolested after the final surrender is evidence that he believed Weatherford guiltless. At the battle of the Holy Ground, in the following December, he was defeated and narrowly escaped capture by the troops under General Claiborne. When the last hope of the Creeks had been destroyed and their power of resistance broken by the bloody battle of the Horseshoe bend, March 27, 1814, Weatherford voluntarily walked into General Jackson's headquarters and surrendered, creating such an impression by his straightforward and fearless manner that the general, after a friendly interview, allowed him to go back alone to gather up his people preliminary to arranging terms of peace. After the treaty he retired to a plantation in Monroe county, where he lived in comfort and was greatly respected by his white neighbors until his death. As an illustration of his courage it is told how he once, single-handed, arrested two murderers immediately after the crime, when the local justice and a large crowd of bystanders were afraid to approach them. Jackson declared him to be as high toned and fearless as any man he had ever met. In person he was tall, straight, and well proportioned, with features indicating intelligence, bravery, and enterprise. *Authorities:* Pickett, Alabama, ed. 1896; Drake, Indians, ed. 1880; Woodward, Reminiscences, 1859.

(37) REVEREND DAVID BRAINERD (p. 104): The pioneer American missionary from whom the noted Cherokee mission took its name was born at Haddam, Connecticut, April 20, 1718, and died at Northampton, Massachusetts, October 9, 1747. He entered Yale college in 1739, but was expelled on account of his religious opinions. In 1742 he was licensed as a preacher and the next year began work as missionary to the Mahican Indians of the village of Kaunameek, twenty miles from Stockbridge, Massachusetts. He persuaded them to remove to Stockbridge, where he put them in charge of a resident minister, after which he took up work with good result among the Delaware and other tribes on the Delaware and Susquehanna rivers. In 1747 his health failed and he was forced to retire to Northampton, where he died a few months later. He wrote a journal and an account of his missionary labors at Kaunameek. His later mission work was taken up and continued by his brother. *Authority:* Appleton's Cyclopædia of American Biography, 1894.

(38) REVEREND SAMUEL AUSTIN WORCESTER (p. 105): This noted missionary and philologist, the son of a Congregational minister who was also a printer, was born at Worcester, Massachusetts, January 19, 1798, and died at Park Hill, in the Cherokee Nation west, April 20, 1859. Having removed to Vermont with his father while still a child, he graduated with the honors of his class at the state university at Burlington in 1819, and after finishing a course at the theological seminary at Andover was ordained to the ministry in 1825. A week later, with his newly wedded bride, he left Boston to begin mission work among the Cherokee, and arrived in October at the mission of the American board, at Brainerd, Tennessee, where he remained until the end of 1827. He then, with his wife, removed to New Echota, in Georgia, the capital of the Cherokee Nation, where he was the principal worker in the establishment of the *Cherokee Phœnix*, the first newspaper printed in the Cherokee

language and alphabet.   In this labor his inherited printer's instinct came into play, for he himself supervised the casting of the new types and the systematic arrangement of them in the case.   In March, 1831, he was arrested by the Georgia authorities for refusing to take a special oath of allegiance to the state.   He was released, but was rearrested soon afterward, confined in the state penitentiary, and forced to wear prison garb, until January, 1833, notwithstanding a decision by the Supreme Court of the United States, nearly a year before, that his imprisonment was a violation of the law of the land.   The *Cherokee Phœnix* having been suspended and the Cherokee Nation brought into disorder by the extension over it of the state laws, he then returned to Brainerd, which was beyond the limits of Georgia.   In 1835 he removed to the Indian Territory, whither the Arkansas Cherokee had already gone, and after short sojourns at Dwight and Union missions took up his final residence at Park Hill in December, 1836.   He had already set up his mission press at Union, printing both in the Cherokee and the Creek languages, and on establishing himself at Park Hill he began a regular series of publications in the Cherokee language.   In 1843 he states that "at Park Hill, besides the preaching of the gospel, a leading object of attention is the preparation and publication of books in the Cherokee language" (Letter in Report of Indian Commissioner, p. 356, 1843).   The list of his Cherokee publications (first editions) under his own name in Pilling's Bibliography comprises about twenty titles, including the Bible, hymn books, tracts, and almanacs in addition to the *Phœnix* and large number of anonymous works.   Says Pilling: "It is very probable that he was the translator of a number of books for which he is not given credit here, especially those portions of the Scripture which are herein not assigned to any name. Indeed it is safe to say that during the thirty-four years of his connection with the Cherokee but little was done in the way of translating in which he had not a share." He also began a Cherokee geography and had both a grammar and a dictionary of the language under way when his work was interrupted by his arrest.   The manuscripts, with all his personal effects, afterward went down with a sinking steamer on the Arkansas.   His daughter, Mrs A. E. W. Robertson, became a missionary among the Creeks and has published a number of works in their language.   *Authorities:* Pilling, Bibliography of the Iroquoian languages (articles Worcester, Cherokee Phœnix, etc.), 1888; Drake, Indians, ed. 1880: Report of Indian Commissioner, 1843 (Worcester letter).

(39) DEATH PENALTY FOR SELLING LANDS (p. 107): In 1820 the Cherokee Nation enacted a law making it treason punishable with death to enter into any negotiation for the sale of tribal lands without the consent of the national council.   A similar law was enacted by the Creeks at about the same time.   It was for violating these laws that McIntosh and Ridge suffered death in their respective tribes.   The principal parts of the Cherokee law, as reenacted by the united Nation in the West in 1842, appear as follows in the compilation authorized in 1866:

"AN ACT AGAINST SALE OF LAND, ETC.: *Whereas,* The peace and prosperity of Indian nations are frequently sacrificed or placed in jeopardy by the unrestrained cupidity of their own individual citizens; *and whereas,* we ourselves are liable to suffer from the same cause, and be subjected to future removal and disturbances: Therefore, . . .

"*Be it further enacted,* That any person or persons who shall, contrary to the will and consent of the legislative council of this nation, in general council convened, enter into a treaty with any commissioner or commissioners of the United States, or any officer or officers instructed for the purpose, and agree to cede, exchange, or dispose in any way any part or portion of the lands belonging to or claimed by the Cherokees, west of the Mississippi, he or they so offending, upon conviction before any judge of the circuit or supreme courts, *shall suffer death,* and any of the aforesaid judges are authorized to call a court for the trial of any person or persons so transgressing.

" *Be it further enacted*, That any person or persons who shall violate the provisions of the second section of this act, and shall resist or refuse to appear at the place designated for trial, or abscond, are hereby declared to be outlaws; and any person or persons, citizens of this nation, may kill him or them so offending at any time and in any manner most convenient, within the limits of this nation, and shall not be held accountable to the laws for the same.   .   .   .

" *Be it further enacted*, That no treaty shall be binding upon this nation which shall not be ratified by the general council, and approved by the principal chief of the nation.   December 2, 1842."—Laws of the Cherokee Nation, 1868.

(40) THE CHEROKEE SYLLABARY (p. 110): In the various schemes of symbolic thought representation, from the simple pictograph of the primitive man to the finished alphabet of the civilized nations, our own system, although not yet perfect, stands at the head of the list, the result of three thousand years of development by Egyptian, Phœnician, and Greek.   Sequoya's syllabary, the unaided work of an uneducated Indian reared amid semisavage surroundings, stands second.

Twelve years of his life are said to have been given to his great work.   Being entirely without instruction and having no knowledge of the philosophy of language, being not even acquainted with English, his first attempts were naturally enough in the direction of the crude Indian pictograph.   He set out to devise a symbol for each word of the language, and after several years of experiment, finding this an utterly hopeless task, he threw aside the thousands of characters which he had carved or scratched upon pieces of bark, and started in anew to study the construction of the language itself.   By attentive observation for another long period he finally discovered that the sounds in the words used by the Cherokee in their daily conversation and their public speeches could be analyzed and classified, and that the thousands of possible words were all formed from varying combinations of hardly more than a hundred distinct syllables.   Having thoroughly tested his discovery until satisfied of its correctness, he next proceeded to formulate a symbol for each syllable.   For this purpose he made use of a number of characters which he found in an old English spelling book, picking out capitals, lower-case, italics, and figures, and placing them right side up or upside down, without any idea of their sound or significance as used in English (see plate v).   Having thus utilized some thirty-five ready-made characters, to which must be added a dozen or more produced by modification of the same originals, he designed from his own imagination as many more as were necessary to his purpose, making eighty-five in all.   The complete syllabary, as first elaborated, would have required some one hundred and fifteen characters, but after much hard study over the hissing sound in its various combinations, he hit upon the expedient of representing the sound by means of a distinct character—the exact equivalent of our letter *s*—whenever it formed the initial of a syllable.   Says Gallatin, "It wanted but one step more, and to have also given a distinct character to each consonant, to reduce the whole number to sixteen, and to have had an alphabet similar to ours.   In practice, however, and as applied to his own language, the superiority of Guess's alphabet is manifest, and has been fully proved by experience.   You must indeed learn and remember eighty-five characters instead of twenty-five [*sic*].   But this once accomplished, the education of the pupil is completed; he can read and he is perfect in his orthography without making it the subject of a distinct study.   The boy learns in a few weeks that which occupies two years of the time of ours."   Says Phillips: "In my own observation Indian children will take one or two, at times several, years to master the English printed and written language, but in a few days can read and write in Cherokee.   They do the latter, in fact, as soon as they learn to shape letters. As soon as they master the alphabet they have got rid of all the perplexing questions in orthography that puzzle the brains of our children.   It is not too much to say that a child will learn in a month, by the same effort, as thoroughly in the language of Sequoyah, that which in ours consumes the time of our children for at least two years."

Although in theory the written Cherokee word has one letter for each syllable, the rule does not always hold good in practice, owing to the frequent elision of vowel sounds. Thus the word for "soul" is written with four letters as *a-da-núñ-ta*, but pronounced in three syllables, *adanta*. In the same way *tsá-lúñ-i-yu-sti* ("like tobacco," the cardinal flower) is pronounced *tsáliyustĭ*. There are also, as in other languages, a number of minute sound variations not indicated in the written word, so that it is necessary to have heard the language spoken in order to read with correct pronunciation. The old Upper dialect is the standard to which the alphabet has been adapted. There is no provision for the *r* of the Lower or the *sh* of the Middle dialect, each speaker usually making his own dialectic change in the reading. The letters of a word are not connected, and there is no difference between the written and the printed character. *Authorities:* Gallatin, Synopsis of the Indian Tribes, in Trans. Am. Antiq. Soc., II, 1836; Phillips, Sequoyah, in Harper's Magazine, September, 1870; Pilling, Bibliography of Iroquoian Languages (article on Guess and plate of syllabary), 1888; author's personal information.

(41) SOUTHERN GOLD FIELDS (p. 116): Almost every valuable mineral and crystal known to the manufacturer or the lapidary is found in the southern Alleghenies, although, so far as present knowledge goes, but few of these occur in paying quantities. It is probable, however, that this estimate may change with improved methods and enlarged railroad facilities. Leaving out of account the earlier operations by the Spanish, French, and English adventurers, of which mention has already been made, the first authentic account of gold finding in any of the states south of Mason and Dixon's line within what may be called the American period appears to be that given by Jefferson, writing in 1781, of a lump of ore found in Virginia, which yielded seventeen pennyweights of gold. This was probably not the earliest, however, as we find doubtful references to gold discoveries in both Carolinas before the Revolution. The first mint returns of gold were made from North Carolina in 1793, and from South Carolina in 1829, although gold is certainly known to have been found in the latter state some years earlier. The earliest gold records for the other southern states are, approximately, Georgia (near Dahlonega), 1815–1820; Alabama, 1830; Tennessee (Coco creek, Monroe county), 1831; Maryland (Montgomery county), 1849. Systematic tracing of gold belts southward from North Carolina began in 1829, and speedily resulted in the forcible eviction of the Cherokee from the gold-bearing region. Most of the precious metal was procured from placers or alluvial deposits by a simple process of digging and washing. Very little quartz mining has yet been attempted, and that usually by the crudest methods. In fact, for a long period gold working was followed as a sort of side issue to farming between crop seasons. In North Carolina prospectors obtained permission from the owners of the land to wash or dig on shares, varying from one-fourth to one-half, and the proprietor was accustomed to put his slaves to work in the same way along the creek bottoms after the crops had been safely gathered. "The dust became a considerable medium of circulation, and miners were accustomed to carry about with them quills filled with gold, and a pair of small hand scales, on which they weighed out gold at regular rates; for instance, 3½ grains of gold was the customary equivalent of a pint of whisky." For a number of years, about 1830 and later, a man named Bechtler coined gold on his own account in North Carolina, and these coins, with Mexican silver, are said to have constituted the chief currency over a large region. A regular mint was established at Dahlonega in 1838 and maintained for some years. From 1804 to 1827 all the gold produced in the United States came from North Carolina, although the total amounted to but $110,000. The discovery of the rich deposits in California checked mining operations in the south, and the civil war brought about an almost complete suspen-

sion, from which there is hardly yet a revival. According to the best official estimates the gold production of the southern Allegheny region for the century from 1799 to 1898, inclusive, has been something over $46,000,000, distributed as follows:

North Carolina	$21,926,376
Georgia	16,658,630
South Carolina	3,961,863
Virginia, slightly in excess of	3,216,343
Alabama, slightly in excess of	437,927
Tennessee, slightly in excess of	167,405
Maryland	47,068
Total, slightly in excess of	46,415,612

Authorities: Becker, Gold Fields of the Southern Appalachians, in the Sixteenth Annual Report United States Geological Survey, 1895; Day, Mineral Resources of the United States, Seventeenth Annual Report United States Geological Survey, part 3, 1896; Nitze, Gold Mining and Metallurgy in the Southern States, in North Carolina Geological Survey Report, republished in Mineral Resources of the United States, Twentieth Annual Report United States Geological Survey, part 6, 1899; Lanman, Letters from the Alleghany Mountains, 1849.

(42) EXTENSION OF GEORGIA LAWS, 1830 (p. 117): "It is hereby ordained that all the laws of Georgia are extended over the Cherokee country; that after the first day of June, 1830, all Indians then and at that time residing in said territory, shall be liable and subject to such laws and regulations as the legislature may hereafter prescribe; that all laws, usages, and customs made and established and enforced in the said territory, by the said Cherokee Indians, be, and the same are hereby, on and after the 1st day of June, 1830, declared null and void; and no Indian, or descendant of an Indian, residing within the Creek or Cherokee nations of Indians, shall be deemed a competent witness or party to any suit in any court where a white man is a defendant."—Extract from the act passed by the Georgia legislature on December 20, 1828, "to add the territory within this state and occupied by the Cherokee Indians to the counties of DeKalb et al., and to extend the laws of this state over the same." *Authorities:* Drake, Indians, p. 439, ed. 1880; Royce, Cherokee Nation of Indians, in Fifth Ann. Rep. Bureau of Ethnology, p. 260, 1888.

(43) REMOVAL FORTS, 1838 (p. 130): For collecting the Cherokee preparatory to the Removal, the following stockade forts were built: In North Carolina, Fort Lindsay, on the south side of the Tennessee river at the junction of Nantahala, in Swain county; Fort Scott, at Aquone, farther up Nantahala river, in Macon county; Fort Montgomery, at Robbinsville, in Graham county; Fort Hembrie, at Hayesville, in Clay county; Fort Delaney, at Valleytown, in Cherokee county; Fort Butler, at Murphy, in the same county. In Georgia, Fort Scudder, on Frogtown creek, north of Dahlonega, in Lumpkin county; Fort Gilmer, near Ellijay, in Gilmer county; Fort Coosawatee, in Murray county; Fort Talking-rock, near Jasper, in Pickens county; Fort Buffington, near Canton, in Cherokee county. In Tennessee, Fort Cass, at Calhoun, on Hiwassee river, in McMinn county. In Alabama, Fort Turkeytown, on Coosa river, at Center, in Cherokee county. *Authority:* Author's personal information.

(44) MCNAIR'S GRAVE, (p. 132): Just inside the Tennessee line, where the Conasauga river bends again into Georgia, is a stone-walled grave, with a slab, on which is an epitaph which tells its own story of the Removal heartbreak. McNair was a white man, prominent in the Cherokee Nation, whose wife was a daughter of the chief, Vann, who welcomed the Moravian missionaries and gave his own house for their use. The date shows that she died while the Removal was in progress, possibly

while waiting in the stockade camp. The inscription, with details, is given from information kindly furnished by Mr D. K. Dunn of Conasauga, Tennessee, in a letter dated August 16, 1890:

"Sacred to the memory of David and Delilah A. McNair, who departed this life, the former on the 15th of August, 1836, and the latter on the 30th of November, 1838. Their children, being members of the Cherokee Nation and having to go with their people to the West, do leave this monument, not only to show their regard for their parents, but to guard their sacred ashes against the unhallowed intrusion of the white man."

(45) PRESIDENT SAMUEL HOUSTON, (p. 145) : This remarkable man was born in Rockbridge county, Virginia, March 2, 1793, and died at Huntsville, Texas, July 25, 1863. Of strangely versatile, but forceful, character, he occupies a unique position in American history, combining in a wonderful degree the rough manhood of the pioneer, the eccentric vanity of the Indian, the stern dignity of the soldier, the genius of the statesman, and withal the high chivalry of a knight of the olden time. His erratic career has been the subject of much cheap romancing, but the simple facts are of sufficient interest in themselves without the aid of fictitious embellishment. To the Cherokee, whom he loved so well, he was known as Kâ′lanû, "The Raven," an old war title in the tribe.

His father having died when the boy was nine years old, his widowed mother removed with him to Tennessee, opposite the territory of the Cherokee, whose boundary was then the Tennessee river. Here he worked on the farm, attending school at intervals; but, being of adventurous disposition, he left home when sixteen years old, and, crossing over the river, joined the Cherokee, among whom he soon became a great favorite, being adopted into the family of Chief Jolly, from whom the island at the mouth of Hiwassee takes its name. After three years of this life, during which time he wore the Indian dress and learned the Indian language, he returned to civilization and enlisted as a private soldier under Jackson in the Creek war. He soon attracted favorable notice and was promoted to the rank of ensign. By striking bravery at the bloody battle of Horseshoe bend, where he scaled the breastworks with an arrow in his thigh and led his men into the thick of the enemy, he won the lasting friendship of Jackson, who made him a lieutenant, although he was then barely twenty-one. He continued in the army after the war, serving for a time as subagent for the Cherokee at Jackson's request, until the summer of 1818, when he resigned on account of some criticism by Calhoun, then Secretary of War. An official investigation, held at his demand, resulted in his exoneration.

Removing to Nashville, he began the study of law, and, being shortly afterward admitted to the bar, set up in practice at Lebanon. Within five years he was successively district attorney and adjutant-general and major-general of state troops. In 1823 he was elected to Congress, serving two terms, at the end of which, in 1827, he was elected governor of Tennessee by an overwhelming majority, being then thirty-four years of age. Shortly before this time he had fought and wounded General White in a duel. In January, 1829, he married a young lady residing near Nashville, but two months later, without a word of explanation to any outsider, he left her, resigned his governorship and other official dignities, and left the state forever, to rejoin his old friends, the Cherokee, in the West. For years the reason for this strange conduct was a secret, and Houston himself always refused to talk of it, but it is now understood to have been due to the fact that his wife admitted to him that she loved another and had only been induced to marry him by the over-persuasions of her parents.

From Tennessee he went to Indian Territory, whither a large part of the Cherokee had already removed, and once more took up his residence near Chief Jolly, who was now the principal chief of the western Cherokee. The great disappointment which seemed to have blighted his life at its brightest was heavy at his heart, and he sought forgetfulness in drink to such an extent that for a time his manhood seemed to have departed, notwithstanding which, such was his force of character and his past reputation, he retained his hold upon the affections of the Cherokee and his standing with the officers and their families at the neighboring posts of Fort Smith, Fort Gibson, and Fort Coffee. In the meantime his former wife in Tennessee had obtained a divorce, and Houston being thus free once more soon after married Talihina, the youngest daughter of a prominent mixed-blood Cherokee named Rogers, who resided near Fort Gibson. She was the niece of Houston's adopted father, Chief Jolly, and he had known her when a boy in the old Nation. Being a beautiful girl, and educated above her surroundings, she became a welcome guest wherever her husband was received. He started a trading store near Webbers Falls, but continued in his dissipated habits until recalled to his senses by the outcome of a drunken affray in which he assaulted his adopted father, the old chief, and was himself felled to the ground unconscious. Upon recovery from his injuries he made a public apology for his conduct and thenceforward led a sober life.

In 1832 he visited Washington in the interest of the western Cherokee, calling in Indian costume upon President Jackson, who received him with old-time friendship. Being accused while there of connection with a fraudulent Indian contract, he administered a severe beating to his accuser, a member of Congress. For this he was fined $500 and reprimanded by the bar of the House, but Jackson remitted the fine. Soon after his return to the West he removed to Texas to take part in the agitation just started against Mexican rule. He was a member of the convention which adopted a separate constitution for Texas in 1833, and two years later aided in forming a provisional government, and was elected commander-in-chief to organize the new militia. In 1836 he was a member of the convention which declared the independence of Texas. At the battle of San Jacinto in April of that year he defeated with 750 men Santa Ana's army of 1,800, inflicting upon the Mexicans the terrible loss of 630 killed and 730 prisoners, among whom was Santa Ana himself. Houston received a severe wound in the engagement. In the autumn of the same year he was elected first president of the republic of Texas, receiving more than four-fifths of the votes cast. He served two years and retired at the end of his term, leaving the country on good terms with both Mexico and the Indian tribes, and with its notes at par. He was immediately elected to the Texas congress and served in that capacity until 1841, when he was reelected president. It was during these years that he made his steadfast fight in behalf of the Texas Cherokee, as is narrated elsewhere, supporting their cause without wavering, at the risk of his own popularity and position. He frequently declared that no treaty made and carried out in good faith had ever been violated by Indians. His Cherokee wife having died some time before, he was again married in 1840, this time to a lady from Alabama, who exercised over him a restraining and ennobling influence through the stormy vicissitudes of his eventful life. In June, 1842, he vetoed a bill making him dictator for the purpose of resisting a threatened invasion from Mexico.

On December 29, 1845, Texas was admitted to the Union, and in the following March Houston was elected to the Senate, where he served continuously until 1859, when he resigned to take his seat as governor, to which position he had just been elected. From 1852 to 1860 his name was three times presented before national presidential nominating conventions, the last time receiving 57 votes. He had taken issue with the Democratic majority throughout his term in the Senate, and when Texas passed the secession ordinance in February, 1861, being an uncompromising Union man, he refused to take the oath of allegiance to the Confederacy and was accordingly deposed from the office of governor, declining the proffered aid of federal troops to keep him in his seat. Unwilling either to fight against the Union or to take sides against his friends, he held aloof from the great struggle, and remained in silent retirement until his death, two years later. No other man in American history has left such a record of continuous election to high office while steadily holding to his own convictions in the face of strong popular opposition. *Authorities:* Appleton's Cyclopædia of American Biography, 1894; Bonnell, Texas, 1840; Thrall, Texas, 1876; Lossing, Field Book of the War of 1812, 1869; author's personal information; various periodical and newspaper articles.

(46) CHIEF JOHN ROSS (p. 151): This great chief of the Cherokee, whose name is inseparable from their history, was himself but one-eighth of Indian blood and showed little of the Indian features, his father, Daniel Ross, having emigrated from Scotland before the Revolution and married a quarter-blood Cherokee woman whose father, John McDonald, was also from Scotland. He was born at or near the family residence at Rossville, Georgia just across the line from Chattanooga, Tennessee. As a boy, he was known among the Cherokee as Tsan-usdi′, "Little John," but after arriving at manhood was called Guwi′sguwĭ′, the name of a rare migratory bird, of large size and white or grayish plumage, said to have appeared formerly at long intervals in the old Cherokee country. It may have been the egret or the swan. He was educated at Kingston, Tennessee, and began his public career when barely nineteen years of age. His first wife, a full-blood Cherokee woman, died in consequence of the hardships of the Removal while on the western march and was buried at Little Rock, Arkansas. Some years later he married again, this time to a Miss Stapler of Wilmington, Delaware, the marriage taking place in Philadelphia (author's personal information from Mr Allen Ross, son of John Ross; see also Meredith, "The Cherokees," in the Five Civilized Tribes, Extra Bulletin Eleventh Census, 1894.) Cooweescoowee district of the Cherokee Nation west has been named in his honor. The following biographic facts are taken from the panegyric in his honor, passed by the national council of the Cherokee, on hearing of his death, "as feebly expressive of the loss they have sustained."

John Ross was born October 3, 1790, and died in the city of Washington, August 1, 1866, in the seventy-sixth year of his age. His official career began in 1809, when he was intrusted by Agent Return Meigs with an important mission to the Arkansas Cherokee. From that time until the close of his life, with the exception of two or three years in the earlier part, he was in the constant service of his people, "furnishing an instance of confidence on their part and fidelity on his which has never been surpassed in the annals of history." In the war of 1813–14 against the Creeks he was adjutant of the Cherokee regiment which cooperated with General Jackson, and was present at the battle of the Horseshoe, where the Cherokee, under Colonel Morgan, of Tennessee, rendered distinguished service. In 1817 he was elected a member of the national committee of the Cherokee council. The first duty assigned him was to prepare a reply to the United States commissioners who were present for the purpose of negotiating with the Cherokee for their lands east of the Mississippi, in firm resistance to which he was destined, a few years later, to test the power of truth and to attain a reputation of no ordinary character. In 1819, October 26, his name first appears on the statute book of the Cherokee Nation as president of the national committee, and is attached to an ordinance which looked to the improvement of the Cherokee people, providing for the introduction into the Nation of schoolmasters, blacksmiths, mechanics, and others. He continued to occupy that position till 1826. In 1827 he was associate chief with William Hicks, and president of the convention which adopted the constitution of that year. That constitution, it is believed, is the first effort at a regular government, with distinct branches and powers defined, ever made and carried into effect by any of the Indians of North America. From 1828 until the removal west, he was principal chief of the eastern Cherokee, and from 1839 to the time of his death, principal chief of the united Cherokee Nation.

In regard to the long contest which culminated in the Removal, the resolutions declare that "The Cherokees, with John Ross at their head, alone with their treaties, achieved a recognition of their rights, but they were powerless to enforce them. They were compelled to yield, but not until the struggle had developed the highest qualities of patience, fortitude, and tenacity of right and purpose on their part, as well as that of their chief. The same may be said of their course after their removal to this country, and which resulted in the reunion of the eastern and western Cherokees as one people and in the adoption of the present constitution."

Concerning the events of the civil war and the official attempt to depose Ross from his authority, they state that these occurrences, with many others in their trying history as a people, are confidently committed to the future page of the historian. "It is enough to know that the treaty negotiated at Washington in 1866 bore the full and just recognition of John Ross' name as principal chief of the Cherokee nation."

The summing up of the panegyric is a splendid tribute to a splendid manhood:

"Blessed with a fine constitution and a vigorous mind, John Ross had the physical ability to follow the path of duty wherever it led. No danger appalled him. He never faltered in supporting what he believed to be right, but clung to it with a steadiness of purpose which alone could have sprung from the clearest convictions of rectitude. He never sacrificed the interests of his nation to expediency. He never lost sight of the welfare of the people. For them he labored daily for a long life, and upon them he bestowed his last expressed thoughts. A friend of law, he obeyed it; a friend of education, he faithfully encouraged schools throughout the country, and spent liberally his means in conferring it upon others. Given to hospitality, none ever hungered around his door. A professor of the Christian religion, he practiced its precepts. His works are inseparable from the history of the Cherokee people for nearly half a century, while his example in the daily walks of life will linger in the future and whisper words of hope, temperance, and charity in the years of posterity."

Resolutions were also passed for bringing his body from Washington at the expense of the Cherokee Nation and providing for suitable obsequies, in order "that his remains should rest among those he so long served" (Resolutions in honor of John Ross, in Laws of the Cherokee Nation, 1869).

(47) THE KETOOWAH SOCIETY (p. 156): This Cherokee secret society, which has recently achieved some newspaper prominence by its championship of Cherokee autonomy, derives its name—properly Kĭtu′hwă, but commonly spelled Ketoowah in English print—from the ancient town in the old Nation which formed the nucleus of the most conservative element of the tribe and sometimes gave a name to the Nation itself (see Kĭtu′hwagĭ, under Tribal Synonyms). A strong band of comradeship, if not a regular society organization, appears to have existed among the warriors and leading men of the various settlements of the Kituhwa district from a remote period, so that the name is even now used in councils as indicative of genuine Cherokee feeling in its highest patriotic form. When, some years ago, delegates from the western Nation visited the East Cherokee to invite them to join their more prosperous brethren beyond the Mississippi, the speaker for the delegates expressed their fraternal feeling for their separated kinsmen by saying in his opening speech, "We are all Kituhwa people" (Ani′-Kĭtu′hwagĭ). The Ketoowah society in the Cherokee Nation west was organized shortly before the civil war by John B. Jones, son of the missionary, Evan Jones, and an adopted citizen of the Nation, as a secret society for the ostensible purpose of cultivating a national feeling among the fullbloods, in opposition to the innovating tendencies of the mixed-blood element. The real purpose was to counteract the influence of the "Blue Lodge" and other secret secessionist organizations among the wealthier slave-holding classes, made up chiefly of mixed-bloods and whites. It extended to the Creeks, and its members in both tribes rendered good service to the Union cause throughout the war. They were frequently known as "Pin Indians," for a reason explained below. Since the close of the great struggle the society has distinguished itself by its determined opposition

to every scheme looking to the curtailment or destruction of Cherokee national self-government.

The following account of the society was written shortly after the close of the civil war:

"Those Cherokees who were loyal to the Union combined in a secret organization for self-protection, assuming the designation of the Ketoowha society, which name was soon merged in that of "Pins." The Pins were so styled because of a peculiar manner they adopted of wearing a pin. The symbol was discovered by their enemies, who applied the term in derision; but it was accepted by this loyal league, and has almost superseded the designation which its members first assumed. The Pin organization originated among the members of the Baptist congregation at Peavine, Going-snake district, in the Cherokee nation. In a short time the society counted nearly three thousand members, and had commenced proselytizing the Creeks, when the rebellion, against which it was arming, preventing its further extension, the poor Creeks having been driven into Kansas by the rebels of the Golden Circle. During the war the Pins rendered services to the Union cause in many bloody encounters, as has been acknowledged by our generals. It was distinctly an anti-slavery organization. The slave-holding Cherokees, who constituted the wealthy and more intelligent class, naturally allied themselves with the South, while loyal Cherokees became more and more opposed to slavery. This was shown very clearly when the loyalists first met in convention, in February, 1863. They not only abolished slavery unconditionally and forever, before any slave state made a movement toward emancipation, but made any attempts at enslaving a grave misdemeanor.

The secret signs of the Pins were a peculiar way of touching the hat as a salutation, particularly when they were too far apart for recognition in other ways. They had a peculiar mode of taking hold of the lapel of the coat, first drawing it away from the body, and then giving it a motion as though wrapping it around the heart. During the war a portion of them were forced into the rebellion, but quickly rebelled against General Cooper, who was placed over them, and when they fought against that general, at Bird Creek, they wore a bit of corn-husk, split into strips, tied in their hair. In the night when two Pins met, and one asked the other, 'Who are you?' the reply or pass was, 'Tahlequah—who are you?' The response was, 'I am Ketoowha's son.'"—Dr D. J. MacGowan, Indian Secret Societies, in Historical Magazine, x, 1866.

(48) FAREWELL ADDRESS OF LLOYD WELCH (p. 175): In the sad and eventful history of the Cherokee their gifted leaders, frequently of white ancestry, have oftentimes spoken to the world with eloquent words of appeal, of protest, or of acknowledgment, but never more eloquently than in the last farewell of Chief Lloyd Welch to the eastern band, as he felt the end draw near (leaflet, MacGowan, Chattanooga [n. d., 1880]):

"*To the Chairman and Council of the Eastern Band of Cherokees:*

"My Brothers: It becomes my imperative duty to bid you an affectionate farewell, and resign into your hands the trust you so generously confided to my keeping, principal chief of the Eastern Band. It is with great solicitude and anxiety for your welfare that I am constrained to take this course. But the inexorable laws of nature, and the rapid decline of my health, admonish me that soon, very soon, I will have passed from earth, my body consigned to the tomb, my spirit to God who gave it, in that happy home in the beyond, where there is no sickness, no sorrow, no pain, no death, but one eternal joy and happiness forever more.

"The only regret that I feel for thus being so soon called from among you, at the meridian of manhood, when hope is sweet, is the great anxiety I have to serve and benefit my race. For this I have studied and labored for the past ten years of my life, to secure to my brothers equal justice from their brothers of the west and the United States, and that you would no longer be hewers of wood and drawers of water, but assume that proud position among the civilized nations of the earth intended by the Creator that we should occupy, and which in the near future you will take or be exterminated. When you become educated, as a natural consequence you will become more intelligent, sober, industrious, and prosperous.

"It has been the aim of my life, the chief object, to serve my race faithfully, honestly, and to the best of my ability. How well I have succeeded I will leave to history and your magnanimity to decide, trusting an all-wise and just God to guide and protect you in the future, as He will do all things well. We may fail when on earth to see the goodness and wisdom of God in removing from us our best and most useful men, but when we have crossed over on the other shore to our happy and eternal home in the far beyond then our eyes will be opened and we will be enabled to see and realize the goodness and mercy of God in thus afflicting us while here on earth, and will be enabled more fully to praise God, from whom all blessings come.

"I hope that when you come to select one from among you to take the responsible position of principal chief of your band you will lay aside all personal considerations and select one in every respect competent, without stain on his fair fame, a pure, noble, honest, man—one who loves God and all that is pure—with intellect sufficient to know your rights, independence and nerve to defend them. Should you be thus fortunate in making your choice, all will be well. It has been truthfully said that 'when the righteous rule the people rejoice, but when the wicked rule the people mourn.'

"I am satisfied that you have among you many who are fully competent of the task. If I was satisfied it was your wish and for the good of my brothers I might mention some of them, but think it best to leave you in the hands of an all-wise God, who does all things right, to guide and direct you aright.

"And now, my brothers, in taking perhaps my last farewell on earth I do pray God that you may so conduct yourselves while here on earth that when the last sad rite is performed by loved friends we may compose one unbroken family above in that celestial city from whose bourne no traveler has ever returned to describe the beauty, grandeur, and happiness of the heaven prepared for the faithful by God himself beyond the sky. And again, my brothers, permit me to bid you a fond, but perhaps a last, farewell on earth, until we meet again where parting is never known and friends meet to part no more forever.

"L. R. WELCH,
"*Principal Chief Eastern Band Cherokee Indians.*

"Witness:
"SAMUEL W. DAVIDSON.
"B. B. MERONY."

(49) STATUS OF EASTERN BAND (p. 180): For some reason all authorities who have hitherto discussed the status of the eastern band of Cherokee seem to have been entirely unaware of the enactment of the supplementary articles to the treaty of New Echota, by which all preemption and reservation rights granted under the twelfth article were canceled. Thus, in the Cherokee case of "The United States *et al* against D. T. Boyd *et al*," we find the United States circuit judge quoting the twelfth article in its original form as a basis for argument, while his associate judge says: "Their forefathers availed themselves of a provision in the treaty of New Echota and remained in the state of North Carolina," etc. (Report of Indian Commissioner for 1895, pp. 633–635, 1896). The truth is that the treaty as ratified with its supplementary articles canceled the residence right of every Cherokee east of the Mississippi, and it was not until thirty years afterwards that North Carolina finally gave assurance that the eastern band would be permitted to remain within her borders.

The twelfth article of the new Echota treaty of December 29, 1835, provides for a pro rata apportionment to such Cherokee as desire to remain in the East, and continues: "Such heads of Cherokee families as are desirous to reside within the states of North Carolina, Tennessee, and Alabama, subject to the laws of the same, and who are qualified or calculated to become useful citizens, shall be entitled, on the certificate of the commissioners, to a preemption right to one hundred and sixty acres of land, or one quarter section, at the minimum Congress price, so as to include the present buildings or improvements of those who now reside there; and such as do not live there at present shall be permitted to locate within two years any lands not already occupied by persons entitled to preemption privilege under this treaty," etc.   Article 13 defines terms with reference to individual reservations granted under former treaties.   The preamble to the supplementary articles agreed upon on March 1, 1836, recites that, "Whereas the President of the United States has expressed his determination not to allow any preemptions or reservations, his desire being that the whole Cherokee people should remove together and establish themselves in the country provided for them west of the Mississippi river (article 1): It is therefore agreed that all preemption rights and reservations provided for in articles 12 and 13 shall be, and are hereby, relinquished and declared void."   The treaty, in this shape, was ratified on May 23, 1836 (see Indian Treaties, pp. 633–648, 1837).

BIOGRAPHICAL NOTES

James Mooney was born in Richmond, Indiana, on February 10, 1861. Like other nineteenth-century anthropologists, he was largely self-taught, his formal education being limited to the public schools of Richmond. He also taught in Richmond for two terms before joining the staff of the *Paladium*, a local newspaper. Mooney's parents were Irish immigrants and he maintained a keen interest in Irish nationalism throughout his life, but his real love was the American Indian. He would probably have remained an obscure Indiana newspaperman, however, had it not been for a visit he made to Washington in 1885 to talk with John Wesley Powell, founder of the Bureau of American Ethnology. Powell was so impressed with the earnest young man that he hired him immediately. It was a wise appointment, for Mooney proved to be a tireless and diligent worker. Before his death in 1921, he produced scores of manuscripts ranging from brief essays to lengthy monographs. Willing to learn the language of his informants and to endure the deprivations and hardships associated with field work in the nineteenth century, he quickly became one of the foremost authorities on American Indian life and history. The Cherokees interested him most. In fact, his first major contribution as an ethnologist on the staff of the Bureau of American Ethnology was an essay entitled "The Sacred Formulas of the Cherokees," published in the Seventh Annual Report (1885–86). Twelve years later he published in the Nineteenth Annual Report his "Myths of the Cherokees," perhaps his greatest accomplishment as an ethnologist. This reprint is taken from the first section of that publication.

Richard Mack Bettis was born in Spiro, Oklahoma, in 1934. He is currently employed in Tulsa as a Personnel Management Specialist and Labor Relations Officer for the Southwestern Power Administration of the U.S. Interior Department. Mr. Bettis received his B.A. in Sociology from Northeastern State College in Tahlequah, Oklahoma, and his law degree from Oklahoma City University. He practices law part-time and teaches political science at Tulsa Junior College. Both his parents are of Cherokee extraction, and he is involved in many tribal activities. He is president of the Tulsa Tsa-La-Gi-Ya Cherokee Community and a member of the Medicine Springs Tribal Town near Gore, Oklahoma. The goal of both groups is the preservation of the Cherokee heritage for future generations. Mr. Bettis dedicates his remarks in this book to his daughters, Tiffany and Dandre.

INDEX

Abbott on effect of Georgia anti-Cherokee laws, 112

Abraham, murder of, 55–56

Adair, James, on Cherokee dialects, 4
on Cherokee population, 24
on Cherokee sufferings from small-pox, 26
on Cherokee war of 1759–61, 31
on Christian Priber's work, 27
on decay of Cherokee ritual and traditions, 8
on effects of Cherokee war (1760–61), 35
on horses and swine among Cherokee, 72, 221
on name Cherokee, 4
on peace towns, 215, 216

Advocate, Cherokee, see Cherokee Advocate

Â'ganstâ'ta, see Morgan, Washington; Oconostota

Alabama in Texas, union of, with Cherokee, 140
migration across the Mississippi by, 90

Alabama, production of gold in, 228, 229
Removal forts in, 229

All Bones, see Ka'lahu'

Allegheny River, origin of name of, 6

Almanac, Cherokee, establishment of, 104

American Blood among Cherokee, 73

American Board of Commissioners for Foreign Missions, work of, among Cherokee, 95–96, 131

Anadarko, see Ṇadako

Ani'-Kitu'whagĭ, see Kitu'whagi

Ani'-ku'sa, see Creeks

Ani'-tsa'lăgĭ', Ani'yûñ'wiyă', see Tsa'-lăgĭ, Yûñ'wiyă'

Annuities, Cherokee, 71, 75, 118
apportionment of, 97, 134, 182
withholding of, 134

Apache, murder of party of, by scalp hunters, 217
use of language of, as trade language, 191

Appleton's Cyclopedia of American Bibliography on Rev. David Brainerd, 225
on Col. Benjamin Hawkins, 220
on Chief McGillivray, 218
on Col. R. J. Meigs, 220
on General Robertson, 213
on John Ross, 107
on St. Clair's defeat, 220
on Tecumtha, 224
on Nancy Ward, 214
on Wayne's victory, 221

Aquaquiri, see Guaquili

Arbuckle, General, on adoption of Cherokee constitution, 130

McMinn, Gov. Joseph, effort to cause Cherokee removal by, 96
  emigration under direction of, 94
  figures of, on Cherokee emigration, 97
  treaty signed by, 94
McNair, David, grave of, 229–230
Mahican, separation of, from Delawares, 7
Mañterañ, meaning of name, 4, 201
  see also Catawba
Marion, aid given to, by Sevier, 219
Marshall, John, decision of, in Worcester v. State of Georgia, 113–114
Martin, Joseph, on Cherokee temper in 1786, 53
  on encroachments of Tennesseans, 54
  on French and Spanish encouragement of Cherokee hostility, 52
  on Sevier's expedition (1781), 49
  treaty signed by, 51
Martin, Gen. —, expedition against Cherokee under, 55
Martin, —, on expedition from Virginia through Cherokee country, 20
Maryland, production of gold in, 228
Maryville, attack on, 55
Mason, J. M., on Cherokee opposition to removal project, 122
Maumee Rapids, effect of battle of, 71
  participation of Cherokee in battle of, 69
Mauvila, battle of, 86, 199
Mayes, Chief J. B., proposition for land cession made to, 155
Mechanic Arts among Cherokee, 95–104
  among East Cherokee, 170–171
Medill, W., on Catawba among East Cherokee, 169
  on East Cherokee censuses, 171
Meek on De Soto's route, 200, 201, 205, 206
Meherrin, habitat and migrations of, 5
Meigs, Gen. R. J., aid given to missionary work by, 74
  delegation brought to Washington by (1898), 97
  instruction to, to cause removal of

Cherokee to the West, 92
  life of, 222–223
  on Cherokee attitude in War of 1812, 79
  on Cherokee services in Creek War, 88
  on secret article of treaty of 1807, 76
  recommendation for Cherokee citizenship by, 107
  treaties brought about by, 74–75
Memphis, surrender of Spanish post at, 71
Menendez, establishment of fort by, 17
  on Pardo's expedition, 18, 19
Meredith on adoption of Cherokee constitution, 106
  on John Ross, 107, 232
Merriwether, Gen. David, treaty signed by, 94
Messenger, Cherokee, *see* Cherokee Messenger
Methodists, work of, among East Cherokee, 170
Mexico, alleged Cherokee agreement with, 141–142
Mexico, Cherokee in, 143
  grant to Cherokee by, 140
  proposed Cherokee emigration to, 157–158
Migrations, Cherokee, 5–9
Miller, Governor, efforts for Osage-Cherokee peace by, 133
Milligan, —, on Catawba in Cherokee war, 34
Mills among Cherokee, 75, 95
Mines, Spanish, in Alleghenies, 19, 210
Miro, Gov. Estevan, on Cherokee migration across the Mississippi, 91
Missionaries among Cherokee, arrest of, 113, 114
  and missions among Cherokee, 27–28, 73–74, 95–96, 98, 117, 131, 149, 153, 157, 169
Mission Ridge, cause of name of, 96
Missouri, settlement of, on Cherokee strip, 151
Missouri, Kansas and Texas Railway, construction of, 151
Mobile, Spanish possession of, 58